Social Work: Themes, Issues and Critical Debates

Other titles by Robert Adams:

A Measure of Diversion? Case Studies in IT (co-author)
Prison Riots in Britain and the USA
Problem-solving with Self-Help Groups (co-author)
Protests by Pupils: Empowerment, Schooling and the State
Quality Social Work
Self-Help, Social Work and Empowerment
Skilled Work with People
Social Work and Empowerment
The Abuses of Punishment
The Personal Social Services: Clients, Consumers or Citizens?

Other titles by Malcolm Payne:

What is Professional Social Work?
Social Work and Community Care
Linkages: Effective Networking in Social Care
Modern Social Work Theory: A Critical Introduction
Writing for Publication in Social Services Journals
Social Care in the Community
Working in Teams
Power, Authority and Responsibility in Social Services: Social Work in Area Teams

Other titles by Lena Dominelli:

Community Action and Organising Marginalised Groups
Women in Focus, Community Service Orders and Female Offenders
Love and Wages: The Impact of Imperialism, State Intervention and Women's Domestic Labour on Workers Control in Algeria
Anti-Racist Social Work
Feminist Social Work (co-author)
Women and Community Action
Women Across Continents: Feminist Comparative Social Policy
Gender, Sex Offenders and Probation Practice
Getting Advice in Urdu
International Directory of Social Work
Anti-Racist Perspectives in Social work (co-author)
Anti-Racist Probation Practice (co-author)
Sociology for Social Work

Social Work
Themes, Issues and Critical Debates

Edited by

**Robert Adams, Lena Dominelli
and Malcolm Payne**

Consultant editor: Jo Campling

MACMILLAN

First published 1998 by
MACMILLAN PRESS LTD
Houndmills, Basingstoke, Hampshire RG21 6XS
and London
Companies and representatives
throughout the world

ISBN 0–333–68818–X paperback

A catalogue record for this book is available
from the British Library.

This book is printed on paper suitable for recycling and
made from fully managed and sustained forest sources.

10 9   8   7   6 5   4   3   2
07 06 05 04 03 02 01 00 99 98

Editing and origination by
Aardvark Editorial, Mendham, Suffolk

Printed in and bound in Great Britain by
Creative Print & Design (Wales), Ebbw Vale

Contents

List of figures and tables

Figures

Tables

Notes on the contributors

Robert Adams is a qualified social worker who worked in the penal system for several years, latterly as Deputy Governor of a young offenders' institution, before running a community-based social work project for Barnardo's. He has written extensively about youth and criminal justice, social work and the personal social services, and protest and empowerment. He is currently Professor of Human Services Development at the University of Lincolnshire and Humberside.

Suzy Braye is Assistant Community Social Services Manager with Derbyshire County Council. She has a range of professional experience in practice, education, staff development and management, with professional interests in children's services and mental health. She is joint author, with Michael Preston-Shoot, of *Practising Social Work Law*, 2nd edn (1997) and *Empowering Practice in Social Care* (1995). Since 1990, they have published articles exploring partnership, empowerment, anti-oppressive practice and social work law.

Beverley Burke is Senior Lecturer on the DipSW course at Liverpool John Moores University. Her current work includes teaching and training on anti-oppressive practice to students and practitioners. Trained as a generic social worker, her main practice has been largely in the area of child protection. She has recently been involved in therapeutic work with women survivors of sexual abuse.

Katy Cigno is a Senior Lecturer at the University of Hull and a Specialist Practice Teacher for Wakefield Community and Social Services Department. She was a founder member of the Behavioural Social Work Group, which she currently chairs.

Helen Cosis Brown is Head of Department of Social Work, Counselling, Learning Disabilities and Mental Health Nursing at the University of Hertfordshire. She was a social worker and team leader for ten years in an inner London borough. She has continued to offer training in the field of fostering and adoption and has a number of publications relating to social work practice with lesbians and gay men.

Mark Doel is Professor of Social Work and Head of the School of Social Work and RNIB Rehabilitation Studies at the University of Central England in Birmingham. He trained as a task-centred practitioner in 1981 and has used the task-centred method extensively in his practice, teaching, writing and research. Since

1994, he has has been developing task-centred programmes at post-qualifying level with colleagues at Sheffield University and Wakefield Social Services Department.

Lena Dominelli is Professor of Social and Community Development in the Department of Social Work Studies at the University of Southampton where she is the Director of the Centre for International Social and Community Development. She is also currently the President of the International Association of Schools of Social Work. Besides being an educator and researcher, she has had practice experience as a social worker, probation officer and community worker. She has published numerous articles and 14 books, the most recent being *Anti-racist Social Work*, 2nd edn and *Sociology for Social Work*.

Angela Everitt is an Honorary Research Fellow at the University of Durham and, with her partner Pam Carter, runs 'Reading Lasses', a second-hand radical bookshop in Wigtown, Scotland's Book Town, specialising in women's studies and social studies. For a number of years, she worked in social work education and in social research, undertaking research and evaluation studies with a wide variety of statutory and voluntary organisations and community groups.

Philomena Harrison is Senior Lecturer on the DipSW course at Liverpool John Moores University. Her current work includes teaching and training on anti-oppressive practice to students and practitioners. Trained as a psychiatric social worker, her main practice experience has been with children and families. She is currently undertaking direct work around issues of identity with black children who are using Personal Social Services.

David Howe is Professor of Social Work at the University of East Anglia, Norwich. His research and writing interests include child maltreatment, family support, attachment theory and adoption. He is the editor of the journal *Child and Family Social Work*. His two most recent books are *Attachment Theory for Social Work Practice* and *Patterns of Adoption*.

Chris Jones is Professor of Social Policy and Social Work at the University of Liverpool, and head of the Department of Sociology, Social Policy and Social Work Studies. He is a Marxist academic whose recent publications have been concerned with current developments in Britain's social work policy and education.

Mary Langan is Senior Lecturer in Applied Social Sciences at the Open University. In the early 1970s, she was an inner city social worker and an active participant in the radical social work movement. She has written extensively on social policy, social work and health in *Crises in the British State 1830–1930* (1985, with Bill Scharz), *Radical Social Work Today* (1989, with Phil Lee), *Women, Oppression and Social Work* (1992, with Lesley Day), *Criminological Perspectives – a Reader* (1996, with John Muncie) and *Welfare Needs, Rights and Risks* (1998). She is also general editor of the Routledge social policy series, *The State of Welfare*.

Joyce Lishman is Professor and Head of the School of Applied Social Studies at the Robert Gordon University, Aberdeen. Her practice experience was with children and adolescents, including children with cancer and leukaemia, and their families. She has taught on social work courses at non-graduate, degree and post-graduate levels. She was lead assessor in the quality assessment of social work in Scotland in 1995. Her research has been primarily in client perceptions and the analysis of social work interviews, and more recently on the role of volunteers within the social services. She is general editor of the *Research Highlights in Social Work* series.

Janice McGhee is Lecturer in the Department of Social Work in the University of Edinburgh, with responsibility for teaching law and human development on the Master of Social Work course. She qualified as a social worker in 1979 and has worked in a local authority social work team and in a social work department emergency duty team providing an out-of-hours service. Much of her career has involved direct work with children and families, although she has also been employed as a senor social worker in a large London teaching hospital.

Wendy Marshall was Senior Lecturer in Social Work at the University of Huddersfield and was the coordinator of the MA in child protection. She has been a qualified social worker since 1976 working in a variety of settings. She was particularly interested in the development of poststructural and postmodern theory in psychology and was engaged in research of children's accounts of power in adult/child relationships.

Marjorie Mayo is a Reader in Community Development in Professional and Community Education at Goldsmiths College, University of London. She has taught, carried out research and written about community participation and community development and she has also worked in a variety of practice settings.

Audrey Mullender is Professor in Social Work at the University of Warwick and Editor of the *British Journal of Social Work*. She has a professional background in the statutory social services, and a longstanding interest and involvement in the voluntary sector. She is the author of over 70 publications in the social work field, including (with David Ward) *Self-Directed Groupwork: Users Take Action for Empowerment* (1991) and *Rethinking Domestic Violence: The Social Service Probation Response* (1996). She is currently producing, jointly with Brendah Malahleka, a new edition of Veronica Coulshed's *Management in Social Work* (1998).

Joan Orme is Reader in Social Work Studies at the University of Southampton. She has taught on social work courses for many years, providing core courses on gender. Research interests include the organisation and delivery of social services, social work practice and gender issues in community care.

Nigel Parton is Professor in Child Care at the University of Huddersfield. A qualified social worker, he has been involved in social work education for 20 years. He has a particular interest in child welfare and child protection, and social theory and social work. In recent years, he has published a number of papers on the general area of postmodernity and social work.

Malcolm Payne is Professor of Applied Community Studies, Manchester Metropolitan University, having previously worked in probation, social services departments and the national and local voluntary sector. He is author most recently of *Social Work and Community Care* (1995), *What is Professional Social Work?* (1996), *Modern Social Work Theory*, 2nd edn (1997) and *Teamwork in Multiprofessional Care* (1998).

Stella Perrott is a Social Work Services Inspector with the Scottish Office. She was previously an Assistant Chief Probation Officer and part-time lecturer in Management. Her publications include 'Working with men who abuse women and children' in Lupton, C. and Gillespie, T. (eds) *Working with Violence* (1994).

Michael Preston-Shoot is Professor of Social Work and Social Care at Liverpool John Moores University. He has a background in social work and family therapy, and has recently completed research on user and carer views of community care services and on equal opportunities in education and training. He is currently undertaking research on practice teachers and social work law. He is joint author, with Suzy Braye, of *Practising Social Work Law*, 2nd edn (1997) and *Empowering Practice in Social Care* (1995). Since 1990, they have published articles exploring partnership, empowerment, anti-oppressive practice and social work law.

Lena Robinson is Lecturer in Psychology at the University of Birmingham and has been in social work education for many years. She is the author of *Pyschology for Social Workers: Black Perspectives* (1995) and *Race, Communication, and the Caring Professions* (in press) and has researched on issues related to racial identity and children in care.

Steven Shardlow is Senior Lecturer and Director of Social Work Studies at the Department of Sociological Studies, University of Sheffield.

David Smith is Professor of Social Work in the Department of Applied Social Science, University of Lancaster.

Neil Thompson teaches in the School of Health and Community Studies at North East Wales Institute of Higher Education and is a Principal Consultant with Ashely Maynard Associates. He is the author of several books, including *People Skills* (1996) and *Anti-Discriminatory Practice*, 2nd edn (1997).

Alan Walker is Professor of Social Policy in the Department of Sociological Studies at the University of Sheffield. He has researched and written extensively on the fields of poverty, inequality, social exclusion, disability, ageing and European social policy.

Carol Walker is Professor of Social Policy in the School of Health and Community Studies at Sheffield Hallam University. She has researched and published widely in the fields of poverty and social security, and services for people with learning difficulties.

Dave Ward is Professor of Social and Community Studies at De Montfort University, Leicester. The Centre for Social Action at De Montfort University promotes and undertakes practice, training and research within the principles of the anti-oppressive groupwork advocated in his chapter.

Lorraine Waterhouse is Professor in the Department of Social Work at the University of Edinburgh with responsibility for child-care teaching. She qualified as a social worker in 1972. She has worked in child and family psychiatry and is currently on the Parole Board of Scotland.

Introduction

ROBERT ADAMS, LENA DOMINELLI AND MALCOLM PAYNE

This book introduces the main currents of theory, research and practice in social work, but it does not provide only a single and prelimi-
nary summary of the important features of social work. The book is
introductory, in the sense of being an invitation: we invite the reader
into the territory of social work contexts, values, approaches and
practices. We introduce into this territory some of the ideas that
participate in current debates in social work. Readers should feel free
to be swept into these debates. You should apply your mind and
experience to understand, evaluate and criticise the positions taken.
In this way, you are introducing yourself into social work and introducing social work into your thinking and action.

We have provided chapters which are more than pure expositions
of each topic, based simply on asking experts to summarise their
research or their major book in their specialism. Each chapter offers
an 'insider' perspective on its particular topic, but also adopts a critical 'outsider' position. This makes it possible to examine issues,
engage in debates with other aspects and sustain throughout the
book the spirit of what Lena Dominelli (Chapter 1) calls 'dialogue
over controversies'.

Whilst some readers of this book will be new to social work, no-
one should regard themselves as a beginner. The backgrounds of all
readers will impinge on its contents. Students will bring their life
experiences and academic and personal preparations for social work
to bear on the book's coverage of essential aspects of social work;
practitioners will be able to illuminate its analysis of current debates
with their own experiences; general readers from other disciplines
and professions, with an interest in social work, will find easy access
to its subject matter to chart against their own perspectives. In every
case, readers bring themselves to the book and can examine the effect
of reading it on their understanding and practice.

Many edited collections of essays achieve a degree of integration
through the selection of contributors from a single network or a

shared, unifying perspective. This book, in contrast, arises from Macmillan bringing together three editors of different experience and stance, who have in their turn recruited a group of 21 authors from diverse backgrounds and traditions, and who have enabled this diversity of experience and perspective to interact and, on occasions, bite on each other.

We are living and working in a period when, in the UK at any rate, the monolithic social services department is about to disappear. It is more realistic to participate in continuing debates about the future of social work than to invest in the fallacy that the structures and organisations which sustain it will continue for ever. However, irrespective of how the personal social services are labelled, and how their staff are designated, social work will not disappear. This book contributes to the affirmation of the centrality of knowledge and values of social work, irrespective of such changes as the deconstruction of social services departments.

In the way we have set about creating this book, it occurs to us in retrospect that we have put into practice several core values of social work: respecting other people's views, active listening and not competing with someone else over their point of view, and rejecting conflict and anger, whilst valuing difference and diversity. Such values have a quality which in our view transcends some postmodern perspectives, asserting the fragmentation of all realities. We are doubtful of the view that all reality is ephemeral. We believe that in social work, to say nothing of other aspects of life and work, people share their dreams, visions, ideals and continuities, for example in the personal and professional values they espouse. To be human is to go beyond the ultimate fragmentation of individualism and competition, by collectively creating and ordering responses to the world. Social work, as a socially constructed project aiming to tackle oppression, is in this sense a perpetually changing and unfinished project. It faces enduring divisions and inequalities in societies throughout the world, where problems such as poverty and a lack of access to other resources such as education affect people's ability to fulfil themselves and others. Poor people, for example, cannot get a purchase on participation, no matter how professionals go on about empowerment. We give these ideas about poverty – from an historical perspective (Chapter 3) and informed by contemporary research (Chapter 4) – due prominence in Part I of the book, but these are not matters for academic debate alone. They are aspects of widespread human need which require challenging in ways not always recognised adequately from the vantage point of a postmodern perspective.

Therefore, we believe that social justice is a theme woven into everything we do, as a way of approaching social work, not as part of a hierarchy of knowledges and objects 'out there', or a reductionist set of ideas, but as a perspective which informs our thoughts and feelings. For justice to be done to the ideas and experiences addressed in this book, practitioners' passions as well as their intellectual attentions are likely to be engaged. Authors' views also interact with their feelings about their subjects. There should be no segregation either between academic and practitioner perspectives. Viewing knowledge in a broader sense, as crossing personal, professional and disciplinary among many other boundaries, is difficult but worthwhile, since in the process intellectual and experiential knowledge – academic and practice wisdom – interact, sometimes very creatively. Where appropriate, we have deliberately encouraged the authors to display their commitment and, by implication, their individuality through the strength of the cases they advance for their viewpoint on their topics. This also is a feature of social work: the capacity to allow individuals to express their diversity and their uniqueness, the quality of their ideas and experiences, through their work.

All three of us believe in academic discourse being essential. None of us can describe the nature of social work in a simple way, but we are convinced of its existence being shaped and influenced continually by a number of key debates. During the process of developing the book, we have met and engaged in such debates. The purpose of this book is to create wider opportunities to share in and extend those debates. This book sets out to provide more than a 'reader' of someone else's ideas, by involving you and us in the issues and debates within it. Such debates are open-ended, since they are ongoing, with no starting or finishing point. They do not converge on a set of guidelines on what social work is and how to do it. They involve a continual journey, whose outcome will never be complete understanding or a finished project. This is an anxiety-provoking reality, but it is also exciting, because, like work with clients, it offers people practising social work the reality of engaging in a profession which is in the ferment of continual change and continually in the process of considering, and sometimes taking, new directions. Some subject matter crops up in more than one place in the book. This reflects the reality that we can approach some aspects of social work from more than one direction, and that more than one view of them exists. We have cross-referenced – in the text and through the index – many of the places where this occurs, rather than artificially attempting to edit out the differences and discontinuities which result. Unsurprisingly, therefore, having set the diversity of social work themes and debates going in this book, the fact that we offer no conclusion to the book mirrors the reality that social work offers no global solutions in work with people, and refle holding the mirror up to our own practice – no final answ question of what social work consists of.

The structure of the book reflects our view that we draw on social work approaches in our practice, in a societal context which affects us at every turn. Thus, Parts I, II and III deal respectively with social work contexts, approaches and practice. Part I offers a number of major topics which interact to a greater or lesser degree with anti-oppressive practice (Chapter 1), which provides its linking theme. Part II sets against the linking theme of encouraging reflectiveness on theory in practice (Chapter 10) a selection of those social work approaches we view as generating debates and controversies. Part III considers social work with the major client groups – children and families, adults and offenders – against the backcloth of unfinished debates on social work processes (Chapter 21). Thus, the structure of the book offers the reader the opportunity to use the introductory chapters to the three parts in dialogue with the other chapters in them.

PART I

Social Work in Context

1

Anti-oppressive practice in context

LENA DOMINELLI

Anti-oppressive practice: an old–new paradigm

The role and purpose of social work has been hotly contested since its inception. The diverse answers which have been provided can be categorised as follows into roughly three types:

- therapeutic helping approaches;
- 'maintenance' approaches;
- emancipatory approaches.

Therapeutic approaches to social work are best exemplified by counselling theories, of which Carl Roger's work stands paramount (Rogers, 1980). In these, the 'client'[1] is assisted by the counsellor to better understand him/herself and his/her relationships with others, particularly close relatives and friends, and to move on to a more effective way of dealing with their situation. Yet its long history and wide currency means that it is most readily understood by readers as 'those people with whom social workers work'. Therapeutic approaches focus on individuals and their psychological functioning as the basis of intervention. The role of the counsellor as helper is to listen actively to what is being said and to facilitate a process of exploration which enables people better to address their life circumstances. Any change which takes place is in the individual who is being counselled as they either learn or develop more effective strategies for dealing with the problems they encounter.

The 'maintenance' approach is best explicated by Martin Davies (1994) in his book, *The Essential Social Worker*. In this, he argues that the social worker's main preoccupation is that of ensuring that people can cope or deal adequately with their lives. Under this approach, social workers do not adopt a therapeutic helping role.

Their interventions are much more pragmatic – usually passing on information about resources and possibilities. They are guided in their interventions by 'practice wisdoms' or the accumulated experience of 'what works'. Probing deeply into the individual's psyche does not, therefore, form part of the concerns of those following this approach. The 'maintenance' approach relies on the expert practitioner adopting a largely neutral attitude towards 'clients', although this may involve the use of authority that may be resisted by the 'clients', as for example when the social worker receives a child into care or a probation officer recommends custody for an offender. Engaging in political issues, particularly those which challenge the existing social order, falls outside the remit of the 'maintenance' practitioner, who views society as being basically benign.

Those endorsing an emancipatory approach to social work have an explicit commitment to social justice and to engage in overt challenges to the welfare system if it is seen to thwart this goal. Whilst some see service users as 'victims' of unjust social relations (for example, Bailey and Brake, 1975), others focus on their strengths (for example, Collins, 1990). However, both schools of thought aim to empower those with whom they work by helping them to understand their situation, make connections between their personal plight and that of others, examine power relations and their impact on the specifics of their daily routines and acquire the knowledge and skills for taking control of their lives. Many of these activities draw on the consciousness-raising techniques advocated by Freire (1972).

Social change at both the individual and societal levels lies at the heart of an emancipatory approach. Practitioners may adopt an openly political stance which can create complications between the social workers' professional roles and their activities as social change agents. In this context, gaining the support of sympathetic others outside the social work remit is an important facet of the job undertaken by practitioners endorsing emancipatory forms of social work. In recent times, women, black activists, disabled people, gay men, lesbian women and older people have worked to develop forms of social work practice which seek to empower users and enable them to participate in their own emancipation when in receipt of official assistance. Anti-oppressive practice, with its value commitment to the realisation of social justice, is one variant of a range of emancipatory approaches to social work.

Social justice has provided a thread of historical continuity running through social work practice. The modern variant of a concern with its implementation has been expressed by appealing to 'social work's value base' and through the range of progressive social work paradigms. These began with radical social work in the 1970s, moving on to feminist social work and anti-racist social work in the 1980s and to anti-oppressive practice in the 1990s. The development of anti-oppressive practice has been a fragmented and highly contentious affair as different groups jockey to define and influence its meaning.

The supporters of anti-oppressive practice – white women, black men and women, lesbian women, gay men, disabled people, older people and others – have sought to articulate their questions about its place in and relevance to social work as well as to shape the replies proferred by practitioners. They have argued that its role is one of highlighting social injustice and finding ways of eradicating at least those forms of it which are reproduced in and through social work practice (see Corrigan and Leonard, 1978; Dominelli, 1988; Dominelli and McLeod, 1989; Ahmad, 1990). Securing social change that is in keeping with this goal is, therefore, the aim of anti-oppressive practice.

Its opponents have endeavoured to trivialise its stances and undermine its achievements (see Phillips, 1993, 1994). A large part of their argument is based on claims that those endorsing anti-oppressive practice have exaggerated the extent to which social inequality pervades society. In addition, they believe that anti-oppressive practice has been imposed through draconian measures upon unwilling victims (see Appleyard, 1993; Phillips, 1993, Pinker, 1993), thereby conflating good anti-oppressive practice with poor practice, which should not be condoned regardless of what it purports to be doing.

This chapter focuses on anti-oppressive practice because this book is committed to providing readers with an understanding of the knowledge base and tools that social workers use to engage in progressive practice which takes the side of people who have been subjugated by structural inequalities such as poverty, sexism and racism and seeks to assist them in their desire to reverse the position they are in, that is, to move in emancipatory directions. It is one paradigm for practice among others which vie for the practitioners' attention. Practising in accordance with the principles of anti-oppressive practice requires a commitment to doing so. It can also be very hard work. Given social work's age old concern with the underdog, anti-oppressive practice is an old–new paradigm for practitioners and academics to follow. Its spread has been marked by a problematic reception brought about by the mode of its introduction into training and the barriers that impede its growth. These hurdles include the resistance which has ironically been engendered through the successes that anti-oppressive practice has achieved in the field. I also argue that these obstacles have to be transcended for anti-oppressive practice to become firmly embedded in practice.

Anti-oppressive practice, insofar as it is preoccupied with the implementation of social justice, is intimately bound up with notions of improving the quality of life or well-being of individuals, groups and communities. This concern lends it a holistic mantle which encompasses all aspects of social life – culture, institutions, legal framework, political system, socio-economic infrastructure and interpersonal relationships which both create and are created by social reality. In its early days, anti-oppressive practice highlighted specific social divisions, that is, personal attributes such as 'race',[2] class, age, gender and sexual orientation, that acquire specific social meanings which are rooted in unequal power relations based on the creation of oppositional pairs in which one part is dominant over the other, as in the case, for example, of men over women. This concern gave rise to particular practice paradigms aimed at addressing these social divisions: class in radical social work (Corrigan and Leonard, 1978), women in feminist social work (Brook and Davis, 1985; Hanmer and Statham, 1987; Dominelli and McLeod, 1989) and 'black people'[3] in anti-racist social work (Cheetham *et al.*, 1986; Dominelli, 1988; Ahmad, 1990) among others.

More recently, the realisation that individual identity and social existence are more complex than can be dealt with by focusing on a single social division expressed as a dichotomous pair, and the need to prevent the nihilistic fragmentation of social life, has led black women, white women, people in the disability movement, older people, gay men, lesbian women and those in the ecology movement to look for bonds of solidarity which acknowledge the different starting points held by groups of people working towards a common aim (Collins, 1990; Dominelli, 1997). Their shared objective of securing social relations which endorse social justice can be articulated as one of sustaining a people-oriented social environment which allows each person, community or group to develop their full potential whilst cherishing their cultural traditions and respecting the rights and dignity of others. Moreover, there is a refusal to endorse a hierarchy of oppressions and a commitment to recognising diverse identities as being on an equal footing (Collins, 1990).

As a result of its all-encompassing orientation, anti-oppressive practice is concerned with inputs, outputs and processes. Indeed, its holistic approach to practice can become a barrier to its implementation because individual practitioners can feel overwhelmed by the multiple dimensions of reality which they need to engage with at any one time. However, overcoming this problematic does not have to be undertaken by a single individual. Teamwork and working collectively with others to cover its various aspects in the course of delivering an anti-oppressive service are more realistic solutions to this dilemma. I will now turn to defining anti-oppressive practice.

Defining anti-oppressive practice

Dominelli (1993) has defined anti-oppressive practice as:

a form of social work practice which addresses social divisions and structural inequalities in the work that is done with 'clients' (users) or workers. Anti-oppressive practice aims to provide more appropriate and sensitive services by responding to people's needs regardless of their social status. Anti-oppressive practice embodies a person-centered philosophy, an egalitarian value system concerned with reducing the deleterious effects of structural inequalities upon people's lives; a methodology focusing on both process and outcome; and a way of structuring relationships between individuals that aims to empower users by reducing the negative effects of hierarchy in their immediate interaction and the work they do together. (Dominelli, 1993, p. 24)

Thus, there is a pervasiveness about anti-oppressive practice which permeates all aspects of social work policy and practice. It impacts on service delivery, 'client'/worker relationships, employer/employee relationships, relationships between employees, agency culture and the social context. In defining anti-oppressive practice in liberationist terms, Dominelli (1993) has firmly located anti-oppressive practice within the longstanding tradition of humanism with which social workers are familiar. In drawing upon these antecedents, anti-oppressive practice forms part of an old practice paradigm.

The emphasis of anti-oppressive practice on a holistic approach to social work intervention has directed it towards the development of a new practice paradigm which guides practitioners beyond the traditional goal of controlling 'clients' for the purposes of helping them to adjust to existing power relations or, as a 'maintenance' practitioner might put it, to 'cope' with life as they find it. Based on egalitarian principles, the moral and ethical positions of anti-oppressive practice are those which ask social workers to both understand and engage with the harsh realities within which they work and their 'clients' live, and to seek to change them. Because anti-oppressive practice has to facilitate both coping and change strategies, I argue that anti-oppressive practice constitutes an old–new practice paradigm.

Being able to operate effectively in this *milieu* requires practitioners working in anti-oppressive ways to be both experiential and research-led. Being rooted in peoples' lived-in reality ensures that anti-oppressive practice responds to the issues and questions which are identified by oppressed groups themselves. This approach is important if anti-oppressive practice is *not* to be imposed on reluctant service users. Moreover, this concern with validating the significance of everyday experience as a legitimate source of information in designing services endorses experiential knowledge as an important source of data. Anti-oppressive practice's capacity also to draw upon a more traditional research base in the social sciences will lend an empirical aura to experiential reality, thereby enabling well-informed 'client'-led social work practice to take place more readily.

'Client'-centeredness forms the basis on which anti-oppressive practice offers a paradigm for practice that is highly relevant to practitioners working in contexts in which political hostility to marginalised groups is the norm. Having clearly established empirical or 'hard' facts on which to base service provision also facilitates a more thorough refutation of the arguments posed by the critics of anti-oppressive practice and empowers social workers to advocate more forcefully alongside their 'clients'. In addition, research can, as Everitt shows in Chapter 9, contribute to the development of a reflective practitioner who uses research as an integral element of improving their practice and monitoring its compliance with anti-oppressive practice principles.

Working in ways that are consistent with anti-oppressive practice has implications not only for service provision, but also for the professionals engaged in delivering an anti-oppressive service. To begin with, anti-oppressive practice calls for a redefinition of professionalism, with expertise being rooted in more power-sharing egalitarian directions and making explicit the value system to which the professional subscribes. Hence, anti-oppressive practice challenges traditional or 'maintenance'-oriented views of professionalism in which a neutral expert is required to exercise power over the 'client' and other workers lower down the labour hierarchy through rules which endorse deferential responses to those in 'superior' positions.

Under the auspices of anti-oppressive practice, 'client'-centeredness acquires a different meaning, that is, one based on power-sharing and an empathy which has the 'client's' position as its starting point. A 'client'-centered approach which seeks to reverse inegalitarian relations between the 'client' and worker facilitates the practitioner's ability to work with the messy realities that 'clients' bring with them in more sensitive and relevant ways. It also uses relationship-building to secure change and places the practice value system under the spotlight to reveal the room for ambiguity contained in seemingly straightforward statements about social work's value base and ethical stances. However, as Shardlow demonstrates in Chapter 2, this complexity in value positioning can be a strength which social workers can use constantly to engage in revisiting their own values and how they use them in their practice.

Understanding social relations and how power operates within them through the relationships they establish with their 'clients' enables practitioners more readily to apply the principles of egalitarianism which are both explicitly and implicitly expounded in anti-oppressive practice. Living up to this expectation in practice is immensely difficult, given the competing discourses identified by Parton and Marshall in Chapter 20, and calls for an open acknowledgement of the constraints which hinder its implementation. This may mean that securing egalitarian relations in a pure form is an unreachable goal and that the best that can be achieved is a constant lowering of the power imbalance through a continual process of identifying the sources of power differentials and eliminating as many of these obstacles as possible. The tensions that social workers seeking to implement this approach have to deal with are explored throughout Part 1 of this book. Their impact in 'client'/worker relationships is, however, most clearly evident in Chapter 16, where Doel considers task-centred social work. Here, he indicates that there is more to power than meets the eye. Nonetheless, social workers have the duty of exploring these difficulties in an open and frank manner with their 'clients', so that, together, they may move forward in partnerships that the 'clients' feel they can own.

Processual considerations or questions of *how* relationships are conducted, and on whose terms, are also crucial to the realisation of anti-oppressive practice. Furthermore, process provides the means whereby the experience of anti-oppressive practice or its absence will be confirmed. This is in contrast to traditional understandings of 'client'/worker relationships in which ethics focus more on the ends to be achieved than on the mechanisms whereby these are to be reached.

The emphasis on outcomes in the current competency-based approaches to social work is consistent with an ethical standpoint that ignores process. This is a position which practitioners following anti-oppressive practice would eschew. For them, substance and form are integral parts of one whole, process providing the link between them. For this reason, the adding-on of 'social work's value base' to a competence-based approach is doomed to be incapable of delivering anti-oppressive practice, despite its avowed intention of doing so (Dominelli, 1996). The collaring of social work education and training at the qualifying level by the Diploma in Social Work (DipSW), which encapsulates the competence-based approach, therefore puts the two on a collision course except at the most tokenistic level in which form stands for substance. The issue of competency in doing a professional job well is another, albeit related, matter. Working in anti-oppressive ways requires skills and expertise. Practitioners must know what they are doing and why they adopt one course of action over another and consistently reflect on how they can improve the services they are making available to others.

Those advocating anti-oppressive practice have a responsibility to develop theories and concepts which reflect its principles in practice. As Burke and Harrison demonstrate in Chapter 19, this requires academics to move beyond dualistic thinking and approach their study in an holistic manner. Theorising anti-oppressive practice is an important aspect through which the integration of theory and practice is retained. Social work, uniquely among the social science disciplines, is compelled to maintain the link between theory and practice. Moreover, working in one area of anti-oppressive practice can lead to innovation and theory-building in others. For example, feminist work with women has contributed to a rethinking of masculinity (Bowl, 1985; Connell, 1995), and black and anti-racist perspectives have had implications for the way in which white identity and whiteness is understood (Roediger, 1991).

Practising equality requires the practitioner to value 'difference' in lifestyles and identities instead of settling for a clone of oneself as expressed by demanding a uniform conformity in others. Valuing 'difference' is one dimension of the complexities of life to be addressed explicitly by practitioners subscribing to anti-oppressive practice. For, as Lorde (1984) says, unless individuals follow this path, their reaction to 'difference' is not to value it, but to do one of three things – exercise the wish to control or dominate it, copy it or exterminate it.

Thus, valuing 'difference' goes against commonsense socialisation which portrays difference as 'inferior' or deems it in pathological terms as a 'deficit'. The casting of people different from oneself in a subordinate status is central to the process of 'othering' them (de Beauvoir, 1974; Rutherford, 1992). The 'othering' of individuals or groups withdraws them from the circle of humanity and facilitates the denial of their human, social and political rights. It also permits their being treated as dependent beings who can have others (that is, those who are 'superior' to them) take decisions on their behalf, allegedly for their own good, and authorise their being able to act in this manner without having to justify it. 'Othering' people is, therefore, inimical to anti-oppressive practice.

Transcending commonsense attitudes about 'difference' requires the exercise of an empathy which goes beyond placing oneself in another's shoes by daring to put these on and wear them for a while to develop a deep understanding of the other person's position whilst at the same time reflecting on the privileged nature of one's own. The importance of knowing oneself in order to engage effectively with others who are different is, as Lishman reveals in Chapter 8, essential to carrying out anti-oppressive practice but immensely difficult to do. Challenging inequality and transforming social relations is an integral part of anti-oppressive practice. Knowing oneself better equips an individual for undertaking this task. Self-knowledge is a central component of the repertoire of skills held by a reflective practitioner (Schön, 1983; see Chapter 10). Moreover, reflexivity and social change form the bedrock upon which anti-oppressive practitioners build their interventions.

The commitment to social justice and its capacity to challenge existing social relations of inequality are key features of anti-oppressive practice. From these two elements come anti-oppressive practice's ability profoundly to affect social work practice and the society in which it is conducted. As Jones demonstrates in Chapter 3, poverty is a principal manifestion of the structural inequalities that social workers encounter. Challenging this state of affairs through anti-oppressive practice antagonises social workers' paymasters within the local state and can lead them to lose their jobs, as the Community Development Project (CDP) workers discovered, for example (Loney, 1983; Dominelli, 1990, 1997). Nonetheless, anti-oppressive practice's focus on social divisions and its aim to reduce inequality through the delivery of the personal social services contributes to social workers' capacity to address the issue of poverty in their work. Their doing so is also linked to anti-oppressive practice's potential to transform society. Although lending credibility to grass-roots-oriented social workers, this commitment is a major source of fear for those who oppose the spread of anti-oppressive practice.

For those individuals who lack allegiance to anti-oppressive principles, this fear is rooted in a loss of taken-for-granted privileges accorded to them through an inegalitarian social order (Rutherford, 1992). With this fear comes their desire to obliterate or destroy anti-oppressive practice rather than witness the realisation of its threat to realign the *status quo*. The backlash to anti-oppressive practice stems from resistance to the transformation of social relations demanded by oppressed people on the part of those who can see their assumed privileges vanish were such change to be implemented. For they know that the benefits they have enjoyed thus far have been possible because others who have been oppressed by them have been excluded from legitimating their claim to material resources and collectively distributed forms of power. In other words, the backlash is a struggle aimed at preserving the privileges of those accustomed to having them.

The struggle over anti-oppressive practice – an old–new controversy

Anti-oppressive practice began in the late 1960s/early 1970s as a critique of casework methods in social work practice as practitioners, particularly those in community work, began to challenge class-based privileges within the ambit of social work itself (see Corrigan and Leonard, 1978; Loney, 1983). This critique spread in the late 1970s/early 1980s to encompass women (Brook and Davies, 1985) and black people (Dominelli, 1988). The recent media emphasis, however, has rested largely on what was happening with 'race', the field in which black activists had been mobilising more generally since the 1960s.

The spread of anti-oppressive practice in academic social work circles was slow, although it achieved greater prominence in the late 1980s when the Central Council for Education and Training in Social Work (CCETSW) published its Paper 30. Paper 30 itself concentrated mainly on 'race', the area in which black and white practitioners had been organising to challenge CCETSW's neglect of the topic since the late 1970s. Opposition to these developments ran alongside these initiatives (see Davies, 1994; Pinker, 1993). The impetus for expansion in this area of anti-oppressive practice was threefold. One of these was the activities of the 'new social movements', particularly those involving women and black people. Another force was Paper 30. The third was the policies on equal opportunities and the legislation around their implementation. These began with the Race Relations Act, 1968 (amended in 1975) and later encompassed the Sex Equality Act, 1975 and Disability Discrimination Act, 1996 as these spread into social work agencies under the aegis of equal opportunities policies. The opposition's arguments against anti-oppressive practice in social work have consistently been based on the notion that social workers as professional beings have no right to engage in political action which challenges the existing social order in the way that anti-oppressive practice purports to do by demanding egalitarian social relations (Davies, 1994; Phillips, 1994).

The struggle between the adherents of anti-oppressive practice and those seeking to eliminate it from the domain of social work is a contest about the role of social work in society and the tasks that caring professionals should undertake. As such, it constitutes an old refrain in a new guise. In earlier times, it might have been depicted as the 'maintenance' school of social work against those arguing for social change through social work (see Davies, 1994). The new version of this debate has been framed in the language of 'political correctness' over what rightly characterises the heart and soul of the profession. The backdrop against which the current debate is taking place is one in which social work is feeling the impact of globalisation (Dominelli and Hoogvelt, 1996), the privatisation of the welfare state including the personal social services (Oakley and Williams, 1994), and a deepening polarisation in the social structure of British society as indicated by an increasing gap in wealth between rich and poor (Oakley and Williams, 1994; *Social Trends*, 1996).

Moreover, the British government is using social policy and legislative instruments to restructure the context within which social work has to operate. The Children Act, 1989, the National Health Service and Community Care Act, 1990 and the Criminal Justice Act, 1991 have fundamentally altered the statutory environment within which practitioners operate. In giving more choice to consumers and casting these in terms of citizens' rights, these developments have provided a supportive backdrop for anti-oppressive practice (Braye and Preston-Shoot, 1995). However, these initiatives have been promoted at a time which has coincided with severe cutbacks in public expenditures in the welfare state, including the personal social services, and a significant expansion in the implementation of privatisation measures driven by 'contract government' (Greer, 1994) . These have meant that the progressive thrust of the legislative forces has been undermined by a more conservative one which has placed economic rather than social priorities at the top of the political agenda. In seeking to reverse this trend in the field through their practice, the supporters of anti-oppressive practice have been caught in the cross-fire between the two opposing sides.

Social policy has a crucial role to play in either endorsing or rejecting the development of anti-oppressive practice. Moreover, as Carol and Alan Walker argue in Chapter 4, social policy can assist social work to make a major contribution in reducing the 'growing divide' between the rich and poor people of this country. It can identify the plight of poor people, pinpoint their skills in devising survival strategies and provide the research material for strengthening their case for securing social justice. In supporting such efforts, social policy can make a substantial contribution to putting antioppressive practice on a firmer footing and embedding it in the political arena. Anti-oppressive practice can achieve more rapid progess if there is political support from those currently controlling society's political and economic resources.

Moreover, the *structural* changes being brought about by powerful economic and political forces provide the context which gives this old debate a new potency. For there is more at stake than the provision of services for needy people. At the heart of the matter lies the question of how the post-war welfare state can be transformed to provide a fertile breeding ground for entrepeneurs who can ensure that capitalist relations enter a hitherto sacrosanct area to promote capital accumulation under new conditions in new arenas (Dominelli and Hoogvelt, 1996). Alongside this issue is another one which draws on the anti-intellectual tendencies apparent in popular consciousness (Jones, 1994). This is tied to the question of how professionals can be made to comply with government dictat rather than promote the interests of society's most marginalised groups as they see fit. That poor people lose out as a result of this struggle is an unfortuate consequence, possibly even unintended at the ideological level, of the developments which flow from the restructuring of the welfare state which is being progressed by free-market advocates.

In this context, the perpetuation of anti-oppressive principles and practice as discussed in terms of poor people taking control of their lives, and using their right to fulfil their welfare needs as a basis for challenging existing inegalitarian social relations, is not something that power-holders would wish to encourage. Bureaucratised forms of empowerment through the appeals and complaints procedures, which can be activated once a service which has been delivered is shown to have failed to live up to expectations, are excluded from the attack being mounted against anti-oppressive practice. Indeed, bureaucratic forms of involvement are actively being fostered by the state. The apparatus for processing customer complaints has been rapidly put into place as agencies seek to comply with provisions outlined in the National Health Service and Community Care Act, 1990 and the demands of the various citizens' charters promoted by the Conservative government headed by John Major.

These mechanisms have been exempted from the attacks being mounted against anti-oppressive practice because they are consistent with top-down forms of control exercised by those in power. Moreover, they are neither intended to nor do they challenge the present order of things. Law, as Braye and Preston-Shoot suggest in Chapter 5, has a similar form of ambiguity. It can be very useful in challenging unlawful inequality but, at the same time, can be used to restructure social relations only to a limited extend. Its tendency to individualise collective problems can only mean that redistributive justice remains beyond its scope. Yet it is precisely this form of justice which black activists, women and other oppressed groups are demanding.

The 'backlash' – a rejection of anti-oppressive practice by its opponents

The backlash against anti-oppressive practice, led by government ministers at the highest levels, reached its height in the summer of 1993 (see Appleyard, 1993; Pinker, 1993; Phillips, 1993, 1994). Their attack has to be understood as a rejection of anti-oppressive practice because it is inconsistent with using the welfare state to meet economic rather than social needs. For a social needs-based welfare state would have to encourage the bonds of solidarity encompassed in the pooling of risks to ensure that all members requiring services receive them free at the time of need. This collective strategy for welfare, however, is anathema to privatisation initiatives (Gilder, 1984; Murray, 1984, 1990, 1994) and the consolidation of market principles through the purchaser–provider split. This latter approach can only allow those with money a real choice about what personal social services they can call upon when they need them.

The economic relations underpinning these developments are camouflaged under an ideological cloak which focuses attention on the value system of those supporting anti-oppressive practice. Moreover, because language and access to the mass media have provided the terrain upon which the struggle surrounding the aims of social work is being conducted, it has been easier for traditional power-holders and media pundits to define the terms under which the encounter between the two opposing groups is being carried out. In it, given their greater hold on formal power and control over the media, the traditionalists opposing anti-oppressive practice seem to have gained the upper hand.

This appearance, however, to some extent belies reality in the field. Anti-oppressive practice has gained a strong foothold in the agencies in the form of equal opportunities policies which expanded across the whole of the welfare sector during the 1980s. A greater awareness of the existence of oppressed peoples and their demands for justice have followed this. The theory and practice of anti-oppressive practice also has generalised support among academics who see the value of confronting structural inequality in and through social work.

Thus, those at the vanguard of the backlash cannot count on things going completely their way. Indeed, some of them were astonished at the amount of support that anti-oppressive practice received among mainstream academics, policy-holders and practitioners when the issue hit the popular media in a big way in 1993. Rather than see the complete demise of anti-oppressive practice, these opponents had to content themselves with a restructuring of the mechanisms of CCETSW, which they had identified as being the culprits promoting the most obvious form of anti-oppressive practice – anti-racist practice. This they achieved by replacing the academic head of CCETSW's governing council with a lawyer, abolishing the Black Perspectives Committee which had spearheaded CCETSW's anti-racist initiatives and getting rid of a paragraph stating that racism is endemic in British society. This latter statement was contained in Annex 5 of Paper 30, which regulated the requirements for the DipSW. Paper 30 has now also been revised to expunge anti-racist ideology from its midst (Black Assessors, 1994). In the probation service, an area of social work practice which had taken anti-oppressive practice to heart in a fairly positive way and over which the government had financial control, the relevant ministers decided to withdraw its training programme from the university setting despite almost unanimous resistance to its proposed plan of action (Sone, 1995). Thus, within a short period of time, anti-oppressive practice was deemed to have been effaced from social work training and, in consequence, from practice.

Reality is, of course, more complicated. What the opponents of anti-oppressive practice ignored is that anti-oppressive practice did not achieve popularity because a few academics and practitioners wrote texts which identified what it was and proposed guidelines for practice. Anti-oppressive practice caught the imagination of academics, practitioners and policy-makers alike because it responded to the needs of oppressed people who objected to the failure of *their* services to meet *their* needs as they defined them. In short, anti-oppressive practice represented a small attempt made by social work academics and practitioners to respond to the agendas for practice being set in the field by members of the 'new social movements' led by women and black people. Oppressed people had created these organisational entities for themselves to challenge the inadequate services being meted out to them under the prevailing system.

These 'new social movements' and their demands for relevant services will not go away just because the government decrees that they should, nor will they die just because professionals fail to support their demands through anti-oppressive practice. They will continue with action that will produce oppositional forms of practice regardless of what happens within the mainstream system. And, regardless of the outcome of this struggle, they will continue to put pressure on mainstream policy-makers and professionals to respond to their agendas. A very good current example of this trend is the disability movement. Its adherents are asking practitioners to step aside if they cannot support their demands on their terms (Oliver, 1990). For unless they do so, these professionals are deemed to be working against them and they wish to have nothing to do with them. At the same time, disabled activists maintain their prerogative to constantly criticise whatever professionals do or claim to do on their behalf. As Mayo demonstrates in Chapter 13, community organisers have a long history of working collectively to challenge the *status quo* by subjecting professional practice to public scrutiny. Their activity is not diminishing simply because anti-oppressive practice is being challenged by the establishment.

Structural constraints limiting the spread of anti-oppressive practice

Despite the continuing struggle over anti-oppressive practice and its place in social work practice, its spread is limited by structural constraints which would exist irrespective of the ideological attack on it. Many of these have to do with the resourcing levels necessary to ensure that anti-oppressive practice permeates the whole of an organisation's workforce, culture and structures. To begin with, workers need to be trained in anti-oppressive practice. They will not acquire it from the air through osmosis. It needs to be learned, thought about, debated and absorbed into one's practice. Teaching anti-oppressive practice in a thorough and reflective manner requires highly skilled specialists who know their material to teach it to others in a way that engages with their fears about working in accordance with its principles as well as their aspirations for better practice.

Making these resources available will cost money. Anti-oppressive practice cannot be taught on the cheap. Yet CCETSW sought to introduce anti-oppressive practice in the DipSW without appropriate training being provided for either practitioners or academics teaching this subject. The net result of this policy was a patchy and inadequate outcome as poorly prepared academics and practice teachers tried to teach students and assess them on something that many were incapable of delivering, even when they had the desire to do so. Consequently, much inappropriate learning occurred as people grasped the form without knowing the substance, thereby endorsing tokenism of the worst kind. Those who had been antagonistic to the whole enterprise had their hostility confirmed.

Thus, no real dialogue over the issues involved ensued. Yet, a dialogue about anti-oppressive practice is essential for carrying the hearts and minds of those committed to it and to engage those opposed to it in confronting and reflecting upon its content. For anti-oppressive practice requires practitioners to integrate their understanding on three levels:

- intellectually, to grasp its central principles and methods of working;
- emotionally, to feel secure about and confident in working in anti-oppressive ways, or at least to be able to own up to and learn from the mistakes they make when reality falls short of their ambition to work in this way; and
- practically, to be able to implement the principles they have learnt and feel they own in their practice.

This is a tall order, which needs to be met in total rather than being skimped upon by focusing solely on the mind in the manner that has been evident in CCETSW's past endeavours on the anti-racist front. Worthy as the texts which have come out of the Northern Curriculum Development Project's efforts have been, they have, on their own, been insufficient. Anti-oppressive practice is a specialism with specialist knowledge which, as in other specialisms, must be learnt fully. But it differs from other specialisms in that everyone needs to know about it and how to use it in their practice in a way that infuses the whole of their work with anti-oppressive principles, regardless of the 'client' group. Moreover, it requires a commitment to it from the individual at the emotional and intellectual level as well as the abilities for implementing it in practice. Since these needs on the training front have yet to be met, these constraints will continue to impede the progress of anti-oppressive practice in the field.

The feasibility of such resourcing becoming available is unlikely given the current political context. Hence, new ways of approaching the problem will have to be invented. One way of doing this could be a system of secondments whereby those academics and practitioners with the requisite skills could help to train their colleagues in anti-oppressive practice. Another could be the active exchange of models of best practice, not as exemplars, but as models for discussion with an eye to constant improvement for those who have developed them. Such exchanges should be coupled with the possibility of seeing how to adapt them to meet the specific circumstances of those who are struggling to develop them. Forging collaborative partnerships of this nature within hard-pressed agencies and universities is asking a lot in today's climate. The pressures of the private market in both the field and academy will exact a toll which discourages their formation.

Agencies will have to take on such responsibilities knowing that obtaining additional resources to arrange cover is improbable, regardless of the training needs they can demonstrate. Social work academics will still have to produce the goods that count alongside their other colleagues when teaching quality assessment and research assessment exercise forms are completed. In other words, the busy work of getting through each day is a substantial barrier that those wishing to develop anti-oppressive practice and live up to its principles have to overcome. Moreover, the time in which to contemplate their next move is also at an all-time low.

Then, there is the business of engaging in organisational change both within the agencies and the universities, if an anti-oppressive working environment is to prevail. Organisational change favouring anti-oppressive practice will make demands of everyone within the institution regardless of rank. As Mullender and Perrott argue in Chapter 6, changing the inegalitarian culture of an organisation is also an important structural constraint to be transcended if anti-oppressive practice is to be realised in the workplace. This goal is a particularly problematic one to achieve as it does not rely solely on having the resources necessary for its implementation. It also requires management and workers to move in new directions, including a rethinking of how people relate to one another on both the individual and collective levels to promote egalitarian relations as the norm. Achieving this state of affairs also requires the transformation of the existing organisational value system, which tends to devalue 'difference' and perpetuates structural inequalities of various kinds.

Finally, changing organisational structures is also more than a matter of acquiring additional material resources, although having these to hand helps. It is also about promoting a different vision about what an organisation stands for and how it can be organised to accomplish its new aims successfully. In this sense, changing the organisational structure also draws upon changes in the organisation's culture (Broadbent *et al.*, 1993). Changing management and the accompanying managerial structures is central to securing this change.

Management relations, workplace relations among employees and relationships between workers and their 'clients' have to incorporate more egalitarian ways of working with each other. In other words, there is a flattening of hierarchies followed by the ultimate goal of reducing them to the lowest possible level so that egalitarian relations can flourish as a source of creative energy and innovation in developing better and more relevant services for those who need them. Service users also have to be brought on board as equal participants in the enterprise. Anti-oppressive practice, therefore, relies on teamwork in the best sense of the word and is hard work. Having an awareness of the obstacles to be overcome can also be a major barrier to embarking upon anti-oppressive practice for those who think it is an easy option.

The future of anti-oppressive practice

Anti-oppressive practice has yet to fulfil its potential in social work. What lies in store for it in the current bleak climate? Will anti-oppressive practice surive into the new millenium, despite the pessimistic prognosis being advocated by its opponents? I am cautiously optimistic for its future because it is rooted in the needs of oppressed people and their visions for alternatives to mainstream services. But the future of anti-oppressive practice will not be assured without a struggle. The forces seeking to undermine it are powerful ideologically, socially, economically and politically. In this context, it is important that those favouring anti-oppressive practice take a leaf from this text and engage in what I call *a dialogue over controversies* about its meaning and substance. This will require its proponents to undertake a number of initiatives to transform social relations and publicly present their case for anti-oppressive practice, thereby winning new adherents to the cause. These initiatives are outlined below.

To begin with, the supporters of anti-oppressive practice must form stronger alliances between the professionals who advocate anti-oppressive practice and the activists involved in the 'new social movements' so that they can know very clearly what their critiques of existing services are and what ideas they have for improving them. Anti-oppressive services should in a very real sense *belong to them* as the users. This will require anti-oppressive practitioners to be accountable to the users for their professional behaviour in a way that has not been practised very well in the past. Because of this, it may take a while for anti-oppressive practitioners to establish their credibility with users, for it will have to be earned. User involvement only becomes empowerment when there is a level playing field between the professionals and the service users. Thus, professional relationships with users should model the anti-oppressive practice being sought.

Anti-oppressive practice should be seen as a normal part of citizenship entitlements. People requiring access to the personal social services should not feel that they are charity cases begging from the bowl of mercy. They should have their welfare needs met as a right and should be assured that they will be responded to with dignity and respect. Moreover, they should also know that the services they receive will be appropriate to their needs. Their requests for assistance should not become further barriers which disenfranchise them from their rights as citizens. Academics and practitioners will need to present the arguments necessary for this state of affairs to become reality.

Achieving this objective would be much easier if anti-oppressive practitioners could establish better relationships with the media. Having supporters located within them would facilitate the proactive publicising of progressive social work activities, promote knowledge of existing good practice in this area and encourage the debate to be conducted on terms advocated by anti-oppressive practitioners and not just those of the opposition. Anti-oppressive social workers will also have to engage in anti-oppressive practice in many more areas than is currently the case.

The anti-oppressive cause can be strengthened if its adherents can become more involved in research and theory-building to develop a theoretical base that emanates from anti-oppressive practice carried out in the field. This can become suited to enhancing the status of social work theory and practice in its own right. Social work practitioners acting as social anthropologists who have a strong research orientation can amass the data for arguing in defence of an anti-oppressive practice which responds to the needs of service users as they see them. Were they to succeed in this, social workers acting in the role of intermediaries between policy-makers and 'clients' could more powerfully serve the needs of the disenfranchised groups they purport to represent.

On the training front, anti-oppressive practitioners will have to perform more effectively than they have done to date. Courses which have established good practice in this area should be encouraged to share their models with other courses that are struggling to implement anti-oppressive practice without the resources and knowledge base that this requires. Such exchanges can assist the process of learning from the mistakes others have made without having to revisit them in their own practice. Dialogue between courses can also enrich the models of good practice in those places which originated them. For complacency acts as a barrier to reflexivity in practice and the constant improvement in ways of working that anti-oppressive practice demands.

Finally, anti-oppressive practitioners need to develop a coherent professional organisation for social work. It will have to have the support of the profession as a whole and be able to defend its interests in the political arena. To do this effectively, it will have to be independent from government and encompass the academics, policy-makers, practitioners and service users who endorse its activities. A continuous dialogue with others about the role and purpose of social work in society ought to feature constantly on its agenda. Such an organisation could play a crucial role in promoting anti-oppressive practice and advocating its adoption in the field as well as monitoring its achievements on a regular basis.

Conclusion

Anti-oppressive practice is occurring in a controversial context and continues to develop despite the hostile climate that has surrounded it. However, its continued growth depends on much more work being carried out to constantly ensure that it meets the needs of those whom it is intended to serve and that it can be adopted more widely. Only in this way can its long-term future be assured. Thus, it is important that its supporters find ways of raising its profile and increasing the number of people committed to its being extended as a model of good practice.

The chapters which follow in this book continue the dialogue begun here by focusing on specific issues, dilemmas and controversies. Those which comprise Part I demonstrate how the contexts within which anti-oppressive practice is developed and practised are constantly shifting in response to external forces generated through the activities of services users and policy-makers, and the aspirations of practitioners and academics within the profession. Readers are invited to contribute to this process by reflecting on their own life experiences in relation to what is being said through the written word. To give you maximum space, there is no predetermined order which the chapters will follow. Your choice in what to read first will prevail. Hence, I have resisted describing the structure of this section in sequential order, preferring instead to outline the content of a particular chapter as an element within an organic whole at the point at which a particular topic is being explored. This way of proceeding also means that chapters from other sections of the book can be brought in without erecting artifical boundaries between one part and another. Through this means, I also hoped to encourage you to make links between the different chapters in the book for yourself.

Notes

1. I use the word 'client' here in quotation marks to denote the problematic usage of this term.
2. I use 'race' in quotation marks to highlight the social construction of racial and ethnic attributes.
3. The term 'black people' is used in a political sense and should not be taken to mean a homogeneous and ungendered category.

Further reading

Braye, S. and Preston-Shoot, M. (1995) *Empowering Practice in Social Care* (Buckingham, Open University Press).

This text is primarily about community care. However, it focuses on issues of empowerment and working in anti-oppressive ways within this context.

Dalrymple, J. and Burke, B. (1995) *Anti-oppressive Practice: Social Care and the Law* (Buckingham, Open University Press).

Although this book focuses largely on using the law as a tool for progressive practice, it threads the principles of anti-oppressive practice and the empowerment of service users throughout the discussion. Thus, it can be used by readers to deepen their knowledge and understanding of anti-oppressive practice in a particular area of practice.

Dominelli, L. (1997) *Sociology for Social Work* (London, Macmillan).

This text explores the theoretical underpinnings of anti-oppressive practice, examines the struggle over policy developments favouring its spread, provides case study examples of how anti-oppressive practice is used in holistic ways to address a range of different oppressions which exist in any one intervention and integrates theory and practice within it.

2

Values, ethics and social work

STEVEN SHARDLOW

Introduction and context

Getting to grips with social work values and ethics is rather like picking up a live, large and very wet fish out of running stream. Even if you are lucky enough to grab a fish, the chances are that just when you think you have caught it, the fish will vigorously slither out of your hands and jump back in the stream. Values and ethics similarly slither through our fingers for a variety of reasons: we don't try hard enough to catch them, preferring the practical business of doing social work; the subject matter, if we really investigate it, may sometimes seem complex, hard to grapple with and possibly obscure; there is a lack of conceptual clarity about many of the terms used that form part of the lexicon of 'social work values and ethics'; the boundaries of 'social work values and ethics' are imprecise and ill-defined, so the notion of what should constitute 'social work values and ethics' is itself part of a discussion about the nature of social work values. No doubt there are other reasons for not picking up this particular fish! Yet despite these difficulties in picking up the 'fish', there is something that intuitively suggests that social work is bound up with values and ethics. Is not ethics, according to the *Oxford English Dictionary*, 'the science of morals in human conduct', and is not social work about human relationships and behaviour? This conjunction is suggestive of a duty upon social workers to understand both ethics *and* social work.

This chapter considers both the nature of current debates about values and also reviews the context of those debates. It is grounded on the presumption that no consensus exists about value questions in social work. Evidence of the contested nature can be seen by looking at recent debates, for example over the nature of contracts between clients and social workers, and the extent to which they do or do not empower clients (Cordon, 1980; Cordon and Preston-Shoot, 1987, 1988; Rojek and Collins, 1987, 1988); the extent to which social work is grounded in Kantian ethics (Downie, 1989; Webb and McBeath, 1989, 1990; Gould, 1990); the significance of ideology and knowledge in social work (Dominelli, 1990-91; Webb, 1990–91a, 1990-91b; Smith, 1992), part of which was summarized by Shardlow (1992); and the extent to which a social worker is responsible or accountable when something goes wrong (Hollis and Howe, 1987, 1990; Macdonald, 1990a, 1990b). These debates are inevitably open-ended where social work itself is intrinsically political, controversial and contested, and where the nature of practice is subject to constant change, for example through the emergence of 'care in the community' (see Chapter 23) or the restructuring of work with children and families after the passing of the Children Act, 1989 (see Chapter 22).

The scope of 'social work values'

If, as suggested, the boundaries of the subject 'social work values and ethics' are themselves subject to different interpretations, under-standing the scope of these different interpretations may be the first step to keeping hold of the 'fish'. A narrow or 'restricted description' of the scope of social work 'values and ethics' might focus on:

- social workers' behaviour with clients (ethics).

A 'mid-range description' would add to the above:

- the role of social work as a profession (professional ethics and the sociology of professions);
- the role of social work in society – political philosophy and polit-ical sociology (see Chapter 3);
- the interface between social work and the law (see Chapter 5);
- the nature of social work organisations and their influence on the behaviour of individual social workers (see Chapter 6).

A 'broad definition' might further add:

- the nature of social work knowledge (epistemology);
- the construction of social work as an activity (for example post-modernism);
- the relationship of social work to religious belief systems (theology).

This attempt to delineate three different interpretations of the scope of 'social work values and ethics' is indicative of a broad range of notions and disciplines that might legitimately fall within the rubric of 'social work ethics and values'. From these interpretations (some of which have received much greater analysis than others), it is evident that the subject matter of 'social work values' is frequently, although not exclusively, defined by the interaction of different branches of philosophy and social work practice.

Understanding values and ethics

Philosophy is about asking questions and is concerned as much with finding the best questions as with complete or incontrovertible answers. Likewise, in trying to understand values and ethics in social work, we should be as much concerned with the questions we ask as the answers we might find – not perhaps a satisfying position for the busy practitioner in search of help in dealing with a particular client. Over time, the questions that philosophers ask have changed: similarly, for social work values – a dynamic and evolving subdiscipline with the broader field of social work itself. In the rest of this chapter, three central themes in social work values and ethics will be examined:

- work with service users;
- the role of social work in society;
- newly emerging professional values.

These themes define core elements within social work values and illustrate current concerns where social work practice and values intersect.

Ethics and work with service users

The first question to ask ourselves might be framed in words such as:

How should social workers behave towards their clients?

This is obviously a useful question and one that social work practitioners need to answer for their everyday practice – such as 'What are the boundaries of acceptable behaviour?'; is it, for example, acceptable for a male social worker to touch and provide comfort to a female client in distress (see, for example, Doel and Shardlow, 1998).

Yet such apparently simple and straightforward questions immediately spawn a whole raft of other more problematic questions. Is the language in which the question is framed sufficiently neutral or are terms used which have powerful emotional connotations, prejudicial implications for individuals or groups, highly contested meanings and so on? If any of these factors apply, it becomes even more difficult to think carefully about how to answer questions about how to behave with clients. In this example, the word 'clients' is problematic and other terms such as 'service user' or 'customer' might perhaps be preferred by some. The problem about using *any* of these words – 'client', 'service user' or 'customer' – is that they all carry implications about how people should be treated in everyday discourse. For example, 'customers' have certain legal rights and expectations about treatment when receiving services. Assuming that we can frame questions about how social workers should behave with their 'clients' in ways that do not presuppose answers on account of commonly held understandings of the terms used, other definitional problems arise, for example, who are the clients: is it people who are receiving help from social workers, clients' families, those who might receive help and so on? Thus, to make sense of the original question, we need to be able to define carefully the situations and people to whom the question refers. Despite the apparent prevarication about meaning and not wanting to wallow in difficulties, we can turn our attention to how others have sought to answer these questions concerning how social workers ought to behave towards their clients (using 'clients' as a generic term to refer to all who do or who might use social work services) by examining three of the most important types of response: the 'traditional list' of values, the professional code of ethics and the 'principle' approaches.

Lists of values

Biestek, a Catholic priest, stands as the originator of a set of values that seek to define how social workers ought to behave with their clients. His list, a set of values, included individualisation, the purposeful expression of feelings, controlled emotional involvement, acceptance, a non-judgemental attitude, client self-determination and confidentiality (Biestek, 1961). Each of these terms refers to a principle describing how social workers ought to behave. Therefore, the list lays down a moral code that is determinate, apparently absolute and grounded in Christian theology. The list approach to social work values has been extensively criticised by Timms on the ground that as the various lists contain different values (Timms, 1983), how can they therefore claim to universality for the social work profession as an entirety? Similarly, how can the list be justified? Does it represent anything more than one individual's beliefs – a personal view of what social work values ought to be? Despite the difficulties in justifying 'lists of values', they have had and continue to exert considerable influence on practice. Some of the values contained within the 'lists', such as 'confidentiality' or 'self-determination', chime persistent chords within the social work profession.

Professional codes of ethics

A development from the 'list' approach is to be found in the professional codes of ethics adopted by many national professional associations, for example the British Association for Social Workers (BASW, 1987), National Association of Social Workers (NASW, 1990) and the International Federation of Social Workers (IFSW, 1988). These codes of ethics are broader in scope than the 'list of values'. They represent consensus of the organisation's membership to define the nature and purpose of social work, to positively espouse some features of expected behaviour by professional social workers and to prohibit others. For example, the BASW code of ethics is typical in requiring that social workers:

> will respect their clients as individuals and will seek to ensure that their dignity, individuality, rights and responsibility shall be safeguarded. (BASW, 1986)

Equally, according to the NASW code of ethics, social workers are required not to 'exploit professional relationships for personal gain' (NASW, 1990).

Such statements are typical of the content of professional codes of ethics (see, for example, Banks, 1995 who compares the contents of 15 national professional codes of social work ethics). As can be seen from these examples, the contents of the codes of practice are highly general and do not in themselves provide much help to the social worker, or client for that matter, who wants to know how social workers ought to behave toward clients, for example, the codes do not provide any immediate answer to questions such as 'Is it a social worker's duty to inform the police if they discover that a client has committed a crime?' The statements in the codes of ethics seem to prompt other questions, such as 'How do I respect clients as individuals?' Codes of practice have as much to do with the establishment of a sense of professional identity for national or international social work professional organisations as providing answers to questions such as 'How ought social workers behave toward their clients?' Yet the codes purport to provide such help! Yet, despite these limitations of codes of practice, they can only be truly effective if they are part of a fully regulated profession – the establishment of a general social services council is a matter currently under debate in the UK (see, for example, Parker, 1990; NISW, 1992; Guy, 1994).

Fundamental moral principles

A third approach to answering the question surrounding how social workers ought to behave toward their clients is to be found in the use of a fundamental moral principle to determine desired behaviour. Within professional social work practice, 'respect for persons' is the most frequently employed such principle. This moral notion was fully explored by Downie and Telfer (1969). As a moral principle, 'respect for persons' is derived from the Kant's moral principle of the *categorical imperative*. This is variously written, but among the best known formulations are:

> I ought never to act except in such a way that I can also will that my maxim should become a universal law. (Kant, 1785, in Paton, 1948, p. 67)

> Act in such a way that you always treat humanity whether in your own person or in the person of any other, never simply as a means but always at the same time as an end. (Kant, 1785, in Paton, 1948, p. 91)

Through following these two principles, social workers are 'respecting persons'. Rather than having a set of prescribed or proscribed actions, this approach requires that if social workers wish to know how they ought to behave with their clients, they should consider the proposed action in the light of these two moral principles. This type of approach requires that social workers are fully able to engage in moral reasoning to determine how they ought to behave with their clients.

Having explored three different examples as ways of approaching the question, we may legitimately ask whether we are any nearer to being able to answer the question 'How should social workers behave with their clients?' The answer is yes we are; we now know some of the different ways in which the question has been approached. What we do not have is much of an answer about what a social worker should do in any particular situation – which is just answer the practitioner needs. Answers may also be found by looking to clients themselves, who have defined their expectations of social workers as evidenced in a long series of research studies dating back to the seminal work by Mayer and Timms (1970). For recent summaries, see, for example, DoH, 1995; Lindow and Morris, 1995.) One can also look to legal or procedural guidance provided by the government, as exemplified in the fields of care management (DoH, 1991a; SSI, 1991a, 1991b), child protection (DoH, 1991b) and child care (DoH, 1993). Some of these governmental statements tend to reduce professional autonomy and restrict the arena for independent professional decision-making and might, therefore, be seen as an attempt to deprofessionalise social work, removing the need for decision-making based on professional values by substituting a bureaucratic and procedural requirement (see Chapter 5). Yet they leave social workers fearful of making mistakes.

Social work and society

Our second group of questions is concerned with the function of social work, for example:

> **What is the purpose of social work as an activity in modern society?**
> **Why do we have social work?**

Is it possible to conceive of a society without social work? Some of the newly emergent states of eastern and central Europe functioned under communism without a social work profession (Deacon, 1992; Constable and Metha, 1993). In recent years, these states have moved quickly to establish social work – just as they are seeking to develop non-command-style economies and to introduce market mechanisms. This drive to develop social work in such states does not of itself establish that social work is a necessary function of modern industrial societies. However, it may well be that there is a functional need for social work in modern industrial societies, for example as Lorenz writes:

> Broadly speaking, social work's origins coincide with the formation of modern Western nation states and are directly related to the internal stability that these states need. (Lorenz, 1994, p. 4)

He thus argues that social work is necessary and contributes to the maintenance of social order, while Cannan *et al.* (1992) point to comparative and historical similarities in the emergence of social work in northern Europe.

Perhaps the most persuasive argument that social work is functionally necessary to modern society has been propounded by Davies (1994). He argues, from a humanist perspective, that the function of social work is to help to maintain the fabric of society, a fabric that would otherwise be brittle and likely to fracture, as exemplified in the following quotation:

> In so far as there are common elements in social work they are best described by the general notion of *maintenance*: society maintaining

itself in a relatively stable state by making provision for and managing people in positions of severe weakness, stress or vulnerability; and society maintaining its own members, without exception by commitment to humanist endeavour. (Davies, 1994, p. 40)

Interestingly, in the first edition of the book, Davies continued with a bold statement about the underlying purpose of social work:

and its [social work's] emphasis on the idea of respect for the client, optimism for the future, and faith in the essential or at least potential unity of society. (Davies, 1984, p. 3)

We can only speculate about the reasons for the lost vision of a social work striving for a unified and harmonious society. Yet Davies' vision of the function of social work emphasises the need to maintain the social order while seeing the operation of the state in the promotion of social work as being to further humanist ideals. The 'maintenance theory' of social work found in Davies' writings is essentially benign: he expresses a broad approval of the motives of the state and the consequent role of social work to maintain the social fabric. When a similar argument (in the sense that social work helps to maintain existing social structures) about the role of social work in society is advanced from a Marxist perspective, the timbre alters dramatically:

Since its modern origins in the middle of the last century, social work has been one of the many strategies developed and deployed by the ruling class and the state for intervening in the lives of working people... social work has to be considered as one of the agencies of class control and regulation. (Jones, 1983, p. 9, as quoted in Rojek *et al.*, 1988, p. 64)

Leonard takes this argument further, suggesting that social work promotes a more compliant labour force and seeks the re-education of the 'underclass clientele who are seen as irresponsible and immature' (Leonard, 1976, p. 261). Here, social work is portrayed as a malignant force assisting dominant élites to maintain political and economic power over groups in society who are deemed to be a threat. In such a vision, social work is not acting in the interests of those it helps but is part of a set of social structures that oppress. However, these two different opinions – the Marxist and the maintenance theorist – do not diverge over what social workers actually do in society. It is in the significance, meaning and value of those actions, not for individuals but at the level of sociological or political explanation, that they differ. The type of position adopted by Leonard, which is critical of the position and role of adopted by social work within society, leads relatively easily to the view that social work should strive for social change, in other words to refute the notion that social work is about the maintenance of society. Similar critical and radical views about the function of social work in society are located with a variety of other different intellectual traditions, notably feminism (see, for example, Wise, 1985; Graham, 1992) and anti-racism (see, for example, Dominelli, 1988; Ahmad, 1990).

New values: empowerment, consumerism, structural challenge

In the past 15 years or so, a new set of ideas, such as advocacy (for example, Simons, 1992), consumerism (for example, Allen, 1988), empowerment (for example, Adams, 1990), participation (for example, Biehal, 1993), partnership (for example, Marsh and Fisher, 1992), user involvement (Managment, 1994) and so on, have influenced social work ideology. Braye and Preston-Shoot (1995) characterise these new and emerging 'radical' values, which are concerned with challenging oppression, as distinct from 'traditional values' which emphasise the individualised nature of the relationship between the social worker and individual receiving help. Yet there should be no presumption that the emergence of these new values or the development of older, more traditional ones will lead to changes in professional practice. Without organisational backing or changed professional education, practice is likely to remain relatively fixed.

Let us consider as an example one of these 'radical' values in a little more detail.

Empowerment

Empowerment has been persuasively and powerfully defined by Braye and Preston-Shoot in terms of:

- extending one's ability to take effective decisions;
- individuals, groups and/or communities taking control of their circumstances and achieving their own goals, thereby being able to work towards maximising the quality of their lives;
- enabling people who are disempowered to have more control over their lives, to have a greater voice in institutions, service and situations which affect them, and to exercise power over someone else rather than simply being the recipients of exercised power;
- helping people to regain their own power (Braye and Preston-Shoot, 1995, p. 48).

Such a definition of empowerment is centrally about people taking control of their own lives and having the power to shape their own future. For Braye and Preston-Shoot, the concept seems to imply a general broadening and deepening of citizenship, but for others the context is more circumscribed and refers only to the articulation and meeting of needs (Stevenson and Parsloe, 1993). In essence, in its more restricted sense, 'empowerment' as an idea may not be so very different from 'self-determination' as proposed by Biestek (1961). The social context and the social construction of professional social work practice are different, but when we use words like 'empowerment' or 'self-determination', we should ask how these professional concepts are linked or related to longstanding philosophical debates about the nature of freedom or liberty. Part of the difficulty with such terms as 'empowerment' is their very slipperiness – just like our fish! These values are defined in different ways and hence mean different things to different people. There is a considerable danger with 'radical' values such as 'empowerment' that they vanish as quickly as they came and become mere ephemera: whatever their eventual durability as professional values, they stand in need of justification for adoption by the profession. Otherwise, 'radical' values are susceptible to the same counterarguments as those advanced by Timms against the 'list approach'. They become, in essence, just another item on a list!

If we were to explore the other radical values we might find similar problems with regard to definition, scope and potential for meaningful application to practice: for example, according to Stevenson and Parsloe, 'partnership is very vague since it suggests an equality which is rarely possible' (1993, p. 6). Debates about the nature of concepts such as 'partnership' or 'empowerment' are highly significant, as these debates denote the rise of user-led definitions of the nature of professionalism that stand in contention with the profession's own views.

Endnote – netting the fish

From this brief overview of professional values and ethics in social work, we may emerge in despair about the possibility of providing definitive answers to the questions posed. If this is so, however, the nature of the enterprise is misunderstood; it is not so much final answers but better refined questions that are required. This will help to establish an ethically mature professional stance for social work. Moreover, there is a great diversity and liveliness about the emerging topics for debate in this field: see, for example, the role of social workers in organ donation (Geva and Weinman, 1995), the need for social work to adopt a pacifist stance (Verschelden, 1993) or the importance of religion in social work (Amato-von Hemert, 1994; Clark, 1994). There have recently been an increasing number of published materials concerning postmodernism and social work (for further discussion of this aspect of values, see Chapter 20). There is an inevitability that 'professional values', however defined, will mediate between forms of social work practice that are essentially procedural and forms of practice that are individualised and highly creative.

Further reading

Banks, S. (1995) *Ethics and Values in Social Work* (London, Macmillan).

A brief general overview of social work values designed specifically for practitioners.

Hugman, R. and Smith, D. (eds) (1996) *Ethical Issues in Social Work* (London, Routledge.)

An edited collection containing an exploration of a range of current issues in professional ethics for social workers.

Jones, C. (1983) *State Social Work and the Working Class* (London, Routledge & Kegan Paul).

An exploration of the political context of social work.

Reamer, F. G. (1993) *Ethical Dilemmas in Social Services: A Guide for Social Workers*, 3rd edn (New York, Columbia University Press).

A thorough exploration of professional values for social workers from a US perspective.

Rhodes, M. L. (1986) *Ethical Dilemmas in Social Work Practice* (London, Routledge & Kegan Paul).

A book which takes a series of practical examples of value problems and explores the implications.

Shardlow, S. M. (forthcoming) *Social Work Values and Knowledge* (London, Macmillan).

A detailed overview of professional values from a UK perspective.

3

Social work and society

CHRIS JONES

Introduction

Try and find a clear definition of social work. It is no easy task, although in recent years it would appear that, for some, social work is best described as that activity undertaken by those people employed as social workers by state social service departments. This is the position taken for example by the CCETSW in its national curriculum for social work education. It is not a helpful definition in that it captures nothing of the history of social work or its essence independent of a specific context and suggests that social work can be almost anything if it is called such by a state agency. Such an unsatisfactory definition is a reflection of a real difficulty. For social work is a diverse and shifting activity, undertaken by various kinds of welfare worker, many of whom are currently employed by statutory local authority social service departments, others by voluntary and charitable agencies, still others being genuine volunteers offering social work through a wide range of community-based organisations and groups. Moreover, until the mid-1970s, the majority of people employed as social workers in Britain had no specialist training or education.

Not only is the location of social work diverse in contemporary society, but so too is its practice. It embraces a spectrum of activities along a wide continuum, with counselling and support at one end and statutory powers to remove liberties at the other. Furthermore, as any social work student will tell you, clients of social work, or in modern parlance service users, are in some respects equally diverse. Clients can be drawn from across the life cycle, from the oldest to the youngest, men or women, black or white, from the able-bodied to those with special needs.

This diversity of social work is one of its salient characteristics. For some clients, social work is an activity that brings solace and comfort at times of acute need; for others, it is an activity to be avoided because of the threat it poses to their liberty. Moreover, it is not a static activity. The work of social workers in contemporary social service departments has changed considerably from the pre-Seebohm days of child care and health and welfare departments (Clarke, 1993), and there have been further profound changes since the implementation of the Children Act, 1989 and community care legislation in the early 1990s (Hadley and Clough, 1996).

However, such diversity and dynamism does not mean that it is impossible to talk about social work and society in a more general sense, although one needs to be sensitive to its lack of uniformity. Social work is no different from other social activities in that it is possible to reveal much of its purpose and character by exploring its origins and its development. After all, the personal social services in which social work has taken a lead role has grown to become a very significant part of Britain's welfare system. One presumes that this expansion, particularly since 1945, is based on some understanding of social work's more general role, purpose and function in society. Second, whilst not wishing to diminish the significance of social work's diversity and even its paradoxical nature with respect to its involvement in both social care and social control, there is a need to challenge social work's own in-house appreciation of itself, in which it has glorified its diversity in order, I would argue, to obfuscate some of its more essential and enduring features.

Social work, class and poverty

For all the attention to diversity, social work has, since its modern origins in the Charity Organisation Society (COS) which was formed 1869 through to the present day, been overwhelmingly a class-specific activity. Current social work texts might wish to avoid this conclusion by using other labels and categories for its clients, but the evidence overwhelmingly indicates that, whether the client is old or young, able-bodied or with a special need, an offender, a single parent, an abused child or partner, black or white, clients are most likely to be poor and most likely to be drawn from those sections of the population which enjoy the least status, security and power (Becker and MacPherson, 1988; Schorr, 1992). In Britain at least, it is unusual to find those with wealth and privilege making use of social workers, and one suspects that they would recoil at the prospect. This class-specificity of social work is of great importance. Its focus on and preoccupation with those at the bottom of the social hierarchy is one of the distinguishing features of social work and is a common factor through its historical development. Ironically, the modern social work enterprise, whether expressed through its courses, its professional organisation or its various organisational settings, attempts to play down this class specificity.

The COS, during the period of its greatest influence between 1869 and 1908, was not so coy about its class-specific credentials and mission. Concerned by the threat to social order and progress posed by widespread poverty and destitution – especially in the rapidly expanding industrial and commercial centres of British capitalism – the COS developed casework as *the* method of social reform. Central to the development of casework was the idealist perspectives of the leading members of the COS, of whom Bernard Bosanquet was particularly notable. For the Bosanquets (Bernard and Helen) and Charles Loch, social work was the practical expression of idealist philosophy (Jones, 1978). Idealism gave primacy to the realm of ideas in the determination of social and economic conditions just as casework gave primacy to character and morality with respect to an individual's social and economic position and well-being. 'In social reform', Bernard Bosanquet argued, 'character is the condition of conditions' (1895, p. vii). In a later text, he wrote:

> Here then, seems to be the true meaning of social work. Wherever it may start its goal is the same; to bring the social mind into order, into harmony with itself. Social disorganisation is the outward and visible form of moral and intellectual disorganisation. (Bosanquet, 1901, p. 297)

Casework was developed as an idealist welfare practice and did much to set the tone for all subsequent social work practice and theory. The logic was impeccable once one accepted the taken-for-granted assumption that the plight of the working-class poor and destitute was not related to the fundamental nature of capitalism and its machinations. Indeed, industrial capitalism was taken as a progressive force. The dislocations incurred by its expansion and urbanisation were not problems of capitalism but rather the backwardness of people to adapt and shift, to modernise.

The problems posed by the poor and destitute were defined according to the idealism of the COS as problems of character and morality rather than of lack of resources and power. Social work in its modern origins and subsequent development, whilst focused on the most impoverished and disadvantaged, was neither practised nor conceived of as an activity concerned primarily with the material conditions of clients' lives. Its principal, long-term concern has been with either the moral education of clients or, where this is impossible, with their supervision in order to minimise their nuisance and cost to the state. Material circumstances are considered largely as an external measure of personal and familial morality. Drawing on social

Darwinism, the COS insisted that one's location in the social and economic world was in large measure a reflection of character, those at the bottom of the pile being the most deficient and disorganised. The contribution of the COS to these popular debates and under-standings about social conditions and the plight of the working class in late Victorian society was the manner in which it contributed significantly to the sophistication and quality of these commonplace assumptions of the privileged towards the powerless.

The leadership of the COS was formidable. The Bosanquets in particular matched in intellectual stature and publications their coun-terparts the Webbs in the Fabian Society. Helen Bosanquet's work on the family had a significant impact on social policy in general and social work in particular. Her book (Bosanquet, 1906) marks one of the first systematic accounts of the importance of the family as the basic social unit. The family, Helen Bosanquet argued, was the critical institution which influenced and informed character and morality. The problems of destitution, of crime, of poor labour discipline, of alcoholism, of lack of thrift and so forth were not to be sought in social structural arrangements but in poor and inadequate parenting, especially mothering. This, rather than lack of money or influence, was the problem, and social work was created and developed as a 'mental' activity and welfare practice with overwhelming attention being given to family life and parenting. In essence, casework involved social workers taking on the role of 'good' parents with the clients as 'children'.

Social work as conservative welfare

The COS's creation of casework within an idealist paradigm and a central focus on the family established social work as a conservative welfare practice. Despite many changes in the language and know-ledge base of social work since the end of the nineteenth century, social work has remained an activity that is not only class-specific, but has also continued to practise as if the primary causes of clients' problems are located in their behaviour, morality and deficient family relationships. Mainstream social work, despite its immersion in poverty and amongst the least powerful sections of the population, has rarely ventured to seek explanations for these difficulties beyond family and interpersonal relationships and dynamics. Questioning the legitimacy of social, economic and political systems and the manner in which patterns of inequality and oppression systematically disadvantage women, minority ethnic groups, people with disabili-ties, children and young people, especially when located within the working-class poor, has not been part of social work's agenda.

For all its trappings of liberalism and concern, there has been no sustained or substantial tradition of radicalism within British social work. It is also probable that had social work acquired such a perspective, it would have not enjoyed state sponsorship since 1945. That is not to deny, however, the presence of critical impulses within social work, in particular the influence of feminist and anti-racist perspectives, especially since the mid-1970s (Ahmed *et al.*, 1986; Marchant and Wearing, 1986; Dominelli, 1988; Langan and Day, 1992). For many practitioners and students, the materials generated from these perspectives provided highly valuable insights, under-standings that influenced their practice with clients. Their contribu-tion to highlighting systems of institutional racism and the manner in which much social work practice was both gender-specific and sexist has been considerable.

Nevertheless, throughout its short history, progressive ideas which seek to move the locus of explanation and intervention from the family or individual client to wider social and political systems and processes have tended to be resisted and treated by the key state agencies managing social work as contagion and dangerous. The removal of community work from social work's repertoire during the 1970s is probably one clear example of potentially troublesome perspectives and practices being eradicated. The social work estab-lishment itself has devoted considerable energy and attention to the management of social workers in order to avert the threat of what it perceives as radical contamination. As I have argued elsewhere, many developments in social work education since 1975 can be read in part as being concerned to ensure the reproduction of a conserva-tive and manageable workforce (Jones, 1996a, 1996b). This in turn highlights a further characteristic of social work as a site of ongoing debate, controversy and contest, and as an acitivity whose trajectory is, and has been, influenced by conflicting perspectives on the nature of social problems and appropriate responses.

From the point of view of clients, the history of social work has been marked by suspicion and hostility (Jones, 1997). Social work remains one of the few welfare activities that has at no time been the subject of working-class demands for expansion and development (Wardman, 1977). On the limited occasions when the voices of clients are heard, it is notable that many complain of the moralising and interfering nature of social work investigations and the sheer unsuit-ability of the agencies' responses to their difficulties. This is hardly surprising when many clients have concerns associated with lack of material resources but the agency reinterprets the problem as one of attitude, character or parenting and management skills. The Claimants Unions in the 1970s reckoned that social workers were worse than the social security for their snooping and the conditions which were applied to the giving of small sums of money (Carmichael, 1974). Handler (1968), in his study of children's departments, came to the conclusion that the 'operative social work principles... are remarkably similar to those the Charity Organisation Society, founded about 100 years ago. The close supervision of spending money is little different from the old system of relief in kind; poor people cannot be trusted to spend money that isn't "theirs"'(Handler, 1968, p. 487; see also Davis and Wainwright, 1996). As Bryan and her co-authors (1985) note, add racism to social work's underlying class hostility and the result is that 'black women's relationships with social workers have been fraught with... antagonisms... ':

> Whether we are single parents, homeless young women or the parents of children in care, we are constantly confronted with racist, classist or culturally biased judgements about our lives. The social background of most social workers and the training they receive give them no real understanding of our different family structures, cultural values and codes of behaviour. It is so much easier for them to rely on loose assumptions and loaded stereotypes of us than to try seriously to address the root cause of our problems. These assumptions become the justification for everything from secret files and surveillance to direct intervention of the most destructive kind. (Bryan *et al.*, 1985, p. 112)

That people mostly become clients through third-party referral (for example by the police, schools, health services or social security) rather than through self-referral further illustrates the low regard and suspicion with which social work is held amongst those in need (Schorr, 1992). Social work appears to be one of those welfare services which people seek to avoid wherever possible, and where entanglement has come to be associated with failure and stigma. However, remembering the caveats about diversity and dynamism noted in the introduction, it is important to note that not all clients are treated in the same manner. Social work reflects and in significant ways reinforces the moral hierarchies prevalent at any particular time. This can impact significantly on client experiences of social work, with those who are generally perceived as more deserving – single and abandoned poor fathers, some older poor people for example – having a more positive response than those held in low regard – black young offenders, young poor black single mothers and so on. Moral judgements about worth and deservedness structure social work practice with the working-class poor just as they did a century earlier. Social work, for all its claims of being a liberal and caring occupation, tends to reflect rather than challenge prevailing social mores, which again reflects its social conservatism.

Unloved social work

Paradoxically, despite this conservative tradition, social work has not enjoyed unconditional support from élite groups either. The renaissance of state social work in Britain after World War II was marked by a long process of struggle for legitimacy and acceptance, and it was not until the Seebohm Report in 1968 that social work was granted its own discrete agency. Even then, medicine was most reluctant to give up its stewardship of social work (Leonard, 1973) and has continued to demand that social work be returned to its ambit of control.

Part of social work's problem rests with the status of its client population. In contrast to the COS, which insisted that social work was only possible with those who had shown some semblance of morality prior to their destitution – namely the deserving poor – British social work since 1945 has been principally targeted at those whom the COS described as the residuum or the undeserving poor and whom it regarded as beyond help. (Today, the New Right term 'underclass' is commonly used to describe that segment of the population from whom most clients are drawn; Novak, 1997). This shift in focus during and immediately after World War II marked an important break with COS social work.

Influenced by eugenics and social Darwinism, it was commonplace for the undeserving poor to be condemned as human refuse incapable of being assisted and for whom close supervision and containment was the only reasonable strategy. Whetham, a prominent eugenicist at the turn of the century, represented this perspective when he wrote of the residuum:

> In dealing with men and women of this character, where we cannot hope to accomplish individual radical cure, we must, as with the feeble minded, organise the extinction of the tribe. In the old days the law attempted this extinction by hanging, a preventative of the sternest and most effective nature... For us... the old methods are impossible. We must attain the same result by the longer and gentler system of perpetual segregation in detention colonies, and with all mitigations that are practicable. (Whetham, 1909, pp. 214-15)

By 1945, although these ideas were never expunged – as their re-emergence with the New Right's underclass concept demonstrates – they were no longer acceptable. As with the defeat of the

Conservative government in 1997, popular opinion following World War II was revolted by such inhumanity and demanded compassionate social welfare, the state taking greater responsibility for regulating the excesses of capitalism. In contrast to social work's lack of vision and profile between 1979 and 1997, British social work after World War II enjoyed a quality of leadership which both seized upon and reflected the growing dominance of and consensus around social democracy and the promise of the Keynesian welfare state. Buoyed up by the work of Freud and the neo-Freudians, social work leaders such as Eileen Younghusband were confident that social work had the knowledge and skills to ensure that even the lowest of the low were capable of becoming full participants – citizens – in society. All that was required was that social work be given the remit and resources to intervene.

Psycho-analysis liberated casework from the straitjacket imposed by the biological pessimism of COS, and there was tremendous optimism within social work about the contribution that a psycho-analytically informed casework could now make to resolving a range of deep-rooted social problems (see Morris, 1964; Younghusband, 1970). It was considered that such casework could eradicate the problem of the problem family, strengthen working-class families and thereby reduce the need for residential provision for children and make major inroads into reducing juvenile delinquency. These were no cautious claims. Social work leaders believed that their occupation could, with appropriate funding and training, attend to some of the most pressing social problems of the post-war period. With these claims, social work captured much of the optimism of social policy-makers through the 1950s and 60s. It believed that the Keynesian welfare state had eradicated the principal material causes of poverty, such that those who were still locked in poverty were there because of psychological problems and thereby required social work. It was quite a different context from that of the COS period, but there was no less an insistence within social work that those problematic groups at the 'bottom' of society were there largely because of the consequences of poor parenting and mothering.

Needless to say, the gradual expansion of social work, driven largely by concerns over the working-class family and children (and much less by concerns with those who were poor and old or disabled), did not bring about the sorts of dramatic improvement envisaged by social work commentators. Moreover, there were many groups and organisations, both within the state system itself and elsewhere, which became increasingly critical of what they saw as the softly, softly approach of social work. The police and sections of the magistracy were vociferous in their opposition to the new powers granted to social workers in the 1960s for the management and control of juvenile offenders (Jones, 1978, pp. 304–6). Reactionary critics attracted considerable attention then, as they do now, in pointing to young offenders being given opportunities seemingly to enjoy themselves when placed under the supervision of social services departments following conviction. Social security officials likewise complained that too much of their time was taken up haggling with social workers who were attempting to secure more generous benefit settlements (when there was discretion in the social security system) for those whom they believed were no more than scroungers and layabouts. Despite advances in the social sciences, in which valuable insights have been gained into the manner by which life chances and opportunities are considerably influenced by class position, gender and ethnicity, over which the individual has no control, it seems that many people continue to hold negative views of clients and public opinion is soon excited when it is suggested that they are being treated generously.

Many of these criticisms of social work's apparent tolerance towards some sections of its client population (particularly young offenders and some families) were readily seized upon by the New Right during the 1980s and contributed to the tabloid media's onslaught on social work as the epitome of 1960s moral relativism (Franklin, 1989). In these quarters, there was no understanding that this apparent liberalism was essentially not a reflection of social work's sympathy with the problems and difficulties of clients, but rather a reflection of a particular method in which a sympathetic and caring approach was considered to be essential in order to bring about a change in their clients' behaviour and moral outlook. That is not to deny that many individual social workers have been attracted to the occupation because of their concern and compassion for clients, but as an institution, state social work is sadly not a reflection of society's compassion for its most vulnerable and disadvantaged members. Instead, it is a reflection of a drive to develop strategies which manage some of the principal human casualties of a grossly unequal social and economic system in a manner which locates the problem with the casualties rather than with the system.

For mainstream social work, causes of clients' problems remain principally located within the so-called deficiencies of their family histories and relationships, and there has been virtually no attempt in British social work theorising and writing to understand or explain why it is that the majority of clients, irrespective of their immediate problems, are overwhelmingly drawn from the most impoverished and disadvantaged sections of society. When practitioners have attempted to draw attention to systemic features of their clients' problems, be they related to the perpetuation of class inequalities, patriarchy or racism, they have been rapidly confronted by ridicule and hostility. The furore over child sexual abuse in Cleveland was in large measure due to the manner in which some of the social workers and health professionals involved were seen to be highlighting the abuse of male power at precisely the moment when the Conservative government had embarked on a campaign to raise the profile and status of fathers (Campbell, 1988). There was a similar outburst in the early 1990s when right-wing critics and government ministers caught up with the attention that social work education was then giving to anti-racist perspectives. They were aghast that social work could suggest that racism was endemic and pervasive in British society (Humphries, 1993).

That social work persists as a paradoxical occupation in Britain should come as no surprise. It has always contained elements of genuine concern for some of the most vulnerable in society. For all its contact and immersion in this context, it has only on the rarest of occasions been prepared to question seriously the legitimacy of the society in which such difficulties are perpetually reproduced. Of course, had it done so, state social work would have been abolished a long time ago. In the meantime, it thrives chameleon-like, changing its outer shape and appearance in keeping with the temper of the time. It survives, despite all the attacks, because it appears to have some impact on the management and control of the disadvantaged and distressed. It could and should be more than this.

Further reading

Clarke, J. (ed.) (1993) *A Crisis in Care* (London, Sage).

　Useful edited collection on social work and society.

Holman, B. (1993) *A New Deal for Social Welfare* (Oxford, Lion Publishing).

　Polemical renunciation of the New Right's impact on state social work.

Loch, C.S. (ed.) (1904) *Methods of Social Advance* (London, Macmillan).

　It pays to have an appreciation of the historical roots of British social work.

Mullaly, R. (1993) *Structural Social Work* (Toronto, McClelland and Stewart).

　Provides a lucid and critical analysis of contemporary social work and its possibilities.

Schorr, A. (1992) *The Personal Social Services: An Outside View* (York, Joseph Rowntree Foundation).

4

Social policy and social work

CAROL WALKER AND ALAN WALKER

Introduction

> To claim that economic and social policy, the prevailing political
> ideology and a particular location within the social structure, concep-
> tualised in class terms have a direct bearing upon day-to-day living,
> would hardly be contentious today. (Bailey, 1988, p. 197)

So wrote Roy Bailey in 1988. While few in social work would disagree
with this statement in principle, in practice it is all too easy for the
context within which social workers, and other professionals, work to
be overlooked in the pressures of their everyday lives. In particular, it
is too easy for social workers, the majority of whose service users are
poor (Becker and MacPherson, 1986), to focus on the differing abilities of individuals to manage and cope within the constraints of their
personal circumstances rather than to compare their circumstances
with those enjoyed by the wider population.

In this chapter, we focus on the social policy context within which
social workers operate and their service users live. Social policy is of
particular importance because it sets both the framework and
constraints within which professionals work and the type and level of
service they can provide. It also has an impact on the number of
people seeking or being referred to social services departments, in
particular on their ability to cope independently.

The current social policy context

Over the past two decades, there have been major changes in British
social policy. In particular, successive governments have sought to
role back the frontiers of the state in order to:

- increase individual and family responsibility;
- move from public to private provision;
- decrease public spending on the welfare state.

All these objectives impact most seriously on the most vulnerable people in Britain because it is they who require total or partial support from the state, yet they have been the main losers. It is the poor who have lost most in the changes which have been made in the structure and administration of public welfare services. This is illustrated in a number of different services:

- Housing policy was more concerned with changing tenure than with meeting housing need.
- The introduction of market principles into the NHS and social service provision through the purchaser–provider split and the establishment of fund-holding GPs led to two levels of NHS provision, in which those living in the most deprived areas gained least.
- In education, the introduction of the local management of schools (LMS) and the national curriculum, in particular the publication of league tables, has exacerbated divisions between pupils in poor and affluent areas and penalised those working in areas of social deprivation.
- The focus in the probation service has shifted much more towards an active involvement in punishment and control.
- Changes in local authority social services saw a dramatic shift of social services departments away from providers to being managers and regulators of care.
- In response to the growing number of people dependent on social security, social security policy has focused on getting people off benefit through punitive measures and ignored the continuing poverty of those dependent on benefit, in the vast majority of cases through no fault of their own.

All of these changes have occurred within the context of huge cuts in social spending, which has led to a diminution of confidence in public services, and increasing numbers of people opting into the private sector, for example in health, education and pensions. Before considering how government policy in other areas of welfare state provision has impacted on vulnerable people, we will consider the growth and persistence of poverty in Britain and its implications for social work.

Poverty and social work

The majority of social work service users are poor, yet poverty as an issue is too often marginalised in social work training, even though it is a greater cause of social exclusion than are 'race' and gender, with which it also overlaps (Walker and Walker, 1997). In social work practice, there is a danger that poverty and deprivation can be overlooked precisely because they are so common and are somehow seen as 'normal' for social work service users. However, the fact remains that a significant proportion of the British population are living on incomes substantially below the average for the rest of the population and are, as such, at risk of malnutrition, hypothermia, homelessness, restricted educational opportunities, poorer health, earlier death and of being victims of crime. For example, a child born into a poor family is four times as likely as a child from a better-off family to die before the age of 20.

Since the late 1970s, the UK has experienced an increase in income inequality that is unparalleled, with the sole exception of New Zealand, in the industrialised world (Hills, 1995). Between 1979 and 1993/94, the real incomes (after housing costs) of those in the poorest tenth of the population fell by 13 per cent, the average rose by 40 per cent, while the richest enjoyed a huge increase of 63 per cent (Oppenheim, 1997). Despite this, Conservative governments were reluctant to acknowledge the problem, to the extent that, in the 1980s, the word 'poverty' was banned from official publications. Increasingly, the political debate generally has shifted away from the problem of poverty towards the 'problem' of the poor. Policy has tended consequently to concentrate on influencing the behaviour of the poor, in particular to reduce their dependence on state benefits, rather than tackling the underlying factors, such as unemployment, which cause poverty.

Britain does not have an official measure of poverty. However, two sets of statistics are useful in determining the extent of poverty and the groups most affected.

Low-income families statistics

These figures show the number of people living on incomes below, at and just above the levels of income support (IS) – the 'safety net' minimum social assistance levels. The level of IS varies according to the type of family, the number and ages of children and a number of other criteria, such as disability and age. The weekly income of £118.65 (after housing costs) paid to a family of four (two adults, two children under 11) in 1996/97 is considerably lower than either the average weekly household expenditure of £272 per week (1993 figure, before housing costs) or the average manual earnings of £274.30 (1993 figure). An independent study concluded that prevailing IS rates would only meet 33 per cent of a 'modest but adequate' budget for a lone mother with two young children, 46 per cent of that of a couple with two small children and 34 per cent of that of a single person (Bradshaw, 1993).

Despite the low level of the social assistance rates, the low income statistics (see Table 4.1) show that, in 1992 (the latest year for which figures are available), one-quarter of the population were living on incomes at or below IS rates, and 33 per cent were living on incomes less than 40 per cent above these rates (commonly accepted as being on the 'margins' of poverty).

Table 4.1   Number of people living in or on the margins of poverty in 1979, 1989 and 1992

	1979	*1989*	*1992*
Below SB/IS*	3,170 (6%)	4,350 (7%)	4,740 (8%)
On or below SB/IS	7,740 (14%)	11,330 (20%)	13,680 (24%)
140% of SB/IS and below	13,010 (24%)	16,520 (29%)	18,540 (33%)

*Income support (IS) replaced supplementary benefit (SB) in 1988

Source: Re-presented from Oppenheim and Harker, 1996 (Figure 1).

One of the most worrying aspects of these figures is the number of people living on incomes even lower than the government's social assistance (IS) rate. In 1992, 4,740,000 people fell into this category. Some people's incomes are considerably below this line. For example, Oppenheim and Harker (1996, p. 31) have estimated that couples with children living on incomes below IS level have incomes on average just under two-thirds of income support.

There are two main reasons why people live below the so-called state safety net level of income. First, they are in full-time work but receiving poverty level wages. Second, they are not claiming the social security benefits to which they are entitled. According to the government's own estimates of non-take-up, up to 4.3 million people may be missing out on benefits to which they are entitled, valued at up to £3.2 billion a year.

Households below average income

The government replaced the low income statistics, described above, with a new series entitled *Households below Average Income* (HBAI) in

1985 (DSS, 1996). The HBAI statistics do not reveal anything about actual living standards and incomes but present only a hierarchy of earnings. (Most commonly, figures based on 50 per cent of average income are used as a definition of poverty by commentators, as this figure is used in many international studies, particularly when making comparisons across the European Union.) A poverty line based on 50 per cent of average income in 1992/93, expressed at 1995 prices, would have been £65 for a single person, £196 for a couple with three children under 11 and £118 on average (Oppenheim and Harker, 1996, Table 2.3). According to this measure, the number of people living below these levels rose from 5 million, or 9 per cent of the population, in 1979 to 13.7 million, or 24 per cent of the population in 1993/94.

Who are the poor?

Poverty is not confined to any particular group or place, but it is not a random experience. Certain groups of people are particularly vulnerable because of their economic or family status. Employment is the key to avoiding poverty: those in full-time work are at less risk than those working part time, who are in turn less at risk than a household where no-one is in paid employment. The unemployed account for more than a fifth of those in poverty (according to the half-average income definition), whereas couples with two working partners make up only 2 per cent (Oppenheim and Harker, 1996).

Although, overall, people in work are better off than those not in work, there is considerable inequality within the working population. The gap between the low paid and the highest paid is 'now wider than at any time in the century for which we have records' (Hills, 1995, p. 42). According to the Low Pay Unit (1996), in 1996 over 10 million people in Britain earned less than the Council of Europe Decency Threshold (£5.88 per hour), and 2 million people earned less than £3 per hour.

Vulnerability to poverty is closely associated to family status. Having children increases the risk of poverty for both couples and single people. Lone parents are the group most likely to experience poverty. A feature of growing poverty amongst families is the increase in the number of children living in poor households, which has risen even more steeply than the overall figures. In 1979, 1.4 million children (10 per cent of all children) were living in poverty (according to the half-average income measure); by 1993/94, this had risen to 4.2 million (32 per cent). After lone parents, the group most vulnerable to poverty are single pensioners. Women make up the majority of both of these groups.

A number of other factors increase an individual's vulnerability to poverty; these include gender, 'race', age and disability. Official measures of poverty, and much social research, underestimate women's poverty because data are based on household rather than individual income. Webb (1993) has estimated that, in 1992, two-thirds of adults in poor households were women and that the women in these households had about half as much independent income as the men. Poverty amongst women inevitably has a knock-on effect on their children. Like 'race', age and disability, gender increases one's propensity to poverty because individuals within these groups are disadvantaged in the labour market and are more likely to be dependent on inadequate state benefits for a larger proportion of their income and for a longer period in their lives. People from black and minority ethnic groups are more likely to be unemployed than are white people, and when in work are likely to be lower paid (Bloch, 1997). The poverty of disabled people is exacerbated by the extra expenses which many have related to their illness or disability, which are not reflected in their incomes.

But are the poor really poor?

A report commissioned by the Joseph Rowntree Foundation (Hills, 1995) revealed increasing polarisation between 'a prosperous majority and a growing minority of people living on low incomes'. A subsequent review of numerous qualitative research studies, which looked at the lifestyles of people living on low incomes, confirmed the persistence of poverty and the deprivation of poor families (Kempson, 1996, p. ix).

Irrespective of how they define 'poverty', no-one reading this report can be left in doubt that life on a low income in 1990s Britain is a stressful and debilitating experience. People who rely on IS, in particular, face a struggle against encroaching debt and social isolation, where even the most resilient and resourceful are hard pressed to survive.

In a study of social workers and poverty, Becker (1988, p. 248) found that 'As a group [social workers] appear supportive... But as individuals their poverty awareness has tendencies towards hostility and prejudice'. In particular, his respondents tended to regard the poor both as victims and also as contributing to their situation by an inability to cope. However, as Bailey (1988) has written, there is no spare capacity in a poor household to cope with crises. Its members live their lives on a knife edge; any new crisis can tip them over the edge.

Living on a fixed income takes skill and determination. The remarkable thing is *not* that some people fail to make ends meet but that many people succeed. People who fail to manage their weekly budget and who get into debt are often accused of being feckless. However, Kempson found no evidence to support this:

No matter how resourceful, those living on social security benefits generally find that no amount of forward planning and bill juggling is enough. They face a difficult choice between cutting back drastically on food, fuel and other essentials or falling into debt. (Joseph Rowntree Foundation, 1996)

Debt and poverty are now inextricably entwined. Poor people's debts are most frequently for basic household bills – rent, mortgage, gas, electricity, water and council tax. Because of the nature of their debt, poor people are at risk of serious sanctions, such as disconnection of essential services or the loss of their home (see Kempson, 1997).

Food and diet

While food is one of the most basic essentials, it is in practice often the most flexible part of family expenditure. Consequently, when money is short, the food budget suffers: cheaper food is bought, families cut down on fresh fruit and vegetables, and mothers tend to go without to ensure that their children and their partners are fed (Charles and Kerr, 1985). A National Children's Home study (NHC Action for Children, 1991) found that not one of the 354 low-income families surveyed was eating a diet which met current nutrition guidelines:

Additionally, one in five parents missed food in the last month because they did not have enough money for food; nearly half had gone short in the last year; and one in ten children under the age of five years had gone without food in the last month. Parents knew the diet was inadequate but could do little about it. (Lang, 1997)

The poorer diets of the poor have often been blamed on ignorance, famously so by the former Conservative government minister Edwina Currie. However, it has been calculated that a healthy diet which meets government nutrition guidelines actually costs over one-third *more* than the average cost of the food intake of a low-income household (Cole-Hamilton and Lang, 1986). As a result of poor people's inability to follow a rich, nutritional diet, people in social classes IV and V are at greater risk of undernutrition, failure to thrive, vitamin and mineral deficiencies and poor dental health (Cole-

Hamilton and Lang, 1986). Diet is a crucial factor in the ill-health of poor people, as discussed below.

Family relationships

One of the first sacrifices that poor people make is to cut out 'luxuries', even if they might not be defined as such by the general population: these include leisure and social activities. This self-imposed exile means that many people lose contact with family and friends. They cannot afford to go out and may be reluctant to visit other people's homes because they cannot afford to reciprocate. This isolation, together with the constant worries about making ends meet, can put a strain on family relationships. Kempson (1996) found that this could be a contributory factor to a couple separating or to an older child leaving home:

> Little things that never mattered before are suddenly major issues and you fight over them. I fight with him (her husband), I shout at the kids, he does as well and the kids cry.

Policies on poverty

The main instrument used by governments to tackle the issue of poverty is the social security system. Social security cannot prevent poverty; it can at most only alleviate it. Over the past 20 years, there has been a decisive shift away from insurance-based benefits to means-tested benefits. Between 1978/79 and 1995/96, expenditure on the latter increased from 17 per cent of all benefits to 30 per cent. Over a similar period, the number of people receiving social assistance (supplementary benefit, later replaced by IS) increased from 4.4 million to 9.8 million, that is, one-sixth of the population. Eighty-one thousand families received family income supplement in 1979; by 1995, 648,500 families were receiving its successor, family credit (Piachaud, 1997). Means-tested benefits are an inefficient way of reaching the poor because a significant minority of people do not claim them.

The total social security budget is now £90 billion per year, yet this total disguises over £20 billion of cuts which have been made since 1979. The main cuts were achieved by increasing benefits only in line with prices rather than earnings, but many other small and large cuts have been made to reduce the benefits bill by reducing either entitlement or eligibility to benefits: these have included the replacement of unemployment benefit with job-seekers allowance,

the replacement of invalidity benefit by incapacity benefit, the abolition of reduced-rate national insurance benefits, the replacement of
supplementary benefit with IS and the social fund, and the successive
rounds of cuts to housing benefit (Howard, 1997). These cuts have
been accompanied by a much tighter administrative regime, in particular by a much sharper focus on fraud detection and prevention.
While fraudulent claiming is a legitimate target for action,
overzealous rhetoric – often seen at party conferences – can have a
deleterious effect on the public perception of claimants, and this
activity has not been accompanied by any efforts by government to
get people who are eligible to claim the up to £3 billion of benefits
which go unclaimed each year.

Social policy and social exclusion

Government social policies relating to social security and employment have an obvious impact on poverty. However, there is also a
close relationship between poverty and other social policies, in particular health, housing and education.

There has been a growing body of evidence on inequalities in
health since the publication of the Black Report in 1980. However, the
Conservative government did not accept such a link until 1994
following the recommendations of a Health of the Nation working
group set up by the Department of Health. The link between poverty
and health is symbiotic: ill-health makes people vulnerable to poverty
because sick and disabled people have a more tenuous relationship
with the labour market and because they may have higher costs
related to their condition. However, poverty itself can contribute to
ill-health. Poor diet and homelessness or inadequate housing are
major contributory factors to ill-health. Money worries, together with
the circumstances which cause them – job loss, onset of ill-health,
relationship breakdown – can affect people's mental health and can
lead to anxiety and depression.

Despite nearly half a century of the NHS, committed to providing
health care free at the point of access on the basis of need, a health
gap between rich and poor persists and is widening. People who live
in disadvantaged circumstances have more illness, greater distress,
more disability and shorter lives than those who are more affluent.
The greater propensity of the poor to ill-health is not reflected in their
use of health services. The most recent report on inequalities in health
revealed that health resources are still not distributed equitably
between areas in proportion to needs and that formal health care
services do not respond appropriately to the health care needs of
different social groups (Benzeval *et al.*, 1995). As a result, poorer

people receive less health care relative to their health needs than do better-off people: they are less likely to see a doctor, more likely to have shorter consultations and less likely to have their children vaccinated or to receive health screening.

The significant health reforms which have been introduced over the last decade to address the growing demands on the NHS have done nothing to address inequalities in health. In some respects, they have made matters worse by creating a two-tier health service (Wilkinson, 1996) between patients in a fund-holding practice and those who are not. However, people with the highest health needs may be unattractive to those general practitioners who have to operate within a budget. The increasing incidence of charging, for example for prescriptions, which have increased in price over 14-fold since 1979, and for optical and dental charges, also puts an extra burden on many poor people.

Housing is a key parameter of social exclusion. In Britain, renting is regarded as a poor second-best to owning one's own home, and housing tenure is therefore an important source of social division and an important indicator of deprivation. Between 1980 and 1993, the average income of household heads in council housing fell from 48 to 35 per cent of the average income of household heads in mortgaged owner-occupation (Wilcox, 1996). As a result of very actively pursued and subsidised 'right to buy' policies in the 1980s and 90s, council housing tends to be concentrated on the poorest people, which 'reinforces the image of social rented housing as a residual and stigmatised provision for poor people, who have little political clout in bidding for adequate housing management and maintenance' (Ginsburg, 1997).

Another obvious indicator of poverty and social exclusion is homelessness. After peaking at 151,720 people in 1991, the number officially accepted as homeless by local authorities fell to 125,500 in 1995. However, many homeless people are not included in this statistic because they fall outside the remit of local authority responsibility. An analysis of the 1991 census (Holmans, 1996) suggested that 'on census day there were approximately 110,000 concealed families (such as having to live with parents), 50,000 would-be couples living apart, 140,000 sharing households, as well as the 22,000 families accepted as homeless and living in hostels and bed and breakfast accommodation' (Ginsburg, 1997). This does not count the people who are literally 'roofless' and forced to sleep rough.

There have been several important educational reforms, particularly over the past decade, which have concentrated on finance, structure and curriculum. The reduced educational opportunities open to children in poor families have not been addressed, instead having been exacerbated by the trend towards the reinstatement of grammar schools and so-called parental choice. Partly because of the social segregation caused by the housing market, the children of poorer families tend to go to schools in poorer areas. They often have access to the worst, most deprived schools. Their parents are unable to subsidise school funds and activities to the extent that this happens in more affluent areas. Children from poor families are less likely to stay on at school beyond the minimum school-leaving age and are much less likely to go on to higher education. Evidence indicates a link between educational performance and social disadvantage, both among junior school pupils (Brooks *et al.*, 1996) and at GCSE level (Smith *et al.* 1997):

> educational opportunities and results have become more unequal in social terms. It cannot be the case that 'every child, regardless of background (now has) the chance to progress as far as his or her abilities allow'.

Community care

Long-term care is of critical importance to older people and their family carers. Since the early 1980s, Conservative governments have implemented a policy designed to reduce the direct provider role of public services and to increase that of the private sector. This has resulted in a huge increase in residential and nursing home provision and a resulting rise, from £10 million to £3 *billion*, in social security provision for board and lodgings, which the NHS and Community Care Act (1990) was designed to control. As a result of the changes following the Act, community care is, as we write, in a state of crisis: too little home care and no preventative work, which means that older people in particular are having to enter residential homes, despite the policy of community care; lack of choice between providers; lack of consultation with users and carers about appropriate provision; an overreliance on family carers, often to the point of breakdown; and, in the past year, some 40,000 older people having had to sell their houses to fund their long-term residential care. Thus, the ideal of community care as a means of supporting care by families, of *preventing* carer breakdown and of providing a source of social integration in local communities is farther than ever from being realised.

The tighter budget constraints within which both health and social services departments work has created tensions between the two sectors. As hospitals endeavour to discharge (normally older) patients who are deemed to need only 'social' care, and social services departments are obliged, but unable, to fund suitable care packages for all those assessed as being in need, an unseemly tug-of-war has developed in which each sector is trying to avoid taking responsibility.

Conclusion

Social policy provides the context within which both social work professionals and their service users live and work. The development of welfare states is particularly relevant (if not the beginning and end of social policy). If housing, employment, income or health needs are not being met by the relevant service, the individual is more likely to turn to social services departments as the source of last resort assistance. The key to social workers finding a resolution to family crises may involve addressing a material need – such as adequate housing – without which family stress cannot be relieved.

The pressures of recent years to reduce the role of the welfare state, for both ideological and financial reasons, have made it much more likely that vulnerable people will find themselves in need and that they are much less likely to find support or material help within the state welfare system. In this climate, it is particularly important for those working with the poor to look beyond individual hardship – and sometimes inadequacy – to the structural factors which exclude the poor from sharing in the lifestyles of the wider society.

Further reading

Hill, M. (1996) *Understanding Social Policy*. (Oxford, Blackwell).

   A useful text, very broadly covering British policy processes.

Kempson, E. (1996) *Life on a Low Income*. (York, Joseph Rowntree Foundation).

   A research report vividly demonstrating the realities of poverty today.

Oppenheim, C. and Harker, L. (1996) *Poverty: The Facts*, 3rd edn. (London, Child Poverty Action Group.)

   A useful analysis of the statistics of poverty, updated periodically.

Walker, C. (1993) *Managing Poverty: The Limits of Social Assistance*. (London, Routledge).

   A helpful general text on social security policies.

Walker, A. and Walker, C. (eds) (1997) *Britain Divided: The Growth of Social Exclusion in the 1980s and 1990s*. (London, Child Poverty Action Group).

   A collection of articles showing how poverty leads to social exclusion and disadvantage.

5

Social work and the law

SUZY BRAYE AND MICHAEL PRESTON-SHOOT

Introduction

The relationship between social work and the law remains strongly contested. The law can be problematic in terms of its purposes and outcomes. The law can be used for social engineering, the promotion of particular ideologies and the preservation of power structures. Certain social groups are overrepresented in prisons, care and psychiatric hospitals. How should social work respond?

Louis Blom-Cooper declared that the law was social work's defining mandate (Beckford Report, 1985). Olive Stevenson (1988) countered by arguing for an ethical duty of care as social work's mandate, of which the law is only one component. Both positions in fact simplify a relationship of considerable complexity (Braye and Preston-Shoot, 1990) wherein practitioners and managers must determine in each situation the account to be taken of both polarities. Three developments have assisted them with this task: the emergence of a discipline 'social work law'; the construction of a conceptual frame informed by values and knowledge (Braye and Preston-Shoot, 1997) within which to address dilemmas of practice; and the articulation of academic and practice curricula (Ball *et al.*, 1995; Braye and Preston-Shoot, 1997), and methods of teaching and assessing competence (Braye and Preston-Shoot, 1991; Ward and Hogg, 1993), which counteract uncertainty about knowledge of the law and its relationship to practice.

Social workers experience stress when in contact with the law (Jones *et al.*, 1991) and believe that they are perceived as having limited credibility or standing in that arena (DoH, 1994; Foster and Preston-Shoot, 1995). Moreover, whilst there is evidence that training has improved (Ball *et al.*, 1995), the emphasis given to law in qualifying training is problematic. Practice teachers often do not feel competent to provide students with the necessary learning opportunities to develop competence in social work law (Preston-Shoot *et al.*,

1997). Yet CCETSW, in its revised requirements (1995), requires students to demonstrate, within both academic and practice curricula, competence in applying knowledge and understanding of statutory responsibilities. They must be able to work in accordance with legal requirements and to adhere to policy and organisational procedures. That law is the only subject so emphasised gives it prominence, if not pre-eminence, in the definition of competent practice. The debate on the relationship between law and social work would appear to have come full circle.

Context

Regardless of how the relationship between the law and social work is balanced, there are relevant legal rules. These are the absolute and discretionary duties, and the powers which mandate preventative, protective and coercive interventions with particular service user groups. They are accompanied by central government guidance, some advisory and some directive when issued under section 7 of the Local Authority Social Services Act, 1970. A distinction is drawn between social work law, which may be argued to include those powers and duties which expressly mandate social work activity, and social welfare law, comprising statutes with which social workers should be familiar if they are to respond appropriately to the needs of service users, but which do not permit or require specific actions by them. This distinction also indicates that social workers outside the statutory sector have a different relationship to the law from those who, working in social services departments, are delegated to exercise statutory authority which may have preventative, empowering, protective or controlling purposes. In any setting, however, social workers have a professional obligation critically to appraise the nature and scope of the statutory provisions and, with service users, to advocate for change, the translation of social rights into legal rights and the provision of services which meet need.

These legal rules are translated into operational policies and procedures by local authorities and other agencies undertaking statutory duties. Organisations can be held accountable for the definition and administration of policy, and for social work practice derived from it, through complaints procedures, judicial review and the Commissioner for Local Administration (Ombudsman).

The agency context can be problematic for social workers. The appeals mechanisms available to service users are limited in that, in the event of finding illegality or maladministration, they can quash or criticise decisions made but not ensure or reinstate provision of particular services. Moreover, the conformity which practitioners and managers are expected to demonstrate to organisational policies and procedures sometimes sits uneasily alongside the allegiance to social work knowledge and values, and commitment to the rights and welfare of service users, and may conflict with the legal rules as articulated in statute, case law and guidance. For example, social workers attending law workshops have recounted experiences of being instructed not to inform service users of their rights, and of users being charged for services which fall outside the legal mandate to charge. Practising social work law, therefore, demands not only familiarity with how the law regulates decision-making, but also skills in challenging policies and procedures which are administratively unfair or illegal and/or which run counter to social work values.

The relevant legal rules do not necessarily provide a clear mandate and are not always supportive of social work values. Some social work values have influenced, and may be found, in statute. Section 95 of the Criminal Justice Act, 1991 and section 1(3) of the Children Act, 1989, for example, uphold social work's concern with anti-discriminatory practice. Other legislation, or the guidance associated with it, promotes values and practices that would not be professionally endorsed. One example here would be the restrictions placed on which service users may receive cash from local authorities to purchase their own packages of care (Community Care [Direct Payments] Act, 1996). Thus, the law does not always underwrite anti-oppressive practice, and practising social work law anti-oppressively is a key challenge containing tensions and dilemmas.

The nature of the interaction between social work and the law may be perceived as a continuum (Preston-Shoot *et al.*, 1998), characterised by the extent to which either legal or social work language, methodology and values dominate. Working in court falls at the 'law end' of this continuum. Unfamiliarity with legal language and methodology, together with criticism by the courts of the competence which social workers bring to expert testimony, and of their presentation of evidence (see Foster and Preston-Shoot, 1995), can undermine confidence and create defensive practice.

The context is also increasingly international. For example, in P *v.* S and Cornwall County Council [1996] IRLR 347, the European Court of Justice found that the Equal Treatment Directive could be applied to discrimination arising from gender reassignment. This ruling may require an amendment to the Sex Discrimination Act, 1975 so that complaints of discrimination made by transsexuals are unequivocally covered. The United Nations committee monitoring the Convention on the Rights of the Child has severely criticised the UK for its record on ensuring that policy and legislation complies with the convention's provisions.

Critical themes

Conflicting purposes

Central to social work is a commitment to a value base. Whether this is interpreted traditionally as a commitment to respect for persons, equal opportunity and meeting needs, or radically as a concern with social rights, equality and citizenship, the focus is on change and the goal is to be supported by a specific quality of service. Social work law and social welfare law may facilitate this focus, as when the Court of Appeal held that asylum-seekers had the right to assistance under the National Assistance Act, 1948 (R *v.* Hammersmith and Fulham LBC, *ex parte* M [1997] *The Times*, 19 February). However, social work law is largely expressed as discretionary duties, whether towards groups or individuals. Entitlement is often to unspecified services, such as assessment or a care plan, rather than to a particular service or one of specific quality. Moreover, the local authority may define the extent to which it will exercise discretion, for instance in defining need and taking its resources into account (R *v.* Gloucestershire County Council and the Secretary of State for Health, *ex parte* Barry [1997] House of Lords, 2 All ER 1). Accordingly, it is difficult for service users to challenge local authority practice successfully (for a review, see Preston-Shoot, 1996).

Additionally, the law can express objectives which, rather than counteracting discrimination and meeting needs, oppress or marginalise people. Enactments on asylum, social security provisions, sexuality and housing are examples. The Local Government Act, 1988 proscribes any action by a local authority to promote gay and lesbian lifestyles, referring to such partnerships as 'pretend family relationships'. The reform of the law relating to homelessness (Housing Act, 1996) tightens the definition of intentional homelessness to include unreasonable refusal of an offer of accommodation. It will permit local authorities to avoid obligations on the grounds that alternative suitable accommodation is available in other housing sectors, whilst the duty to provide housing no longer means permanent accommodation.

The law, then, embodies value judgements and ideologies (such as harsh custodial regimes for young offenders) which social work might wish to challenge but to which, because of their position, practitioners are expected to conform. Indeed, the purposes of law are multiple and sometimes contradictory. The law may be harnessed to preserve power structures or to prescribe or proscribe certain lifestyles (for example, favouring marriage in the Family Law Act, 1996). It may be used to shape attitudes and behaviours, as in anti-discrimination legislation, or to express ideology (for example, the primacy of the market in the NHS and Community Care Act, 1990 reforms). It is imbued with discriminatory images of competency to make decisions, and of moral worth, and with prejudicial stereotypes of race, gender, disability and sexuality. The question for social work is how to respond, especially when the purposes and images to which the law is harnessed conflict with social work's value base.

Legalism

Social work is increasingly being regulated through national standards, volumes of guidance and constrained resources. Increasingly, too, it is being judged through inquiries based on the norms and practices of the legal system. This emphasis on legalism is problematic. Essentially, this is because legalism conflates good practice with 'procedurally correct' practice, the latter emphasising apparent certainties rather than acknowledging the imprecisions and choice points inherent in social work tasks. Additionally, legalism presents inherently conflictual notions as if they were complementary and thus minimises debate on the balance to be struck between conflicting imperatives such as rights and risks, needs and resources, autonomy and protection.

The statutory mandate is neither consistent nor comprehensive: it is confused and ambiguous. A child's welfare is not always paramount (compare family proceedings under the Children Act, 1989, to which the paramountcy principle does apply, with financial and accommodation questions in divorce and domestic violence proceedings under the Family Law Act, 1996, in which the needs of, often male, adults can predominate). Children are sometimes denied the right to seek to initiate proceedings (contrast appeals to special educational needs tribunals under the Education Act, 1996, which children have no right to initiate, with section 8 orders in the Children Act, 1989, which they may seek). Government exhortations, prompted by research (DoH, 1995), to alter the balance between child protection and preventative services in favour of the latter, have not been accompanied by official acknowledgement of either the complexity of practice or the social context in which practitioners have operated. Despite recommendations for legislation (Law Commission, 1995) social workers currently have limited powers to protect vulnerable adults from abuse.

The community care mandate boasts choice and needs-led assessments, yet resources control questions of service provision, whilst the differential meanings of partnership, empowerment, choice and quality obscure rather than clarify the objectives to which services should aspire. Both judges (R *v.* Gloucestershire County Council, *ex parte* RADAR [1995] CO/2764/95; R *v.* Gloucestershire County Council and the Secretary of State for Health, *ex parte* Barry [1997]) and inquiries (Ritchie *et al.*, 1994) have criticised government guidance for its lack of clarity and central government for the wretched position into which it has placed councils.

Legalism does not necessarily safeguard service users. First, reliance on the law for resolving questions of welfare may be misplaced. The legal system, with its adversarial nature and narrow emphasis on questions of evidence and procedure, may not be best suited to decide questions of professional practice (King and Trowell, 1992). The more that law becomes the main form of admissible knowledge in social work, the more difficult it may become to address awkward questions about the purpose of provision and to highlight the limitation of judicial procedures in supporting vaguely defined objectives of choice, needs-led assessments and empowerment.

Second, the legislative mandate continues to marginalise the social – whether in social work, social justice or social welfare. The policy emphasis is on individuals rather than the wider system which frequently contributes to the difficulties that people experience. Social work should connect the personal and political, public and private, and from individual cases identify those political and structural issues which require social change as part of problem resolution. Legalism fragments this perspective. It offers officially sanctioned procedures and leaves unaltered the current alignment of power and relationships. Put more starkly, people's needs are not being met (Jordan, 1990), and practitioners inherit a legal mandate characterised by poverty of provision and meanness of spirit (Utting, in Ellis, 1993).

The location of social work

Social work's predominant location in local authorities, on whom statutory functions are placed, has always meant the negotiation of multiple accountabilities – between employers, professional values, professional self, service users and the public. The challenge has always been to hold the dynamic tension that this involves rather than succumb to bureaucracy. Additionally, the challenge has been to find the room for manoeuvre within agencies for anti-oppressive practice and promoting service users' rights and needs. The problem here is not the law *per se* but rather how it is interpreted in policy and practice. One danger for social work is of losing human contact as its core purpose (Barber, 1991; Grimwood and Popplestone, 1993; Drakeford, 1996). For example, users and carers are critical of the loss of relationship, seeing care managers as 'travel agents' rather than 'travel companions' (Onyett, 1992; Buckley *et al.*, 1995). Another danger is the neutralisation of moral concerns and the undermining of moral responsibility, as practice reflects dominant organisational and political interests. The pressures to conform, to practise unquestioningly, are evidenced in reports of bullying by managers and cultures of fear (Mitchell, 1996).

Evidence is accumulating (see Braye and Preston-Shoot, 1997) that agencies are failing to follow guidance and meet their statutory obligations both to children and families and to adults needing care or services. Social work is being drawn into practices which are morally and/or legally suspect – withdrawing services from vulnerable older people and disabled people without the required reassessment and when their needs have not diminished (R *v*. Gloucestershire County Council, *ex parte* Mahfood and others [1995] CO.3507-24), or avoiding formal statements of how children in need will be defined in order to escape any obligation to act (Colton *et al.*, 1995). Indeed, some commentators (Mandlestam with Schwehr, 1995) argue that the uncertainties within statutory duties act as a safety valve, allowing local authorities to escape oppressive obligations. Oppressive for whom?

This is not to underestimate the impact of the consistent under-resourcing of local authorities compared with growing social need and mounting legislative duties. Indeed, the standard spending assessment system, the primary means of funding local government, is confusing, complicated, inequitable and vulnerable to political manipulation. Draconian resource constraints are placed on managers and practitioners, who face the unenviable discomfort of continuing to struggle with irreconcilable demands, or to acquiesce in the gradual erosion of social work values as the only means of survival in the face of such dissonance. That sensitive and innovative practice remains in evidence is a tribute to the strength of commitment and imagination still derived from the professional social work ethos of public service. This discussion must highlight, however, the evidence of services under strain and of the underestimation of people's needs. It cautions that the pre-eminence given in social work training and practice to the law, and to conformity in decision-making to agency policies, can amount to acquiescing in a rationing role and to bypassing political and ethical questions about the purposes of welfare and social work, and about the quality of life that services should promote.

Critical debates

How, then, should social work interface with the law and social policy, and their expression in agency procedures? An empowering

context for practising social work law requires a social work whic
confident in interacting with legislative and local governm
systems, and active in initiating and contributing to debates about tue
goals of practice. This requires frameworks for understanding which
together construct a theory for practice, and which can strike the
balance in the relationship between the law and social work uniquely
in each situation.

Appraising social work law

The different purposes to which the law can be harnessed result in
contradictions which, for social workers, formalise around conflicting
imperatives. Thus, some procedures in child protection have to
balance welfare with justice, where the requirement to promote the
child's welfare conflicts with the parent's right to the justice of a fair
investigative process and trial. The conflict between needs, resources
and rights appears endemic within community care and special
education services, whilst the tension between the rights of an individual to autonomy and the rights of the state to intervene is encap-
sulated within the realm of health care and social care legislation, and
within the Children Act, 1989 and its associated guidance.

These conflicting imperatives are encountered in practice as
dilemmas, for example rights versus risks, care versus control, needs
versus resources, professionalism versus partnership with users,
professional versus agency agendas. Determining the balance to be
struck in each situation will require an understanding of social work
goals and of legal goals, clarity about where social work and legal
purposes overlap and where they diverge, and an approach to decision-making which weighs up the claims of each polarity.

Creative practice in the arena of social work law is thus characterised by identification and exploitation of the spaces left by vague
legislative drafting and unclear concepts or principles for practice,
such as need or partnership. It connects different areas of the law,
and of a social services department's organisational structure, and
utilises case law and appeals procedures – all with the purpose of
pushing the law's boundaries to maximise a service user's rights and
access to services.

Defining welfare

When social work goals and legislative goals diverge, this divergence
should be introduced into debates about the purpose of welfare.
Social work has, at least, three frameworks for understanding to

advance here. One is an understanding of oppression and how social work can risk being recruited into the task of preserving power structures rooted in inequalities. This understanding is derived from research and service user experiences. It informs practice based on values which emphasise rights and equality, echoes of which may be found in some government guidance (DoH, 1989), and on services which strive for an optimal satisfaction of basic needs.

The second is a critical appraisal of the concepts which underpin social policy – partnership, empowerment, choice, quality and need – with particular reference to how the concepts can be recruited for both a New Right and an anti-oppressive practice agenda. This focuses on the quality of the lives of less powerful people by reference to key values and basic needs, and addresses awkward questions about the issues involved in need satisfaction, rights and resources, autonomy, protection and empowerment. It seeks to give substance to the rhetoric by asking how social workers' accountability to different stake-holders should be managed, what a professional ethical duty of care should be, how welfare should be interpreted and needs defined, and how the legal mandate might be used with and for users. Practising social work law will involve accessing research on need in order to argue for services. It will involve enabling people to gain access to political processes by developing partnership and advocacy skills which place service users centre-stage in articulating need, expressing choice and advocating change.

The third framework draws also from research and from listening to users. This is the identification and active promotion of the core elements of good practice and the active articulation of what presently undermines that practice. Welfare is often presented as ineffective. Social work can reclaim its effectiveness – what is valuable and important between practitioners and service users.

Reviewing organisational behaviour and practice ethics

That agencies, far from solving problems, can maintain or exacerbate them is well known. Healthy organisations, therefore, require staff who will challenge received ideas and explore different possibilities. Equally, given the complicated and contradictory mandates inherent in social work law, competent organisations must engage with rather than defend against the dilemmas posed by their mandates and roles. Practice here may include forming alliances with other organisations and with service users to advocate for change, and providing clear policy guidance about the principles which are to take precedence in practice. It should include 'naming the games' within contemporary social policy, particularly the implications for practice of funding decisions, imprecise legal and policy mandates, and political stereo-types of welfare practice. It should incorporate acknowledgement of the feelings that the work engenders in practitioners and managers. The challenge is to create an organisational culture where responsibility is shared through structures of support, supervision and consultation, where practitioners and managers work together, and with service users, to articulate the impact on people's lives of contemporary social and economic policies, and where it is accepted that accountability to an employing organisation can only be fulfilled with integrity where it is consistent with the higher-order principle of effective, ethical and legal practice.

To intervene in organisations requires a factual understanding of decision-making and policy-making structures and how to gain entry to these. It requires knowledge of the law and guidance which relates to the concerns to be raised in order that the challenging position being taken can be justified. It demands an understanding of how systems work and how organisations respond to demands for change. Practice, then, requires sophisticated change agent skills based around agenda-building, problem-defining, policy-assessing and proposal-making (Jannson, 1994), together with constructing alliances or constituencies for change, and groupworking or building support networks. Such practice requires skills in using legislation and policy provisions to achieve clearly expressed outcomes informed by social work values, theory and practice wisdom, and to advance ways of understanding and tackling issues which enable organisations to perceive room for manoeuvre and to respond positively.

Conclusion

A common question is how social workers might practise anti-oppressively in the context of social control functions, of resource and employment constraints, and of the absence of a legal jurisdiction in key areas of inequality. Part of the answer centres on knowledge and skills which integrate social work and the law. Knowledge includes relevant statute, case law and guidance, together with that from other disciplines which helps to make sense of the 'what' and 'why' of each practice situation. Skills, using this knowledge, include:

- using law and guidance which endorse anti-discriminatory practice;
- using provisions to achieve outcomes informed by social work values;

- challenging how authorities approach decision-making and interpret the legislative mandate;
- presenting a clear rationale for practice, based on connecting knowledge with social work goals and tasks.

The challenge is to address the tensions and dilemmas inherent in social work law, in the relationship between social work, social policy and the law, through a legal, policy and organisational literacy. This engages not just at the level of practice – the 'what', 'why' and 'how' of individual situations – but also at higher levels of context about the objectives of policy and the means by which they will be realised. If social work loses its ability or willingness to question and comment, it will lose its position to promote and empower a difference at the levels of both individual and collective experience, and will become identified with policies, procedures and practices which evade awkward questions, mask inequality and perpetuate disadvantage.

Further reading

Braye, S. and Preston-Shoot, M. (1995) *Empowering Practice in Social Care* (Buckingham, Open University Press).

> This book explains the core components of community care policy and its application to social care practice within a value base that promotes partnership and empowerment.

Braye, S. and Preston-Shoot, M. (1997) *Practising Social Work Law*, 2nd edn (London, Macmillan).

> This book explores the tensions and dilemmas in the complex relationship between the law and social work, and offers guidance to practitioners and managers for legally competent social work practice.

Hill, M. and Aldgate, J. (eds) (1996) *Child Welfare Services. Developments in Law, Policy, Practice and Research* (London, Jessica Kingsley).

> This book reports on research critically analysing child-care legislation, policy and practice.

Jackson, S. and Preston-Shoot, M. (eds) (1996) *Educating Social Workers in a Changing Policy Context* (London, Whiting & Birch).

> This book examines the relationship between social work practice, policy and education, providing innovative and creative responses to the challenges presented by the contemporary policy context.

Kaganas, F., King, M. and Piper, C. (eds) (1995) *Legislating for Harmony: Partnership under the Children Act 1989* (London, Jessica Kingsley).

> This book provides a critical analysis of the concept of partnership, a key component of social policy and practice guidance.

6

Social work and organisations

AUDREY MULLENDER AND STELLA PERROTT

Introduction: the organisational context of social work

Although much organisational and human resource management theory has arisen from industry and commerce, it has a clear relevance to public and voluntary sector welfare bodies. Indeed, social work values can be used to evaluate management theory as we consider what organisations do to the people who work in them and the people they were set up to serve. Furthermore, if services and working conditions are to improve over time, organisations have to change and adapt, so that they foster competence, quality and learning.

Social work in its widest sense is practised in a great variety of organisations. It is quite wrong to think of social work as only happening within social services departments (social work departments in Scotland and health and social services Trusts in Northern Ireland, hereafter all summarised under 'SSDs').

Organisations in which social work activities are undertaken are often thought of as falling into two categories: the statutory and independent sectors. The latter can be further subdivided into the voluntary (not for profit) sector and the private (for profit) sector. Recent political priorities of central government have tended to favour a shrinking of the statutory sector and a proliferation of private and voluntary agencies within a more fragmented 'welfare market'.

The statutory sector covers all publicly funded bodies which employ social workers. In addition to SSDs, it embraces the probation service (where a social work qualification was obligatory for probation officers until 1996), education social work (formerly 'education welfare') and a small number of social workers employed by other public bodies such as some housing departments (who work with homeless families or those housed in bed and breakfast hotels), for example. Where social workers are based in hospitals, they are normally employed by SSDs (although some fund-holding general practitioners' practices are beginning to employ their own social workers or counsellors). Similarly, the probation service has staff working in prisons and other offender institutions.

A different way of subdividing the working contexts of social workers and related professionals since the community care reforms of the early 1990s, particularly in relation to adult service user groups but sometimes also in children's services, has been the so-called 'purchaser–provider split'. Under this formulation, staff are either purchasing (commissioning) services for those who are assessed as being in priority need or are directly providing the commissioned services to meet that need. In broad terms, in social work, SSDs are the purchasers of services. Most SSDs have also retained a considerable role in providing services, such as home care and residential care, to all service user groups, but they increasingly do so in competition with voluntary and private agencies. A broadly equivalent trend in the probation service has been the requirement to fund some service provision, for example employment or housing schemes, in the voluntary sector. There has been government-led discussion of whole areas of social service provision being contracted out altogether. Thus it can be seen that organisational forms and responsibilities can only be fully understood within a political and social context.

Organisational forms and issues

Organisational definitions

> An organization is a consciously co-ordinated entity, with a relatively identifiable boundary, that functions on a relatively continuous basis to achieve a common goal or goals. (Robins, 1990, p. 4)

Organisations encompass or involve workforces and structures of staffing, systems of working and markets of demand for goods or services, as well as less tangible facets such as culture, ethos and patterns of power and influence (Clegg, 1990, p. 3). Organisations are also places where identities can be formed (when introduced to someone socially, the first question is often, 'And what do you do?'), social lives and careers established and political aspirations realised. Work can be the vehicle of achieving personal needs and ambitions, or a site of oppression and unhappiness. Clearly, then, we need multi-layered and complex ideas in order to develop an understanding of how organisations function.

Organisational forms: from hierarchical bureaucracy to feminist collective

We owe to the sociologist Weber the development of organisation theory as a discipline of thought in the modern world. Observing the economically driven society around him, he conceptualised the model of the bureaucratic organisational form and praised it for its efficiency in carrying out large-scale administrative tasks (Weber, 1947).

So dominant did the bureaucracy become that its development explains most forms of working life in the Western world. In manufacturing, bureaucracy led to the differentiation of tasks and the production methods which came to be known as 'Fordism' (in reference to the separated, repetitive jobs on the automobile production line), while, in the professions, it led to specialisation, the development of standardised services, hierarchical lines of management control and the application of rules and procedures, even though professionals retained more autonomy than did factory-floor workers, owing to their specialised knowledge and the influence of their external professional associations and training bodies (Mintzberg, 1989, p. 347). In this regard, social work has always been regarded as something of a hybrid, a 'semi-profession' (Etzioni, 1969; cf. Aldridge, 1996) because, as yet, it lacks some of the key controls over entry to its ranks such as obligatory qualifications and gatekeeping by a body such as a Royal College or General Council (Parker, 1990; DoH *et al.*, 1996). It also involves competing interests. In addition to professional autonomy being constrained through employer control, central government has intervened to direct the work of statutory social work agencies through a body of legislation and policy guidance (see Chapter 5). The workforce, too, has experienced competing identifications, not only with professional bodies, but also with trades unions, special interest groups and personal reference groupings such as women's and/or black workers' groups.

In more recent management thinking, there has been a widescale interest in moving beyond simple bureaucracy to alternative organisational forms which are better able to deal with complexity. As information processing, diversification of operations and interdisciplinary liaison have exerted greater demands, control has spread sideways to section heads in various technological and specialist fields. Other factors influencing change have been a developing awareness of the value of the human 'resource' (as opposed to narrowly defined technical efficiency) and, in industry and commerce, the desire to emulate ways of working thought to underlie the post-war growth of the Japanese and the younger 'tiger' economies. Clegg (1990) identifies the more complex 'postmodern' organisation as one that offers a differentiated service or product but has a dedifferentiated, that is, multiskilled workforce. 'Teamworking' has replaced the production line in many manufacturing organisations, the responsibility for the quality of the output being shared between all members of a multi-skilled and non-hierarchical team. Alongside this, 'quality circles' have been introduced where groups of workers meet to solve common problems and seek ways to improve standards. These 'new' developments represent ways of working which have traditionally been valued by social workers but which have only recently been 'discovered' by others.

Whilst there has been a move to train social workers in core, transferable job competencies (CCETSW, 1995), SSD jobs have actually been becoming more rather than less specialised under a welter of new legislation (the post-Seebohm genericism of the 1970s having all but disappeared, except in out-of-hours teams), and only the burgeoning number of freelance trainers and consultants utilise those other post-Fordist developments of working from home via modem and fax machine in a telecottage environment. Staff in SSDs, voluntary bodies and probation have shared with UK workers in other sectors the job insecurities of wide-scale reorganisations, budget cuts and moves to widen the employment base to those with other kinds of qualifications or none.

'Flexibility' in the labour market, it is true, has tended to lead to the creation of more temporary and part-time jobs, both in industry and in social work, the latter also relying heavily on employment agencies to fill vacancies. Part-time employment in social services increased by 50.4 per cent between 1988 and 1992 (Local Government Management Board and Association of Directors of Social Services [LGMB and ADSS], 1993, p. 27), with women predominating in this 'flexible fringe' (Handy, 1990, p. 77). Part-time middle management (team leader) posts in social services more than quadrupled between 1988 and 1992 (LGMB and ADSS, 1993, p. 28), and over 90 per cent of these are held by women (p. 29). However, part-time working tends not to be offered (or tends to be disadvantageous for career prospects) at the most senior managerial levels, where men still heavily predominate.

Of course, there have always been real alternatives to (as opposed to modifications of) bureaucratic, hierarchical structures, and the voluntary sector of welfare provision in the UK is one of the richest sites of these. Those with the longest history include all-women organisations (Hawxhurst and Morrow, 1984; Dominelli, 1990) such as women's aid and rape crisis, sometimes run solely by black women, as in specialist black refuge services, or by lesbian women as in lesbian helplines. In these, the distinctive organisational form has been that of the feminist collective (Iannello, 1992). Its wider legacy includes rotating the chairing of meetings, delegating tasks, sharing information and equalising access to resources (Freeman, undated). Some of the current interest in tribal/extended family group decision-making (Family Rights Group, 1994), according to Maori, native American and other traditional cultural patterns, relates to a similar search for alternative means of working in partnership, often within a more holistic ethos than Western society retains. Gay and lesbian groups, too, have developed wholly new thinking on organisational principles, such as approaches to recruitment and recording where confidentiality is paramount.

Non-traditional organisations come under tremendous pressure from the more traditional, however, to behave in ways the latter can recognise and understand. If difference is noticed at all, it is registered as some kind of inferiority – as disorganisation, inefficiency or unprofessionalism. Also, at the points where the two organisations need to interact, power, for example through access to funding, may be used to force the smaller to become more like the larger. Increasingly, for instance, local authority contributions to the funding of posts in women's organisations are accompanied by pressure to move away from equality of pay and status, with 'project directors' appearing in former collectives. On a wider scale, voluntary agencies fear that competing for contracts to sustain their funding base will distance them from their pioneering roots and reduce their capacity for advocacy. As only the widest diversity of projects can reflect the more complex understanding of human need we have now acquired, the challenge to the large public agencies is to support and to emulate where appropriate, rather than to impose uniformity.

A culture of excellence and quality

As old-style rationality and bureaucracy have proved inadequate to guarantee efficient performance in complex contemporary organisations, greater interest has begun to be shown in 'softer' concepts such as culture, emotions and even sexuality (Hearn and Parkin, 1995). The human messiness that the Weberian legacy viewed as 'inimical to rational, efficient capitalism' has, ironically, become an essential part of theorising about organisations (Clegg, 1990, p. 150). Organisations are not, after all, peopled by automata – staff bring their personalities, feelings and social roles to work and are affected, in turn, by the way in which they find themselves treated there.

In social work, issues such as a culture of blame, the risk of violence, inadequacies of staff care policies, racism from users and colleagues, and, simply, the degree of stress in the job (NISW, 1995a) all require an awareness of the impact of organisations on the people who work within them. Tribunal cases and out-of-court settlements involving social workers who received no help when their health was suffering under pressure of work (Thompson, 1996b), as well as a national survey indicating that 'half the profession had considered leaving social work in the preceding three years because of stress and frustration' *Professional Social Work*, 1996, p. 1), illustrate recent grounds for concern. There is a need to foster social work agencies as 'competent workplaces' (Pottage and Evans, 1994) rather than environments which can actively contribute to stress (Thompson *et al.*, 1996).

The work of Peters and Waterman (1982) began the exhortation to organisations of all kinds to create and harness a more positive climate. They emphasised people over roles, and the need for value-driven rather than efficiency-obsessed activity. The line of interest in culture and 'quality' has, in general terms, been unbroken from then with the 'Investors in People' (IIP) award scheme currently emphasising the reliance of every successful organisation on each member of its workforce. This is certainly true in social work, where the lowest tiers of workers are all in direct contact with the public.

Widespread efforts to develop 'quality assurance' (DoH, 1992; Kelly and Warr, 1992) – a bottom-up involvement of all members of an organisation in setting and meeting agreed quality standards – have provided many teams with positive opportunities to work towards the improvement of service design and delivery. At its most creative, work on quality has merged with thinking on *equality* (National Association of Race Equality Advisers, 1993, p. 9). This has allowed some groupings of black staff and female staff to incorporate their demands into mainstream rethinking about the accessibility and appropriateness of all services.

Care needs to be taken, however, that programmes claiming to develop wide-scale quality assurance are not masking top-down efforts to increase managerial control (James, 1994). This is not to denigrate the quite proper increase in monitoring, inspection, complaints procedures (DoH/SSI, 1991a; NISW, 1993) and evaluation (Everitt and Hardiker, 1996). However, while the language of quality may resonate with social workers, who well understand the human face of the organisation, the countertrend towards the macho metaphors of lean, mean, goal-oriented and aggressive organisations appears to leave little space for empathy or caring. Those who are expected to draw organisational and individual worker goals more closely together are likely to be the middle managers: team leaders and area or district officers. Effective supervision (Brown and Bourne, 1996) is certainly crucial in keeping a workforce functioning effectively, all the more so if it is linked to a comprehensive system of staff appraisal, staff development and staff care.

Working in organisations: oppressive or empowering?

Equal opportunities

Direct and indirect discrimination against an individual who is a current or potential employee are now unlawful to the extent of the definitions in the Sex Discrimination Acts, 1975 and 1986, the Race Relations Act, 1976 and the Disability Discrimination Act, 1996 (the latter covering physical disability, learning difficulties and mental illness). There is no equivalent legislation covering unfair treatment at work for gay men, lesbians or older workers. Nor does Britain yet have a minimum wage, some of the lowest-paid workers in the country (disproportionately women, disproportionately black, disproportionately deprived of training; Phillipson, 1988) being responsible for the quality of life of many thousands of people in group and domiciliary care settings.

The existing equal opportunities Acts cannot be said to operate particularly effectively, even on their own terms, if we work from a baseline which regards racial and other oppressions as endemic: '[f]ewer than 2,000 people have had their complaints of racial discrimination under the [Race Relations] Act supported by industrial tribunals or courts' (CRE Connections, 1996, p. 1). Furthermore, the legislation depends on individuals taking cases and, by definition, fails to tackle entrenched, structural oppression.

Equality in social work organisations appears to be most effectively pursued – through codes of practice, equality standards and the like – by designated staff in high-level equality units (Thobani, 1995). Formal and informal measures can combine practical supports, such as dependency leave and child-care provision, with personal encouragement through mentoring and coaching, mutual support networks, fostering skill and career development, women-only and black-only management training, appraisal schemes, consultancy, secondments and job swaps, and opportunities to 'act up' to a higher level.

There is a growing literature on the organisational impact on women's careers, and similar work is needed in relation to other oppressed groups. For women, there are studies which identify the problem (DoH/SSI, 1991b), clarify what aids or hinders progression (Coleman, 1991; Allan *et al.*, 1992) and warn that a male backlash is inevitable (Cockburn, 1991). This thinking has begun to work its way through into self-help guides (Clarke, 1992), including those for women's career development in social work (Foster, 1996), and into the social work literature more broadly (Grimwood and Popplestone, 1993). Male-managed environments are recognised as obstructive and often hostile contexts for women, particularly when much of the work itself involves the need to challenge violent and abusive men (Perrott, 1994). Within the above movement for change is some awareness that black women (Martin, 1994), lesbian women and disabled women face compounded forms of discrimination, that they may be more visible, more isolated and less trusted once in management posts, that they may lack appropriate role models, and that there is less scope to make mistakes when many others depend on you to forge a path to the top for them while everyone else expects you to fail. There are also moves to target other groups under-represented in managerial grades, for example through a survey of male and female black managers in public services (Andrew, 1996).

The feminisation of management

Meanwhile, human resource management theory is beginning to explore the hitherto undervalued, especially the 'feminine', qualities such as interpersonal and intuitive skills that can contribute to organisational success. Whereas classical management theory concerned itself with men managing men in masculine ways – controlling, rational – so that women's contributions were invisible (Hearn and Parkin, 1995; cf. Spender, 1980), gendered management thinking reveals that women's ways of interacting – teamwork, running democratic meetings, drawing out each other's strengths rather than competing – can make organisations more effective, particularly in handling more diverse demands and more complex lines of communication. Up to now, men's styles of talk (Tannen, 1996) – 'bantering', putting others down, self-promotion – have made them seem natural leaders, with women avoiding what they regard as boasting, while playing down their own authority and helping others to contribute. Now, organisations are beginning to question whether they need leaders or facilitators (cf. Mullender and Ward, 1991), whether they require so many managers or more project teams devoted to innovative and responsive thinking, and whether relationship skills might not be just as important as business acumen. There is even a new business interest in 'values-aware' and 'responsible' management within an environmental context (Baty, 1997).

The recognition of stereotypical expectations helps to explain why workplaces can be intensely uncomfortable for gay and lesbian staff members. Not only is there crude homophobia and heterosexism in daily conversation (Hearn and Parkin, 1995), but also rigid gender hierarchies devalue women's contributions and reward only those men who act out the 'macho' role. Black people, too, may find themselves valued only in as far as they conform to white norms. The latest formalised manifestation of this has appeared in psychometric testing standardised around white test results, which is associated with lower rates of appointing black staff to posts (Skellington with Morris, 1992, pp. 135–6).

Thus, it is not just (or even predominantly) the traditionally excluded groups who need to change, but those who stereotypically and disproportionately hold the power in organisations. Here, there are emergent theories about the ways in which managements and masculinities reinforce one another and about how both might be transformed (Collinson and Hearn, 1996). Male practitioners are urged to think how they operate in organisations, whether they should absent themselves from whole areas of work such as those directly involving survivors of sexual abuse (Pringle, 1992/93), and whether they have a special responsibility in all settings where men could usefully reconsider prevailing models of masculinity (for example, Bensted *et al.*, 1994, writing about work with offenders). Additionally, accountability to women is viewed as crucial in the direction of projects aimed at changing men (Mullender, 1996, Chapter 9). Again, this thinking could usefully be extended to other anti-oppressive agendas.

Achieving organisational change

Since it is not always possible, or even desirable, to set up wholly new organisations, the wider challenge to professionals is to seek planned change within their own agencies (NISW, 1995b), wherever they observe that services or employment practices are outdated or oppressive.

A parallel stimulus from managers towards organisational change is being triggered by the need to balance increased demand and higher expectations with a shortfall in resources (George, 1996). Restructuring within existing agencies has become the hallmark of the age, so that organisations are needing sophisticated ways to manage, and to help their staff to weather, processes of change. While stable and static organisations concentrate on efficiency and tend to be centralised and bureaucratic as a result (Mintzberg, 1989), those which face greater complexity tend to decentralise and become more organic, developing and adapting as needed.

A number of change techniques are nowadays considered more appropriate than the mere assertion of managerial authority. Styles of change management include (Kotter and Schlesinger, 1979):

- education and communication;
- participation and involvement;
- facilitation and support;

- negotiation and agreement;
- manipulation and co-optation;
- explicit and implicit coercion.

Their deployment depends on the circumstances. Legislative change, for example, is usually interpreted as a need for new information and is managed through education and communication, while imminent budgetary crisis elicits stronger measures in varying degrees of manipulation, co-optation or coercion to impose cost-cutting measures, for example redundancies. It is likely that imposed change techniques will lead to later problems within the organisation, however, as anger and resentment engender resistance and lowered morale. Nor is effective change only a matter of altering what other people do (Pugh, 1993). A rigid or unreflexive approach, that is, one where we are unable to see our own part in what is happening, creates fresh resistances in others and new obstacles in operating systems.

While some organisations are actively empowering, most show some resistance to change (cf. Pernell, 1986, p. 112). Many, for example, are skilled at reinterpreting new ideas in accord with their own norms, demanding compromises and spinning out decisions until momentum is lost. 'Covert resistance' (Whitaker, 1975, p. 426) – verbal assurances without active support – can be far harder to deal with than out-and-out opposition. Also, the change process itself virtually always takes longer and creates more unforeseen problems in existing performance levels (Carnall, 1990) than has been allowed for.

To smooth the way, Pugh (1993, pp. 110–12) has devised a number of 'rules' for the successful implementation of change in organisations which encompass full participation, long-term planning, and the avoidance of change for change's sake. Social work also has its own model of 'managing change through innovation', developed at the NISW (Smale, 1993). Its message involves breaking down both the planning and the actual change process into clearly defined components, and placing considerable stress on the 'people' aspects such as enabling, convincing, reassuring, forming alliances and partnerships on the one hand, and avoiding and bypassing where necessary on the other.

Change is possible, then, but it requires vision, persistence and strong alliances, preferably between staff and service users pursuing shared objectives.

Conclusion

Constant agency reorganisations, expectations on workers to develop transferable competencies, and demanding performance criteria have made 'managing change' an essential skill in professional social work. Within this pursuit of change can be perceived opposing trends in management thinking. On the one hand, resource shortfalls and the need to compete in a 'market' of welfare are encouraging aggressive talk of rationalisation and 'downsizing', that is, imposing cuts. On the other hand, the diversification of service provision to meet a wider range of community needs, the tailoring of standards to the demands of service users and the opening up of management theory to celebrate difference all give cause for hope that social work values may not be totally at odds with the agendas of the future. Furthermore, diversity in the welfare sector continues to allow for experimentation with organisational forms more in tune with an ethos of caring, empowerment and resistance against oppression.

Further reading

Clegg, S. R., Handy, C. and Nord, W. (eds) (1996) *Handbook of Organization Studies* (London, Sage).

A useful organisation 'text book' which covers theories of organisation, current issues and research.

Itzin, C. and Newman, J. (eds) (1995) *Gender, Culture and Organisational Change: Putting Theory into Practice* (London, Routledge).

This book focuses on gender in organisations and on feminising the workplace and service delivery. It provides useful case histories of successful change in and across organisations.

Kelly, D. and Warr, B. (1992) *Quality Counts: Achieving Quality in Social Care Services* (London, Whiting & Birch).

An edited collection which provides the most accessible general introduction to quality assurance in social work and social care.

Mabey, C. and Mayon-White, B. (1993) *Managing Change* (London, Paul Chapman Publishing in association with the Open University).

A widely read and practical introductory text on managing change in organisations.

Morgan, G. (1986) *Images of Organization* (Thousand Oaks, CA, Sage).

An exploration of organisations through metaphor and symbols – for example, the organisation as a brain or a psychic prison – which provides insights into how organisations work and what they mean to their members.

7

Social work through the life course

LENA ROBINSON

Introduction

During the late 1980s, social work education 'became increasingly aware of the impact of oppression and discrimination on clients and communities' (Thompson, 1993, p. 1). For example, CCETSW requirements for the DipSW award attached a high priority to an anti-discriminatory approach in college and placement teaching and assessment (see CCETSW Paper 30, 1991). The CCETSW document which outlined the guidance notes for the teaching of child care in the DipSW course stressed that 'all social work students should have a sound knowledge of human growth and development, [and] the significance of race, culture and language in development must be understood' (CCETSW, 1991, p. 14). The Children Act, 1989 states that the race, culture, language and religion of children and young people must be addressed in the provision of services. In order to meet the needs of and help the development of any child, black or white, it is essential that social workers operate with adequate knowledge, understanding and sensitivity.

Life course study may draw on different theoretical perspectives – sociological, economic, political, biological, anthropological and psychological. Social work has turned to the social sciences, particularly psychology, for accounts of human behaviour which can be applied in practice. This chapter will focus mainly on the psychological perspective. It argues that traditional psychological theories have not had sufficient explanatory power to account for the behaviour of black people. The term 'black' in this chapter has been used to describe people from South Asian, African and Caribbean backgrounds.

The issues discussed in this chapter are offered as the initial steps toward an understanding of some concepts covered in the literature

78

on the life course from a black perspective: attachment theory, black identity development, the family and older people.

Inadequacies of Western psychology

The conventionally accepted paradigms and discoveries of Western psychology do not provide an understanding of black children, adolescents and older people. Even a casual observation of the history of psychology will demonstrate that psychological literature from the past 100 years has been based on observations primarily on Europeans, predominantly male and overwhelmingly middle class. A model of white middle-class personality has been 'utilized as a measuring stick against which all other psychological development is assessed' (Sinha, 1983, p. 7), 'the standard against which others must measure up' (Segall *et al.*, 1990, p. 93).

The formulations of such notable thinkers who have shaped the thought of Eurocentric psychology, such as Sigmund Freud (1953) and Carl Jung (1950), have all directly or indirectly asserted the superiority of European races over non-European races. Despite the diversity of the various schools of Western psychology, they seem to merge unequivocally in their assumption of the Eurocentric point of view and the superiority of people of European descent. It is not surprising, therefore, that the conclusions reached from the application of their concepts and methods are invariably of the inferiority of non-European peoples (Robinson, 1995).

A main feature of Eurocentric psychology is the assumption among psychologists that people are alike in all important respects. In order to explain 'universal human phenomena', white psychologists established a normative standard against which all other cultural groups were to be measured. What appeared as normal or abnormal was always in comparison to how closely a specific thought or behaviour corresponded to that of white people. Hence, normality is established on a model of the middle-class, Caucasian male of European descent. The more one approximates this model in appearance, values and behaviour, the more 'normal' one is considered to be. The obvious advantage for European (whites) is that such norms confirm their reality as the reality and flaunts statements of their supremacy as scientifically based 'fact'. The major problem with such normative assumptions for non-European people is the inevitable conclusion of deviance on the part of anyone unlike this model. In fact, the more distinct you are from this model, the more pathological you are considered to be (Robinson, 1995).

Social workers in Britain and the USA have been influenced greatly by the psycho-analytic approach in psychology. This approach is based on Sigmund Freud's work but has been developed by neo-Freudians (for example, Erikson, Melanie Klein, and Jung). In contrast to the critiques of Freud for sexism (Mitchell, 1974; Frosh, 1987), the racism of the psycho-analytic approach is relatively unknown. Mama (1995) criticises Freudian psycho-analysis for 'its universalism and ethnocentrism... A theory which takes sexual repression and taboo as the bedrock of 'civilisation' is also highly culture-bound' (Mama, 1995, p. 127). Fernando (1991) notes that Freud (1930) 'envisaged the development of civilisation being dependent on suppressing instinctual behaviour under the guidance of the super-ego, elaborated into a 'cultural super-ego'; it was natural for him that the'leadership of the human species' should be taken up by 'white nations'(Freud, 1915, 1930) and that 'primitives' have a lower form of culture' (Fernando, 1991, p. 41). In his book *Totem and Taboo*, Freud (1912–13) refers to the practices and behaviours of African peoples as 'savage' or 'primitive'. However, 'although Freud adhered to racist thinking, it was Jung who integrated racist ideas more fully into psychological theories' (Fernando, 1991, p. 42)

Carl Jung (at one time Freud's star pupil) has been referred to as the father of 'transpersonal psychology'. He believed that certain psychological disorders found among Americans were due to the presence of black people in America. He noted that 'The causes for the American energetic sexual repression can be found in the specific American complex, namely to living together with "lower races, especially with Negroes"' (Jung, 1950, p. 29). Jung identified the modern African as 'primitive' in every sense of the word. Dalal (1988) maintains that Jung considered black people to be inferior rather than just different.

Erikson's (1968) psycho-analytical theory focuses on one distinctive feature of adolescence: the development of a sense of identity. He proposed a process whereby adolescents begin with an unclear sense of their identity, experience a 'crisis' and achieve a clear sense of their identity. He felt that 'identity crisis' was normative to adolescence and young adulthood. Erikson (1964) spoke of ethnic self-doubt and a pathological denial of one's roots as being seminal to Negro identity. He could not conceive that, for some individuals, their colour might actually be a source of pride. In an article 'Memorandum on identity and Negro youth', he states: 'A lack of familiarity with the problem of Negro youth and with the actions by which Negro youth hopes to solve these [identity] problems is a marked deficiency in my life and work which cannot be accounted for by theoretical speculation' (Erikson, 1964, p. 41).

Toward a black perspective in psychology

There is a consensus amongst most black psychologists and professionals that explanations of black behaviour which are alternative to white European perspectives must be developed. A black perspective in psychology is concerned with combating (negative) racist and stereotypic, weakness-dominated and inferiority-oriented conclusions about black people. This perspective is interested in the psychological well-being of black people and is critical of research paradigms and theoretical formulations that have a potentially oppressive effect on black people. Black psychologists (mainly in the USA) have presented alternative perspectives on black child development. However, the research of black scholars, who have unique insights into the problems of minority children and adolescents, has largely been neglected by mainstream developmental psychology (Spencer, 1988).

Attachment

In this section, I will briefly examine the concept of attachment, which is one area of development related to children. This concept refers to the special bond that develops between the infant and the care-giver. Attachment provides the child with emotional security. Once attachment is established, babies are distressed by separation from their mothers (called separation distress or anxiety). Ainsworth *et al.* (1978) have delineated three different styles of attachment: secure, avoidant (children who shun their mothers) and ambivalent (children who are uncertain in their response to their mothers). One of the assumptions about the nature of attachment in the USA and Britain is that secure attachment is the ideal. Cultures differ, however, on their notion of 'ideal' attachment. For example, German mothers value and promote early independence and regard avoidant attachment as the ideal, seeing the 'securely' attached child as 'spoiled' (Grossman *et al.*, 1985).

Some cross-cultural studies (for example, Tronick *et al.*, 1992) also challenge the notion that closeness to the mother is necessary for secure and healthy attachment. Indeed, this notion is prevalent in traditional theories of attachment based on research in the USA. Tronick *et al.* (1992) found the children in their study to be emotionally healthy despite having multiple care-givers.

Theories of attachment appear to be central to social work practice with children and families. However, most of the social work literature on attachment is Eurocentric and does not address issues of working with black children and families. A recent text for social workers, Howe's (1995) *Attachment Theory for Social Work Practice,* refers briefly to 'cultural variations in the distribution of the different types of attachment patterns' (Howe, 1995, p. 78) but takes no account of Britain's black population.

Gambe *et al.* (1992, p. 30) argue that 'the processes of colonization, migration, refuge-seeking and the effect of immigration controls have led to black families developing the capacity to maintain relationships and attachments over vast distances and time'. Attachment theory fails to take into account such issues and fails to appreciate the strengths of black families. Thus, the Eurocentric bias of attachment theory 'can contribute to inappropriate and racist assessments, [and] inappropriate interventions' (Gambe *et al.*, 1992, p. 30).

There is still much to be done to understand the attachment patterns in other cultures. The studies that do exist, however, are clear in suggesting that we cannot assume that what is seen most in Euro-American culture is best or most descriptive for all. Notions concerning the quality of attachment and the processes by which it occurs are qualitative judgements made from the perspective of each culture. Each culture has values different from but not necessarily better than those of others.

Black identity development

This section argues that the model of psychological nigrescence (a French word that means the 'process of becoming black') is more relevant to the psychological life experiences of black adolescents in Britain than are the more traditional psychological theories. It will enable us to gain a better understanding of the difficulties experienced by black adolescents in Britain.

Black identity has been discussed extensively in the social science literature using various terms and measures. According to Looney (1988, p. 41), 'Black identity deals specifically with an individual's awareness, values, attitudes, and beliefs about being Black'. It can also be viewed as 'an active developmental process which is exposed to various influences within and without, and [which] can be selective and/or adaptive' (Maxime, 1986, p. 101). These definitions will be used as the 'operating definition' in the discussion of black identity development.

A perspective that has largely been ignored by traditional Eurocentric psychology is the research on the psychology of nigrescence. Nigrescence models tend to have four or five stages, the common point of departure being not the change process *per se* but an analysis of the identity to be changed. These models are useful as they enable us to understand the problems of black identity confusion and to examine, at a detailed level, what happens to a person during identity change. Perhaps the best known and most widely researched model of black identity development is Cross's (1971, 1980, 1991) model of the conversion from 'Negro' to 'black'.

Cross suggests that the development of a black person's racial identity is often characterised by his or her movement through a five-stage process, the transformation from Pre-encounter to Internalisation–commitment. Briefly, the five stages are:

1. *Pre-encounter.* In this stage, the individual's racial identity attitudes are primarily pro-white and anti-black. That is, the individual devalues his or her ascribed racial group in favour of Euro-American culture.
2. *Encounter.* Encounter attitudes describe the awakening process experienced by black people. This awakening is often the result of a critical incident in one's life that leads the individual to reconceptualise issues of race in society and reorganise racial feelings in one's personal feelings. For example, a white individual with racist attitudes and practices may act as a catalyst to racial identity attitude change.
3. *Immersion–Emersion.* This stage involves learning and experiencing the meaning and value of one's racial group and unique culture. Immersion attitudes are pro-black.
4. *Internalisation.* This is the stage of racial identity in which the individual achieves pride in his or her racial group and identity.
5. *Internalisation–Commitment.* In this stage, the person finds activities and commitments to express his or her new identity.

The internalisation stage and the next stage, internalisation–commitment, are characterised by positive self-esteem, ideological flexibility and openness about one's blackness.

There is an extensive empirical literature that confirms Cross's model of black identity development (see Cross, 1971, 1991). Although Cross' identity development model has been developed with African-American samples in the USA, it is argued by various authors (for example, Maxime, 1986; Sue and Sue, 1990) that other minority groups share similar processes of development. In Britain, Maxime (1986) has used Cross's model in the understanding of identity confusion in black adolescents.

Parham (1989) has expanded Cross's nigrescence model. Parham considers that 'The process of psychological Nigrescence… is a life-long process, which begins with the late-adolescence/early-adulthood period in an individual's life' (Parham, 1989, pp. 194–5). An understanding of Cross's model should sensitise social workers to the role that oppression plays in a black individual's development.

Maxime (1993) has used Cross's model in the understanding of identity confusion in black children and adolescents in residential, transracially fostered and adoptive care settings.

Cross's model serves as a useful assessment tool for social workers to gain a greater understanding of black youth. Pre-encounter attitudes have been linked to high levels of anxiety, psychological dysfunction and depression (Parham and Helms, 1985; Carter, 1991), and low self-regard and self-esteem (Parham and Helms, 1985). Young people's perceptions of the social worker are likely to be influenced by their racial identity development. Thus, young people at the pre-encounter stage are more likely to show a preference for a white social worker over a black worker.

Finally, social workers need to be aware that raising children in a white-dominated society places special pressures on the black parent. Although the basic mechanisms for socialisation are the same for black and white children – reinforcement, modelling, identification and so forth – the transmittal sources and content may exhibit some subtle and some obvious differences for black children. The need for adaptive responses to social, economic and political barriers helps to shape the socialisation of black children (Harrison *et al.*, 1990). Peters (1985) indicated that many black parents focused on racial barrier messages and emphasised learning to cope with and survive prejudice in a white-dominated society.

Social work with black families

This section will focus on the dominance of pathology models of black family functioning – with reference to models of African-Caribbean and Asian family structures in social science and social work literature and practice.

Many social work texts paint crude cultural stereotypes of black families. The 'norm' against which black families are, implicitly or explicitly, judged is white. The norm presents a myth of the normal family as nuclear, middle class and heterosexual. Black families are seen as strange, different and inferior. The pathological approach to black family life is evident in the British research on black people. It is also evident in social workers' perception of black families. Barn (1993) notes that social workers' 'negative perceptions of black families led them to develop a "rescue mentality" which came into force very quickly when dealing with these families' (Barn, 1993, p. 120). Various studies (for example, Barn, 1993) have indicated the high presence of black children in the care system. Social workers tend to rely on Eurocentric theory and practice that devalues the strength of black families (Ahmad, 1990). For example, Stubbs (1988) observed 'the ease with which negative models of Afro-Caribbean culture and family functioning, already prevalent within the social work literature... fit into the frameworks of knowledge held by social workers to be relevant to their task' (Stubbs, 1988, p. 103).

Asian families have also been described in terms of cultural stereotypes. Parmar (1981, p. 21) notes that 'the traditional Asian household organised through the extended family kinship systems is held out to be responsible for a number of problems that Asians face in the context of British society'. It is argued that the 'rebellion' that 'Asian parents face from sons and daughters is... to be expected and deserved particularly if they [Asian parents] insist on practising such "uncivilised" and "backward" customs as arranged marriages' (Parmar, 1981, p. 21). Young people, particularly young women, are said to be torn between two cultures (Anwar, 1976), unable to tolerate strict rules, particularly arranged marriages, and ill-equipped to integrate into British society. Complex family situations tend to be reduced to simplistic, catch-all explanations such as 'endemic culture conflict', which offer no real understanding and fail to give any positive regard to the client's cultural roots (Ahmed, 1986). Implicit in the idea of 'culture conflict', is the assumption that the values of British family are modern and superior while the Asian culture is in some way backward and inferior.

White social workers are more likely to tolerate intergenerational conflict between parents and adolescents in white homes than in black homes. However, the little research that exists suggests that young Asians, for example, are no more alienated from their parents than are any other group of young people (Westwood and Bhachu, 1988).

Dwivedi (1996) argues that if social work perceptions and practice are largely Eurocentric, the Children Act, 1989 can easily work against the best interest and protection of the black child. Thus:

> The instrument of 'race, culture, religion and language' can be easily abused to perpetuate the dominance of professional control as a manifestation of their perception of ethnic minority families as culturally deficient, dysfunctional or pathological from whom the children need to be rescued on the one hand, to a justification of non-intervention even when a child desperately needs intervention and protection, so that the professional could appear to be culturally sensitive in case abuse is culturally acceptable! (Dwivedi, 1996, p. 9)

Social work with older black people

Older people, both black and white, face discrimination on the grounds of age or 'ageism'. Fennell *et al.* (1988) define ageism as follows: 'ageism means unwarranted application of negative stereo-types to older people' (1988, p. 97). Unlike other older people, black elders face additional problems arising from racial, cultural and economic differences and disadvantages.

The comparative literature on black and white elders is domi-nated by the theme of 'double jeopardy'. This concept, first popu-larised in the USA (National Urban League, 1964), asserts that the adverse living conditions of black elderly in America is compounded by the social fact of their overall treatment as minority group members (Jackson *et al.*, 1982). In Britain, the term has been applied to 'emphasise the double disadvantage of being poor (in income, housing, health, status and role) and a member of a minority group which suffers racial discrimination' (Patel, 1990, p. 5). In addition to 'race' and age, gender and social class are also important dimensions to inequality (Patel, 1990). Thus, older blacks could face triple jeop-ardy, which is defined as the combined impact of race, age and social class on the lives of people in disadvantaged minorities (see Jackson *et al.*, 1982).

British research has suggested that the service needs of elderly people from black groups may be considerable as a result of low incomes, poor housing, isolation and comparatively poor health (Askham *et al.*, 1993). However, older black people 'have been virtu-ally neglected by statutory bodies and have seldom found provisions addressing their specific needs (Farrah, 1986; Holland, 1986; Dominelli, 1988, p. 117). Dominelli notes that 'myths about the support of the extended family in caring for its older members have been used by white social workers and their institutions to deny the need for making appropriate provisions available' (Dominelli, 1988, p. 117). This approach ignores the fact that 'immigration controls since 1962 have made it virtually impossible for black family units to exist in their totality in Britain' (Dominelli, 1988, p. 96). Therefore, not all older Asians live with family members, and even when they do, they may still have problems of isolation and lack of daytime support. The strains on the extended Asian families, partly as a conse-quence of cramped accommodation, have been mentioned in many of the reports presenting the need for Asian day centres (for example, Rochdale County Council, 1986). Older black people, especially older Asians, are ill-informed about their welfare rights and the social services. Positive action is, therefore, required by social services departments and other organisations to increase awareness (Askham *et al.*, 1993). However, social work practice in this area is largely ethnocentric, if not colour blind.

The dominant psychological theories on ageing do not provide an adequate understanding of older black people. For example, disen-gagement theory (see Cumming and Henry, 1961) claims to be universal, but the theory is based on a model of middle-class, white, older people living in the US Mid-west (Hochschild, 1975). Blakemore and Boneham (1994) suggest that 'ethnicity and race do make a difference to the experience of ageing, whether this is in connection with... roles in the family... culture-specific needs for care by voluntary and statutory services, or problems of racism and stereotyping' (Blakemore and Boneham, 1994, p. 138). Thus, the main theories on ageing 'need to be reconsidered with ethnic and racial diversity in mind' (Blakemore and Boneham, 1994, p. 137).

Conclusion

The issues discussed in this chapter indicate that black and white people have different experiences at different stages of the life course. Social work training and practice must question whether theories which have originated in Euro-American settings have relevance in working with black clients in Britain. A Eurocentric perspective in psychology has meant certain theoretical deficits when social workers attempt to apply it in practice. Traditional psychology perpetuates a notion of deviance with respect to black people. Social workers need an understanding of the black perspective in psychology and social work theory in order to be able to deliver effective services to black clients and communities.

Research which focuses on attachment theory, identity development, the black family and black elders from a black perspective will enable social workers to gain a better understanding of the difficulties experienced by black children, teenagers and adults in Britain.

Further reading

Blakemore, K. and Boneham, M. (1994) *Age, Race and Ethnicity* (Buckingham, Open University Press).

> This is an important reference book for social workers who want to gain an understanding of ageing among black people in Britian.

Cross, W. E. (1992) *Black Identity: Theory and Research* (Philadelphia, Temple University Press).

> This book provides a detailed discussion of racial identity development models.

Dwivedi, K. N. and Varma, V. P. (eds) (1996) *Meeting the Needs of Ethnic Minority Children: A Handbook for Professionals* (London, Jessica Kingsley).

This book provides social workers with theoretical and practical information on the health, education and social care of black children.

Phinney, J. S. and Rotheram, M. J. (eds) (1987) *Children's Ethnic Socialization: Pluralism and Development* (London, Sage).

This comprehensive book discusses black children's development.

Robinson, L. (1995) *Psychology for Social Workers: Black Perspectives* (London, Routledge).

An essential introductory text for all social workers in training and practice.

8

Personal and professional development

JOYCE LISHMAN

Introduction

> Social Work involves entering into the lives of people who are in
> distress, conflict or trouble. To do this requires not only technical
> competence but also qualities of integrity, genuineness and self
> awareness. (Lishman, 1994)

Discussion of personal and professional development must be set in
the uncertain, demanding, complex and changing context of social
work. The current emphasis on vocational training and the achievement of discrete technical competencies in a culture which promotes
market forces, consumerism and managerialism (Holman, 1993;
Banks, 1995; Clark, 1995; Dominelli, 1996) is at the expense of fundamental aspects of social work including:

- a concern about individual people and the enhancement of their
  lives and relationships;
- a commitment to social justice and the eradication of poverty and
  discrimination;
- a commitment to social work as a moral and ethical activity;
- an holistic approach to practice, where relationships and process
  as well as outcomes are addressed;
- a commitment to partnership and involvement with users in
  developing services to meet their needs;
- a commitment to evaluating practice as a means of developing it;
- a recognition that the worker's use of self is integral to social
  work activity.

Examination of personal and professional development in this
chapter is based on a definition of social work which includes these

fundamental aspects. We cannot, however, ignore the tensions between this holistic approach and the current culture and context in which professional definition and identity are being challenged both by the political ideology of the New Right, with its adherence to managerialism and efficiency savings, and by a competency-driven approach to training and professional development (Banks, 1995; Sheppard, 1995; Vanstone, 1995).

This chapter examines both the context of personal and professional development in social work, and essential elements of personal and professional development. In particular, our motivation for social work, and our capacity to manage complexity, change and uncertainty, involve both personal and professional development, and each is discussed in turn. Three critical aspects of professional development are then examined: the use of supervision, the articulation and promotion of good practice along with the development and evaluation of models of practice and service provision, and the need for commitment to the next generation of entrants to social work.

The context and nature of personal and professional development in social work

The ideological, political, economic and financial context has already been alluded to and is hostile to the concept of reflective professional practice on which this discussion of personal and professional development is based. The complex and uncertain nature of social work, with its ethical base, legal accountability, responsibility for complex decision making and risk assessment, public profile and constantly changing legislation, requirements, structures and organisation requires social workers to engage in ongoing development, personal and professional, if they are to survive, respond effectively to users and clients, and manage the uncertainty which is endemic to the profession.

The ethical issues in social work summarised by Banks (1995) involve tensions between individual rights, public welfare, inequality and structural oppression; they lead to moral dilemmas and a balancing of rights, duties and responsibilities for which there may be no 'right answer'. An ethical response may conflict with financial accountability and resource availability; it may inform or conflict with legal accountability.

Social workers engage in complex decision-making, often about relative risks, safety, harm and protection. They do so in the context of a breakdown of consensus about social and collective responsibility and a rise in the value accorded to individual choice and responsibility. Paradoxically, 'society' is simultaneously experiencing widespread economic insecurity and increasing marginalisation and vulnerability, in particular in relation to people who are unemployed, in poverty or homeless, or have mental health problems (Parton, 1996). Social work is closely interlinked with these changes, and social workers' dilemmas and actions reflect and symbolise wider preoccupations with insecurity, safety, marginalisation, risk and control.

Such inherent complexity in the social work task is compounded by the pace of change which social work has experienced. Change is not unique to social work, although we may feel we have been bombarded by it! Since the late 1980s, policy and legislative change has included: the National Health Services and Community Care Act, 1990; local government reorganisation, 1996; The Children Act, England, 1989; The Children Act, Scotland, 1995; and the overall reorganisation of social work into child care, community care and criminal justice (with the loss in England and Wales of probation as part of social work training) (Criminal Justice Act, 1991; Children Act, 1989, 1995). In social work education and training, new initiatives for qualifying training were introduced in 1990 and changed in 1995 (CCETSW, 1995).

This history suggests that the external environment of social work will constantly change. Internally led change and development in practice and service delivery which is responsive to user/client views and based on the evaluation of practice and service delivery is also essential. However, such rapid policy, legal and organisational change adds to the uncertainty and complexity we experience in our practice.

The context of social work practice has not been favourable to personal or professional development. As Pietroni (1995, p. 38) argues 'a short social work basic training, no nationally recognised career path or consistent professional development structures, an inhibition or an antipathy towards individual authority and excellence and a context is produced which is intrinsically antagonistic to thoughtful practice'. Other barriers to professional development and learning include:

- a tension between a local authority's requirement for a technically competent worker, and a professional requirement for critical reflective practice, which may include criticism of the agency practice;
- a lack of agency recognition in terms of pay and status for the achievement of professional development, the practice teaching award being one example;
- a lack of time allowed for professional development;
- a lack of access to professional development; for example, Dominelli (1997) raises issues about access to higher education for women which are also relevent to professional development in

social work and social care, where women with family commitments may have difficulty in terms of finance and time in pursuing relevant professional developments.

We may ask why we should undertake any professional development when it may not be organisationally valued and is unlikely to be financially rewarded. Professional development is essential to develop, use and promote more effective models of practice and service delivery in a context of rapid change of policy and legislation. Personal development is essential to underpin professional development since our use of self is part of the service we offer to users and clients. The need for continuing professional development is not the prerogative of social work. Qualifying training, in any profession and whatever the length, is inevitably limited in input, both breadth and depth, and in opportunities for application to practice. Professionals also need to update their expertise as knowledge and methods change and develop:

> One central purpose of continuing professional education is to bring practising professionals into contact with new knowledge and ideas. Sometimes this is conceived in terms of general updating, sometimes as a stimulus to critical thinking and self evaluation, sometimes as the dissemination of a particular innovation, sometimes as part of the process of implementing a new mandatory policy... (Eraut, 1994, p. 25).

Put briefly, but too simply, two contrasting models appear to influence continuing professional development: the competency-based approach underpinning the National Vocational system and adopted to some extent by CCETSW for both qualifying and post-qualifying awards, and an approach which values reflective practice and the learning process, and stresses the role of the professional as a reflective practitioner (Schön, 1987).

The 'competency' model is based on functional analysis which 'breaks the job down into functional units and the units into elements each of which has to be separately assessed to cover a range of situations according to a list of performance criteria' (Eraut, 1994, p. 118). This model is inappropriate for education, training and professional development in social work because it results in fragmentation of the complexity of social work and lacks an holistic approach to the necessary integration of knowledge, values and skills and the processes whereby these are integrated and applied.

This chapter bases professional development on the second approach, the reflective practitioner model. Schön (1987) acknowledges the need for academic rigour but also its limitations in the messy reality of practice (see also Payne, Chapter 10 and Adams, Chapter 21). By reflection and analysis, we can adapt and develop the theories we use to new, complex and out-of-the-ordinary situations.

Our motivation for social work

Why do we become social workers, and why should this be relevant to our personal and professional development?

Motivation for social work, like social work itself, is varied and complex. Cree (1996) found that reasons for entering social work training were family background, significant life experience of loss, illness or disability, and adult choice including social work as a vocation to care for individuals, as a means of 'changing the system' and promoting social justice or as a career. Rochford (1991) drew attention to the experience of loss, both normal and exceptional, as a major factor in motivation for social work. Cree (1996) also highlights gender differences in motivation for social work. Men are entering a profession in which their promotion prospects are high but the qualities and abilities required of them are not stereotypically male. For women, the opposite is true.

Why does motivation matter, and why should it be an issue for personal development? Think about your own motivation. Was it political, was it your experience of racial or gender discrimination, or did it arise from your personal experience, as a child or as an adult. How do you think it influences your practice?

We need a personal element in motivation for social work whether it arises from our experience of structural oppression or of personal difficulty. It can give us compassion, empathy and insight into the lives of people with whom we work and a commitment to challenging injustice and discrimination. However, we must not be driven in our practice by our personal experience, attempt to impose the experiences which motivate us on our clients or users, or work out our agendas (personal or political) through their lives.

How may we harness the positive and empowering aspects of our motivation and avoid the potential danger of using our clients or users to meet our own needs rather than responding to theirs? Developing and maintaining self-awareness is one way, supervision, potentially, another.

Self-awareness and reflection

We need to develop our self-awareness and capacity for critical reflection in order to ensure that our motivation and past experience are used to enhance our practice. Self-awareness is also necessary if we are to recognise our impact on others. Do we convey authority and expertise where required? Do we convey a non-judgemental attitude to aspects of clients' lives which are potentially shocking, for example violence, abuse or deprivation? What sense of empowerment do we convey to our users? How do we remain aware of our impact on others?

Self-awareness and critical self-reflection are also necessary to ensure confidence that our responses arise from the client's or user's situation rather than our past or needs. This requires self-awareness and 'awareness of situations and topics which generate most personal anxiety to the worker since intense anxiety is likely to lead to inattention, poor listening, and inappropriate responses and action' (Lishman, 1994, p. 60).

Finally, we need to use self-awareness and reflection to meet the complex demands of social work. Carter *et al.* (1995) suggest that we experience in social work a tension between the uniqueness of each situation and the need to develop generalised responses to 'familiar social work problems'. 'We have to think things through, for every case is unique. When we forget this, problems arise. If we simply label people as a "housing problem" or whatever, and then go through our "housing routine" we are liable to miss all sorts of things... Of course, we rely on routines: it would be intolerable if we had to work things out from first principles for each and every situation. However, these routines have to be open to feedback from the situation' (p. 8). They argue that this requires both 'reflecting in action' and 'reflection on action'.

We need to develop a discipline of reflecting on what we have done and how we have behaved, 'reflection on action' (Schön, 1987) in order to learn, confirm good practice, analyse mistakes and develop alternative actions and responses. Questions contributing to reflection on action include:

- How did I engage with that person or in that situation?
- What previous experiences influenced me?
- What did I do?
- Why did I do it?
- On reflection, how might I have responded differently, if at all?

By practising such discipline, we may increasingly be able to 'reflect in practice', where questions have a more immediate focus and may include the following:

- What am I feeling?
- How am I presenting?
- Do I need to change my approach or focus?
- Why do I feel uncomfortable?

Managing complexity

We have noted the complex demands of social work, but its very essence is complex and ambiguous, involving tensions between a focus on the alleviation of individual distress and misery and on challenging structural oppression and inequality, and between meeting individual need, promoting empowerment, ensuring the protection of vulnerable children and adults, and carrying out functions of social work control. Practice is equally complex. For example, faced with families in poverty, in isolation, with difficulties in child care and control (Walker, 1995), what out of the range of relevant knowledge and theory do we draw on? What focus do we select? What methods do we employ? Equally, how do we manage the complexity of our feelings, of being overwhelmed, of feeling inadequate and helpless, of empathy, of frustration?

Such complexity and need 'stirs up powerful and primitive feeling in all professionals' (Trowell, 1995, p. 195). One danger is that we become paralysed by attempting to manage all the complexity and by our inability to do so effectively. Walker (1995) warns of the dangers of the wish to be omnipotent: 'the belief that I could or should be brilliantly effective' (p. 56). An alternative danger is that we attempt to limit and simplify the complexity, for example, by:

- providing 'concrete responses' such as providing a service or aid but ignoring the feelings and relationships which surround the problem; for example, providing a Zimmer frame may be necessary for the user's functioning but not sufficient for their wellbeing, because issues about dependency and anxiety about 'failing' may need to be addressed.
- 'splitting' and 'projection'. 'Splitting arises from the existence of utterly contradictory feelings that seem impossible to countenance simultaneously and which are therefore kept in separate compartments… Projection occurs when a feeling or characteristic which in reality belongs to the self is first externalised and then ascribed to another person' (Brearley, 1991, p. 52). Splitting and projection are defence mechanisms which began in infancy in order to cope with the powerful good and bad primitive feelings and can be helpful essential mechanisms in coping as adults. As workers, however, if we use splitting and projection in relation to our clients, users and work, we are in danger of distorting a complex reality.

We have to be able to contain, for example: worry and concern for a mother on her own, depressed, in debt and without the very basic material props of parenting, for example a washing machine; our anxiety about her child's emotional and physical needs; our anger with the political and social security system which allows if not promotes this; and resonances with our past and our childhood experience of need and dependency. If we split, for example by focusing entirely on the child's needs and vulnerability, or project, for example by rage at the system, we cannot manage and balance the complex task of addressing ways of improving resources and parental care, and improving the ways in which the parent's and child's needs can be met.

How can we develop this personal capacity to contain and manage such complexity? In part, we need to recognise this as a continuing area of personal and professional development; in part, it requires a commitment to the maintenance and development of self-awareness; in part, it requires a capacity for reflection in and on action; and, in part, we need to be able to analyse practice and therefore learn from and build on previous experience. Practice supervision may offer the opportunity to examine our responses to complex cases with real needs, vulnerability and risks and engage in the same processes for personal development and learning. We also need to be allowed to make mistakes and get things 'wrong' provided that we learn from the experience and are not dangerous to our clients.

Managing uncertainty

Uncertainty faces us in a number of ways. We face uncertainty about our value base as we are challenged to examine, for example, how racism, sexism, heterosexism, ageism and other forms of oppression may influence us, without our necessarily recognising this. In working with users and clients, we face uncertainty about how to respond appropriately, how to choose the 'right' response to the myriad of feelings, impressions, theories and experiences which form our working practice. Uncertainty is not unique to social work but is a component of 'professional' activity. More specifically, uncertainty in social work arises because individuals and their problems are unique, there is no set causal link between a problem, a response and an outcome, risk assessment is problematic (Kemshall and Pritchard, 1996), the organisational context has been constantly changing and the political context is hostile but unpredictable.

Dealing with uncertainty means realising that often there is no right response, although there may be a wrong one. The danger here is that, again, we try to simplify, which may involve:

● demanding certainty and answers where none are available;
● giving answers and information which are definite but may be wrong;

- dealing with the discrete parts of a problem which may have an immediate solution and ignoring the more messy and uncertain areas.

Such strategies for denying uncertainty can be dangerous as they may lead us to impose 'certain' but wrong action on our clients or users.

How may we better deal with uncertainty? Perhaps we first have to recognise it as an essential part of life, not just social work! We need to consider how we deal with uncertainty in our lives, what helps and what hinders. 'We need to avoid jumping to closed conclusions and keep open the possibility of change as a result of reflecting in action and dialogue with others' (Carter *et al.*, 1995, p. 9). We need to use the experience of training, of supervision and of our colleagues to help us examine our own ways of dealing with uncertainty and, where we find they are inappropriate, to explore and practise other ways.

Managing change

We have seen that the recent context of social work has been of rapid, constant and externally imposed change. Change is not unique to social work. In our personal lives, we have to adapt to changes of biological maturation and ageing, and life cycle social and emotional changes.

More generally, we need to be aware (Marris, 1974) that any major change, be it voluntary or imposed, will involve loss for the participants – an initial loss of their previous 'taken for granted' view of the world, sense of security and established sense of meaning and purposes. Such loss is met with ambivalence, analogous to grief, involving conflict between contradictory impulses: to remain the same and keep what is valuable from the past, and to move on. Marris argues that the management of change necessitates the expression of ambivalence and conflicting impulses before the participants can move on to accept the change (whether it involves new perspectives, skills or organisational structures) and integrate it into a continuity of experience and meaning. Such an analysis helps us to understand why change, even where we can see that it brings rewards, is met with apparently irrational resistance. While such resistance to change is not intrinsically bad – for example, it may delay ill-thought out or ill-advised changes (Coulshed, 1991) – change is essential if an organisation is to be responsive to its environment and to develop and thereby survive, and in order to develop better services and practice.

In our personal and professional development, it is important to pay attention to how we manage change. At the extremes, do we totally resist it or embrace it without thought for the past? We need to examine our personal responses because they will influence how we respond to clients or users who are facing change, for example in relationships, dependency or physical location, how we respond to changes in the organisation and delivery of social work, and how open we are to new ideas, without discarding hard-earned knowledge and skills from the past.

Managing complexity, uncertainty and change is demanding and stressful, and it is impossible to prescribe methods and techniques to do so 'successfully'. What can help? At a personal level, we have seen the need to develop and maintain an awareness of our own strengths and weaknesses, a capacity to tolerate and contain our irrational feelings and responses, and a discipline of self-critical reflection.

To support and help us in this, we can use specific training courses, discussion with colleagues, mulling over particular cases and incidents, recording, reflection and evaluation, and perhaps, potentially most importantly, supervision.

Supervision

> Supervision is an effective tool for professional staff development which managers would be foolish not to consider. However, many managers subvert the supervision process into a means of controlling or instructing staff, instead of as a means of developing staff. (Turner, 1995, p. 127)

The above quotation indicates the potential dilemma and danger of supervision. It can become a management tool of accountability and efficiency. Equally, it can be used to enhance professional development and thereby practice and service provision.

What should you expect of supervision? Ideally, it should be provided on a regular and reliable basis. It should involve mutual trust and an awareness of issues of authority and responsibility. It should provide support and an opportunity to express feelings and to go 'below the surface' in the analysis of problems and situations. It should address particular issues which workers identify as problematic, including facing pain, anxiety, confusion, violence and stress. Its content and process should be anti-oppressive and anti-discriminatory, with a professional development focus of empowerment. It should focus on learning.

There is a gap between what should happen and what actually does happen! Areas of discrepancy which will hinder professional development include:

- the unavailability of supervision;
- the abuse of power, for example where the dissemination of information is controlled or supervision is used to exercise the supervisor's power or control as negative power, for instance by blocking and restricting, or by punishment (Grimwood and Popplestone, 1993);
- a lack of emotional or feeling support: 'Supervisors often cut off from the pain in clients' lives. The worker, unable to share and thereby receive support from her line manager, is left on her own with the loss and grief of her clients' (Hanmer and Statham, 1988, in Grimwood and Popplestone, 1993, p. 47).
- a lack of acknowledgement and support in issues connected with violence: often as workers, we are left to deal with fears of and responses to violence as our personal responsibility rather than being offered support and the opportunity for reflection, process and analysis in supervision.

It is important to seek good supervision. In particular, it can help us to manage anxiety and confusion. Turner (1995, p. 126) argues that 'Many workers feel they must appear to be coping well with their work at all times. What they see as their less acceptable thoughts, feelings and actions are suppressed, denied and avoided, for fear of being seen as not a good enough worker. It is important for supervisors to demonstrate in supervision their own capacity to contain anxiety and remain thoughtful about whatever the worker brings, rather than avoiding the painful issues, rushing for solutions, or giving "neat" packages of instructions.' Such a capacity for containment, empathy, reflection and their encouragement of analysis in depth can help us to cope with the pain, violence and anxiety we may encounter. It can also help us to become more able to take responsibility for our own work, to make our own judgements and then to improve them.

As Brown and Bourne (1996) argue, supervision is time for exploration, reflection, learning and problem-solving.

Promoting and developing good practice and service provision

The development of good social work practice and service delivery is a collective responsibility of all qualified social workers. We need constantly to examine critically and review practice and service delivery. We need to identify what are the ingredients of 'good practice' and how can they be applied elsewhere. We need to identify areas for improvement and gaps in service delivery and responses to user need, in order to begin to change services and provide new ones. This is, of course, within a context of lack of resources. *Community Care* (1996) found that most social workers had to refuse services that clients needed because of a lack of resources. However, *Community Care* also regularly provides examples of innovative developments in practice and service delivery to meet gaps in service provision or unmet need.

We need to develop and maintain ways of learning from others: we should not in each unitary authority or voluntary organisation be reinventing wheels. How can we keep abreast of new developments which we may usefully be able to apply? One problem is the overload of information we receive and the need to select from it. Conferences and training courses are specific and therefore targeted clearly for us in terms of application to our particular practice and service development needs, but they are expensive. However, they can put us in touch with other workers' relevant experience in relatively informal but productive ways.

We can learn by reading. *Community Care* provides relevant articles about good practice and service development. It also reviews relevant literature from which we can select what may best apply to and develop our current expertise. More general texts may be useful at post-qualifying level (see further reading).

We can engage in the formal post-qualifying training continuum. CCETSW sets out a framework for post-qualifying training which involves two levels: post-qualifying and advanced. The requirements are difficult to summarise and the details are set out in CCETSW Paper 31 (1990), soon to be revised. The main features of the post-qualifying level are 'the development of competence, confidence and professional credibility beyond the qualifying level' and either the development of specialist expertise in one area of practice or the responsibility for the management of an aspect of social work. At the advanced level, candidates may be assessed in practice, education and training, management or research, but all candidates have to demonstrate a range of competence including the analysis of practice and service delivery, the development and improvement of services, the critical evaluation of values, theories, models, methods and policies, and the management of innovative change.

We need, as the post-qualifying framework requires, to articulate our practice. We need to do this, for example, in supervision in order to learn from what we do and change and develop our practice. We need to articulate our practice to colleagues from other disciplines. We need to articulate our practice so that other social workers can learn from what we do. We may be working on behalf of our users and clients in excellent innovative ways which benefit them, but if we do not articulate this practice, others cannot learn from it and have to reinvent the wheel. We need to articulate practice for the political survival of the profession and our users, in order to demonstrate to the government, press and public what we do well (even though they may not necessarily listen).

We need not simply to identify good practice, but also to evaluate it. As Ian Shaw (1996) argues, evaluating practice has historically been a problematic aspect of social work. However, there are good reasons why we should engage in the evaluation of practice and service delivery. Evaluation examines our effectiveness and can help us improve it, can increase our accountability to users and clients, develops our knowledge and identifies gaps in knowledge, and helps us develop new models of practice and service delivery.

If we develop a new method, project or service, we need to examine how well it works for its users. More problematically, the continued funding of innovative projects is often linked with the evaluation of effectiveness where definitions of effectiveness may not necessarily be shared by funder and the project and its users. Evaluation, we need to recognise, can be part of a political and resource context. Nevertheless, we need to engage with it: as Ian Shaw (1996) argues, 'it holds the promise of keeping social work honest'.

How to evaluate our practice can appear threatening, with connotations of scientific experimental method, although as Everitt *et al.* (1992) suggest and Everitt argues in Chapter 9 of this volume, the social work process of finding and collating evidence, hypothesis-forming and assessment, intervention and hypothesis-testing, review, further assessment, revision of intervention and further review is not dissimilar to qualitative research methodology.

Educating and training the next generation

There are inevitably many valid reasons for not becoming a practice teacher or providing input to social work eduction, including a lack of financial or career recognition, a lack of resources including staff, space and time, and a lack of organisational support where management is preoccupied with service delivery and cuts in resources.

In such circumstances, educating and training the next generation can be seen as a luxury. Why should you become involved in practice teaching or any other teaching input to social work courses? Good reasons include the need to ensure the continuation of professional service delivery to clients and users, the professional and value component of generativity (Erikson, 1965), that we should put back into the profession as we have received, and the enhancement of our learning and expertise. Students question and challenge us in ways that ensure we explore, examine, reflect on and evaluate our practice.

Teaching others often provides the best opportunity to articulate our own practice, to question and examine what we do and why, and, if we are open to challenge, to identify gaps and failures in practice and provision. Students then provide a challenging external scrutiny of what we do. By educating and training them, we provide the future development of our profession, and workers who can learn from and develop our experience.

Conclusion

Personal and professional development, in this context, is a very broad agenda: it lasts a lifetime and depends on definitions of social work and its functions. It can be undermined by ideology (for example, the emphasis on technical competence or managerialism), by a lack of access (by gender, class or ethnicity), by a lack of organisational support and reward, and by a lack of resources including time.

This chapter focuses on themes of self-awareness, reflection and critical self-evaluation which underpin both personal and professional development, and not on models of development involving discrete technical competencies because social work is a complex, uncertain and value-based activity in which we work with people from different backgrounds who are likely to have experienced structural oppression, discrimination, personal difficulty, loss or tragedy. Despite the barriers identified, we owe it to our users and clients to maintain our personal and professional development and thereby contribute to the development and improvement of the social work practice and services they receive.

Further reading

Brown, A. and Bourne, I. (1996) *The Social Work Supervisor: Supervision in Community, Day Care and Residential Settings* (Buckingham, Open University Press).

This book, although focusing on supervision, is invaluable in drawing attention to issues of professional development and support for social workers and potential blocks to them.

Carter, P., Jeffs, T. and Smith, M. K. (1995) *Social Working* (Basingstoke, Macmillan).

This edited collection of chapters by practising social workers identifies major issues in professional development by analysing social work practice from the perspective of experienced social workers, including the main processes: a 'hands-on' approach to examining and articulating practice and learning from it.

Eraut, M. (1994) *Developing Professional Knowledge and Competence* (London, Falmer Press).

This book contains a valuable multidisciplinary analysis of issues in professional development and pressures which deal with complexity.

Shaw, I. (1996) *Evaluating in Practice* (Aldershot, Arena).

This book presents a model of evaluating a practice based on the reality of social work and recent developments in qualitative methodology for doing and learning research.

Yelloly, M. and Henkel, M. (1995) *Learning and Teaching in Social Work: Towards Reflective Practice* (London, Jessica Kingsley).

This edited collection addresses issues in the post-professional education of social workers and related professionals, examining the concepts of professionalism, competence, knowledge and anti-racism, with an emphasis on how professionals learn and maintain a self-critical and reflective approach to practice.

9

Research and development in social work

ANGELA EVERITT

Introduction

Social work has long had a somewhat ambivalent relationship with research. Concerns have been expressed that practitioners do not read research, do not inform their practice with findings from research, do not influence decisions on what is researched, do not commission research and do not undertake research themselves. There is not space in this one chapter to consider all of these issues. Instead, taking account of recent policy initiatives, the chapter suggests some approaches to research and development that might be particularly relevant for social work. In this, social work is understood as a professional activity wherein practitioners engage in their craft to contribute to policy and practice with a view to reducing inequalities in society and to ameliorating the local and personal effects of these.

Enhancing research in practice

A range of initiatives have been introduced in recent years to enhance the relevance of research to policy and practice development. Some, such as the practitioner-research programmes at York University (Whitaker and Archer, 1989) and at the Social Work Research Centre at Stirling University (Fuller and Petch, 1995), focus upon providing opportunities for social workers to undertake small-scale research relevant to their practice. Others, such as the Joseph Rowntree Foundation, in its publication of *Findings* and *Research Matters*, published twice a year by the magazine *Community Care*, concentrate on making the findings of research accessible to practitioners. Still others take the form of action-research projects such as the Department of Health's pilot scheme, set up in 1995 with social services departments in the south west of England designed to promote the use of research findings in practice and to involve practitioners in identifying needs for research.

The state of research in health and the personal social services has been the focus of two working groups established by the Department of Health: the Smith review of personal social services' research reported in June 1994 (Smith, 1994) and the Culyer review of NHS research the following October (Culyer, 1994). Both were partly prompted by concerns about how research and development would fare in the market economy of health and social care. With purchaser–provider changes in the organisation of services, and short-termism in funding and projects, questions were being asked on where and by whom research and development would be undertaken. It was thought that research and development might well diminish, with purchasers attracted by the cheapest and providers driven to reducing costs. Furthermore, a decline in local government research was anticipated as unitary authorities disappeared and others struggled with depleted budgets. Both reviews, acknowledging the gap between research, policy and practice, emphasised the importance of the usefulness, relevance and ownership of research by those expected to be influenced by findings. Both recommended that practitioners should feel ownership of research, be involved in deciding what should be researched and take part in dissemination and implementation exercises. They should be trained to be research literate, and researchers should have a clear responsibility to make research findings accessible. Links between health and personal social services, and other services such as education, should be fostered and partnerships introduced for commissioning and conducting research across professional and organisational boundaries. The Culyer Report recommended that more attention be paid to health research in primary and community health. Both reviews recommended that research and development strategies be developed nationally, regionally and across the personal social services and the health service.

Considerable attention has been paid to developing research-based and informed practice with children in care. Indeed, there is some evidence that the Children Act, 1989 was itself informed by research (Harwin, 1990). Attention has been paid to making child-care research findings accessible to practitioners (Kahan, 1989; DoH, 1996). The development of research-informed practice is key to the Department of Health-funded research and development project *Looking After Children: Good Parenting, Good Outcomes* (Parker *et al.*, 1991; Ward, 1995). This is concerned with assessing outcomes in child-care work and with developing practical instruments, action and assessment records. These records, for social workers to complete with children in care, are intended to ensure that child-care research findings inform practice, that work with children in care is pursued systematically, that data are generated for departmental review and monitoring purposes as well as comparatively across social services departments and that the child growing up in care is able to capture her or his own history. Similar to structured questionnaires, they comprise questions derived from research findings on good parenting which social workers are expected to build into their ongoing conversations with children and young people in their care.

At first sight, to the researcher, the *Looking after Children* project is impressive. It is systematic and meticulous, and care has been taken to include every detail important to the child in care. It has attracted a wealth of expertise from research units and university social work departments, and it is becoming adopted widely by social services departments and by social welfare organisations in other countries. It is interesting and innovatory in its approach to bridging the gap between research and practice. However, it is through this very gap that the project could fall into technical and unthinking ways of working. Whereas some practitioners may, and undoubtedly do, adopt the action and assessment records as valuable instruments for research and professional practice, others may merely engage in it, or alternatively resist it, as yet more of the procedural form-filling that has replaced so much professional practice.

New managerialism in health and welfare has been accompanied, even strengthened, by an array of what might be seen as research and development activities: monitoring, evaluation, inspection, performance review, output and outcome measurement, and evidence-based practice. While the central assumption of this chapter is that social work practice, and the policy context in which it operates, should be systematically subjected to the scrutiny of research and developed to take account of evidence of effectiveness, there is little doubt that these recent initiatives are experienced as a part of increasing managerial control. Rather than approaches designed to enquire into, and ensure the effectiveness of, policies, procedures and practices, they can be more like technical intrusions into what should be professional practice:

> The extravagance of professional expertise was to be replaced by a range of review techniques including quality assurance, clinical audit, performance indicators in various forms and guises. Much of this scrutiny was external to the professions concerned and seen as a direct attack on clinical autonomy. (Rafferty and Traynor, 1997, p. 17)

This technical recording of practice has been exacerbated in social services through departmental defensiveness in the wake of child abuse enquiries and the evidence of abuse experienced by children and adults in their care. It can serve to prevent or obscure the interrogation of professional practice, particularly through the public pretence that services and practices are informed by research. Professional practice must be subject to rigorous scrutiny and public debate, and should itself be concerned with opening up social services and policies to such processes. What is important in professional practice and in closing the gap between research and practice is that social work practitioners are research-minded (Everitt *et al.*, 1992). This is a necessary condition not only for doing research and implementing research findings in practice, but also for ensuring that practice makes a difference for people in trouble. As Utting reminds us:

> To get the best out of research you need an inquiring mind, the desire to improve performance and a critical and sceptical intelligence... Research is a means, not an end in itself – a tool with which to improve and perfect one's business, whether this be making policy, managing services or working face to face with people: it is not a machine which dispenses neat answers on cardboard squares. (Utting, 1989)

The process of researching is one of questioning, of generating and being open to evidence. It is about teasing out values and theoretical assumptions with a preparedness to engage in debate with those who may interpret the evidence differently. It contrasts with polemic, rhetoric and common sense. It disrupts routine and procedure. There is now quite a research literature available for social workers on undertaking research and reading published research critically (for example, Whitaker and Archer, 1989; Everitt *et al.*, 1992; Broad and Fletcher, 1993; Shakespeare *et al.*, 1993; Hart and Bond, 1995). Indeed, the literature on research methods for practitioners generally, teachers (for example, Altrichter *et al.*, 1993; Burgess, 1993), nurses (for example, Sapsford and Abbott, 1992) and leisure (for example, Veal, 1992) is quite considerable, indicating that the problem is with the relationship between research and practice generally rather than with social work in particular.

In nursing, a large part of the problem is attributed to the power of members of the medical profession (Rafferty and Traynor, 1997). It is not only that they decide on research priorities and claim the major slice of the research resource, but also that they set the prevailing ideas of what constitutes respectable and credible research. This has led to a predominance of randomised control trials with little acknowledgment of the value of smaller-scale studies yielding qualitative data. At the same time, claims that qualitative studies are more likely to contribute to social change must be treated with caution. We only have to compare the detailed large-scale studies of poverty and health that have been undertaken over long periods of time (for example, Townsend *et al.*, 1988) with the one hundred and one case studies of people successfully making their journeys back from long-term unemployment (Booth and Mallon, 1994) or with the current prevalence of focus groups falsely occupying the space of research and consultation (Preston, 1996) to be rightly sceptical of seemingly genuine stories of people's lives and concerns. The underlying issue here is power. Processes that are dressed up as research, and come to be accepted as such, are powerful in that they produce knowledge that is thought to be credible, to be 'true'. It is important to be critical, not only of professional practice, but also of research and of knowledge, and to be mindful of the ways in which some explanations and understandings come to be thought of as 'true'. Such truths may serve to maintain the *status quo* and to continue and strengthen oppressive practices.

Theory and practice in research

The 'Wider Strategy for Research and Development relating to Personal Social Services' (Smith, 1994) adopts the official definition of research as used by government in its research policy and funding strategies. It separates 'basic research' (that is, 'experimental or theoretical work... to acquire new knowledge') from 'strategic research' (that is, research that is applied but where no specific applications have been identified) and 'applied research' (that is, 'to acquire new knowledge' but 'directed primarily towards practical aims and objectives').

For social work, the distinction which separates theory from practice is unhelpful. It feeds into practices that do not enhance social science's potential contribution to the amelioration of social problems and the reduction in social inequalities. One effect, for example, of the 'basic' and 'applied' split is the hierarchy that can develop between those who, in élitist and prestigious ways, regard themselves as social science theorists looking down upon those in more applied academic areas and probably not noticing practitioners at all. On the one hand, this serves to let such social scientists off the hook: in the position they adopt they have no need to ensure that their research makes a difference to 'private troubles and public issues' and accept no responsibility for this. On the other hand, it promotes in social workers anti-theoretical and anti-academic feelings voiced as 'they're out of touch', 'not engaged in the real world', 'irrelevant'. This finds expression in social services departments and social welfare projects where there is no time to research, even to read, in order to reflect upon what is happening in practice and to keep up to date with developing knowledges.

In the 1970s, these tendencies separating theory from practice were noted by social theorists and those engaged with radical social work. Alas, Gouldner's opening lines are as relevant today as they were then:

> Social theorists today work within a crumbling social matrix of paralyzed urban centres and battered campuses. Some may put cotton in their ears, but their bodies still feel the shock waves. It is no exaggeration to say that we theorise today within the sound of guns. (Gouldner, 1970, p. vii)

Cohen, reflecting on his encounters with social workers, wrote thus:

> the most familiar reaction we encounter is encapsulated in the phrase (often quite explicitly used): 'it's all right for you to talk.' The implication is that, however interesting, amusing, correct and even morally uplifting our message might be, it is ultimately a self-indulgent intellectual exercise, a luxury which cannot be afforded by anyone tied down by the day-to-day demands of a social-work job. (Cohen, 1975, p. 76)

Gouldner and Cohen had in mind the radical activist, the practitioner with an urgency to change and a commitment to 'the tangible outcomes of pragmatic politics' rather than 'the intangible outputs of theory' (Gouldner, 1970, p. vii). Today, practitioners are often more likely to be concerned with the measurable outcomes of depoliticised practices as they follow departmental and governmental rules, guidance and procedural manuals. Their haste is more likely to be to be generated by a concern to get home, away from their alienating, underresourced, overburdened and ill-regarded places of work.

In contrast, the field of disability politics provides a positive illustration of the coming together of academics and activists. Here, disabled academics have been significant in changing understandings of disability, through theorising, research and personal experiences. Shakespeare (1996) has pointed out that, in the disability movement, academic interventions are closely related to the ongoing struggles of disabled people, social theories of disability arising from the wider political movement of disabled people in the 1990s. Re-theorising disability was necessary to social change. People like Oliver (1990) and Morris (1991) alerted us to ways in which research had shaped how we thought of disabled people within medical labels and categories. Disability was individualised, disabled people pathologised, subjected to treatment, sympathy and charity. Particular professional groups became experts in knowing better about their needs than disabled people themselves, telling them how they should behave, what they should expect from life, how they should feel and how they might improve. Social theorists such as Oliver (1990) conceptualised disability as social, to do with restrictive environments and disabling barriers, rather than to do with individual failure and personal tragedy. This social model of disability disrupted the medical model to become adopted by disabled people's organisations such as the Union of the Physically Impaired Against Segregation. It allowed the experiences of disabled people to be articulated and heard. There is not the space here for all the empirical data, nor the massive social change, that have arisen through disabled people bringing together theory, research and practice. It serves, however, as an exemplar for research and development throughout social work. It is not a rational, technical model wherein research findings are fed into policy and practice, where, unless the *status quo* is socially and/or economically ready for a change, they will hit stony ground (Pahl, 1992). It is a political model of praxis.

It is important that research and development in social work is understand as a process of praxis involving the theorising of practice and the development of theory through practice. The term 'praxis' is used, as in Stanley, to adopt:

> a political position in which 'knowledge' is not simply defined as 'knowledge *what*' but also as 'knowledge *for*'. Succinctly the point is to change the world, not only to study it... [and to engage in] a social science endeavour which rejects the 'theory/research' divide, seeing these as united manual and intellectual activities. (Stanley, 1990, p. 15)

Praxis involves a commitment to understanding in order to take action, a recognition that understanding comes through engagement and debate with others, and a preparedness, through deliberation, to make judgements about 'the good'.

Critical social research

In taking seriously research and development for 'good' practice, practitioners must consider carefully the kinds of research likely to be useful to them and to users of their services that will accord with anti-discriminatory practice. This requires an understanding of theories of knowledge and theories of methods, of epistemology and methodology:

> Epistemology is the study of theories of knowledge. What is knowledge? What can we know about the social world? Who can become knowledgeable. What do we choose to know? These are important epistemological and methodological questions. (Everitt *et al.*, 1992, p. 6)

The prevailing view of both research and policy development assumes processes imbued with objectivity, neutrality and rationality. Bulmer presents this view wherein:

> The task of social research is to provide as precise, reliable and generalisable factual information as possible... This information, when fed into the policy-making process, will enable policy-makers... to reach the best decisions on the basis of the information available. (Bulmer, 1982, p. 31)

The Seebohm Committee, which recommended the establishment of research sections in the new social services departments, talked in similar terms: suggesting that 'better decisions depend on better information' (Seebohm Committee, 1968).

This 'objective' approach is informed by a particular understanding of research (how we come to know about the social world) and of development (how we intervene to bring about change). Here, 'research' and 'development' are seen as separate functions, research informing development. It is an understanding which assumes objectivity in both the research process and the policy process. Research is understood as an activity undertaken under conditions controlled to ensure objectivity as far as possible. It demands and produces expertise and it requires considerable time and resources. The 'scientific method' of such research separates it from policy and practice processes and researchers work from the 'outside', usually located in universities and central government research institutes and centres, but increasingly in private consultancy agencies. This is a top-down model: policy is expected to be informed by research, practice to be informed by policy.

This supposed objectivity in social research is used to justify particular approaches to policy research that bear little resemblance to research as an enquiring activity involving the critical scrutiny of assumptions, values, policies and practices. As already noted in this chapter, research undertaken technically in the form of feasibility studies, monitoring and evaluative studies now accompanies policy initiatives almost as a matter of routine. These are often expedient activities in the name of research to put on a public show that something is being done, and indeed the funding mechanisms of the market place, where outputs are purchased from public, voluntary and private providers, have spawned a considerable 'research' industry in monitoring and evaluation. This may be valuable in providing work for academics, freelancers and private consultants, and in justifying the continuing existence of projects and programmes, but will have done little to bring about much-needed research-informed developments designed to tackle inequalities (Everitt, 1995).

The 'objective' approach to research and development purports that researched knowledge, together with research processes for generating and according credibility to knowledge, is value-free. However, that this very supposition as so generally accepted is itself highly political. Research and policy processes are depoliticised, making both seem rational and disguising the presence and exercise of power. The work of critical social scientists, feminists and members of other new social movements provides social work with credible alternatives that recognise research *and* development as political activities. To suppose that they are not, to fail to reveal the political nature of research, is to leave the prevailing bias of our society untouched and closed to questioning and debate, a bias that is sexist, homophobic, racist, classist, ageist and disablist. The values, assumptions and cultural beliefs of those who shape the research and development agenda, who raise the research questions and who, through observation and interaction, seek data to answer these questions are influential in research and development processes. Unless particularly addressed, the world will continue only to be known through the lenses of those with power and resources. As Harding argues, the perspectives and beliefs of researchers and those who determine the research agenda should be treated, like data, as evidence:

> open to critical scrutiny... Introducing this 'subjective' element into the analysis in fact increases the objectivity of research and decreases the 'objectivism' which hides this kind of evidence from the public. (Harding, 1987, p. 9)

Thus, feminists and other critical researchers attempt to be clear, with themselves and others, about the standpoint from which they understand the world. Furthermore, attention is paid to researcher/researched relations and to the researched becoming researchers so that those usually objectified through research have the opportunity to articulate, become conscious of and develop understandings of their own experiences. Value is placed on revealing and acknowledging the experiences of researchers and the researched, while, at the same time, experience is not treated as unproblematic. It needs to be theorised to understand ways in which it is shaped through structures and processes (Maynard, 1994).

Analysing research as a powerful process, and understanding its power to produce knowledge regarded as credible, raises a number of questions. How do phenomena and people come to be known, identified and categorised in particular ways? Who falls into which categories and with what effect? What views are respected and whose are not? Who decides what should be researched, what questions should be answered, how and by whom? As we have noted from the reviews of research in the personal social services and the NHS (Culyer, 1994; Smith, 1994), government has in recent years turned its attention to such questions and introduced a number of policy initiatives designed to shape research and development. These are now explored a little more to bring them to the attention of practitioners who might be able to shift the research and development agenda towards addressing social problems and inequalities.

Users and beneficiaries of social work research

The White Paper *Realising our Potential* (Cabinet Office, 1993) emphasised the need for government-funded research to produce useful knowledge. Focusing upon science, engineering and technology, the White Paper probably escaped the notice of social work. Yet it has had considerable influence upon the ways in which research priorities are set in all fields, including the social sciences and health and social care. It recommended that decisions about what to research should be made through partnerships of academics, professionals, industrialists and government, and that research designs should take account of those intended to benefit or take account of research findings.

Following the White Paper, all research councils which fund research were required to change their charters, policies and procedures. The Economic and Social Research Council is now committed to funding social science research that is likely to enhance economic competitiveness and public welfare. Each year, it prioritises themes for research. It does this through consultation exercises with learned societies, universities and 'users of research in government, business, public life and the media' (Economic and Social Research Council, 1996) and in response to the government's Technology Foresight Sector Panels. These panels of partners forecast research priorities for sectors of society including, for example, health and life sciences, and leisure and education (Office of Science and Technology, 1994).

There are two key themes within these research and development policy developments: useful research and users of research. The policy changes clearly indicate that research should only be funded from public money if it is seen (by whom?) as potentially useful. Furthermore, those who are expected to make use of research should be involved in deciding on research priorities. It is these same themes that were confirmed and strengthened for social work and social care by the research and development reviews (Culyer, 1994; Smith, 1994). The final section of this chapter will briefly explore these themes for their meaning for research and development in social work.

An awareness of the relationship between knowledge and power, and a recognition of the success of the New Right in shaping our thoughts, our language and our curricula for learning, should make us sceptical of the emphasis upon partnership in determining research agendas. It fits more with Conservative political mechanisms that have served to control the autonomy, creativity and critical thinking of academics and professionals than it does with notions of democracy in science and knowledge. Writers in the field of adult education distinguish 'useful knowledge' from 'really useful knowledge' (Hughes, 1995). They have reminded us of the Society for the Diffusion of Useful Knowledge set up in the early years of industrialisation to provide workers with knowledge useful to the emerging economy (Kelly, 1962). This 'useful' knowledge was contrasted with 'really useful knowledge', which:

> meant knowledge that sought to make sense of the causes of hardship and oppression in working-class people's lives... must help to make sense of intolerable circumstances with a view to their challenge. (Hughes, 1995, p. 99)

Similarly, social workers should be active in influencing research agendas to ensure that all that they learn of the intolerable conditions of poverty and racism through their daily practice is exposed and understood. Practitioners have important roles as 'social investigators' (Sinfield, 1969) to reveal the harmful effects of structures and policies such that some people live in fear in their own homes and neighbourhoods without the means to participate as full members of our society and without hope for the future.

Scrutiny of policy and practice does not, however, exclude the practice of social workers themselves. Power is exercised through all of our practices, including research, and to be research-minded is to be constantly alert to the ways in which our talk, our assessments, our inspections and our behaviours affect others. For example, research on user and carer participation in needs assessment reveals a lack of dialogue with users and carers (Ellis, 1993) and, as Utting points out in his foreword to the research report:

> Occupations which trade on non-judgementalism are shown to be as moralistic in their approach as any lay person. The ways in which some workers discouraged 'dependency' should impress the most fervent advocate of Victorian values, and shows that the Poor Law is alive and kicking nearly 50 years after its official internment. (Utting, 1993, p. 3)

The research demonstrates examples of good practice but also reveals 'stereotyped responses... [and a] 'lack of creativity' (Ellis, 1993, p. 7). If social work is concerned with challenging the discriminatory contexts of the lives of users and of their own practice, then to be enquiring and critical is essential in the repertoire of practice skills. As Utting forcefully points out, the assumptions that social workers can and do make about policies, resources and values would often not stand up to rigorous questioning and scrutiny, and serve to discriminate against users of social services. Furthermore, while social workers engage in anti-oppressive talk, speaking the correct words, any critical analysis of their practice might well reveal a totally different reality.

In reflecting on the users of research in social work, it is perhaps helpful to distinguish between users and beneficiaries. In participating in research and development, through setting research agendas, commissioning research and undertaking research, social workers themselves should be users of research for the benefit of those who use, or are likely to use, their services. They should also, however, develop ways of providing opportunities for users of social services to become users of research in their own right. Feminists, disability researchers and action-research approaches have demonstrated the potential value, to both knowledge and action, in people becoming knowledgeable about their own lives. Hopefully, having read this chapter, you will know that this makes sense theoretically, politically and professionally.

Further reading

Broad, B. and Fletcher, C. (eds) (1993) *Practitioner Social Work Research in Action* (London, Whiting & Birch).

A useful collection of articles giving examples of research by practitioners having a real effect on practice and policy.

Everitt, A., Hardiker, P., Littlewood, J. and Mullender, A. (1992) *Applied Research for Better Practice* (Basingstoke, Macmillan).

A helpful introduction to research for improving practice, with an anti-oppressive focus.

Fuller R. and Petch A. (1995) *Practitioner-Research: The Reflective Social Worker*, (Buckingham, Open University Press).

A thoughtful guide to practice research.

Hart, E. and Bond, M. (1995) *Action Research for Health and Social Care: A Guide to Practice* (Buckingham, Open University Press).

A useful guide to implementing research techniques as part of practice.

Sapsford, R. and Abbott, P. (1992) *Research Methods for Nurses and the Caring Professions* (Buckingham, Open University Press).

Helpfully views research from a multidisciplinary focus.

Theories for Practice in Social Work

10

Social work theories and reflective practice

MALCOLM PAYNE

Introduction: reflecting on reflecting

The first part of this book has presented ideas about the nature of social work and the social and political world in which social workers operate. As Part I has shown, we need to approach such ideas critically because many of them are in debate. Understanding the purposes and context of our work does not, therefore, give us any easy answers, and we must find ways of connecting our knowledge and understanding of society, policy and people with the actions we will take as social workers. Part II examines some examples of important and well-known 'practice theories' which seek to explain in organised ways how social workers may usefully act, using their knowledge about the social world in which they operate. Practice theories are no less debated than the material considered in Part I, so we have to come to a view, as practitioners, not only about the most helpful knowledge of the social world to use, but also what ideas we can use to apply that knowledge to the particular social and interpersonal situations we are dealing with. If we are to practise from this knowledge and theory, we must have ways of thinking which turn thinking into practice action. Reflection is a way of doing this.

When social workers talk about reflective practice, they often simply mean thinking things through carefully before taking any action or making a response to clients' communications. This sometimes encourages a particular style of practice – slow, considered, thoughtful, thinking out all the angles, checking out all the details before taking the plunge. There are several different meanings of 'reflection' in social work and two concepts related to the idea of 'reflective practice'.

Meanings of reflection

Thinking issues through in all their complexity and acting towards clients and others in a considered, thoughtful manner is the common-sense meaning, introduced above. This has relationships with other important ideas in social work theory and practice, and with widely accepted views about the role of social workers. Reflection in this sense connects with study and diagnosis. Modern social work practice replaces the medical associations of these terms with ideas such as 'assessment', but the implication remains of trying to put together a full picture of what difficulties a client faces from a multitude of different pieces of evidence, some of which might not be immediately obvious. Very often, this is a formal responsibility of social workers, for example when they write pre-sentence reports for courts or carry out community care assessments for clients needing packages of services. This means not only reflecting on what is apparent or what is said in the early stages, but also looking for clues to important issues from many different and possibly insubstantial sources.

Boud and Knights (1996), drawing on their previous work, describe a three-phase process of reflection: returning to an experience, attending to feelings connected with the experience and re-evaluating the experience through recognising its implications and outcomes. They include the ideas of reflection in action, that is, while events are going on, and reflection afterwards. Inevitably, in their view, reflection must be grounded in our personal experiences, which have shaped us as a thinker, and our objectives. They give importance to attention, that is, noticing and applying our minds to particular events. Experience helps us to identify when particular aspects of a situation are important.

Being a 'reflective practitioner', according to the ideas of Donald Schön, is a more complex way of understanding reflection. He argues that some professions deal with work (such as building bridges) which use 'technical rationality'; that is, you can calculate through mathematics and scientific thinking exactly what the consequences of your decisions and actions will be (and so be sure that the bridge will not fall down when you have completed it). Some people (such as behaviourists) argue that social work should be developed so that it is like this, but Schön thinks that some kinds of work deal with such complex and variable situations that complete technical rationalism is impossible. Theories in this kind of work offer guidelines for action in the average daily situation, rather than complete rules about what to do. When we come across something new, complex or out-of-the-ordinary, this causes us to stop, think over our guidelines and amend them. Thus, our guidelines (theories) grow every time we deal with a yet more complicated bit of human life, but they will never cover everything.

The implication of Schön's ideas are that people doing jobs like this (for example, teaching and social work) should be educated to expect that their theories and guidelines will only help them so far. We should learn how to identify when existing theories are not helpful enough and should be trained in techniques of reflecting on situations and theory together so as to develop theories further. His particular concern is education for such techniques, and several of his examples use a supervisor, as in social work, for an exploring and questioning discussion. He describes reflection (Schön, 1983, pp. 76–104) as having 'a reflective conversation with the situation'. Issues in our work are reframed into different kinds of problem, so that an alternative way of dealing with them can be worked out. Gould (1996) describes this as 'imaginisation', that is, creating images in our mind of the problems that we are dealing with. In Schön's view, we argue out the implications of our new approach, leaving it open to rethink our rethinking if our new premise does not seem to work. We bring past experience to bear on new unique situations and try out a rigorous 'on-the-spot experiment' to see whether our ideas work.

Schön emphasises that reflection takes place in a 'virtual world' (1983, pp. 157–62) of our own constructions about the problem and possible answers to it; it is not reality and action itself. He takes it for granted, however, that professionals would agree about the most appropriate way of reflecting and the most appropriate outcome and that we are dealing with rational processes which can be understood and explained. In social work, and probably in most other professions, there are different points of view which could be taken about similar situations, and legitimate debate about appropriate professional responses. These points of view and debates are represented by different practice theories, explored in Part II, which suggest different ways in which social workers may interpret and react to the situations they face.

The third, still more complex, idea about reflection comes from Mattinson's (1975) work. She shows, in a study of social work supervision, that social workers very often *reflect their relationships* with their clients in their behaviour towards their supervisor. So if a client is frightened of getting things wrong, and becomes dependent on their social worker, always coming for advice and guidance before doing the simplest thing, the social worker will start doing this, in an out-of-character way, with their supervisor, too. This is also common sense if you think about (reflect – in the first sense – on) it. You, the social worker, are being presented with everything in a complicated life and have to advise someone who is worried about what to do. As a result, you take on all the pressure of being worried. Therefore, you lose some of your own self-confidence, passing on to your supervisor some of the pressure and also, probably unwittingly, some feeling of what the relationship you are dealing with is like. In working with clients, you can use this idea that your relationship with them reflects their relationship with others. If a mother, for example, is making you feel anxious because she is very dependent on you and demanding, this might be a clue to how she experiences her daughter's dependence on her. So, again, being reflective about how you feel about your client as part of what is going on can cause you to think and do something about how she is feeling about her daughter. This view of reflection comes from the psycho-analytic idea of transference which suggests that the nature of relationships with important people in our past influences current important relationships.

These three meanings of being reflective emphasise the point that it is not enough as a social worker to travel along guidelines and conventions. Schön (1983) suggests that much of the time this will be satisfactory. However, any situation may need us to develop and change our guidelines, responding to new aspects of the work and to social circumstances that we meet. We must look underneath the surface relationship and events which are presented to us. Doing this is not a self-indulgent attempt to seek out complexity or dig into private matters which do not concern us. Nor is it, as some managers seem to think, complicating a simple agency task and established procedure that the worker has been given to do. It is, rather, essential to maintaining a critical awareness that at any time we may need to think again and think differently. Because this kind of flexibility is the essence of dealing with any human being and being effective in working on complex human problems, critical awareness and reflection is an important practical implementation of the social work value of respecting human individuality and rights.

However, it is not divorced from the real world in which we practice. Jones and Joss (1995) incorporate the idea of reflective observation into Kolb's model of experiential learning. We have a concrete experience, which we observe and reflect on, construct new ideas about and then experiment, leading us to have a further concrete experience about which we can reflect. This model emphasises the importance of using observation (Briggs, 1995), that is, testing our reflection against what we see and experience, not allowing it to become divorced from, and indeed enabling it to build upon, the real world which we experience. Reid (1994) expands Kolb's model using Gibbs's 'reflective cycle', where we start from description (what happened?), and move to feelings (what were you thinking and feeling?), evaluation (what was good and bad about the experience?), analysis (how can you make sense of what happened?), conclusions (what alternatives did you have?) and an action plan (what would you do if it happened again?).

In summary, then, we can see reflection as taking place in our minds both as we act (reflection in action) and afterwards as we think about and try to understand the events we have experienced. Reflection implies attending to particular situations, and using observation, imagining alternative ways of understanding those situations (imagining and reframing). Reflection, then, leads us to experiment with alternative approaches which eventually become incorporated into our ways of thinking and acting in social work. Practice theories, like those reviewed in Part II, help us to express and identify those alternative approaches in models of practice which we might use when we act as social workers.

Two related concepts

Reflexivity is easily confused with reflectiveness. It means the circular process by which our thoughts affect our actions, which affect the situation we are dealing with and therefore offer feedback through the reactions of others involved, which can affect how we understand and think about the situation. This sets off another cycle in which our thoughts affect our actions. Circularity is important because social work is active. We do not just think and assess but act on the situations we deal with. Reflexivity means that we constantly get evidence about how effective or worthwhile our actions are, and we can change what we are doing according to the evidence of its value. To do so, of course, requires being reflective, because we have to be constantly alert to the possibility that what we are doing needs to change and we have to keep our minds open to changing according to the evidence we see about the effect we are having. Thus, reflexivity gives reflection a chance to work.

Praxis is a Marxist term which takes this idea a little further. It emphasises that our thoughts and the circular reflexive process are affected by our ideology, that is, what we believe the social world is like and how we think it should be. Our ideology causes us to think and therefore act with particular objectives. This interacts with the world, and praxis proposes that we should allow the evidence of how the world is to reform and affect our beliefs. Marxist ideas emphasise the importance of using praxis to experience the inequality and oppression in the world that we deal with, so as to strengthen our ideology of opposition and desire to work within the world effectively to change it.

The ideas of reflexivity and praxis emphasise how our thought interacts with practice to affect clients and service users, and how their reactions and experience come to affect our own view of the world and our thoughts. Reflection, then, is one of the processes through which clients participate in social work. We are forced by our experience of their world and problems to *think* carefully about their experiences and respond to them. Social work does not impose a set of prescriptions on clients. Instead, it reacts to clients and the world in which they live, and it does so through reflection. All three meanings of reflection are involved: thinking things through, questioning our guidelines and developing our theories to respond to new situations, and understanding how our relationships with clients reflect their own experiences and relationships and give us access to how they are experiencing the world.

However, there are some aspects of using theory and knowledge in an organised way which the idea of reflection does not help us with. In the first place, reflection in 'reflective practice' takes place almost in a social vacuum. It is often assumed that the issues that we consider will easily arise out of the problems that we face, that our assessment of clients and their situation will inevitably raise the issues that we must reflect on. Second, it is unclear what the process of reflection actually is and how it connects the practice theories that we want to use. Practice theories are supposed to convert our understanding of the social world and our assessment of the client into ideas for usable action, but we have to integrate our general understanding and our assessment into a view of the situation to which the practice theory can be applied. It is this process that the various chapters in Part II examine. Third, this action must take place in a set of services geared to a range of social needs and organisations; these services are explored in Part III. The remaining commentary in this chapter is therefore concerned to provide a model of the use of reflection in the context of social work practice, first through understanding the aims of social work that we are taking up in our practice, then through understanding how we can reflect on practice theories as we work and finally through integrating knowledge about the social world from Part I in our thinking. We can take this capacity for reflection forward into practice within particular social work services which are considered in Part III.

Reflecting on the social work role

The starting point of using practice theory lies not in the theories themselves but in how we understand social work and its role in society. This is the same distinction that Shardlow (Chapter 2) makes between the narrow scope of social work ethics and mid-range or broad descriptions of the very nature of the thing we are doing. Practice theories are about *effective* behaviour with clients, just as values are about *ethical* behaviour with clients A theory cannot tell us how to be effective unless we can say what our aim is and therefore what direction we want to be effective in.

There are three basic views of the nature and role of social work (Payne, 1996a), the distinctions between them having some support in Harrison's (1991) research on how social workers decide what to do in particular cases. He found that social workers either had one typical approach to all their work based on one of these views, or used two or more in succession if their usual approach was not relevant.

Individualist-reformist views

These views see social work as providing services effectively to help individuals' personal problems and adjust well to the society around them. Dominelli, in Chapter 1, called these 'maintenance' and traditional views. Such practice is prevalent in most official agencies, whose job is to provide efficient social services to meet the needs of members of the public, sorting out their practical and emotional problems, getting other services to respond better to their needs and perhaps raising problems which affect a lot of people to improve the administration or provision of services. Workers would take their functions from the defined responsibilities and role of their agencies, using their interpersonal social work skills to implement a set of well-established conventions and approaches derived from agency policy or conventions of social work practice.

Care management to organise a package of community care services, or effective planning of a network of support to prevent a parent from physically abusing his child, is a typical kind of service. Clients are dealt with mainly as individuals but perhaps in groups and in their community, particularly if, through community organisation, local people can get together to improve services through self-help or improving the general environment. This approach to social work recognises that, in complicated modern societies, many people may need help in hard times or if they are affected by longstanding problems. Individualist-reformist theories, such as task-centred or cognitive-behavioural work, set clear targets and involve the planning and delivery of services and personal help in an organised and focused way.

Reflexive-therapeutic views

These views see social work as helping individuals (and perhaps groups and communities) to achieve personal growth, self-actualisation and personal power over their environment, that is, to identify and fulfil satisfactorily their human wishes and needs. Dominelli, in Chapter 1, called these 'therapeutic' views. Personal growth and fulfilment not only increases the humanity of services and values the humanity of people in need, but also enables people to deal more effectively with the issues that face them. So, these views argue that individualist-reformist work sorting out practical situations and teaching people skills (as in task-centred work) or providing services and checking up on behaviour does not deal adequately with the fundamental problems of people who are struggling with disability or with parenthood. Workers use models of practice such as psychosocial work and counselling to explore clients' views and understanding of their problems, to try to understand and to help clients gain insight into the complex social and psychological origins of the problems that they face and to help them plan new ways of responding to the challenges in their lives. They would develop a warm, relationship with their client, using their personal skills to help the client feel valued and supported. Workers in these approaches would be non-directive, and they assume that the job is about releasing clients' own skills and capacities to achieve what they want.

For example, a colleague works with people dying of brain tumours. There are practical things to do in an individual-reformist way, such as sorting our disability benefits and helping the struggle against increasing illness at home. But there is more besides. She helps very frightened people die in dignity, helps their families prepare for and say goodbye at their death, and tries to set the still living on a path for satisfying relationships in the future. Her director of social services complains about this, because he says there are no criteria by which he can assess whether the right services are being delivered according to quality standards. Actually, this just shows that he has not considered *appropriate* criteria for *all* the services his department provides.

In one case, she helped a West Indian mother dying at 29 with practical and social security matters and developed a relationship with several members of the family. After the death, a nine-year-old son refused to go to the funeral, and the family were very distressed about this. The day before the funeral, she took him to the church where the funeral would be, suggested that she could come with him, showed him where they might sit at the back out of everyone's view and suggested that, as an alternative, they might sit in the park opposite, so as to be there, if not actually in the church. They sat there, and he revealed that he did not want to go because he was embarrassed by the possibility of his aunts giving extravert displays of grief. She thought that he feared breaking down in tears himself. They agreed to sit in the park, and she accompanied him there on the day of the funeral. He decided to go into the church with her. She herself became tearful. This allowed the boy to cry with her. The family appreciated her commitment and help, and the genuineness of her emotion; also, no doubt, the boy was helped to grieve appropriately for his mother and this probably prevented or reduced emotional distress in the future. A consumer evaluation would, without question, demonstrate clients' views of these benefits, and nobody can deny that an effective health and social care should offer such support in circumstances of great distress.

Socialist-collectivist views

These views are transformational; in Chapter 1, Dominelli called them 'emancipatory'. That is, they propose that, rather than helping people to adjust to society to deal with their problems, we should change fundamental structures in society which are the origins of most people's problems. Society is organised so that some people are in groups which are oppressed by inequalities with other groups and the resultant injustices. Such structural problems in society were originally seen as coming from socio-economic inequalities leading to conflicts between social classes. More recently, however, it has been recognised that other social divisions, affecting ethnic minority groups and stigmatised groups such as disabled or mentally ill people are just as powerful creators of inequality. Gender inequality is also important. It arises from the conventions of patriarchy, where there are social assumptions that give men a great deal of social power.

Using feminist, radical and anti-oppressive practice, workers engage in a dialogue of equals with clients to help them raise their consciousness of the ways in which their problems arise from inequality and oppression. The aim is to create cooperative alliances between people with shared problems and other organisations with concerns for injustice and inequality. Thus, people can gain experience of the effectiveness of working together to resolve their own problems, rather than being blamed for their own inadequacies and seen as 'a problem' or becoming alienated from others who share similar difficulties through developing their own personality and skills. Such experiences of cooperation can be empowering and help to overcome feelings of helplessness. Very often, such cooperative work can be successfully developed in particular localities and among groups with shared interests and is an integral part of community work.

For example, a young woman, Sandra, came to a women's refuge having been frequently beaten by her husband. Thinking she was alone and blaming herself for her husband's behaviour, she was surprised to find that many other women shared the same problem.

Her husband found out where she was and other women kept him out of the house, much to Sandra' relief. She welcomed this mutual support and realised that, together, relatively powerless people could defend themselves. Eventually, Sandra was able to help others in similar crises before being rehoused in a different part of town. Some years later, Sandra was confident enough to be part of a group of women who described their own experiences to an audience of mainly men at a trade union conference, which sought to gain support for the refuge and the group that ran it, as well as making an influential group of men more aware of weaknesses in their 'macho' view of themselves. In this way, the women's group sought to make a contribution to changing the social expectations which led to violent patterns of behaviour among men.

Some people criticise socialist-collectivist views because it seems impractical for individual social workers, or even groups, to achieve sweeping social changes. However, such changes are often achieved through many small steps of progress, and socialist-collectivist ideologies help us to keep a long-term perspective in the daily pressure of small-scale events. Moreover, they avoid the tendency of individualist and therapeutic approaches to focus problems on individuals' failings, thus 'blaming the victim' of structural problems, rather than focusing on changing the root causes of difficulties.

These three views are opposed to each other, but also have something in common. Individualist and therapeutic approaches both focus on individuals and are thus often regarded as 'traditional' social work as opposed to 'radical' socialist views. Therapeutic views often criticise the inhumanity of individualist approaches and the tendency of socialists to focus on social change rather than meeting the human needs in front of them. Individualists criticise the socialist idea that social workers employed in an official agency might transform society; a modicum of reform carried out through private political work or campaigning through professional or pressure groups is the most that might be achieved, individualists claim. Reflexive-therapeutic work is also criticised by individualists for its unrealistic ambitions for personal changes through therapeutic means. Both socialist and therapeutic views criticise individualism for a lack of ambition and imagination about what might be possible and the prosaic, rather oppressive, methods of practice proposed.

In some cases, one view joins another to criticise a third, then joins with the third to criticise the former ally. In fact, each of these views is part of a continuing discourse abut the priorities, objectives and value of social work which has been going on ever since it started (Payne, 1996a, Ch. 2). None of them represents a complete view of social work. None of the oppositions among them is full-scale conflict. Aspects of otherwise bitterly critical views are shared: both therapeutic and socialist social work, for example, focus on insight and consciousness-raising.

Social work contains elements of all these three views, and their influence and role is constantly varying and debated. Reflective practice requires us to interpret our role in the world and focus on the particular combination of elements that social work takes up in the situation before us. More widely, politicians, the public and the press constantly debate the role and value of particular occupational groups. Professional groups such as social work negotiate their role with others around them, such as nursing, teaching and medicine, in a constantly changing network of services, legislation, knowledge and value bases, educational and professional structures and clients' views and expectations. Since the role and pattern of social work is uncertain and debated, we inevitably have to reflect constantly on our actions. Practice theories provide organised statements about the world which help us to have our debates and carry forward our reflections with an agreed terminology and some aspects of shared understanding.

Using theory reflectively

Theories are sometimes presented, as in the chapters in Part II, as more or less complete perspectives on how we should try to understand the world or as models of how to respond to particular situations. Theories are said to explain and justify why particular perspectives or models are valuable in acting as social workers. How do we identify which theory or theories to use, and how do we use them? One important basis for this, already considered, is the view of social work that, for the time being, we take among the possible views discussed in the previous section. In this section, we explore how we can reflect on theories as we apply them in three different ways: selectivity, eclecticism and critical engagement.

Selectivity

This approach to using theory proposes that we should select just one, or one group of related theories, and apply that to all the situations that we deal with. The advantage of this approach is that we can go into the ideas of the theory in depth, become comfortable and assured in applying them and act consistently throughout our work. There are, however, problems with this approach, both practical and theoretical.

Among the practical problems are that most social workers operate in (sometimes multidisciplinary) teams with others who may not share the particular theory they use, and the theory may not make sense to clients either. Many workers who operate selectively are supported in doing so because they work in agencies (for example, psychiatric units or specialist centres such as women's refuges) where workers share a theoretical position, often in a fairly small group of people who work together consistently, as in a day or residential care setting.

The theoretical problems with selectivity lie in the difficulty of one theory extending into a wide range of different situations. Many theories, such as psycho-analytic or cognitive-behavioural theories, claim this possibility and some, including these examples, are extensively developed. However, it is often enthusiasts who claim this, and observers often consider that such theories are overstretched, over-complex and hard to follow, or ignore large areas of work which their theory does not fit. For example, both of these examples are primarily therapeutic in character and do not deal well with the practical problems of people in poverty or suffering from racist abuse in an inner city housing estate.

Eclecticism

The eclectic approach suggests *either* that workers should select aspects of different theories and use them together, perhaps all at once or perhaps successively, in a case *or* that workers should use different theories in different cases, depending on which is appropriate. Eclecticism enables different ideas to be brought to bear, helps to amalgamate social work theories when they make similar proposals for action, deals better with complex circumstances and allows workers to compensate for inadequacies in particular theories.

As with selectivity, however, there are theoretical and practical disadvantages. Workers may be unable to decide which set of ideas to select and how they should put them together. Also, it is difficult to know many complex theories well enough to take parts of them and use them appropriately. Social work theories may produce similar action proposals, but this often implies different ways of understanding issues. So, in contrast with the selective approach, eclecticism may confuse clients and workers by bringing together ideas in inconsistent patterns. Epstein (1992), therefore, proposes that eclecticism should be built up by continuing reflection, agreement and debate, and recommends doing this cooperatively in a team rather than encouraging individual flexibility from moment to moment in our practice.

An important focus of eclecticism is systems theory (Pincus and Minahan, 1973). This biologically based perspective on practice emphasises working at different levels in society: the individual, the 'system' surrounding individuals and the more extensive systems which form a context for lower-level systems. This allows practice with agencies and other people and groups on behalf of clients to be theorised, and Roberts (1990) argues that systems theory was part of a trend in the 1970s to integrate many different aspects of social work into a generic form of practice. Systems theory's integration is at least partly eclectic, since it suggests that different theories might be used at different levels (for example, therapeutic theories with individuals, radical theories with social systems) and with different systems (for example, family therapy with a family, task-centred work with peer groups). Since it provides a model for analysing the different systems and levels with which workers might operate, it provides a basis for deciding which aspects of a case might have different theories applied to them. However, it does not help to decide which level or system to work on or which theory to choose and how it may be integrated with the other theories chosen.

Critical engagement

An alternative way of using theories to help in reflection is by using them critically against one another. We have seen already that there are different views of the nature and aims of social work and that many social work theories offer criticisms of other theories. Differences between theories can help reflection in practice by enabling alternative and opposing theories to criticise practice which used a particular theory.

Mrs Jones, for example, is a single parent who is very depressed and is unable to care adequately for her three preschool children. The social worker focused on her depression and found that this comes from isolation and loneliness. Her general practitioner supplied anti-depressants and the worker thought through with her the life she has led so far and plans for the future. Reflecting on this, radical theory would criticise the individualised approach. It does not look at how single parents may be stigmatised, put in the worst housing and blamed for not building up a conventional family. Feminist theory would draw attention to the oppression of women by forcing them into caring roles and not validating their aspirations for the future. Cognitive-behavioural theory tells us that she might benefit from learning different ways of thinking which would enable her to cope better with the world, instead of our approach of being concerned with her feelings and responses to her present situation. By reflecting on these alternative views of the situation, the worker can criticise and develop her approach, even if she does not use them to guide her practice according to their own model of action.

This 'critical contrastive approach' is one of a number of approaches to engaging in critical reflection using theory (Payne, 1996b). A dualities approach looks for conceptual opposites to inform our understanding. For example, if we say that someone's behaviour is childlike, what do we mean by adult-like behaviour, and how does it differ? A special case of this is the 'thinking-feelings' approach. If we are concerned about clients' thinking, we should ask ourselves how their emotions are coming out in this situation, and vice versa. In the case of the bereaved boy described above, we saw how the focus of work was on his feelings in a very distressing situation. A useful counterbalance might well be to progress to rational planning for the future. In every case, using the dualities and thinking-feeling approaches, we should look for what we are *not* doing and for what is *not* coming out.

Another approach to critical engagement is the three views of social work outlined above. If we are focusing on providing a service to an individual, we can ask ourselves how alternative views of social work would criticise this. Are we forgetting about building the client's personal capacity and emotional strength? Are we forgetting to look at the consequences of oppression and the inadequacies of social provision in this case? Our answer may give us clues to alternative social work theories which would pay dividends, or confirm us in the approach that we are currently using.

Reflecting on integration and dissent

So far, we have examined the complexities of the idea of reflection and some related concepts and, following that, some of the difficulties which arise in reflecting on practice theories. The argument has been that the idea of reflective practice is often discussed in a social vacuum and that we need to reflect in a context of awareness about debates around the nature of social work and the value of the practice theories we are considering. We have to incorporate in our reflective practice an understanding of the interaction between the ideas we are using to guide our practice, and we have to have models for thinking the interaction of ideas out.

Our reflection must also include the material considered in Part I about the social. Reflective practice must integrate this into our thinking about action, because our action needs to use this knowledge. Complete integration is neither possible nor desirable, however, because, as Part I demonstrates throughout, there is no agreement about how we should interpret and act on much of this material. So, again, our reflection must incorporate the possibility of dissent and disagreement.

Practice theories and the social world

Theories of the social world allow us to use knowledge from a variety of sources to guide our understanding of how clients might react and why events have turned one way rather than another. In particular settings, we might need to use other theories. For example, in hospital and health-related social work, medical knowledge might be useful, in education welfare work, educational theories and so on.

Some theories of the client world relate closely to social work practice theories described in Part II. Learning theory relates closely to behavioural work, and social learning theories have developed into aspects of modelling and cognitive practice. Attachment theory about child and adult behaviour derives from the interest and work of psycho-analytic practitioners, which also influenced psychosocial theory. Radical, feminist and anti-oppressive practice is strongly influenced by Marxist sociology and political theory, and by feminist and black social and artistic perspectives.

However, much theory and knowledge is not represented directly in social work practice theories. Much of it can be used with any practice theory. For example, research in aspects of the life cycle from different perspectives may be incorporated into most approaches to social work practice. Sociological knowledge about families, groups and communities can influence any form of social work. One important area of debate in social work, however, has been whether the characteristics of particular theoretical positions can incorporate particular areas of knowledge or values. For example, psychosocial theory has sometimes been criticised for its historical tendency to stereotype women as carers and as subordinate to men, and cognitive-behavioural theory has been criticised for its inability to incorporate black and minority ethnic communities' perspectives on behaviour within a structure of thought which assumes a consistent and, some would say, Eurocentric approach to learning and thinking. Some of the inadequacies and strengths of particular theories in taking into account various aspects of psychological and social knowledge form part of the arguments around why one theory is thought better than another. So, weaknesses in its being able to incorporate important knowledge may cause us to be cautious about what a particular theory has to offer. Social workers need to understand in detail what theoretical positions can offer as part of their evaluation of the use of particular theories in practice.

Theory, the law and the agency

One of the difficult aspects of applying theory is understanding its role in relation to the legal basis of social work practice and agency requirements. Part I of this book shows that these two factors influence and constrain how social workers practise. Magistrates and judges reading pre-sentence reports and managers looking at our practice are not likely to concern themselves with which theory was used. Colleagues in a multidisciplinary team are interested in the results we produce, not explanations of how it all came about. Lay people are naturally entitled to have reports and explanations of practice presented in clear, non-technical language, and colleagues are entitled to expect our practice to be competent and successful. This does not, however, make theory irrelevant to our practice.

Everything we do implies a theory about the circumstances that we deal with. Obviously, as we undertake social work activities, we use theory, even if it is not one of the formally stated ones. Knowing about and using the formal statements of theory help to clarify and organise ideas about what we do. It helps report-writing and justifying ourselves to managers and magistrates if we can be clear about why we took this or that action. Occasionally, a particular case goes wrong and there is a formal enquiry. Happy the social worker who can refer to the organised statement of well-established practice contained in a recognised theory as the basis for what they did. Even if this does not happen very often, our practice and everyday activity will display greater self-confidence and consistency if we have an organised view of what we are doing and why. Colleagues and clients will also have their own theories about the world, both formally organised and informal. Our own understanding of theory enables us to see where their theory is situated in the constellation of possible views of the world. We can also identify more easily inconsistencies and difficulties in decisions that they have chosen to make. Where colleagues theories agree with our own, we can cooperate and work together on a more common basis and cement multidisciplinary work more effectively.

Theory, then, can be used for accountability to agencies and external institutions such as the law, because it clarifies our ideas about what we do. Moreover, applying, and being able to refer to, an established form of practice enables us to justify that our practice to outsiders.

Theory in practice

Perhaps the most important group to whom we can justify our practice by using theory is our clients. They are entitled to know that we have an organised view of what we are doing and why and gain understanding and explanation of what we are doing, so that they can agree or disagree with it. This is one of the claimed advantages of such approaches as cognitive-behavioural practice and task-centred work, since a clear and often written agreement is made between worker and client. It is one of the essential features of radical, feminist and anti-oppressive theory, which requires a dialogue between equals rather than an expert therapist helping a disempowered client.

Obviously, clients do not need to be involved in every technicality. However, Secker's (1993) study of social work students suggests that students who succeeded in applying theory with confidence had certain important characteristics. Their skills in using theory were not about intellectual ability, but about skill in working openly with clients. Their use of theory started from the clients themselves. They listened well and responded to what clients told them. They did not put clients in theoretical categories. Instead, they used theoretical ideas all the time in discussing matters with clients. As a client said something, they might say, 'That reminds me of an idea...'. They picked up ideas and talked them over with clients; they did not keep them to themselves. They worked together with clients to test out their ideas, first in discussion and then in what Schön (1983) calls 'on-the-spot' experimentation.

Using theory, then, does not require great intellect, it requires the application of exactly those social and interpersonal skills in working openly with people that social workers most like to claim. It involves reflecting theoretically *with* clients and also with colleagues, making reflection-in-action and reflection after the event an everyday part of what social workers do. Also, it means having the self-confidence to be open about your ideas and willing to experiment, alongside your clients, in putting your ideas into action.

Using Part II reflectively

The chapters which follow, in Part II, offer a beginning in using social work's theoretical ideas. The first three chapters explore three basic forms of social work: counselling, groupwork and community work. None of these belongs to social work alone, and there is debate in these chapters about the extent to which these forms of practice interact with other professionals' practice. These debates draw attention to the way in which social work is increasingly part of multi-disciplinary intervention from a network of allied professions or occupational groups. Nevertheless, social work uses these forms of practice and applies, as Cosis Brown in particular shows, a variety of other theoretical models of practice within them.

The next two groups of accounts of theory describe broadly individualist and therapeutic models of practice (psychosocial, cognitive-behavioural and task-centred) and then socialist-collectivist models (radical, feminist and anti-oppressive). These are not the full range of possible models, and for a more extended review you could refer to Payne (1997). However, these accounts from proponents of and enthusiasts for each model will allow you to begin the process of critical engagement with different models. How far, in the first group, is practice required to be individualist-reformist or reflexive-therapeutic? How far are the ideas of psychosocial theory in conflict with cognitive-behavioural theory? What ideas do they share? You could also examine your own reactions. Would you feel comfortable with the structure and clarity of task-centred work, for example, or do you think that psychosocial theory offers a more rounded view of human beings and their needs? Are all these approaches inadequate? Do they leave you turning towards socialist-collectivist models for a change of focus? Are there links as well as oppositions between the first group and the second? Looking at the second group, what are the crucial differences between radical and later socialist-collectivist models? Do these ideas give you clear concepts of how to practise, or are they just theories which give you a different view of the world? Whatever you think about their clarity as practice models or world-views, which do you find most useful and why?

The final chapter, on postmodernist ideas, proclaims that it is different. It tries to offer a way of thinking about people and the social situations in which they live. These are some of the very latest ideas influencing social work at present. They seek to help us understand and explore the complexity, uncertainty and ambiguity of the world that we inhabit, whereas many of the other theories discussed here try to clarify and organise our thinking about the world according to their own point of view. Amongst other things, postmodernist theory argues that such clarifications and certainties are only limited representations of the world's complexity which we may agree as useful social conventions, but which reflect social and power relationships whose complexities we should try to understand.

This approach to theory suggests we should be cautious and critical of all simplifications of the world. Indeed, it argues that we should be critical and reflective in all our dealing with other human beings. We should never use theory to pigeon-hole and restrict the infinite variety of humanity. Instead, theory should be a guide to be used together with clients to explore, understand and transform the social world in which we live together.

Further reading

Mattinson, J. (1975) *The Reflection Process in Casework Supervision* (London, Institute of Marital Studies).

Although this is a difficult book based in psycho-analytic theory, it is one of the great classics of social work writing which enables readers to see ideas emerging from the extended case examples given.

Palmer, A., Burns, S. and Bulman, C. (1994) *Reflective Practice in Nursing: The Growth of the Professional Practitioner* (Oxford, Blackwell).

Recommending a book about nursing demonstrates the interlocking nature of ideas within the network of related professions, and this book offers a range of practical articles about reflective practice which can be applied to social work.

Payne, M. (1996) *What is Professional Social Work?* (Birmingham, Venture).

This book contains a more extended account of many of the ideas about views of the nature of social work discussed in this chapter.

Payne, M. (1997) *Modern Social Work Theory: A Critical Introduction,* 2nd edn (London, Macmillan).

A more extended critical review of social work theories than is possible here.

Schön, Donald A. (1983) *The Reflective Practitioner: How Professionals Think in Action* (New York, Basic Books).

The classic, creative and easy-to-read book about how some professions benefit from learning how to use 'reflection-in-action' in inform their practice.

11

Counselling

HELEN COSIS BROWN

Introduction

This chapter explores the relationship between social work and counselling, and the use of counselling theories, values and skills within social work practice. It covers the changing context of counselling within social work, the different theoretical underpinnings to counselling ideas and skills relevant to social work, counselling theory and skills within social work practice today and some current issues emerging from counselling and social work. The current context of this exploration is radically different from that which gave rise to the Barclay Report of the early 1980s. The report argued that it was:

> essential that social workers continue to be able to provide counselling and we use the word to cover a range of activities in which an attempt is made to understand the meaning of some event or state of being to an individual, family or group and to plan, with the person or people concerned, how to manage the emotional and practical realities that face them. (Barclay Committee, 1982, p. 41)

Barclay, on the same page, argues that social workers have themselves seen counselling 'as the hallmark of their calling'. Brearley (1995) documents the social, political, legislative and policy changes that have impacted on social work since the mid-1970s that have altered social workers' relationship to counselling. It would today be more likely that social workers would see their hallmark as brokerage or care management rather than counselling. Social work students are often resistant to undertaking direct in-depth work with service users, seeing 'counselling' as something they feel they are neither prepared for nor trained to undertake.

Social work practice is (with a few exceptions) located within a legislative context. Where counselling is employed by its practitioners, it will be alongside other interventions and within a legislative, procedural and organisational context, compromising it as a form of 'pure' counselling, it being instead one of several possible social work methods of intervention. Social work practitioners, in all their various manifestations, have traditionally had a complex relationship with counselling. Bringing together the separate enterprises of counselling and social work has posed theoretical, organisational, ethical, practical and practice dilemmas. They are two separate areas of helping interventions, governed by different professional bodies, underpinned by separate bodies of knowledge and offering different outcomes, while at the same time as sharing many of the same values, intentions, processes, ideas and methods. They are both interested and engaged in the processes of change, and they are both predominately preoccupied with the psychosocial. It might well be difficult to distinguish some social work interviews from a counselling session. Social work training has traditionally drawn heavily on counselling methods when teaching social work interviewing skills. However, it is often argued that, despite the very close relationship between social work interviewing and counselling, they are separate activities, one being the practice of counselling and the other the utilisation of counselling skills. Feltham points to the different views of professional bodies in relation to this distinction, the British Association for Counselling (BAC) arguing that social workers are employing counselling skills rather than practising counselling, whereas the Group for the Advancement of Psychodynamics and Psychotherapy in Social Work have occasionally argued that casework can be not just counselling, but also indeed psychotherapy (Feltham, 1995, p. 72). Historically social casework, as practised by psychodynamically oriented social workers, would hardly have been discernible from counselling. Today, within some social work settings, it is difficult to make a distinction; for example, in-depth work being undertaken by a social worker within a child psychiatric department in a hospital setting with an anorexic young woman may be difficult to distinguish from a counselling session undertaken by a counsellor with a similar young person.

Social work students and practitioners now occupy a post-Thatcher era and are engaged in discourses different from those of the Barclay Report. One change has been the gradual de-emphasis on the 'collective' and the re-emphasis on the 'individual' and the individual's responsibility to facilitate change, whether that be social, economic or personal. The past 20 years have seen the corresponding mushrooming of personal therapies, the increased professionalisation of counselling, the growth in numbers of private counsellors and psychotherapists, and the explosion of related trainings. The same period has seen counselling being relocated within the social work context, into the 'provider sector', and a growing reluctance on the behalf of social workers to undertake counselling with service users, seeing it as outside their remit, theoretical and skills base and outside the realm of the possible, because of time and resource constraints. A cynical observer might comment that one major development in the differentiation between counselling and social work has been that the former is now rarely other than for the benefit of the bourgeoisie and the latter for the working class.

Social work practice today, in its many different forms and contexts, still needs to employ counselling as a possible method of intervention in specific and appropriate contexts, at the same time drawing on counselling theory and skills to inform its knowledge and skills repertoire more generally. Social workers still have to 'do the work' with service users, whether it be in-depth, long-term work or as part of an assessment in order to devise a care plan. Without counselling theory and counselling skills, social work practice is likely to be ineffectual and inefficient.

Theoretical groupings within counselling

Before looking at some of the broad theoretical groupings of ideas underpinning different 'schools' of counselling, it may be important to say something about what counselling is. The word 'counselling' is often used interchangeably with the word 'advice'. For example, it might be more accurate to refer to careers 'advice' given in schools rather than careers 'counselling'. Dryden *et al.*, emphasising the distinction between the spontaneous giving of help and professional intervention, write, 'counselling is a more deliberate activity and in its definition of the term the British Association for Counselling spells out the distinction between a planned and a spontaneous event. "People become engaged in counselling when a person, occupying regularly or temporarily the role of counsellor, offers or agrees explicitly to offer time, attention and respect to another person or persons temporarily in the role of client (BAC, 1985, p. 1)"' (Dryden *et al.*, 1989, p. 4). One of the most comprehensive definitions of counselling is offered by Feltham and Dryden (1993, p. 40), who describe it thus:

> a principled relationship characterised by the application of one or more psychological theories and a recognised set of communication skills, modified by experience, intuition and other interpersonal factors, to clients' intimate concerns, problems or aspirations. Its predominant ethos is one of facilitation rather than of advice-giving or coercion. It may be of very brief or long duration, take place in an organisational or private practice setting and may or may not overlap with practical, medical and other matters of personal welfare.

This definition illustrates why there may be some confusion over what it is, precisely, that makes counselling and social work perceived as being so different, as well as offering some insight into why BAC might need six separate divisions within it adequately to reflect all its constituent parts.

What are the 'psychological theories' that are referred to within this definition? As it pertains to social work practice, counselling has two areas related to it that have been of significance to its practice and knowledge base: the theoretical underpinning of different 'schools' of counselling and their related skills application. There are very many different counselling approaches built on a number of diverse theoretical perspectives. Only some of these have been influential upon social work and they may be grouped under four general headings: psychodynamic, cognitive-behavioural, humanistic person-centred and eclectic and integrative. These headings represent whole sets of ideas separate from counselling, which can be traced in relation to their influence on social work practice, and the ideas related to each heading can be shown to have been influential upon both social work and counselling at similar historical moments. For example, the inter-relationships between psychodynamic ideas and social work and psychodynamic ideas and counselling, seen earlier this century, are similar for both social work and counselling (Yelloly, 1980; Jacobs, 1988; Pearson *et al.*, 1988; Payne, 1992; McLeod, 1993, p. 23; Brown, H. C., 1996). Theoretical developments are part of an economic, social, geographical, historical, racial and gendered context; both social work and counselling have been subject to similar influences in their different processes of professionalisation since the beginning of the nineteenth century. Both professions developed in an often defensive relationship to their more orthodox and (often perceived as) intellectually superior relatives psycho-analysis and psychotherapy. Both social work and counselling have suffered from developing in their shadows, despite their undoubted enrichment as a result of their close liaisons. There is no clear, singular, linear relationship between psycho-analysis, psychotherapy, counselling and social work, neither in their historical development nor in their theoretical underpinning. However, the myth and to some extent the reality of their inter-dependency has had a powerful influence.

Psychodynamic ideas

Jacobs (1988) offers what is still a very useful account of the interrelationship between psychodynamic ideas and counselling. This is one of the most complex theoretical areas drawn on in counselling, utilising a whole range of evolving ideas developed by many different individuals (Freud, Jung, Klien, Bion, Fairbairn, Winnicott and Bowlby to name just a few of the originators) over a considerable period of time. Key psychodynamic concepts relevant to counselling would include the unconscious, the structures of the mind (the id, the ego and the super-ego), the past being relevant and impacting on the present, psychosexual development (oral, anal, phallic (oedipal), latency, adult sexuality), defence mechanisms, envy, depression, transference and countertransference, projective identification, ambivalence, attachment, separation, loss and crisis. It is beyond the scope of this chapter to detail the meaning and different interpretations of these concepts. McLeod offers a useful precis of their development and their application to counselling. Psychodynamic and psycho-analytical ideas have had a profound impact on the way in which we view human development and have been integrated into our cultural heritages in ways that subtly influence our understandings about ourselves and others. These influences have also impacted on counsellors. 'All counsellors and therapists, even those who espouse different theoretical models, have been influenced by psychodynamic thinking and have had to make up their minds whether to accept or reject the Freudian image of the person' (McLeod, 1993, p. 43).

Psychodynamic counselling has attracted much criticism, including its normative and potentially pathologising tendencies and the question of its efficacy. Questioning the outcomes of psychodynamic interventions has been raised alongside the problem of resourcing what was often long-term intervention that had no measurable outcome. The development of 'brief-therapy', associated with such people as Mann, Sifneos, Malan and Davanloo, has been significant in relation to this (McLeod, 1993, p. 38). The development of brief-therapy has been highly significant to counselling, as by its nature it is about facilitating the mobilisation of the client's inner and outer resources to manage a particular life event or set of circumstances, circumstances where limited interventions are often appropriate, as opposed to, in the case of psychotherapy, often long-term intervention focused on personality change. This development has not just affected psychodynamic counselling, but has also had a general impact on counselling (Dryden and Feltham, 1992).

Both humanistic person-centred and cognitive-behavioural counselling developed partly, but not exclusively, in response to some of the perceived difficulties and limitations of the psychodynamic approach.

Humanistic person-centred ideas

The development of humanistic person-centred counselling has its roots located within the broad developments of both phenomenological and existential influences within philosophy and psychology during the post-war period. Its inception is often associated with a talk given by Carl Rogers in 1940 (Rogers, 1942), in which he emphasised clients' potential to find their own solutions. 'The emphasis on the client as expert and the counsellor as source of reflection and encouragement was captured in the designation of the approach as 'non-directive' counselling' (McLeod, 1993, p. 63). Coulshed (1991, p. 52) writes that the 'theory base and important concepts devolve from a philosophical background of the existential tradition which respects an individual's subjective experience and places emphasis on the vocabulary of freedom, choice, autonomy and meaning'. Although this approach can be associated with broad theoretical and philosophical developments outside psychology, it was also part of the so-called 'third force' (the first and second being associated with the work of Freud and Skinner) within psychology, person-centred counselling being one development within that 'force'.

As a set of theories and methods, the person-centred approach is associated with an optimistic view of human nature but tells us little about human development. Although Dryden *et al.* (1989) are right in seeing the necessity of contextualising these theories, with their emphasis on 'self-actualisation', within the Californian culture of the 1960s, they are still important in having established the central significance of empathy, warmth and genuineness as key to the effectiveness of counselling interventions. The emphasis here is on counselling intervention rather than explanation of human behaviour. This approach and its theoretical underpinnings have been highly influential in social work, particularly on ideas relating to social work interviewing skills. Egan (1990) is seen as a bridge between counselling and social work interviewing, and is still highly influential in social work training courses. He is also seen as a bridge between the humanistic person-centred and behavioural approaches (Dryden *et al.*, 1989).

Cognitive-behavioural ideas

Cognitive-behavioural ideas and their influence on counselling have been associated with developments within mainstream psychology, with its emphasis on scientific methods, and the growth of behavioural and cognitive psychology in the post-war period. These ideas built on work undertaken drawing on animal experiments earlier in the century, associated with such people as Pavlov, Watson and Thorndike. From the 1950s onwards, they were built on by Eysenck, Rachman, Skinner, Wolpe and others, who were chiefly interested in behaviour and learning, and with understanding how behaviours are learnt and what interventions will enable behaviour to change. They were not interested in understanding the inner meanings of acts or causation other than how those acts were learnt.

Feltham (1995, p. 83) notes that 'behaviour therapy is based on what can be observed, studied, measured and reliably changed'. These are a different set of criteria from psychodynamic or humanistic person-centred preoccupations. Within this tradition, there are numerous types of behavioural and cognitive counselling interventions, drawing on specific theories including respondent conditioning, operant conditioning, observational learning and cognitive learning to name but a few. These interventions are interested not exclusively in behaviour, but also in thought and feelings, and how these then impact upon and affect behaviour.

There have been moments in the history of social work when it has been fashionable to be derisive about behavioural interventions, but their relevance to social work is important. They have been shown to be effective with specific conditions, for example enuresis, agoraphobia and anxiety. One strength is their capacity to be adopted and practised by ordinary practitioners, be they social workers or community psychiatric nurses, who have not had to receive such an extensive training as would be expected of a psychodynamic counsellor, for example to facilitate an effective outcome. Behavioural interventions are often seen as successful in the short term and focus on management, focused change, measurement and monitoring. In the current climate of social work, these methods might be seen as fairly closely matching the needs of the professional roles.

Social work has traditionally drawn on a wide range of counselling theories and methods, a combination of psychodynamic, person-centred and cognitive-behavioural approaches, often in a haphazard way rather than in a theoretically and therapeutically logical manner that considers efficacy and professional integrity.

Eclectic and integrative approaches

The eclectic approach, which is sometimes referred to as integrative, is where the theory and the corresponding method of intervention are chosen as the most relevant and appropriate to meet the needs presented by the client or service user's specific circumstances. It can be seen as a way of maximising the beneficial aspects of the three different schools. This leads to the potentiality of the practitioner having an underlying psychodynamic understanding, taking a person-centred approach to the counselling relationship, one that is characterised by warmth, respect and empathy, while having the capacity to, where relevant, employ behavioural techniques. This, to many, smacks of heresy, but there is a growing literature looking at the validity of integration. McLeod notes the difference between an eclectic approach, which is a more accurate description of the above, and one that is integrative:

> An eclectic approach to counselling is one in which the counsellor chooses the best or most appropriate ideas and techniques from a range of theories or models, in order to meet the needs of the client. Integration on the other hand, refers to a somewhat more ambitious enterprise in which the counsellor brings together elements from different theories and models into a new theory or model. (1993, p. 99)

For social workers, their approach is likely, more often than not, to fall within the eclectic category, one they are already overfamiliar with and one that is often used against them, reinforcing the perception that social work has a flimsy, incoherent theoretical base in practice, whereas, in fact, eclecticism can be a potential strength.

Counselling and social work

Social work, within the statutory sector, at the tail end of the twentieth century, comprises a set of activities and interventions that are primarily focused on assessment, administration, care management, risk analysis and monitoring. It can be argued that the focus social work did have, or was perceived as having, on the facilitation of change, whether it was at the level of the individual, household, group or community, has slowly been transferred out of the statutory sector and into the provider sector, one that is increasingly private and voluntary. Within the provider sector, social workers both practise counselling and employ counselling skills. Within the areas of drugs and alcohol, palliative care, mental health and family work, there are social workers employed who will be negotiating a counselling component to their overall work with a service user. This counselling work will rarely be 'pure' counselling, as by definition it will, as with social work practice more broadly, be located in the context of a wider intervention context.

It can be argued, and the author is amongst those who do, that counselling has to remain as an integral part of social work wherever its location or context. This is 'counselling' in its broadest sense, focusing primarily on the application of counselling skills and the deployment of specific or integrative theories of counselling. If we examine the processes of assessment, be they in relation to child protection (DoH, 1988), assessment and care management in community care (DoH, 1991c) or the assessment undertaken by the key-worker under the Care Programme Approach in mental health (DoH, 1996), these processes necessitate the social worker having the competence to deploy counselling skills to undertake a full and comprehensive assessment. This link is made explicitly by Smale *et al.* when they consider the skills needed to enable competent work to be done when assessment work is undertaken (Smale *et al.*, 1993). Pearson (1990), from a counselling perspective, also explores what it has to offer to social support and care management. It is interesting to note that two recent publications that look explicitly at social work competence make very little direct reference to counselling (Thompson, 1996a; Vass, 1996).

Egan (1990), over a number of decades, has provided social work educators with a relevant and applicable model for the application of counselling skills to social work interviewing. Utilising both person-centred theory and behavioural ideas, he developed his model. Coulshed lists seven qualities that counsellors (here she is referring to the context of social work) should have, qualities that are often associated with person-centred counselling and ones that are central to Egan, these are empathy or understanding, respect, concreteness or being specific, self-knowledge and self-acceptance, genuineness, congruence and immediacy (Coulshed, 1991, p. 45). Egan's model can be summarised as having four components: exploration, understanding, action and evaluation. It is easy to see why Smale *et al.* have built on and adapted this model for application with assessment and care management in community care. It has real strengths, including its commitment to working with, and not for, the client. It is a model that fits well with ideas of, and emphasises the importance of, engagement, clarity, focusing, planning, prioritising, negotiating realisable and relevant goals, action and review, and evaluation, all aspects of competent social work practice whatever its context, congruent with a culture of increasing openness and practitioner accountability. While the Egan model has received much criticism for its focus, its foundations and its crises-free assumptions, it is a model that can be adapted and built on to enhance effective social work intervention, as demonstrated by Smale *et al.* (1993).

It has been argued that social workers are more likely in the current social work context to offer counselling only within the provider sector, which is increasingly made up of private and voluntary organisations. However, social workers within all contexts, to be effective, need to apply counselling skills and be informed by counselling ideas to be effective. This remains particularly pertinent within the statutory sector, where the majority of assessment work is still concentrated, the application of counselling skills being fundamental to the processes of assessment and care management.

Issues

Egan's model is one that draws on behavioural and person-centred ideas and methods. It largely ignores psychodynamic ideas, and that can mean that it has limited application. To focus on 'a problem', without an understanding of causation, may mean that the intervention has limited effectiveness. Also, to ignore the contribution of systemic ideas to social work could mean that 'the problem' is seen outside its context, again limiting the effectiveness of the intervention. For the model to be effective, it needs to be located within a familiarity with and understanding of both psychodynamic and systemic ideas.

There has been much written recently about the reflective practitioner (see Chapter 10; Schön, 1987; Yelloly and Henkel, 1995; Thompson, 1996a). Thompson writes that the reflective practitioner is 'a worker who is able to use experience, knowledge and theoretical perspectives to guide and inform practice... Reflective practice involves cutting the cloth to suit the specific circumstances, rather than looking for ready-made solutions' (Thompson, 1996a, p. 222). Reflective practice also needs the practitioner to have, what was earlier referred to as self-knowledge. It requires the practitioner to be able, and be committed, to reflecting upon their own perceptions, responses and feelings in any given situation, requiring an understanding of counter-transference. Counter-transference is a complex and fraught area of both psycho-analytic and psychodynamic theories. 'Social work accessible' explanations of these ideas are available (Salzberger-Wittenberg, 1970; Jacobs, 1988, Pearson *et al.*, 1988; d'Ardenne and Mahtani, 1989). Without this theoretical base underpinning the application of counselling skills, we will not achieve reflective practice.

As ideas in counselling and social work have developed, so has there been a growing acceptance by both professions of their limitations in offering an appropriate service to a cross-section of all our communities. Not only have these two professional groups been unable to reach all communities, but they might also have been both overtly and covertly, deliberately and by default, discriminatory and oppressive to both individuals and specific communities. Anti-oppressive practice has become an accepted part of the discourse of social work. Within counselling, as well, there is a developing substantial literature, demonstrating a general acceptance that both, ideas and models may need to be adapted to integrate anti-oppressive practice (Noonan, 1983; d'Ardenne and Mahtani, 1989; Scrutton, 1989; Crompton, 1992; Atkinson and Hackett, 1995; Davies and Neal, 1996). When social work deploys counselling skills and ideas, it needs to take cognisance of the developing literature of counselling and anti-oppressive practice.

Conclusion

A key issue for counselling and social work is social worker's gradual defensive rejection of and timidity towards its use of counselling and counselling skills. It has been argued that both are still and will remain central to the roles and tasks of social work. Counselling skills are integral to the processes of assessment and care management, and there will remain a need for counselling within the social work context, certainly within the provider sector. If we are going to achieve the goal of a profession that is made up of competent and reflective practitioners, we will need to draw on counselling skills and models that enhance effectiveness and make use of counselling theories that inform practice. This could enable professional reflection to take place when working with the needs of specific, unique individuals within their own context and lead to the deployment of sensitive, relevant and effective interventions that facilitate negotiated change.

Further reading

Atkinson, D. R. and Hackett, G. (1995) *Counseling Diverse Populations* (Madison, Brown & Benchmark).

Offers a general coverage of anti-discriminatory practice issues in counselling.

Brearley, J. (1995) *Counselling and Social Work* (Buckingham, Open University Press).

This book covers areas directly pertinent to the content of this chapter.

Dryden, W., Charles-Edwards, D. and Woolfe, R. (eds) (1989) *Handbook of Counselling in Great Britain* (London, Sage).

An excellent general introduction to counselling.

Feltham, C. (1995) *What is Counselling?* (London, Sage).

An accessible introduction to counselling.

McLeod, J. (1993) *An Introduction to Counselling* (Buckingham, Open University Press).

A helpful introduction to counselling theory and practice.

12

Groupwork

DAVE WARD

Where has all the groupwork gone?

How things have changed! My immediate reaction on being invited to contribute this chapter on groupwork was a mild panic. Although I see groups and groupwork as central to much that we do, in both our private and professional lives, 'groupwork' seems, almost without being noticed, to have faded from view. This invitation brought it back to my attention with a start: where has groupwork gone?; why?; what might be its future?

The 1970s were a golden age for groupwork. Students on social work courses would actively seek, and talk proudly about having done, 'groupwork' on placement. Groupwork had a secure place on the curricula of social work training courses within which the four 'methods' – casework, family work, *groupwork* and community work – dominated. These provided a framework for organising a potentially overwhelming mass of material and hinted at an exclusive knowledge and skill base which was seen then as necessary for an aspiring profession.

The late 1970s and 1980s saw an outpouring of British texts focusing on the generic basics of groupwork (for example, Davies, 1975; Douglas, 1978, 1983; Brown, 1979, 1986; Houston, 1984; Heap, 1985; Whitaker, 1985; Preston-Shoot, 1987) and, in 1988 *Groupwork*, the first British journal devoted to the method, was launched. However, this output was failing to keep up with deeper changes that were taking place in society at large.

Little of this vibrancy and expansiveness is visible today. One or two of the established authorities have continued to pursue the method (Brown, 1992; Douglas, 1993), joined by a few others (Adams and O'Sullivan, 1994; Vernelle, 1994), but I see little evidence of its take-up in field practice. *Groupwork* continues as a thrice-yearly publication. However, a scan of its contents since 1990 reveals that, of the more than 100 papers published, over one-third were by foreign authors. Only 11 addressed groupwork practised in the statutory social services. While there are rich veins of practice experience and conceptual analysis, little of this is grounded in the mainstream of social work. Similarly, the basic texts do not address directly the issues faced in the settings in which most social workers work. Much of this literature must seem remote to social work students with prior experience in statutory agencies. As an external assessor to social work qualifying programmes, I have frequently commented on how the few students who do undertake groupwork in their practice placements rarely refer to the basic texts in their practice studies, but rather apply concepts and methods from non-groupwork sources to their work with groups.

The 1990s have seen tremendous changes in the vision and practice of social work as a result of pressures from several directions. In some respects, these forces are in conflict, but, in sum, they have had the effect of putting the notion of a social work organised around the four core methods into terminal decline. They include the drive towards specialisation, the emergence of the law as a central concern, new approaches to the education and training of social workers, the impact of 'new managerialism' and, finally, the searching and scathing critiques of theory and practice from radical, feminist and anti-racist perspectives. This list is neither complete nor exclusive, but will enable me to sketch the context within which I believe an identifiably different groupwork has come into position.

The demethoding of social work

The child abuse scandals in the 1970s and 80s had a profound impact. They cast doubt on whether social workers managed, organised and trained generically had the specialist skills to deal with complex child-care cases (for example, Blom Cooper, 1985). Outcomes traceable to this are a trend towards specialisation and a concern for safety-first practice (DoH, 1995). The law, as the framework within which social work is practised and which provides legitimacy, is given much greater prominence in training and, presumably, in the minds of social workers.

In the probation service, another set of changes were taking place. A national survey (Caddick, 1991) revealed that groupwork was being practised widely in the service, much of it 'providing developmental or enabling experiences for the members' (p. 211). However, in 1992, the punishment-oriented Criminal Justice Act was introduced:

> an offence specific practice developed... decreasing appreciation by practitioners of the dynamics of the groupwork process and concentration on the task in hand rather than the process. (Senior, 1993, p. 35)

Alongside these developments, and reflected in them, have been wider changes in the culture of Britain, developing momentum throughout the 1980s following the Conservative election victory in 1979, but only institutionalised in social work practice in the 1990s. One element is 'new managerialism', with its focus on concrete and measurable outcomes, in a drive towards greater economy, efficiency and effectiveness (McLaughlin and Muncie, 1994). As Youll (1996, p. 39) argues:

> what is not directly observable and therefore easily measured and described gets left out: mindfulness, the process and nature of relationships, managing the affective component of the work, the 'artistry of social work'...

Inexorably, the attention moved away from the 'how' of the job. This is illustrated vividly in a probation text (Raynor *et al.*, 1994) in which a chapter on 'a programme to reduce offending', which is predominantly group based, covers rationale, aims, content and evaluation but nothing on groupwork skills and methods.

Echoes of these developments can be seen in profound changes in social work education. Responding to accusations of indequate training, most stridently made in relation to child-care practice, qualifying training has been reorganised around greater specialisation and a competence framework (CCETSW, 1996). While there is much debate about the efficacy of a competency approach, the fact is that such an approach, consistent with the imperatives of new managerialism, concentrates attention upon precisely framed identifiable and measurable behaviour (Cannan, 1994/95). What is lost is the synergy of bringing skills together to form, collectively, a method.

The final factor I wish to note as influencing the 'demethoding' of social work has been the so-called 'progressive' critique of traditional social work. This has interrogated not only the reactionary policies and practices flowing from the New Right, but also how good intentions can be damaging. It began with the Radical Social Work movement in the late 70s and early 80s, moving on into the trenchant critiques from feminist, disability, gay and lesbian, and anti-racist perspectives from the mid-80s. I do not question the rectitude of the critiques – indeed, I have been an unashamed participant – but merely highlight their impact, alongside other factors, in changing the face of social work.

The four methods were a product of a time that has now passed. They made sense as part of the knowledge base of an aspiring profession which confidently saw itself progressing to enheightened status and security. Battered from all sides, those conditions no longer apply. Social workers' confidence in themselves has been profoundly shaken. It is not surprising that they have come to feel safer operating within instrumental but more clear and defensible frameworks, reflected in such buzz words as 'competencies', 'risk assessment' and 'case management'.

Groupwork and work-in-groups

In contemporary social work, there is a good deal of evidence of a continuing interest in groups. Indeed, there is a considerable amount of work taking place *in* groups. However, it is not recognisable as groupwork. It does not pay substantial attention either to the knowledge base of group dynamics or to the practice base in groupwork method and skills. Nor does it incorporate the democratic and collective values that are, as we will see, at the core of real groupwork. It is to be found in cognitive behavioural work, particularly with offenders; in residential and day care; in 'self-help'; in research and service evaluation; and, organisationally, in teamwork. In some cases, for example in so-called 'What Works' practice with offenders (McGuire, 1995), the guiding texts simply pass over groupwork knowledge and skills. In other areas, for example residential and day care or management, the evidence is that groupwork is not taken seriously, although some theoretical work has highlighted its importance (for example, Brown and Clough, 1989).

Work in groups involves moving away from a notion of the group as an *'instrument'* (Douglas, 1993) or 'medium' (Whitaker, 1985) for help and change, where group members work together to explore and exploit group resources (Douglas, 1993, p.31), to a greater emphasis on the group as *'context'*:

> in which a powerful and knowledgeable resource, usually one leader, operates… in which all group members have a primary relationship to the group leader who works with each individual in turn in the context of the group. (Douglas, 1993, p. 33)

an orientation quite consistent with the changes in social work outlined.

Douglas (1993) sees a close connection between groups as 'instrument' or 'medium' and 'concepts of equality and democracy' (p. 31), and for A. Brown (1996, p. 83):

> Groupwork is anti-oppressive in its context, purpose, method, group relationships and behaviour.

Indeed, what has historically distinguished groupwork from forms of practice focused on the individual has been:

an emphasis on the commonalities of problems and situations and the concomitant commonality of feelings to which they give rise. In groupwork each issue that is raised, even when that issue at first glance seems to have no relevance to others in the group, does have applicability for all. The worker who practises real groupwork draws out that applicability and elicits the commonalities and asks members to examine the issues of others. (Kurland and Salmon, 1993, p. 10)

At its best, groupwork can offer (Coulshed, 1991, p. 161, summarising Yalom, 1970):

- a source of power for members;
- mutual support;
- an exchange of information;
- motivation and hope;
- opportunities to learn and test interpersonal and other social skills;
- a sense of belonging;
- role models;
- feedback on behaviour and coping attempts;
- a chance to help as well as be helped.

Furthermore, if affiliated to a purpose which explicitly rejects the splintering of public issues from private troubles and also to a set of practice principles which stress the potency of self-directed action and non-élitist leadership, groupwork can be the preferred method for anti-oppressive practice. Bringing together people with common needs and problems to work together on their own behalf represents the essence of empowerment (Mullender and Ward, 1991, p. 12).

Instead, we find predominantly, in the mainstream, groups that are 'one-to-one treatment with the rest of the members acting as bystanders'. Such groups are boring, suppressing and run by people who must maintain control. Process is used to enhance conformity; dissenters may be humiliated; revealing is required, with punishment if refused (Konopka, 1990, cited by Kurland and Salmon, 1993, p. 8).

Although Kurland and Salmon are writing about the American scene, British writers have similar observations. Brown (1994, p. 45) notes a trend towards groups that are increasingly task-oriented, with decreasing emphasis being paid to process: 'reducing groupwork... to a rather sterile exercise in which group members receive packaged group programmes of limited usefulness, making no real impact on them as unique individuals often caught up in oppressive social conditions of poverty'. Senior (1993) acknowledged that the individualised task focus had produced some high-quality training materials (for example, Martin, 1997) but was concerned that:

unless groupworkers were skilled enough to use the group process appropriately, opportunities for personal development of clients were left undone. (Senior, 1993, p. 35)

As an example, Cowburn and Modi (1995) critically evaluate approaches, predominantly based *in* groups, to working with male sex abusers. They see in the prevalent cognitive behavioural programmes and, in particular, in the practice of individual confrontation, oppressive Eurocentric and heterosexist assumptions, grounded in conformity and obedience, which are potentially dangerous in reinforcing abusers' minimalist views of their own responsibility and the harm their actions have caused. Effective practice, they argue:

> needs to help to develop a person's positive sense of identity as a firm base from which knowledge, skills and understanding about offending behaviour can be brought together to avoid re-offending... it needs to be experienced within a context that is not oppressive (Cowburn and Modi, 1995, pp. 204–5).

Real groupwork may have become unfashionable precisely because it acknowledges that groups develop a life of their own over which the worker cannot ever have complete control. In a group, the agenda is likely to be holistic. Group members will raise what is important and significant to them, no matter what 'ground rules' and boundaries have been set. Such free-flowing characteristics are out of kilter with the current climate, emphasising, as it does, discipline, individual responsibility and, at an organisation level, preset objectives and audited outcomes. The outcome is many projects and workers for whom the ideas of real groupwork are unfamiliar and regarded with suspicion (Drakeford, 1994, p. 237).

However, there is a danger of casting out the baby with the bath water. The drive for efficiency seeks, wherever possible, economies of scale, and this means gathering people together. Whenever this happens, group process and the need for groupwork skills will come to the fore.

A continuing need for groupwork

Sustaining Caddick's (1991) findings, work-in-groups has continued to develop as a vital activity across the probation service, but along the dimension of 'the modification of offending or offence related behaviour' rather than 'towards providing developmental or enabling experiences for members' (Caddick, 1991, pp. 210–11). Cognitive-behavioural approaches developed in North America have provided the received model (Ross *et al.*, 1989). Cowburn and Modi (1995) have highlighted the risk of deconstructing fragile identities in such group-based work with sex abusers. They urge, instead, a groupwork approach which 'allows offenders to feel power and consequently a strong sense of self... [which]... will allow them to develop non-offending ways of finding self-affirmation (Cowburn and Modi, 1995, p. 205). As noted, recent texts on 'What Works' cognitive-behavioural practice pay minimal attention to group dynamics, group process and groupwork methods and skills.

Likewise, in residential and day care, sometimes called *group* care, there is a dearth of literature with a groupwork base and practice examples. Exceptions have been Douglas (1986) and, particularly, Brown and Clough's (1989) *Groups and Groupings: Life and Work in Day and Residential Centres*. Brown and Clough built on the premise that better practice lies in understanding the complexities of the 'mosaic' of more or less formal groups which straddle the experiences of users and staff in day and residential settings. A particular contribution of this work was to extend attention beyond inter- and intra-group processes (Douglas, 1986) to the 'rediscovery' of the open and large group as contexts which require special consideration and skills (see also Ward, 1993).

In the organisation and management of social services, the problem is not the lack of literature on groups, organisations and management *per se*. Rather, it is the failure to apply the knowledge and understanding of group process, and to use groupwork skills, in the management of social work agencies as 'mosaics' and of front-line teams as groups. The culture of 'new managerialism' has led to a top-down style preoccupied with obedience, performance indicators and output measures, features which are an antithesis of groupwork. According to one former senior civil servant, this leads to a narrowing of vision, driving out initiative and distorting priorities, a flattening of the levels of performance leading to conformism, a reluctance to question received ideas and 'ultimately to secrecy and defensiveness' (Faulkner, 1995, p. 69). The capacity of groupwork, applying techniques of problem analysis, objective-setting, prioritisation and evaluation to enhance creativity and to generate team spirit and enthusiasm for the tasks in hand, goes unconsidered in such a culture.

In the rapidly expanding field of 'self-help', much initiative takes place in group settings. There are two sides to the self-help movement. Negatively, it can be seen as substituting for properly resourced, high-quality welfare services, providing an ideological smokescreen for further cuts, contracting out and, at worst, the unpaid and unsupported care of the poorest by the poorest. On the other hand, self-help groups, besides providing the quality of empathy and support that only those in the same predicament can extend to their peers, have raised the profile of hitherto unmet need and brought about significant changes in policy and provision. Adams (1990, 1996a) shows the importance of an understanding of group process if workers are to mobilise and empower, rather than stifle, the creativity and commitment of those involved. Crucially, Adams (1996a) goes beyond a checklist approach (see, for example, Wilson, 1986, 1988, 1995), to assert and explain how, to achieve these purposes, groupwork skills must be set within a paradigm of practice principles which is explicitly anti-oppressive (pp. 117–18).

Finally, I have come increasingly to note the use of groups in research and evaluation (Ward, 1996). This has come into public view with the prominence given to the use of 'focus groups' by political parties in devising their appeals to the electorate. Whilst there is a technical literature on focus groups (for example, Morgan, 1988; Krueger, 1994), there is little acknowledgement of group and group-work matters in the research methods literature, even where partici-pative, ethnographic, feminist and other anti-oppressive approaches are advocated. It is self-evident that the knowledge of group process and a measure of groupwork practice skill should be components in such methodologies. Indeed, the potential impact of research on groups studied, and indeed its capacity to empower or oppress, should be central ethical considerations for all researchers (Fleming and Ward, 1996; Taylor, G., 1996).

Re-establishing groupwork

A. Brown (1996, p. 90) identifies three key considerations for the future of groupwork: values, practice-based model-building and sustaining groupwork and groupworkers into the millennium. Up to this point, I have identified forces which have undermined the pres-ence of groupwork in mainstream social and probation work and how this may be counterproductive from both ethical and practice perspectives. What I would like to propose now is a practical reasser-tion of groupwork which can encompass the three considerations set out by Brown. A recent briefing by the NISW (1996) highlights that a major cornerstone for social policy, and challenge for social work, in the new enlarging Europe is the fight against social exclusion. The briefing argues:

> The challenges of reducing social exclusion through working with those individuals and groups currently denied access to employment or services demands new approaches... The absence of such an aim in the United Kingdom has profound implications for the practice of social work.

In this context, I am prompted to recall Douglas's (1993) observation, cited earlier, of the historical connection between groupwork and equality and democracy. I discern in other countries of the European Union, where mass unemployment, demographic changes and the apparent inability of governments to sustain their welfare provision have created various forms of social exclusion, conscious efforts being made to reframe welfare services in ways which enhance an inclusive group-oriented approach. In contrast, in the UK, we have barely begun to address 'the role of social workers as agents in the fight against social exclusion and the development of a model of practice that can incorporate a broader community focus as well as an individual or family approach' (NISW, 1996).

The challenge of social exclusion demands that we take account of what we have come to know about the systematic oppression of excluded groups, about anti-discriminatory practice and about empowerment (Mullender and Ward, 1991; Rees, 1991; Thompson, 1993; Adams, 1996a), and, in this context, groupwork reasserts its significance. This is because the group can be (Butler and Wintram, 1991, p. 77):

- a source of immediate support, of friendship, where the knowledge that a meeting will take place regularly provides a safety net in itself;
- a place to recognise shared experiences and their value;
- a way of breaking down isolation and loneliness;
- the source of a different perspective on personal problems;
- a place to experience power over personal situations with the capacity to change and have an effect on these.

Also, beyond these foundations, 'in groups there is a better chance of addressing the inseparability of private troubles and public issues' (Breton, 1994, p. 31). Even though matters may surface as private troubles, in groups these private troubles soon become shared troubles, providing the ground for the *analysis* of their structural sources, and *action* together to bring about change (Mullender and Ward, 1991).

Butler and Wintram (1991), Lee (1994) and Mullender and Ward (1991) have articulated specific models for practising anti-oppressive groupwork. What is distinctive is their insistence on taking account of an interconnectedness of values, methods and skills right through practice. Helpful guidance can be found in Brown (1992), who provides an invaluable inventory of areas for attention, but one which – distinctive and essential to anti-oppressive groupwork – must be set within a searching exploration of underpinning values (Mullender and Ward, 1991). Brown (1992, pp. 152–80) draws attention to: group composition; supervision and consultation; style format and group culture; ground rules; putting race and gender on the agenda; confronting racism, sexism and other forms of discrimination when they occur within the group; co-working; worker self-preparation; and work within the group and within its external environment.

To illustrate what is possible, I will conclude with practice examples from arguably the least promising areas of social work practice.

Butler (1994) writes about a group for women whose children were adjudged by social services as at risk of significant harm from their parents. She explores how the 'facilitation' style of groupwork engendered an atmosphere of equality, enabling the women 'to explore the humour, sadness and strains of family life and no longer remain silent about these' (Butler, 1994, p. 178). Central to the group agenda emerged structural dilemmas facing members: women's sexuality and relationships with male partners, which were entangled with the processes of racism and the difficulties of bringing up mixed-parentage children. Faced with relentless hardships, the women easily identified the politics of poverty. Unpacking structural and individual issues was critical to these women's empowerment and the creation of their own solutions to the threats and dilemmas they faced (Butler, 1994, p. 163).

In the completely different setting of a young offenders penal institution, Badham (1989) and colleagues worked with the inmates to develop a through-care service which the young men would see as useful and relevant by enabling them to raise issues and complaints within the institution and to prepare themselves for release. The workers sought to draw out of the young men, and to provide opportunities for them to learn, skills and knowledge which would help them survive both 'inside' and after release. Confronting racist and sexist attitudes was part of this, and the worker team included women and black workers. The young men controlled the group's programme producing, amidst wide-ranging discussions, advice booklets and arranging speakers on welfare rights, housing, parole and temporary release. For invited speakers, including the governor, the group prepared their briefs, organised invitations and devised questions so that they acquired the information they wanted. The governor acknowledged the value of the forum and saw in this different context hitherto unrecognised capacities in these inmates. One young man said on leaving the group, 'It made you feel as though you *can* do something with your life while you are inside' (Badham, 1989, p. 35).

This, then, is the shape of an anti-oppressive groupwork practice to tackle the processes of exclusion. Like so many other catch words that have gone before – participation, citizenship and, sadly, empowerment – there is, of course, the ever-present danger of the 'fight against exclusion', being co-opted and watered down to become meaningless, ideological deodorant. Some insurance against this can lie in interlinking with an anti-oppressive approach grounded in the practice of 'real' groupwork. It is an opportunity to begin to bring British social work with groups back in from the cold.

Further reading

Brown, A. (1992) *Groupwork*, 3rd edn (Aldershot, Ashgate).

> This remains the best basic text on practising groupwork, with an excellent bibliography for further reference.

Brown, A. (1996) 'Groupwork into the future: some personal reflections', *Groupwork* **9**(1), pp. 80–96.

> This article identifies an agenda for groupwork into the twenty-first century, with an emphasis on empowerment and anti-oppressive practice as key aspects.

Adams, R. (1996a) *Social Work and Empowerment* (London, Macmillan).

Breton, M. (1994) 'On the meaning of empowerment and empowerment oriented social work practice', *Social Work with Groups*, **17**(3), pp. 23–38.

Mullender, A. and Ward, D. (1991) *Self-Directed Groupwork: Users Take Action for Empowerment* (London, Whiting & Birch).

> These three texts are most helpful in unravelling the notion of empowerment and providing practical guidelines for practising groupwork in that direction in mainstream social work settings.

13

Community work

MARJORIE MAYO

Introduction

'Community work has a long history as an aspect of social work' (Payne, 1995, p. 165). Essentially, community work brings a focus upon helping 'people with shared interests to come together, work out what their needs are among themselves and then jointly take action together to meet those needs, by developing projects which would enable the people concerned to gain support to meet them or by campaigning to ensure that they are met by those responsible' (Payne, 1995, p. 165). Community work has generally been associated with holistic, collective, preventative and anti-discriminatory approaches to meeting social needs, based on value commitments to participation and empowerment.

'As stated,' Payne continues, 'this looks innocuous.' Public policy statements, both in Britain and internationally, abound with commitments to the values of participation and empowerment. In practice, however, as Payne goes on to point out, 'community work has proved controversial and problematic', having the capacity to draw 'attention to inequalities in service provision and in power which lie behind severe deprivation' and so to become part of struggles 'between people in powerless positions against the powerful' (Payne, 1995, pp. 165–6) This has been offered as an explanation for the British government's decision to conclude its own experiments in community development (the Community Development Projects – CDPs) in the 1970s, for example (Loney, 1983).

Why then, given its potentially controversial and problematic characteristics, has community work not merely survived from the 1970s, but taken on an apparently new lease of life in the 1990s? This chapter starts by exploring some aspects of this question. Having summarised key features of the current context, this chapter will move on to provide some 'mapping', including a brief discussion of different definitions of key terms, together with a rapid summary of the recent history of debates around community work as an approach to social work.

The discussion will then focus on issues and debates in community work today. What are the main theoretical perspectives, and what are their varying implications for community work practice? At what levels, and in which types of practice setting, is community work most relevant and appropriate? What are the key areas of knowledge and skills which are required? This chapter will also consider a number of the more negative features and some of the key dilemmas of the contemporary context, in terms of both policy and practice. This will then provide the basis for concluding with an overall appraisal of community work's contribution, both actual and potential. What has community work to offer as an approach to reflective social work practice? And what changes in social policy might be required if community work's contribution were to be enhanced?

The context

The economic and social policy context within which social work and community work operate has changed significantly since the 1970s. These changes have been characterised in terms of 'globalisation', an expression which has become increasingly fashionable since the 1980s, 'when it began to replace words like "internationalization" to denote "the ever intensifying networks of social and economic relationships"' (Dominelli and Hoogvelt, 1996, p. 46) These changes have also been described in terms of a number of 'posts' – post-industrialism, post-fordism, post-structuralism and postmodernism (Taylor-Gooby, 1994; Dominelli and Hoogvelt, 1996; Penna and O'Brien, 1996). There are key differences between these terms, as Penna and O'Brien point out, the first two referring predominantly to debates within political economy, the latter two having been more concerned with debates within cultural studies. These differences are beyond the scope of this chapter.

What these different terms share in common, however, is a common sense that the old order of 'modern' industrial society is in a state of flux and transition, on a global scale, whether this is in terms of economic change, or in terms of social, political and cultural change. These changes have fundamental implications for welfare states in general, and more specifically for the social policy context for social work and community work.

In summary, despite national and local differences, there are powerful global trends, it has been agued, including trends towards increasing marketisation, increasing privatisation, increasing fragmentation of services and the technocratisation of social work itself, in the contract culture (Dominelli and Hoogvelt, 1996). These changes pose significant threats. They also pose new contradictions. For community work in particular, the current focus upon the role of the community sector, within the mixed economy of welfare, could be seen to represent new opportunities as well as new challenges. Only, this increased emphasis upon the role of the community sector is taking place within the wider context of reduced public resources, including reduced public resources for the support and development of the community sector itself. Similarly, the current focus upon the promotion of self-help, diversity and choice offers new opportunities for some, against a background of reduced opportunities and choice for others. This makes it more important than ever that those engaged in community work are actively aware of these divergent tensions and critically reflective in their practice.

'Mapping' community work: definitions and recent history

This need for clarity starts with the concept of 'community' itself, a term which has over time been the subject of confusion and contestation (Crow and Allen, 1994; Mayo, 1994a; Payne, 1995). The uses of the term 'community' which have greatest relevance for community work can be broadly summarised as follows:

'community' as shared locality – a common geographical area, for example a neighbourhood, a housing estate in an urban or suburban context, or a village in a rural area;

'community' as shared interests – these might be interests based upon cultures and identities, as in the case of ethnic minority communities, or upon common identifications of particular needs (as in the case of the parents of children with special needs, or ex-users of mental health services, for example).

The term 'community' is frequently applied to services to differentiate them from institutional forms of provision (for example, community care services for the elderly in their own homes and/or in day centres in their localities, rather than in residential homes or geriatric hospitals). The term 'community' is often contrasted with 'state', as in the case of the 'community sector', which has been associated with small, relatively informal and 'bottom-up' forms of service provision, in contrast to the larger, more bureaucratic forms of service provision typically associated with the public sector. Community-based services have been associated with the promotion of unpaid caring and self-help (often in response to widening gaps between shrinking services and increasingly unmet social needs). Also, community-based services have been associated with more participatory and more empowering approaches to social welfare provision, based upon enhanced respect for the diversity of users' and carers' own perspectives.

As has already been pointed out, community work has a long history as an aspect of social work, predating the current focus within the mixed economy of welfare. Broadly speaking, community work has been defined as being concerned 'with enabling people to improve the quality of their lives and gain greater influences over the processes that affect them' (AMA, 1993, p. 10). Twelvetrees has suggested that, at its simplest, community work is 'the process of assisting ordinary people to improve their own communities by undertaking collective action' (Twelvetrees, 1991, p. 1). Community work has been particularly concerned with the needs of those who have been disadvantaged or oppressed, whether through poverty or through discrimination on the basis of class, race, gender, sexuality, age or disability.

Community work developed from the late nineteenth-century settlement houses, starting with Oxford House (founded in 1883) and Toynbee Hall (founded in 1885), linked to social work as well as to community education. Through the work of the community association movement in the inter-war period, and community work in the New Towns, after World War II, community work developed as a professional activity, alongside the unpaid work of volunteers and activists in community organisations and social movements. At the end of the 1960s, the government launched its own Community Development Project as part of its efforts to combat poverty and deprivation through more holistic and more preventative approaches to social welfare (Loney, 1983), approaches which were emphasised in the Seebohm Committee's conception for the future of the social services, 'directed to the well-being of the whole community and not only of social casualties, seeing the community as the basis of its authority, resources and effectiveness' (Seebohm Committee, 1968, p. 147) Similar arguments were put forward by the Barclay Committee's Report in the early 1980s (Barclay Committee, 1982).

This emphasis upon the role of the community, and the need for partnerships between social service departments and the local communities they served, re-emerged, at the end of the 1980s, in the changing context for social work in the mixed economy of welfare (Bamford, 1990). In particular, the Griffiths Report on care in the community took up the theme of closer partnerships between statutory services and local communities as part of the new welfare pluralism. The NHS and Community Care Act, 1990 enshrined both increasing marketisation, and a potentially increasing emphasis upon community work, at least in theory if not necessarily in practice. Whatever the varying outcomes in reality, following these and related changes in social policy and in local government, it is hard to imagine social work reverting to previous models within all-encompassing local authority social service departments, as the Seebohm Committee had envisaged. This all goes to demonstrate the significance of the challenges for community work.

Community work and social work

Community work has a long history as an approach to social work. In the context of the NHS and Community Care Act, 1990, there has been particular interest in community work in relation to community care, promoting care in the community, as well as enabling service users and carers to participate in planning, monitoring and evaluating community care services. Community social work has not, however, been confined to community care. Community-based social work has been and continues to be relevant across a wide range of social work practice, including preventative work with children and their families, for example, as studies by Cannan and others have demonstrated (Cannan, 1992; Smith, T., 1995).

Whilst community work has a continuing role, as an approach to social work, however, community work has not been confined to social work. Community work has featured as an approach to youth work, and community work has featured and continues to feature within other professional settings, including housing and planning. In addition, community work has also been carried out, and continues to be carried out, by volunteers and unpaid activists within communities.

There have been long-running debates on whether or not community work should be defined as a professional activity at all, professionalisation having been posed as potentially undermining to community activism and autonomous community movements (Banks, 1996). In summary, then, community work has its place as an approach to social work, but community work is not confined to the social work profession.

Alternative perspectives and implications for practice

By this time, it should have become apparent that community work can be and has been based upon competing perspectives, associated with both right and left positions on the political spectrum. Community work has been promoted to encourage self-help and informal caring, to compensate for reductions in public service provision within the context of the increasing marketisation of welfare, to support strategies to combat poverty and oppression, and to facilitate community participation and empowerment.

Texts such as Twelvetrees have distinguished between alternative community work perspectives, contrasting the 'professional' approach, which seeks to promote self-help and to improve service delivery within the wider framework of existing social relations, with the 'radical' approach. This latter 'radical' approach seeks to go further, contributing to shifting the balance of existing social relations through empowering the relatively powerless to question the causes of their deprivation and challenge the sources of their oppression, 'drawing upon insights from neo-Marxist structural analyses, together with insights from feminism and from anti-racist analyses' (Twelvetrees, 1991). This is the type of approach which supports minority ethnic communities, for example, in drawing attention to inequalities in service provision and 'in power which lie behind severe deprivation' (Payne, 1995, p. 166).

Whilst these distinctions have relevance, the terms 'professional' and 'radical' have inherent problems, in the current context, as Twelvetrees himself has also recognised. In particular, in recent years, the term 'radical' has become even more confusing, since its adoption by the 'radical' right. The use of the term 'professional' to describe one perspective could also be taken to imply that the alternative perspective was in some way 'non-professional' or even 'unprofessional' (although this was not actually suggested by Twelvetrees himself). Given that professional values, knowledge and skills are essential to community work, whatever the perspective in question, it has been suggested that it would be less confusing to categorise community work perspectives in terms of a 'technicist' approach on the one hand, and a 'transformational' perspective, emphasising community empowerment and social transformation, on the other hand' (Mayo, 1994b).

These two broad types of community work perspective have also been broken down into further subdivisions and related to the different types and levels of community work practice. Dominelli, for example, has characterised the traditional, 'neutral' views of community work in ways which are comparable to the 'technicist' approach. She defines these views in terms of their assumptions that 'the system' is basically sound, although individual and community pathologies need to be ironed out through the community work process; she quotes Biddle and Biddle's comment that 'the poor and the alienated must overcome their inner handicap practically through activation of their own initiatives' as a classic text to illustrate approach (Dominelli, 1990, p. 8).

Table 13.1   Two perspectives on community work

Perspective	Goals/assumptions
'Professional' 'Traditional' 'Neutral' 'Technicist'	To promote community initiatives, including self-help To improve service delivery (*within the framework of existing social relations*)
'Radical' 'Transformational'	To promote community initiatives, to improve service delivery and to do so in ways which empower communities to challenge the root causes of deprivation and discrimination, and to develop strategies and build alliances for social change (*as part of wider strategies to transform oppressive, discriminatory, exploitative social relations*)

Dominelli then goes on to characterise three models of community work – community care, community organisation and community development – in terms which can be related to this broad type of 'traditional', 'neutral' or 'technicist' approach. Community care schemes based on the use of unpaid and typically white, middle-class women volunteers to cover gaps in statutory provision would fit into this 'neutral' approach, for example, although the effects may be far from neutral, in terms of reinforcing inequalities of race, gender and class, in service provision. Similarly, Dominelli places community organisation – or community work which focuses on improving the coordination between various welfare agencies – as typically forming a tool of corporate management rather than a tool for more fundamentally challenging the inequalities in resource allocation (including the specific inequalities experienced by women and black people). Third, Dominelli considers the community development model, which focuses on the promotion of self-help skills, and fits this, too, into this broad type of approach; this is especially the case, it is suggested, when leadership in community development programmes is provided by outside professional experts brought into so-called problem areas to tackle social problems as defined by the state. However, Dominelli also points out that, where community development involves collective struggles to achieve groups' demands, this community development model may turn into 'community action'.

In contrast, Dominelli considers three models which would be more consistent with the 'transformational' approach, as outlined above – class-based community action, feminist community action and community action from a black perspective. These models are all, in their different ways, about more fundamental social change (including a change in the consciousness of those affected), whether focusing upon addressing inequalities of class, gender and/or race. Dominelli describes class-based community action in terms of bringing people lacking power together 'to reduce their powerlessness and increase their effectiveness' (Dominelli, 1990, p. 11), typically using conflict, direct action and confrontation as well as negotiation to achieve their ends. Feminist community action has 'transcended the boundaries of traditional community work by challenging fundamentally the nature of capitalist patriarchal social relations between men and women, women and the state and adults and children' (Dominelli, 1990, p. 11). Community action from a black perspective has made the struggle for racial equality central to their work – whilst anti-racist feminist community work has been committed to eliminating both racial and gender inequality.

Table 13.2   A continuum of community work models?

Model/level of work	Perspective typically associated with model
Community care Community organisation Community development	'Professional' 'Traditional' 'Neutral' 'Technicist'
Community action Femininist community action Community action from a black perspective	'Radical 'Transformational'

As Dominelli and others have also recognised, however, there is, in practice, a degree of overlap between these different models, 'particularly in the areas of techniques and skills adopted' (Dominelli, 1990, p. 7), and there have been continuing debates, including debates about differences within both femininist and anti-racist approaches, which are beyond the scope of this particular chapter. (For a guide to these debates, see, for example, Williams, 1989.)

As it has already been suggested, in the context of the particular pressures and tensions of the mixed economy of welfare, this makes it

. the more important that community workers are critically aware
: the potential implications of different models and reflective in their
practice. More specifically, this context requires increasing knowledge
and skills, as community workers have to operate within the more
complex and more fragmented environment of the mixed economy of
social welfare provision. Whatever the history of community organisation, in terms of whether or not this model has necessarily implied
a more traditional, less structurally challenging/transformational
perspective in the past, in the current context community workers
neglect community organisation work at their peril (not to mention
the potential peril of the communities they work with professionally).
The local authority, although a key player with overall responsibility,
can no longer be expected to be the key provider of relevant services.
Communities may need to negotiate with a wider range of agencies,
public sector agencies, quangos, private sector agencies, voluntary,
not-for-profit and other community sector organisations. Community
workers have a potentially more vital role than ever, not only in
enabling, but also in empowering communities to address these situations effectively. Community workers need to be effective, then, at
the levels of interagency work and at the levels of local and regional
planning, as well as at the level of grass-roots neighbourhood work.

Similarly, I would argue that, in the current context of the mixed
economy of welfare, a considerable proportion of community
workers will be needing to address community care issues, whatever
their own perspectives. Models of community work practice, which
place community care at one end of the spectrum, through to community action and to feminist, black and anti-racist community work at
the other end of the spectrum, need to be reconsidered in the light of
these changing conditions (Popple, 1995).

Community care can be approached, in any case, from different
perspectives – from traditional perspectives which focus upon the
promotion of self-help and volunteering in ways which substitute for
rather than enrich public service provision, or from more transformational perspectives which address issues of immediate needs within
the context of wider strategies for community empowerment,
supported by anti-discriminatory, anti-oppressive community work
practice. Such an approach has been set out, for example, in the
chapter by Shaw which addresses the possibilities as well as the problems for community care, drawing upon the Scottish experience
(Shaw, M. 1996). The point to emphasise here is that, whether community workers are focusing upon community care issues and/or
tackling interagency community organisation issues, they need to
reflect upon their practice critically. Is their practice informed by relatively traditional, 'technicist' perspectives on community work,
which focus upon managing social problems and containing social

needs? Or, alternatively, how far is their practice informed by more transformational perspectives, geared not only towards meeting social needs, but also towards addressing the causes of oppression and discrimination and promoting community empowerment?

Table 13.3   Beyond a continuum? Alternative perspectives on community care, community organisation and community development

Models	*Alternative perspectives and practice*	
	Traditional/technicist *for example:*	Radical/transformational *for example:*
Community care	Promote volunteering	Empower users and carers
Community organisation	Promote interagency coordination	Negotiate /campaign for organisational change to improve services/support for the community sector
Community development	Promote self-help to tackle concentrations of deprivation	Empower communities to develop strategies to tackle deprivation and disadvantage

Whatever their underlying perspective, however, community workers need an increasingly sophisticated core of background knowledge, techniques and professional skills (see Beresford and Trevillion, 1995). Broadly speaking, as a starting point, community workers need to be confident of their skills in the following areas:

- engagement (with a range of individuals, groups and organisations);
- assessment (including needs assessment, via area profiles);
- research (including participatory action research with communities);
- groupwork;
- negotiating (including working constructively in situations of conflict);
- communication (across a wide range of contexts);
- counselling;
- the management of resources (including time management of self);
- resourcing (including grant applications);
- recording and report-writing (for a wide range of purposes);
- monitoring and evaluation.

These are, of course, typically skills which are widely transferable. In addition, community workers need a sound background knowledge of social policy and welfare rights, together with a specific knowledge of the fields in which they are predominantly operating, fields such as health and welfare policies and practice in relation to community care, child protection legislation for those concerned with children and families in the community, and housing and planning legislation for community workers involved in housing, planning and urban or rural regeneration programmes, for example. In addition, as it has been argued elsewhere:

> community workers need to have knowledge and understanding of the socio-economic and political backgrounds of the areas in which they are to work, including knowledge and understanding of political structures, and of relevant organisations and resources in the statutory, voluntary and community sectors. And they need to have knowledge and understanding of equal opportunities policies and practice, so that they can apply these effectively in every aspect of their work. (Mayo, 1994b, p. 74)

Some current issues and dilemmas

In recent years, community work has had to respond to the criticism that it is an area of practice that is 'both imprecise and unclear' (Popple, 1995, p. 1). In a period of increasing pressure to target scarce resources more precisely, with clearer performance indicators, there has been decreasing scope for generalist, preventive community work, the type of work with children and families in deprived areas that Holman (1983), for example, has carried out and analysed so effectively and with such inspiration. Crisis management in child protection, for example, has tended to divert resources from community-based approaches to the support of children and families in need (for example, through community-based family centres and through particular initiatives such as child-care projects and credit unions).

More specifically, community work tends to be promoted within particular, short-term initiatives, such as projects to promote community participation in government-initiated urban regeneration schemes such as the 'City Challenge' and 'Single Regeneration Bid' programmes. By their very structure, as short-term schemes, these have a focus upon short-term outcomes and very specific performance indicators (such as the numbers of trainees attending training courses). The point to emphasise here is absolutely not that there is a case for exempting community work from the fullest public account-ability. However, the contemporary emphasis upon short-term inter-ventions, evaluated by overly narrow performance indicators, risks being ultimately self-defeating, marginalising the more holistic, preventive, longer-term approaches to community work – the type of community work which has been pioneered by Holman, for example, and developed, for instance, in the more community-based family centres (Holman, 1983; Cannan, 1992; Smith, T., 1995; Durrant, 1997).

These short-term programmes can be potentially divisive in communities, too, where community groups find themselves competing against each other for limited resources. The point to emphasise here is that, even if particular groups and individuals take a more positive view of programme outcomes, communities overall could be left even more fragmented and alienated following commu-nity regeneration interventions. Community workers need to be criti-cally aware of this potential for negative as well as for positive outcomes. This is a key point and one which relates to a long history of debates over how far community work, like other approaches to social work, can be controlling rather than caring and enabling. There are parallels here with debates around contemporary notions of communitarianism, including debates about how far this actually focuses upon responsibilities rather than rights, upon communities policing themselves and/or competing with neighbouring communi-ties for limited resources, eked out via self-help, rather than working together to challenge the policies in question.

Conclusion

In the contemporary context of the mixed economy of welfare, community work has a potentially more vital contribution than ever to make. Community workers can support communities in coming together to work out their needs, and then take action together to meet those needs. Also community workers can work in ways which empower communities to develop strategies to challenge inequalities in service provision and indeed to begin to challenge the underlying causes of discrimination and deprivation.

Conversely, however, this contemporary context is also more prob-lematic than ever, with the risk of further fragmentation and increasing inter- and intracommunity conflicts. This means that community workers need greater professional expertise than ever. Most particularly, their practice needs to be informed by critical theory if they are to address these challenges as reflective practitioners.

Without significant changes in the wider context, including significant changes in the social policy context, however, community work risks remaining severely constrained as an approach to social work. It will continue to be hampered by the short termism which has reduced rather than increased support for the community sector and focused upon crisis management, to the detriment of longer-term and more holistic strategies of meeting social needs in preventive and anti-discriminatory ways, ways which are both participatory and empowering.

Further reading

Beresford, P. and Croft, S. (1993) *Citizen Involvement: A Practical Guide for Change* (London, Macmillan).

A discussion of user involvement.

Bulmer, M. (1987) *The Social Basis of Community Care* (London, George Allen & Unwin).

The background to sociological and social policy debates.

Cannan, C. and Warren, C. (eds) (1997) *Social Action with Children and Families* (London, Routledge).

Readings in community social work with children and families.

Dominelli, L. (1990) *Women and Community Action* (Birmingham, Venture Press).

Issues of gender, race and class in community work.

Popple, K. (1995) *Analysing Community Work* (Buckingham, Open University Press).

A textbook on community work.

14

Psychosocial work

DAVID HOWE

Introduction

It would be possible to argue that, in essence, social work *is* psychosocial work if by psychosocial we mean that area of human experience which is created by the interplay between the individual's psychological condition and the social environment. Psychosocial matters define most that is of interest to social work, particularly people who are having problems with others (parents, partners, children, peers and professionals) or other people who are having a problem with them. There is a simultaneous interest in both the individual and the qualities of their social environment.

For example, a woman neglected as a child may have low self-esteem, feel anxious and agitated in close relationships, becoming depressed when she feels unable to control what is happening to her. She needs to be loved and valued but can never take other people for granted or trust them. Her partner comes from a similarly adverse 'socio-emotional' background. Their relationship is characterised by mutual anxiety as each fears that the other may abandon them, and mutual anger as each believes that the other is capable of causing them hurt. The result is that their relationship is full of conflict and turbulence, anxiety and depression. The emotional needs of both people are so great that any children of their union are, in their turn, likely to experience an emotionally disturbed upbringing. The woman's past social experiences affect her emotional make-up. These influence the way she approaches and handles *current* social experiences. The way her partner and children react to her behaviour then creates yet another round of family life to which she has to respond. And so on.

The basic dynamic between psychology and setting can be used to explore all aspects of people's psychosocial functioning. The developmental frameworks that help to analyse social behaviour and the quality of people's past and present relationships provide social workers with a powerful theory to guide all aspects of practice, including observation, assessment, evaluation of risk, decision-making, the choice of methods of help and treatment, worker reflectivity and models of practitioner supervision.

Although the research and knowledge base which underpin this perspective continue to develop apace, the main features of the approach were recognised and described as early as the 1920s and 30s. Perhaps the most articulate and coherent rendition of the psychosocial approach was, however, made by Florence Hollis, best captured in the second edition of her book *Casework: A Psychosocial Therapy,* published in 1972. In this work, she defines the essential elements of a psychosocial approach, in which she argues that clients and the contexts in which they find themselves have to be thought about and handled simultaneously. Using the knowledge bases of her time, Hollis was inclined to use Freudian psychology to inform the 'psycho' element of the approach, and social systems theory to develop the 'social' component of the practice.

Attacks during the 1980s by Marxists, early feminists and behaviourists on much of social work's traditional knowledge bases, including psycho-analytic theory, dealt a severe blow to the use of psychosocial outlooks in welfare work. A few core concepts and practices remained, including those of loss, grief and mourning, but the basic approach went into steep decline, at least in social work. However, in psychology, particularly developmental and clinical psychology, the concept of the 'psychosocial' continued to develop and grow, playing a major part in providing the discipline with a powerful perspective on understanding people's psychological development and behaviour in various social and cultural contexts (see, for example, Rutter and Smith, 1995). It is ironic that social work, which had such early claims on the 'psychosocial', now finds itself turning to other social sciences to rediscover the rigour, relevance and usefulness of adopting socio-emotional outlooks on human relationships.

The socialness of self

Although the idea that we are 'social selves' whose being and personality form within social relationships is not new, there has been a resurgence of interest in the 'socialness of self' in the social sciences (see, for example, Bakhurst and Sypnowich, 1995; the phrase 'the socialness of self' is used by Mulhall and Swift, 1995). The self and personality form as the developing mind relates with and tries to make sense of the world in which it finds itself. As it does this, it takes on many of the properties of the environment which it seeks to understand and negotiate. How we understand, think, feel, see and conceptualise, although heavily influenced by inherited temperamental and biological dispositions, is also shaped by our social, cultural and linguistic experiences.

Individuality is socially based, and personality forms as social understanding develops (Burkitt, 1991, p. 2).

The developmental implications of this perspective are that the *quality* of relationships with other people during childhood has a direct bearing on the development of personality and the emotional make-up of the individual. The poorer the quality of people's relationship history and social environment, the less robust will be their psychological make-up and ability to deal with other people, social situations and emotional demands:

> it seems that the postulate that a lack of continuity in the loving committed parent–child relationships is central has received substantial support... What has stood the test of time most of all has been the proposition that the qualities of parent–child relationships constitute a central aspect of parenting, that the development of social relationships occupies a crucial role in personality growth, and that abnormalities in relationships are important in many types of psychopathology. (Rutter, 1991, pp. 341, 361)

Therefore, the way in which different personalities handle and develop their *current* social environment is in large measure a product of *past* relationship experiences. Current social performance hints at people's earlier social experiences. Past relationship histories help us to understand current levels of social competence.

Inner working models

Different types of personality indicate the different ways in which people attempt to make sense of and adjust to their relationship environment. Adverse environments which lack love, mutuality and empathy are less conducive to the formation of secure and confident personalities. Children who lack responsive, consistent and predictable relationships find it more difficult to handle the emotional stresses that life inevitably throws up. The coherence of people's psychological organisation reveals the type of psychological adjustments which they have had to make in order to cope with their social environment. The models used to represent relationships gradually become internalised, forming the basis of personality (Bowlby, 1988). The individual's personality is judged by the characteristic ways in which he or she makes sense of and handles social relationships and experiences. In our development, what is on the social outside therefore establishes itself on the psychological inside. In this sense, external relationships become mentally internalised (Howe, 1995, p. 24).

As they seek to understand what is happening around them, babies create mental representations to interpret the confusion of experience.

Once established, these models act as templates within which subsequent experiences of that type are interpreted. Of central concern is the infant's need to understand the relationship she has with her prime care-givers. Attachment figures (in the first instance, usually, but not necessarily or only, the mother) provide the child with security and her first opportunity to be in a relationship. To be a competent player in the relationship, the child needs to make sense of the selected attachment figure emotionally and socially. In order to do this, however, she has to understand her own self, other people and their shared relationship. For this to be possible, the young mind has to build up an internal working model of the mother so that her actions, feelings, beliefs and intentions can be read (Bowlby, 1988). Here are the beginnings of social understanding. The more open, full and accurate the communication between mother and child, the more the child learns to understand the mother, her own self and their shared relationship. Such mutuality encourages reciprocity, empathy, responsiveness, cooperation, regard and respect. Experience helps to generate the models, and the mental models then aid in the interpretation of future experience. In this way, *past* experiences influence how *present* experiences are approached and understood (Bowlby, 1988; see also Howe, 1995).

Everyday life is a matter of understanding and negotiating the world of other people. The more children are able to make sense of their social world and understand their own place within it, the more adept, skilled and relaxed they can be in social relationships. In turn, this improves their chances of developing mutually rewarding friendships, entering reciprocally based intimate relationships, becoming caring parents and emerging as socially competent beings.

Frith (1989, p. 169) reminds us that, 'The ability to make sense of other people is also the ability to make sense of one's self.' Children learn about their own psychological states within relationships. The more sensitive, empathic and reciprocal the communication within relationships, the more fully will children learn to understand the nature and effect of their own mental states on themselves and those around them. The more they can understand the basis of their own thoughts and feelings, the more skilled will they become at understanding and interacting with other people. Imbalances, insensitivities and inconsistencies in the care-giver/child relationship mean that the infant's attempts to model interpersonal experience are more difficult to achieve. Not being able to make sense of experience is confusing, stressful and anxiety-provoking. When other people are unpredictable and not susceptible to influence or control, children are less able to learn how to conduct themselves socially. The argument is that, if human beings are social beings, the ways in which we develop social understanding and become socially competent are of great relevance to those who work with parents and their children.

Attachment and relationship-based theories as examples of a psychosocial perspective

Attachment theory is a good example of how a psychosocial perspective can help us to understand and assess the quality of people's social relationships. The success with which people relate with others is a measure of their 'social competence'. Attachment theory provides us with a coherent, well-researched and elegantly argued set of ideas about the feelings, behaviours and psychological strategies we all use in our dealings with others, particularly if those others are our partners, parents or children (see Bowlby, 1979, 1988). Parents are the people most likely to provide children with their early, close relationship experiences. Attachment theory explores how the qualities of children's relationships with their carers affect their socio-emotional development, which then influences the way in which they relate to and deal with other people. Therefore, if we are to understand the quality of children's social environment, we also have to understand the parents, their personalities and the kinds of relationship they generate with each other and their children. If the social outside influences the child's psychological inside, we need to pay careful attention to the quality of the relationship between the two.

Attachment behaviour

Attachment behaviour is a biologically adaptive response designed to ensure that babies get into close, protective relationships. They need to get into such relationships at times of danger and when they feel anxious. They also need to be in close relationship with their prime care-givers in order to develop social understanding, interpersonal competence and language. By the time they are one year old, most children have established strong *selective attachments* to one or more adults or older children.

Attachment behaviours are triggered when children experience stress or anxiety. At such times, children seek out their attachment figure. This person is experienced as a 'secure base' – a place of safety and comfort. When children are not anxious or in need of comfort, they are free to explore and learn about their environment. It follows that children who experience a lot of anxiety have less time and emotional energy to explore and learn how to become socially adept.

Four types of relationship experience and their impact on psychosocial development and competence

Researchers and clinicians who have studied interactions between parents and their children have observed that the type of relationships they form depend on the parent's physical and emotional availability, sensitivity, reliability, predictability, responsiveness, level of interest and level of concern. Children who experience their attachment figures as usually available and responsive feel *secure*. Those who do not experience their attachment figures as reliably available and responsive feel varying degrees of *insecurity*. Ainsworth *et al.* (1978) worked with many of Bowlby's ideas and were the first to formulate an attachment classification system. Others have added to and refined the original classification, but the basic framework remains in good shape and of great relevance to social workers.

Although there are now many refinements, we might recognise four basic types of attachment experience. Each type represents a certain kind of emotional relationship within which a child has to make particular kinds of psychological adjustment if he or she is to cope and survive in the social world. We have already said that aspects of the child's personality and ability to develop social understanding form within these important relationships. Natural temperaments, degrees of resilience and cultural contexts certainly have a strong part to play, but the classification remains extremely useful in helping child-care workers to understand children's emotional experiences and psychosocial functioning. The theory insists that many features of our personality and emotional life form within the history of our relationships with others. Therefore, the different patterns of attachment lead to particular personality and relationship styles during childhood and beyond into adulthood. We might consider four types of attachment:

1. secure attachments;
2. insecure, ambivalent attachments;
3. insecure, avoidant attachments;
4. disorganised attachments.

A basic understanding of these four relationship environments helps practitioners to make sense of the way in which children and adults react to and deal with the social and emotional demands of others.

Secure attachments

In secure parent/child relationships, care is loving, responsive, predictable and consistent. There is a sensitivity to children's needs, thoughts and feelings. Communication between care-givers and children is busy and two-way. There is mutual interest and concern in the thoughts and feelings of the other. Within such relationships, children begin to understand and handle both themselves and social relationships. They feel valued, socially competent and interpersonally effective. Other people are seen as trustworthy and available.

These children are usually sociable and well liked by peers. They cope reasonably well with the conflicts, upsets and frustrations of everyday life. As they mature into adulthood, they continue to feel good about themselves. In Main *et al.*'s terms (1985), these are 'autonomous' and 'secure' people who have a broadly realistic, accurate and workable view of themselves, other people and the relationships between them. Such people are only likely to come the social worker's way at times of great environmental stress (hospitalisation, a disaster, the physical demands of a disability or old age) or in the guise of a resource (foster carer, adopter or volunteer).

Insecure, ambivalent attachments

When parental care is inconsistent and unpredictable, children begin to experience increasing levels of anxiety. The problem is one of neglect and insensitivity rather than hostility. Parents often fail to empathise with their children's moods, needs and feelings. Misunderstandings and inaccurate communications abound. The child is never quite sure where he or she is within the parent/child relationship. The child becomes increasingly confused and frustrated. Distress and anxiety lead to a clingy dependence. To this extent, children feel that the world of other people is hard to fathom and impervious to their influence and control. Love comes and goes in what seems an entirely arbitrary way. This generates a fretful, constant anxiety. Children become demanding and attention-seeking, angry and needful. They create drama and trouble in an attempt to keep other people involved and interested. Feelings are acted out.

Insensitive and inconsistent care is interpreted by children and adults to mean that they are ineffective in securing love and sustaining comforting relationships. Their conclusion might be that they are not only unworthy of love, but also might be unlovable. This is deeply painful. It undermines self-esteem as well as self-confidence. Thus, there is a need for closeness but a constant anxiety that the relationship might not last: 'I need you, but I am not sure I can trust you. You may leave me and cause me pain, so I feel anger as well as fear.' Such feelings provoke jealousy, conflict and possessiveness in relationships. Children, indeed adults, who have grown up in such relationships are racked by insecurity. There is a reluctance to let go of others, yet a resentment and fear that they may be lost at any time. The result is that people cling to relationships, yet conduct them with a high level of tension and conflict.

No matter how fraught, for those who feel anxious and insecure, it often feels better to be in an 'active', noisy relationship with the world. Silence and isolation trigger feelings of emptiness and despair. Lives, therefore, are full of drama and crisis, many of which will appear on the social worker's doorstep.

Insecure, avoidant attachments

Children who develop avoidant patterns of attachment have parents who are either indifferent, hostile, rigid or rejecting. Although these parents may respond reasonably well when their child appears content, they withdraw when faced with distress and the need for comfort and attention. The clinging, complaining behaviour of children in ambivalent attachment relationships serve no purpose in these cooler styles of parenting. Attempts at intimacy only seem to bring rebuff and hurt. Carers encourage independence and de-emphasise dependency. When separated from their parents, these children show few signs of distress. Upon reunion, the children either ignore or avoid their attachment figure. Adults cannot be trusted or relied upon. It seems better to become emotionally self-reliant. Feelings are suppressed. To experience such rejection must mean that the self is unlovable or even bad. Self-esteem is very poor.

Lack of emotional involvement and mutuality mean that both children and adults find it hard to understand and deal with feelings. Empathy is poor. Anxiety and frustration easily lead to anger and aggression. These may not be popular people. They can be unfeeling, even cruel. They may find it difficult to form intimate, emotionally reciprocal relationships. Getting too close brings the fear of rejection and pain. As children, they may bully and try to get their way through physical force rather than social skill.

Disorganised attachments

Many children suffer physical abuse and maltreatment seem to show a confused mixture of resistant and avoidant patterns of attachment (Main and Solomon, 1986). The parent may not be wholly hostile or rejecting, but there are times when they are either dangerous or very frightening to the child. Relationships of this kind produce *disorganised* and *disturbed* attachment patterns in which the parent's violent or scary behaviour causes the child to feel extremely anxious. Anxiety normally triggers attachment behaviour in which the child approaches the parent for comfort. But in these cases, the attachment figure is the cause of the anxiety, so to approach him or her actually raises the level of anxiety. The child is therefore faced with a dilemma. There is an urge both to *approach* and to *avoid* the attachment figure. The result is that the child is deeply confused and either physically or emotionally 'freezes'. This confusion extends to dealings with other people. Distress and undirected, agitated behaviour is often the result when children find themselves in close relationships. They do not know how to seek comfort nor do they seem to know how to respond to other people's warmth and concern. There is a general air of helplessness and disorientation.

Assessments

Using a psychosocial approach places a great deal of emphasis on making thorough, carefully observed, theoretically informed assessments of people, their relationships and their sociocultural environment. We need to know how people act and relate with each other, how they behave with their children, neighbours and officials, how children respond to parents, peers and teachers, and how they play and react to demands and difficulties. How people react to 'outer world' events tells us about their 'inner world'. Indeed, among the 'people professions', social work remains peculiarly well placed to appreciate how people bring feelings to situations and how situations provoke feelings in people (Winnicott, 1964; Schofield, 1996). There is a need to identify the stresses in people's lives. Do they have unsupportive partners, live in poverty or experience isolation? What children and adults say and do, then, needs to be interpreted within the logic of a psychosocial framework. The character and quality of people's current behaviours and relationships tell us about their internal working models, defensive inclinations, emotional states and personality. Although working within a psychosocial perspective does not require social workers actively to enquire about people's past experiences, large amounts of information will in practice be acquired about their childhoods, relationships with others, including sexual partners, encounters with authority, emotional states, material problems and interpersonal ups and downs. This information can be fed into the assessment to help the social worker understand the way people are relating to their social and material environment.

Practice

A detailed psychosocial assessment allows social workers to begin to make sense of what people say and do. It sees links between past and present relationship experiences. Connections can be made between the emotional and behavioural impact of people on each other. The ability of people to feel in control of their own mental, social and economic state is recognised as fundamental to their general well-being. When control is absent, anxiety rises. And when anxiety mounts, a variety of feelings and behaviours may be triggered, including anger, despair, worthlessness, aggression, denial and avoidance, which brings them to the attention of social agents. Using a psychosocial approach allows social workers to understand and 'stay with' the apparent confusion and complexity that seems to characterise the lives of so many clients. The ability to make sense of what is going on allows practitioners to respond calmly and clearly. In this way, they are able to contain difficult emotional situations and continue to be available to people who feel frightened and confused, angry and impotent. Such client/worker relationships provide the opportunity for reflection, emotional growth, rational planning and decision-making.

Working within a psychosocial perspective defines two major areas of interest for the practitioner. The first concerns the notion of *risk factors* – what elements of the individual's psychosocial environment place their development, emotional well-being and social competence at risk. Social workers and clients need to identify such risks so that they may be avoided, decreased, changed or removed. Risks range from the obvious (for example, physical and sexual abuse) to the more subtle (for example, marital discord, the absence of emotional support, neglect, social isolation and financial worries). The second requires the social worker to identify the *protective factors* in an individual's psychosocial environment – what elements are promoting their well-being, sound socio-emotional development and social competence. Social workers and clients seek to increase, introduce and improve factors which strengthen and protect psychosocial functioning. *Emotional, social and economic support* are amongst the most effective protective measures we can receive (see, for example, Brown and Harris, 1978). Such support may be introduced in a variety of ways. Conflict may be reduced between parents. Depressed mothers may be encouraged to meet other women at a family centre. Social workers may provide frequent, low-intensity visits (Jones, 1985). Attempts may be made to increase social security benefits. In extreme cases, in order to reduce risks to psychosocial functioning, clients may need to be removed to new social environments, as happens in the case of the adoption of older children or the transfer of an old person into a residential home.

Conclusion

At a deep level, a psychosocial approach taps into important contemporary debates about the development of behaviour and personality, and the social nature of being human. Increasingly, social scientists are recognising that our natures and development are the exclusive result of neither genes nor experience. Rather, there is a complex interaction between the two in which the way our inheritance expresses itself and develops depends on the physical and social environment in which we find ourselves, and the way in which our environment is shaped and reacts depends on our individual characteristics (see, for example, Plomin, 1994). These insights provide the basic intellectual outlook of a psychosocial approach. Not surprisingly, psychosocial theory has been seen to have greatest relevance in child care and family work. However, the perspective is being increasingly used in work with other client groups. The quality of the social environment appears to be an important factor in understanding the onset and experience of those at biological risk from either schizophrenia or depression. Social developmental models might help us to understand the various kinds of relationship that develop between elderly parents being cared for by their adult children, bearing in mind that the children themselves are the product of the care and attachment environments generated by their parents.

Always at the heart of practice, psychosocial theories are being revitalised in social work as other disciplines, particularly in the psychological sciences, are exploring how people develop (or fail to develop) social understanding and interpersonal competence. If social work is about people's emotional well-being, personal development and social behaviour, a psychosocial approach provides theories which help both to explain personal experience in a social context and to guide practice.

Further reading

Dunn, J. (1993) *Young Children's Close Relationships: Beyond Attachment* (Newbury Park, CA, Sage).

A stimulating read, written by a leading developmentalist, that takes a well-rounded look at young children's development in the ever-changing context of family, peer and cultural relationships.

Durkin, K. (1995) *Developmental Social Psychology: From Infancy to Old Age* (Oxford, Blackwell).

A solid, comprehensive introduction that provides a good understanding of personal growth and the role of developmental processes in building social relationships throughout the lifespan.

Howe, D. (1995) *Attachment Theory for Social Work Practice* (London, Macmillan).

A broad outline of the main features of attachment theory, backed by a comprehensive review of the research literature, and aimed at social workers both in training and in practice.

Mattinson, J. and Sinclair, I. (1979) *Mate and Stalemate* (London, Institute of Marital Studies).

A first-hand account, backed by analytic and attachment-oriented theories, of working with marital problems in a social services department, packed with case examples.

Rutter, M. and Rutter, M. (1993) *Developing Minds: Challenge and Continuity across the Life Span* (Harmondsworth, Penguin).

An examination and review of the research literature that looks at human development over the course of life, paying particular attention to the continuities and discontinuities in the psychological growth process.

15

Cognitive-behavioural practice

KATY CIGNO

Introduction

The rapid expansion in recent years of theoretical and empirical research in applications of learning theory has not been matched to the same extent by a growing awareness and interest of social work practitioners. Fischer's (1974) 'quiet revolution' has not, in the British context at least, gained in vigour. Later in this chapter, we shall consider some of the reasons for this.

During this same period, terminology has changed, reflecting shifts in emphasis. For example, Payne, writing in 1991 about theories in social work, divided the cognitive from the behavioural and discussed their theoretical bases in separate chapters. The journal *Behavioural Psychotherapy* changed its name to *Behavioural and Cognitive Psychotherapy* in 1993 with volume 21, number 2. Sheldon revised his 1982 text *Behaviour Modification* and published it in 1995 as *Cognitive-behavioural Therapy*, including sections on the role of cognition in the development of problems and in helping to determine which behaviours will be performed. It should also be noted that the hyphen denotes a linking of cognition and behaviour: an indication of a consideration of how the one informs the other and how both elements are important for therapeutic practice.

A careful examination of the role cognition plays in deciding whether a behaviour will be repeated or not, or how it helps, on the one hand in the learning of behaviours, and on the other in eliminating unwanted behaviours, is a particular contribution which social workers (although, of course, not uniquely; see, for example, Herbert, 1987a, 1987b; Falloon, 1988; Falloon *et al.*, 1993; Webster-Stratton and Herbert, 1994) have made and should make to the literature as well as to the enhancement of practice skills. Social workers' broad remit, attention to both the immediate and wider environment and their tradition of intervention in the client's own home setting put them in an ideal position for developing applications of cognitive-behavioural theory to the real and often untidy, oppressive world of clients of social welfare in local authority and other non-clinical settings. This chapter will concern itself with such applications.

The policy context of social work

Superficially, the current political and social policy climate would seem favourable to the advancement of the principles of behavioural practice. The pragmatic concentration on presenting situations and problems, planned, focused work, contracts, the attention to goals, outcomes and evidence for 'what works': does this not fit in with value for money, managerialism and performance indicators of effectiveness? Furthermore, current legislation and procedures, while rarely acknowledging the influence of learning theory and competency-based approaches, have nevertheless absorbed several of their essential principles. Some examples are:

- the Children Act, 1989 and its 'Guidelines', with their emphasis on working in partnership with professionals, parents and children, clear assessments, written, negotiated plans and systematic reviewing;
- the National Health Service and Community Care Act, 1990, with its user involvement and needs-led assessments within a context of what is realistic and possible;
- CCETSW's Paper 30 (CCETSW, 1991) and the revised version (CCETSW, 1995); its evidence-based approach to assessment incorporates the direct observation of student social worker skills, identifies knowledge and values necessary to the social work task and lists progress indicators for judging the success or otherwise of a student's work with clients.

While some of these factors in the world of social work have 'good guy' and some 'bad guy' connotations, the fact remains that social workers have not embraced behavioural approaches to a greater degree than before the reverses of the welfare state during the years of Thatcherism (Hutton, 1996). We need to consider why this should be so. There could be several reasons.

First, many misconceptions prevail about learning theory approaches: they are mechanistic; they are about punishment; they are concerned with institutions and token economies. This view ignores the many British texts published over the past decade or so (for example, Hudson and Macdonald, 1986; Falloon *et al.*, 1993;

Sutton, 1994; Iwaniec, 1995; Scott *et al.*, 1995; Sheldon, 1995) as well as the smaller but significant number of case studies written by social workers from the position of mainstream social work and social services (Iwaniec *et al.*, 1985a, 1985b; Bunyan, 1987; Bourn, 1993; Cigno, 1993).

This leads to the second point: keeping up with the research on effectiveness of different social work approaches is hard work, although there are some reviews available to make the task easier (for example, Macdonald *et al.*, 1992; Macdonald, 1994; Sheldon, 1994). It requires considerable commitment to seek after truth and carry out our ethical duty of using only those approaches where there is evidence that they work in that situation, with this family or person, with those problems (Cigno and Wilson, 1994), rather than following our own predilections. Apart from a love affair between social workers and 'family therapy', Payne (1991) notes that social workers still use psycho-analytic theory and do not find cognitive-behavioural theory attractive. Decisions to use one approach rather than another do not appear to be based on research evidence of 'what works' (Newman *et al.*, 1996).

The third reason is that some North American research is based on clinical studies of what hard-pressed local authority social workers would rightly regard as esoteric problems unlikely to come their way in their work with the disadvantaged, poor, oppressed, multiproblem section of the population in crowded inner cities or isolated, amenity-deprived rural areas. This, of course, ignores the important and ground-breaking studies by social work academics such as Thomas (1974), Fischer (1978) and Gambrill (1983).

Sheldon sums up why many practitioners are reluctant to use cognitive-behavioural therapy as part of their repertoire of helping approaches. The objections are:

> on vague philosophical grounds – aesthetic grounds might be a better phrase, since objections are rarely accompanied by the disciplined logical analysis that real philosophy requires. In short, they just don't like the look and sound of anything 'behavioural' because of what they think it implies about the nature of human existence. (Sheldon, 1995, p. 31)

Others (for example, Hollin *et al.*, 1995) point out that client resistance is much less than that of practitioners. The latter need to accept that an evidence-based approach should inform what we do, both at the level of understanding the aetiology of problems and in our approach to them.

We now go on to consider more precisely what we mean by cognitive-behavioural practice, its underpinning theories and how an understanding of it can help us to identify people's problem behaviours as well as work out programmes with them to improve significant aspects of their lives.

Cognitive-behavioural practice

Before describing procedures and giving examples of their relevance to social work settings, I shall attempt, in the space available, to define and discuss what is meant by learning theory (or, more properly, theories) on which cognitive-behavioural intervention is based.

Behaviour is, largely, a result of prior learning, and what we learn is acquired in different ways. Sometimes we learn, so to speak, inadvertently or without deliberate intention. This kind of learning by association is known as classical conditioning: Pavlov's dogs produced saliva at the sound of a bell or approaching footsteps which they had learned to associate with the bringing of food; a child's fear of the dentist who has drilled into a tooth after an unpleasant injection may spread to fear of other people in white coats in laboratory-like settings.

We also learn through others' reactions to our behaviour or through environmental consequences: our behaviour is established and maintained by reinforcement, which we sometimes like to think of as a 'reward', although it may not necessarily look 'rewarding'. A volunteer may work in an Oxfam shop because she finds it a pleasant environment in which to meet people and also because it makes her feel good to be doing something worthwhile, but many of us would not work unless we got paid. This kind of learning is known as operant conditioning. Here we can already see how our thoughts, or cognitions, have a role to play in deciding whether a behaviour will be repeated or not, as well as whether it is reinforced.

Many behaviours, such as the way we talk (regional accent?), walk (swagger or glide?), cook or drive a car, are acquired by watching or listening to someone we like or respect doing it. This is called modelling or vicarious learning. We may think about others' performances and talk it over with ourselves (what effect will we have?, will we be able to imitate the behaviour successfully?) before we repeat the action. Sutton (1994) uses the term 'social learning theory' which encompasses as good deal of what we have briefly outlined above. She describes it in a clear and useful statement:

> Social learning theory comprises a large body of concepts which, happily, are recognised by researchers in the disciplines of both psychology and sociology. It concerns how children and adults learn patterns of behaviour, as a result of social interactions, or simply through coping with the environment... it suggests how to focus

upon the practical rather than the pathological, upon people's strengths and potentials rather than upon their weaknesses or short-comings, and upon how to empower those with whom we work. (Sutton, 1994, pp. 5–6)

Clearly, the effects of what we do are going to determine which behaviours will be repeated and in which circumstances. It is this knowledge of how and why we learn that enables the cognitive-behavioural practitioner to make a thorough assessment of a 'problem' behaviour which, according to its possessor or to one or more significant others, needs changing. It may be that more of the behaviour is desired, as for example in cases of non-school atten-dance, or less, as in cases of adults who have difficulty in controlling their anger. Scott (1989) has written about social work with parents where the focus is on controlling anger, leading to the potential or actual abuse of children, and where techniques include relaxation, role-rehearsal and self-talk. Getting a child back to school often entails changing the parent's or the teacher's behaviour, which may be the reason for the child's absence from the classroom in the first place. Fear of maths or sports, worsened by a teacher's sarcasm or shouting, may be the antecedent to sickness or truanting.

Fundamental to behaviour therapy is the observation that being aware of our thinking does not necessarily alter behaviour. Under-standing, achieving 'insight' into why we do what we do, by no means inevitably leads to behaviour change. We may think 'This is bad for my teeth' as we reach for another chocolate, or 'These harm my health' and 'I must see about giving this up' as we smoke, or 'This never really works and I shouldn't do it' as we raise a hand to smack a child. We listen to the sound of our voice as we quarrel with our loved ones and think 'This is awful; I'm making things worse.' Scott *et al.* (1995) give examples of how cognitions – anxious thoughts, maladaptive interpre-tations of self, unrealistic expectations of others and disturbing rumina-tions – affect behaviour in many, often serious, ways.

An awareness of these processes is a start, but a consideration of our own, our friends' and our clients' experiences tells us that this alone does not usually lead to the desired behaviour change. Crucially, strategies are also required. Cognitive restructuring – chal-lenging, for example, negative thoughts about ourself ('I'm no good') and teaching others to do so – has been described and applied by social workers, such as Scott and colleagues (1995); much cognitive-based work derives from the studies of Beck (1976) and Beck *et al.* (1985). There is currently a great deal of work being done in this area, but most practitioners would argue that a mainly cognitive approach needs to be evaluated by indicators of behaviour and environmental change. One has only to think of the implications of a client with a serious addiction or of a parent whose child has been identified as being at risk of overchastisement telling the worker, 'I think things are better now', and of the practitioner going away satisfied that the intervention has been a success on this evidence alone. In social work, therefore, a careful combination of cognitive and behavioural techniques can be useful and appropriate provided that clearly defined behavioural goals are identified to ensure that an evaluation of practice as 'a success' is soundly based.

Areas of practice and links with effectiveness

There are, then, many areas where research and experience indicate that help with behaviour problems is required. Herbert (1987b), in his preface to a book on helping children and their parents with problem behaviours, describes his conversion to a behavioural approach. When he was practising as a child psychologist, a despairing mother told him that she wanted to know what to *do* when her child screamed and cried. As we have said, understanding is not enough; people want strategies to help them cope.

One area where families of children with learning difficulties do not get sufficient help is behaviour problems (Burke and Cigno, 1996). Sinclair *et al.* (1995) report that 30 per cent of children in the care system are referred because of problematic behaviour. Research shows that helping parents to learn different responses to their child's behaviour and teaching them parenting skills can help to prevent abuse or stop it escalating (see Cigno, 1995, for a review of the literature, and Chapillon, 1996, for a student social worker's account of a parenting skills group).

Social skills training (SST) has been used effectively with different client groups, including people with various degrees of learning difficulty (for example, McBrian and Felce, 1992; Cullen *et al.*, 1995), with adults in different situations and with diverse problems (Hollin and Trower, 1986), with people with mental health problems (Hudson, 1982; Oliver *et al.*, 1989), with young people leaving care (Biehal *et al.*, 1994) and with young offenders and alcohol-related crime (McMurran and Hollin, 1993). Some undesirable results of a certain kind of punitive 'training' were discovered by Gendreau and Ross (1987) in their research on 'boot camp' rehabilitation. After such treatment, there is evidence that the young offenders become leaner, fitter criminals. The authors conclude that cognitive-behavioural intervention, rather than short, sharp shocks, works.

Old people are not often thought of as having goals or indeed as being suitable for the attention of social work intervention. Gambrill (1986), however, reports a successful, step-by-step approach to helping older people in the community express what they would like to achieve. They can be assisted to improve the quality of their lives by, for example, making telephone calls to friends and organisations to increase social contacts. Cigno (1993) describes a behavioural programme carried out in residential care with a 70-year-old woman to decrease unwanted aggressive behaviour and increase helpful acts and contacts in the wider community (see below).

Motivational interviewing (see Rollnick and Miller, 1995) has developed from learning theory principles such as the use of positive modelling, cognitions and selective reinforcement of self-statements to change the behaviour of adults, including young offenders, with addictions (Tober, 1991; McMurran and Hollin, 1993). Indeed, motivational interviewing, because of its promising results, is now used widely in the field of addictions.

In the area of child welfare, what is familiarly known as the Dartington research has drawn attention to key criteria for assessing outcomes with young people (Bullock *et al.*, 1993; DoH, 1995). In order to evaluate outcome, it is not only important to take into account factors such as maturation and other variables which operate externally to the intervention (Hill and Aldgate, 1996b), but also to draw up a baseline on basic features of well-being such as health, educational achievement, level of social skills and troubled behaviour of the person concerned prior to intervention and service provision. It is possible, for example, to assess outcomes for children and young people according to how far they conform to accepted social norms of behaviour.

Consumer research, from the early British study of Mayer and Timms (1970) to the many studies now available, confirm that clients of all ages value attributes such as reliability, openess, honesty and clarity in their social worker quite apart from any particular approach adopted (Stein and Carey, 1986; Howe, 1989). Happily, these qualities are the basis for the client/worker relationship within which cognitive-behavioural social work is practised. Freeman *et al.* (1996) report the feelings of young people on being let down by social workers over such matters as cancelled visits and postponed meetings. Some missed visits may be inevitable in the busy schedule of local authority social services, but many are due to poor planning and lack of consideration of the meaning of such disappointments for vulnerable and relatively powerless clients. Similar findings of appreciated practitioner attributes are found in a study by Cigno (1988) of the views of mothers attending a family centre.

The evocative accounts of users of being on the receiving end are important feedback as long as other, more objective outcome criteria are employed alongside (Cheetham *et al.*, 1992). All the technical skills in the world are to no avail if the practitioner lets the client down by oppressive practice such as missed appointments and lack of openess over further action. It is crucial that students learn this during their practice placements, for one of the ways we learn is by modelling ourselves on others' behaviour. 'Show me' is a reasonable position for a student to take *vis-à-vis* experienced, qualified practitioners. It is very common often not to connect one's own behaviour with those to whom we are close and over whom we have influence. As a parent once said apologetically of her child, 'I don't know why he **** swears like that. I'm always telling the little **** not to **** well do it.'

Assessment and intervention

The key to good practice is thorough assessment. In the case of behavioural approaches, this needs to detailed. Apart from adhering to basic social work values such as those mentioned above, social workers need to practise from within a relationship of Rogerian warmth, genuineness and empathy. Assessments may vary, but a good starting point for many situations where the aim is behaviour change is an ABC (Antecedents, Behaviour, Consequences) analysis. It has the advantage of being easy to remember and is an excellent guide to the questions to be asked. In brief, these are as follows:

- *Antecedents:* What are the circumstances in which the behaviour takes place? What happens just before the behaviour in question?
- *Behaviour:* How can the actual behaviour be described? What does the person do?
- *Consequences:* What happens immediately after the behaviour?

The worker and the client together discuss the relationship between the three. Many of our clients, living in poor housing, jobless, ill-educated and often suffering from health problems, exhibit what Seligman (1975) has called 'learned helplessness'. They do not think or feel that they can make any impact on their situation; it is their destiny to suffer the 'slings and arrows of outrageous fortune'. In some areas of their life, and in the immediate term, this may be true; however, if they can learn to take action in one small part of their life, the results can be greatly reinforcing, can increase self-esteem and can encourage the client to take small steps to improve other aspects of living:

Ms A's three children were on the child protection register because of her ex-partner's abuse and her own lack of parenting skills. The children, aged three, five and seven, were, according to their mother, 'out of control' and 'did what they liked'. She attended a parenting skills course where she constantly said 'Things are no better'. Gentle exploration of this statement by the worker revealed that she was now managing to get the children to school and that she was thinking of taking a course at the local college, 'but I'm thick'. She was surprised when the worker praised her for her efforts and discussed how she might go about getting information about courses. A home visit indicated that Ms A was now talking to the children and had some control over them. She subsequently went to the library to obtain leaflets about part-time courses. Pointing out to her and giving her credit for the changes she was making to her own behaviour and how she was able to influence her children's to their benefit made her smile. She was further encouraged by the other parents in the group 'evaluating' her progress by telling her 'You should have seen how you were a month ago'.

Pointing out that Ms A's negative self-statements were not true was a start. Tracing her attempts to improve her management of the children, praising her for getting them to school and talking to them at home, and observing how they responded to this encouraged her to continue with these new behaviours. She began to see that, with encouragement, she could take steps to change some elements in her environment and was not forever destined to be a 'bad mother' and 'thick' (for a discussion of these issues from a user self-help perspective, see Adams, 1994).

The above is an example of challenging learned helplessness of a mother where there was risk of neglect and abuse to children, and of shaping coping behaviour mainly through cognitive restructuring and positive reinforcement. The next example is of a case where careful observation of a person's environment, behaviour and its consequences led to an ABC assessment, hypotheses, intervention plan, review and evaluation.

The problem concerned a young man, C, attending a centre for adults with learning disabilities. Various activities took place; and, as well as participating in these, service users, were encouraged to take responsibility for other tasks. C was often asked to take messages from one member of staff to another. He was willing and pleased to do this but usually returned after a long while with the message undelivered. The staff could not understand why this was so and renewed their attempts to impress upon him where he had to go. One worker volunteered to study the problem, observing C over the space of two weeks. Her analysis was as follows:

● *Antecedents:* An activity room, often the education room (because one of C's goals is to improve his literacy skills). C is asked to take a message to someone in another part of the building.

- *Behaviour:* C sets off. Talks to the manager on the way. Walks round the building, sometimes stopping at different rooms. Returns to where he started, message undelivered.
- *Consequences:* Staff express disappointment. C misses much of the teaching/activity session. C cannot tell why he has not delivered the message. C's learning goals are not achieved.

One hypothesis is that C enjoys wandering about rather than participating in an activity. If so, it is good that he is having a pleasant time but less good that he is not achieving his own learning objectives. The second is that he fails to understand the instructions given or understands but forgets. Further observation showed that the first hypothesis is partly right. C likes being entrusted with a message but also enjoys chatting to the manager and walking about. Nevertheless, he is not happy when he realises that he has failed to carry out the task, nor when he misses an activity.

The volunteer discovered that the instructions given to C did not follow the same pattern. This is related to the second hypothesis. Here are some of the instructions he was given over the observation period:

Take this to Mr Jones
Take this to Mr Jones' room
Tell Mr Jones the forms are here
Take this to the craft room
(and so on, with the substitution of another name or room)

So he is sometimes directed to a person and sometimes to a room in a fairly random way. After a while, and particularly after a chat with the manager, C would either have forgotten where he was going or would not remember the name of the person to whom to give the message. Writing the name down for others to read would reduce C's responsibility. This longstanding problem was solved by giving C, along with the message, something to remind him of his destination: a piece of wood, a cotton reel, a tube of paint, a book and so on. The manager was also asked to prompt him by asking to see the object he was carrying. This programme worked: messages were delivered, C's pride in his achievement and competence increased and he spent more time on improving his literacy and other skills.

Putting this plan into operation required working together as a staff team in order to achieve a coherent response. Otherwise, C's wandering behaviour and failure to complete a given task would have been intermittently reinforced, perpetuating his confusion over what was expected of him.

The next situation also demonstrates how important it is to try to make sure that anyone involved in a behavioural programme is aware of how essential it is not to respond in different ways to a target behaviour for elimination or increasing. (Parents will be well aware that the child refused sweets, staying up late, going out to play and so on by one parent may achieve success by making the same request to another parent or to a grandparent!)

Gambrill (1983, 1986) writes about how professionals often do not consider that old people have goals. Neither are they often the subject of 'casework' but rather of the allocation of resources, important though the latter may be. Similar points, albeit from different perspectives, have been made by Wilkes (1981) and Erikson *et al.* (1986). Yet, in both field and residential settings, the quality of life of older people and their family or co-residents can be improved.

A detailed account of the case of Miss B, a resident in a home for elderly people, is given by Cigno (1993). Miss B's problems were that she shouted, upsetting and frightening other residents as well as exasperating staff. For example, she would throw things on the floor during mealtimes. This got her attention from staff, while at other times, when she was calm or helpful to others, she tended to be ignored. The places where these behaviours took place could be almost anywhere and could be triggered by a look perceived as hostile (antecedents). Miss B would then shout, swear, insult someone or argue (behaviour), resulting in complaints from residents and scolding from staff, sometimes ending in a shouting match (consequences). Further consequences were exclusion from a social event because of fears that she would make a scene.

Miss B was helped, by the use of a chart, to record periods free from outbursts and, by rewards which she selected, to reduce her aggressive behaviour and increase her social skills. Gradually, the charts were withdrawn as the changes in Miss B's behaviour began to alter the way in which residents and staff reacted to her. In other words, enough reinforcements were present in the natural environment to render the use of a chart redundant.

Devices such as charts and other symbolic rewards and monitoring systems are useful for clarifying and establishing desired behaviours with some clients – a diary is often a good way of recording and reviewing progress – but these should be withdrawn once the behaviour has been firmly established or eliminated. Tangible rewards, such as special outings, comfort food and so on, should always be accompanied by social rewards like smiles and praise.

Conclusion

Therapeutic approaches have a place in mainstream social work. There is a case for thoughtful, systematic intervention – what used to be called 'casework' – as part of a 'package of care' to be carried out by the practitioner and not referred to other professionals (Sinclair *et al.*, 1995). Once the therapeutic component of social work is lost through privatisation or loss of competence, it is doubtful whether it will ever be regained. As our American colleagues advocate, 'Say you're a social worker!' (not a therapist or a case manager).

Although social work and social services will continue to go through many changes, social workers should resist learning helplessness and make sure that their work is as competent as it can be in the light of current knowledge of what works. To do this, we need the best prepared people to practise social work: to paraphrase Pearson (1983), if this is élitist, so should we all aspire to be.

Acknowledgement

I am grateful to Professor Brian Sheldon of the University of Exeter for his comments on a draft of this chapter.

Further reading

Behavioural Social Work Review

Published three times a year for its members by the Behavioural Social Work Group, it is also available in many university libraries. It contains practitioner accounts of intervention as well as more academic articles, information and book reviews.

Iwaniec, D. (1995) *The Emotionally Abused and Neglected Child: Identification, Assessment and Intervention* (Chichester, John Wiley).

A major and timely contribution to the literature as more attention is focused nationally and internationally on the lasting damage caused by the prolonged emotional abuse and neglect of children.

Sutton, C. (1994) *Social Work, Community Work and Psychology* (Leicester, British Psychological Society).

The author, whose practice and research have roots in social work and psychology, provides an account of human development across the life span and of evidence-based practice, covering different settings in the context of a multicultural society.

16 Values Essay

Task-centred work

MARK DOEL

Introduction

One of the biggest challenges facing the social work profession is how to square professional practice with the 'circle' of organisational constraints. The break-up of social work into its constituent tasks and the increasingly proceduralised nature of the work of agency practitioners are two factors which lead back to Brewer and Lait's question of 1980, *Can Social Work Survive?* (Brewer and Lait, 1980).

This chapter will present task-centred social work not as *the* answer to the question of survival, but as one of the best available. It will also seek to clarify what task-centred social work is, in the light of misconceptions deriving from its name.

Task-centred social work has its roots in North American casework practice. It is widely known that Reid and Shyne's (1969) research project, *Brief and Extended Casework*, looked at the effectiveness of short-term casework, but perhaps fewer understand that what they experimented with was a curtailed form of long-term work, cut short after a number of sessions. They found that the interventions which were allowed to run their full course were no more and no less effective than those which were foreshortened. It was Reid and Epstein (1972) who made a virtue of the short interventions by developing a short-term therapy, making positive use of a time limit to achieve a 'goal gradient effect'; in other words, the closer we approach a deadline, the more motivated we are to take action.

From these beginnings in the mainstream of social casework, the model has grown and adapted to a wide variety of contexts. It has been tried and tested in work with children, families and elders; in large public welfare agencies, small voluntary agencies, probation, school and hospital settings; in fieldwork, day, domiciliary and residential work; by students, experienced practitioners and managers; with individuals, groups and communities; with a wide range of difficulties and problems; and with people from diverse cultures and backgrounds (see Doel and Marsh, 1992, pp. 118-22 for a comprehensive guide to the task-centred literature). In short, task-centred social work is a generic practice method whose effectiveness has been subject to more evaluation and scrutiny than any other social work practice method.

In the process, task-centred casework has become task-centred practice, an indication of its development from individualised, therapeutic beginnings to a broader stage; a move away from conservative practices into more radical territory, embracing notions of partnership, empowerment and anti-oppressive practice, and signalling practical ways of realising these ideas.

Task-centred work and other social work ideas

The influences on task-centred social work have been broad and various. From its inception in the psychosocial tradition, it soon became embroiled in the heat of the inquisition over behaviourism – just how behaviourist was task-centred work? In a debate which now seems as unfashionable as loons and flared trousers, task-centred work was seen as merely 'soft' – as opposed to the 'hard' behaviourism of those whom traditionalists considered beyond the professional pale. What these questions served to show was the growing influence of learning theory as a way of understanding why people behave as they do. This in turn led to consideration of alternative patterns of behaviour and an increasing focus on outcomes and the ways in which these can be defined and measured (Jehu, 1967). All of this was consistent with the developing technology of task-centred practice, with its aim for a more precise statement of problems and goals, and a philosophy of 'small successes rather than large failures'.

As the behaviourist controversy faded, systems theory became the latest fashion statement, its essential design being detailed by Pincus and Minahan (1973). The systems approach in general, and the task-centred one in particular, contributed much to providing a unified approach to social work practice. More recently, in an example of 'retro' style, Tolson *et al.* (1994) make a strong case for task-centred as a generalist practice, using concepts from systems theory to demonstrate how task-centred practitioners can move within and between systems at different levels. This approach places the problem centre-stage, so that it is the problem rather than the person which is 'the client'.

Task-centred practice is a member of the family of problem-solving models. In addition to developing its own techniques, such as the task planning and implementation sequence (Tolson *et al.*, 1994, p. 73), it borrows from many others (such as 'positive reframing' from family therapy). The vogue for social skills training in the late 1970s and early 80s made its mark on the task-centred methodology, for example in the use of techniques such as 5W+H (what? when? who? where? why? and how?) when investigating the specific nature of the problem, and coaching and rehearsal methods to help people achieve success with tasks (Priestley *et al.*, 1978).

technique

consultation

In the 1980s, task-centred practice was well placed to give voice to the clients' rights/consumer choice movement (BASW, 1979). With its emphasis on working with people around issues which they considered prime, it provides a strong counter to paternalistic professional practice. Its links with open and shared recording (Doel and Lawson, 1986) and the requirement for explicitness about the purposes of the work, gave task-centred practice an ambiguous attraction to both radical and managerial elements in social work. This tension continues into the 1990s; task-centred practice provides a visible means of shaping the good intentions of partnership and the concrete expression of anti-oppressive principles, whilst also attracting interest from agency managers keen to have measurable outcomes and explicit systems of accountability.

humane

A.O.

Task-centred practice is primarily about learning. Indeed, the task-centred encounter between social workers and service users can be likened more to a teaching session than, say, a medical consultation, an administrative interview, a salesperson's pitch or a therapy session. The task-centred encounter has the feel of a highly participative workshop.   *need for relationship*

The essence of task-centred work

A brief description of the components of the task-centred model will help to place in context the themes and issues which are raised in this chapter. For a detailed exposition of the British variant of the task-centred model, see Doel and Marsh (1992). In addition, briefer summaries are available in Doel (1994) and Marsh (1991).

Task-centred casework was first described as a method to help people with 'problems of living' (Reid and Epstein, 1972). It is a systematic model of social work with a coherent and explicit value base. It has a 'practice technology' which has developed out of a body of research to examine what works well and what works less well. There is, therefore, a 'how to' aspect of the model, in addition to a clearly expressed 'why'. Its value base is anti-oppressive in that it addresses issues of power and oppression, both in the immediate encounter between worker and service user and in the broader social context.

There are three phases in task-centred social work, plus entry and exit.

Entry

The point of entry for a social worker is often muddy. The purposes of any contact may be unclear for the worker, the service user or both. Conversely, the participants may have clear but contrary purposes. Unlike most other services, the social work service might be unwelcome.

It is essential that practitioners use a method of work which accommodates these complex factors. It should not enforce consensus where none exists, but should ease the process of reaching agreement where one is possible. Above all, it should be sensitive to the service user's 'world' – the context in which the work occurs and the relative power of the participants.

There is, rightly, a debate about the extent to which partnership is really possible. Dominelli (1996, p. 157) writes that 'the real extent to which "clients" gain control through task-centred approaches remains a matter of controversy'. She sees financial constraints, policy imperatives and the practitioner's value base as setting boundaries which pre-empt the possibility of real power-sharing. Of course, these are factors common to all social work interventions, whichever method is used. However, the task-centred model ensures that discussion of power is part of the work itself.

Phase 1: Exploring problems

There is no neat 'cut-off' between the entry period and the first phase of exploring problems. In many instances, the early parts of the investigation of problems will confirm or challenge the mandate for further work. The worker may have spent much time helping the person to 'engage with the problem'; de Shazer (1988) uses the term 'visitors' for those people who think that the problem is someone else's.

The encounter between the task-centred worker and the service user is a systematic approach which links areas of concern to desired changes, which are achievable through a relatively brief and intensive plan of action. As well as an outcome, there is an explicit attempt to learn from this particular experience of problem-solving, in order to generalise to other circumstances. The learning is mutual; the service user learns to generalise to problem-solving with other life difficulties, and the practitioner evaluates this example in the light of other task-centred encounters in order to learn what works and what does not work.

This first phase is composed of a number of smaller stages:

- Problem scanning, which involves a wide review of problematic areas (the 'headlines') and a deliberate avoidance of explanations and solutions.
- Additional problems, consisting of problem areas evident to the practitioner but not mentioned by the service users.
- Detailing each of the identified problems, with an investigation focused on the problem in order to gain a better understanding of it, rather than to provide causal explanations or fodder for a social diagnosis. Questions such as 'What will be the first sign that you are overcoming the problem?' and 'What are you doing that stops things from being worse?' help the person to colour in the details (George *et al.*, 1990, p. 10).
- Selecting a problem (or, to use the jargon, 'targeting'), in which the service user makes a choice about the problem area they want to work on, based on their informed judgement and having considered factors such as the feasibility of working on the various problems. There may also be 'mandated' problems, which the worker is sanctioned to work on, even though they are not recognised as a problem or a priority by the client.

Phase 2: Agreeing a goal – the written agreement

Having focused on difficulties, problems and concerns, the work now turns to what it is the person wants. Goals may already have been mentioned, and they have often been confused with problems ('I need to get out of this house' sounds like a problem but it is in fact a goal, and it may not be the best way to address the problems it is intended to resolve). All involved in the work need to be aware of how the the agreed goal(s) will resolve or alleviate the selected problem(s). The goal must be one which is within clients' control to achieve, one which they are well motivated to work towards and which workers consider ethically desirable (in other words, they can lend their support to it).

A significant factor in the success of the goal is to decide a time limit by which the goal will be achieved, an agreed pattern for contact between worker and client, and concrete indicators of how success will be recognised. The time limit sets the work in a framework, and the indicators for success allow all involved to pace their progress and gauge the distance to achievement.

Together, the selected problem(s), the agreed goal(s), the time limit and frequency of contact make up the agreement. This should be recorded (usually written, with copies for all involved), but other formats should be considered in work with people with a visual impairment or difficulties with literacy.

Phase 3: Planning and implementing tasks

Once the written agreement is in place, the rest of the task-centred work follows a recognisable pattern from one session to another, in which past tasks are reviewed and evaluated, and future tasks are developed and implemented.

The 'task' is a central construct of task-centred social work, yet there is much confusion over this notion. The everyday English use of the word carries misleading implications, for example that tasks are always 'physical doings' when, in task-centred practice, they can be cognitive reflections, mental lists, a log of feelings and so on. Everyday tasks are usually free-standing ('My task today is to get the ironing done'), which is why many practitioners consider that they are working in a task-centred way when all they are doing is performing tasks. In task-centred work, tasks are carefully negotiated steps along the path from the present problem to the future goal. They build in a coherent fashion, sometimes completed in the session itself, sometimes completed between sessions, some for the user and some for the worker, some repeated, others unique (see Doel and Marsh, 1992, pp. 60–79, for a full account of the significance of task development and review).

The importance of task-development to the service users' success in achieving their goal has led to a five-stage task planning and implementation sequence (Tolson *et al.*, 1994). This is based on research into what promotes task achievement.

Exit

The end of task-centred work has been planned from the beginning; indeed, the built-in time limit is a powerful motivator for success, whether the intervention is a short, intensive burst over a few days or a number of sessions spread over several months. The length of work is a judgement based on how long it is likely to take to achieve the goal. Any change should be negotiated explicitly rather than allowing a sense of drift.

In situations where there is long-term contact between the service user and the agency (for example, in residential care), task-centred agreements can be negotiated periodically.

Issues

A systematic practice method

It is evident from the preceding description that task-centred work is a systematic method of practice. One way of illustrating what is meant by 'systematic' is to consider one task-centred practitioner acting as 'a fly on the wall' watching the work of another. Although the observer has not been involved in the work and knows none of the background or context, he or she will recognise the practice as task-centred, identify the particular phase of the work and any specific technique being used, and predict the shape of the next sequence of work. For example, the observer might state:

> This is the middle phase of the work. They have been reviewing the work on the tasks agreed at their previous session, using the scoring method to help the clients make a judgement about their success. They are now developing new tasks. The practitioner is helping them to generate these by using the Headlines technique, usually associated with the earlier problem exploration stage. The practitioner might provide some coaching later, depending on the nature of the tasks, and the tasks will certainly be recorded so that they all have a copy. They will agree a time by which the tasks should be completed and the practitioner will probably refer back to the original agreement, so they are all clear about when the work will end.

The observer will even be able to make some comments and judgements about how well the work was progressing and how skilled the observed practitioner was:

> I've never seen the Headlines technique used at this stage – that was very imaginative and I'm going to try it myself. I liked the way the practitioner asked '*What* changes have happened since I last saw you?' rather than '*Have* any changes happened since I last saw you?' I think the worker should have been clearer about the reasoning behind the scoring – even when a task has not been completed, there are things to be learned from that failure and the practitioner came over as half-hearted at that stage... and so on.

Although each task-centred encounter is recognisable as such, it is not a question of 'painting by numbers'. The mood and feelings of the clients, their particular circumstances and the context of the work all guide the practitioner, so that each encounter is unique. It has been likened elsewhere to a tidal progress, often slow and with one pace back for each two forward, but overall there is movement (Doel, 1994, p. 23).

Who is task-centred work for?

In an earlier section, we explored how task-centred practice has been influenced by psychosocial, behavioural, systems and problem-solving theories, in addition to broad movements such as clients' rights and anti-oppressive practice. Is the task-centred model, therefore, a coat of many colours?

There is certainly anecdotal evidence that many practitioners subscribe to task-centred practice. Payne (1995, p. 119) suggests that it is 'a popular model of social work, widely used in the UK'. In a survey of 25 student placement reports, 17 mentioned that task-centred practice had been used. (Second was counselling, mentioned in seven reports.) However, there is a suspicion that if social workers wish to convey a sense that their work is purposeful and active, they label it 'a task-centred approach'.

Task-centred practice is fast becoming the new eclecticism, popular but undifferentiated. In the audit of practice undertaken in the *Social Work in Partnership* action research, which employed a task-centred model of practice, Marsh and Fisher (1992, p. 41) found that the initial response from participants was 'We do all that already.' It is an irony that its apparent simplicity makes task-centred practice a victim of its own success, yet the explicitness and clarity of the process of task-centred work should not be mistaken for easiness.

If social work is appropriate and possible, task-centred work is appropriate and possible. Social workers find themselves in situations where they are not practising 'social work' (for example, when they are policing or administering), and task-centred work will not be appropriate in these circumstances. Similarly, if the service users' capacity for rational thought is severely limited, the use of the method will be similarly limited, as will other methods of social work practice.

Task-centred work and empowerment

In using a problem-solving approach, task-centred practice links us all, clients of social work or not. The task-centred philosophy does not

[margin: Why use it?]

pathologise service users but sees them as fellow citizens who are encountering difficulties. These difficulties are often more severe and more enduring than those which non-service users experience (and clients have fewer resources at their disposal to overcome them), but the problem-solving techniques used in task-centred practice are universal, even if the specific application in task-centred work is unusually systematic. In effect, the service user undergoes a training course in problem-solving techniques, and – with appropriate coaching from the worker – can use this method independently when the agency leaves. *[margin: empowered]*

[margin: Mainly individual]

Although the focus of task-centred work is primarily with individuals, families or groups, the method recognises the significance of context on individuals' problems (Tolson *et al.*, 1994, p. 395). In other words, there is often a dissonance between the level at which analysis takes place (structural) and the level at which effective action can be taken (local). The reasons a person is without a job might be analysed at a macro-economic level, but the possibility of doing something about it remains micro. Task-centred work helps expose the subtle relationships between these different systems.

Conclusion

Professional practice in an organisational context

Task-centred social work helps the practitioner and the service user by providing a framework to consider whether there is just cause for the work to begin. Whatever methods practitioners use for the ensuing encounter with the client, the idea of developing a mandate for the work is one of the most valuable contributions which the task-centred model has made to social work practice. Social workers practise in diverse fields, with a broad range of systems and in uncertain circumstances, and task-centred practice offers a unifying model of practice for social work in all these circumstances.

[margin: balance]

Practitioners must behave professionally. This means an ability to handle uncertainty, to use discretionary power and responsibilities, and to subscribe to a code of ethics drawn from outside any particular employer. Practitioners are under equal pressure to behave bureaucratically, by following procedures established in large organisations, driven increasingly by administrative and financial considerations. In these circumstances, it is necessary to establish ways of working which allow professional practice to engage with agency realities. Task-centred work can provide the cog which gears profession to organisation. *[margin: cog]*

Task-centred work lends itself to professional practice because of the skills needed to negotiate with the service user in ways which are truly empowering and anti-discriminatory. The explicit focus on power and discrimination, and the emphasis on qualitative outcomes, means that it is significantly more than a systematic procedure.

There are also aspects of task-centred work which could fall foul of professional practice, if not properly exercised. For example, it could be seen as routinised practice, in which the instruments of the model are used to exercise 'pure' social control, and tasks (or failure to complete tasks) become sticks with which to beat the client or to provide evidence of the client's incompetence or lack of motivation.

tension

There are aspects of task-centred work which fit well with agency imperatives, such as the accountability of an explicit approach, the potential to quantify outcomes and the economy of time-limited interventions. However, the emphasis on negotiation could be problematic if it implied a willingness to work on issues which might not, at first sight, be defined as the kinds of problem with which the agency dealt. Moreover, the need for relatively 'short, fat' interventions, rather than 'long, thin' ones, might not fit well with agency culture.

The task-centred model has proved itself to be an effective method which is popular with practitioners and service users. It has the potential to maintain professional practice whilst satisfying agency requirements. However, this degree of accommodation can appear ambiguous and perhaps explains why the task-centred method is described, on the one hand, as 'supporting managerialist objectives' (Dominelli, 1996, p. 156) and on the other as 'offering much potential for empowering clients' (Ahmad, 1990, p. 51).

A systematic strategy of training in the task-centred method, from pre-qualifying to post-qualifying levels, is the best way to retain a clear understanding of what it means to undertake work which can be called 'task centred'. Only when there is confidence that task-centred work *is* task-centred work can agencies, practitioners and service users benefit from experiences which are commonly understood.

Further reading

Doel, M. (1994) 'Task-centred work', in Hanvey, C. and Philpot, T. (eds) *Practising Social Work* (London, Routledge).

Offers a brief overview of the task-centred method.

Doel, M. and Marsh, P. (1992) *Task-Centred Social Work* (Aldershot, Ashgate).

Offers a detailed account of the task-centred model in contemporary British practice.

17

Radical social work

MARY LANGAN

Introduction

Although the moment of radical social work has now passed, many of its defining values – of community and commitment, of equality and empowerment, of feminism and anti-racism – have entered the mainstream of social work practice. Indeed these values have been endorsed by recent child protection and community care legislation and have become a feature of the 'rules and requirements' for social work qualifications promulgated by CCETSW. Despite the fact that supporters of the principles of radical social work have many reservations about recent developments in the field of social services, they have broadly welcomed the adoption of these principles by the authorities as an indication of the potential for shifting practice in a progressive direction.

Is this a postmodern paradox: that radical social work has triumphed despite the demise of the movement that launched it? Or is it a more familiar irony: that the rhetoric of radical social work has survived the containment of the movement's radical impulse? To grasp the ambiguous legacy of radical social work, it is necessary to trace its evolution over the past three decades.

By the early 1990s, the discourse of radical social work, a movement loosely mobilised around *Case Con*, published between 1970 and 1977 and self-styled as 'a revolutionary magazine for social workers', seemed to have permeated the highest levels of the system (Bailey and Brake, 1975; Langan and Lee, 1989). Olive Stevenson recalls how 'many, including myself, were astonished to see the idea of empowerment articulated in government guidance in community care' (Stevenson, 1994, p. 175). She quotes guidelines published by the Department of Health Social Services Inspectorate, which define the policy objective as 'the empowerment of users and carers' (DoH/SSI, 1991a). 'This is revolutionary stuff', comments Stevenson, greeting it

207

as a 'very influential' statement which gave 'authority and impetus' to radical initiatives within social services departments.

The trend towards the official endorsement of what were formerly regarded as radical causes had been gathering momentum for some time. Frost and Stein welcomed as one of the 'progressive aspects' of 1989 Children Act the imposition on local authorities of a duty to consider a child's 'religious, racial, cultural and linguistic' heritage (Frost and Stein, 1990). The 1991 Criminal Justice Act and the 1990 NHS and Community Care Act contained similar formulations reflecting official acknowledgement of issues of oppression and discrimination.

The ascendancy of feminist and anti-racist principles in the world of social policy reflected their wider rise in public approval in the early 1990s. Unions and employers drew up codes of conduct on issues of sexual and racial harassment, and local authorities promoted high-profile campaigns proclaiming 'zero tolerance' of violence against women. The police and the courts adopted a more sympathetic approach towards victims of rape and domestic violence, and the judiciary arranged courses in 'race awareness' for its members. The Football Association, together with individual clubs, took a firm stand against racist chants on the terraces.

It was in this climate that the controversy in 1992–93 around CCETSW's statement on anti-racism took place (CCETSW, 1991, p. 46). A number of journalists and academics condemned the formulation in Paper 30 that 'racism is endemic in the values, attitudes and structures of British society', accusing CCETSW of 'political correctness' (see Jones, 1993, 1996b, 1996c; Dominelli, 1996). In response, some Conservative politicians exploited the populist potential of the issue, accusing CCETSW of being excessively preoccupied with 'ologies and isms' (Tim Yeo, then social services minister) and of pushing equal opportunities 'to extremes' (Virginia Bottomley, then Minister for Health). This barrage prompted the newly installed CCETSW chief executive to organise a prompt review of the statement.

An editorial in *Community Care* (9 September 1993) expressed bemusement at the furore over a statement which had been adopted in 1988 and considered uncontroversial: 'Paper 30 has been almost unanimously supported by senior social work professionals. It was revised in 1991 without any objection.' Indeed, the first official reply to complaints about Paper 30 was that 'the Department of Health fully shares CCETSW's commitment to equal opportunities for all' (*Sunday Times*, 11 October 1992). Thus, although some found social work's radical anti-racist policy a convenient target for sniping, the substance of the policy was approved not only by the professional social work authorities, but also by the government itself.

The radical response to the right-wing attack on CCETSW's anti-racist stand was uneven, fragmented and mostly defensive. Many agreed that there had been some excesses in 'race awareness training' and grudgingly accepted a more anodyne redraft of the anti-racist statement, notably omitting the word 'endemic'. On the other hand, the broad approach of anti-discriminatory practice continued to enjoy official approval. In fact, far from signalling a major conflict within the world of social work, the Paper 30 controversy revealed the extent of the convergence between the radical critics of the 1970s and the social services authorities of the 1990s. To understand this convergence, we need to consider the roots of radical social work.

The roots of radical social work

According to David Marsland, CCETSW's anti-racist policy was 'the final folly of the sixties' (*Daily Mail*, 21 June 1993). In the sense that many of the values associated with radical social work originate in the upsurge of youthful radicalism in the 1960s, there is some truth in this.

In the late 1960s, the movement that emerged out of the struggle for civil rights in the American South and gathered momentum in the campaign against the Vietnam War reached a crisis. Writing in 1966, two activists summed up the prevailing sense of frustration and the quest for a political alternative:

> As it becomes more difficult to carry The Movement with freedom songs and slogans, and as the complexities of social change in the overdeveloped society become apparent, the early idealistic non-political thrust has been blunted. To function 'out there' demands the use of politics. (Jacobs and Landau, 1967, p. 78)

For some, the way forward lay in the 'community organising movement', which, according to one authority, 'established far more clearly than any other actions or tendency a coherent set of ideas for the New Left as a movement' (Young, 1977, p. 56). Young summed up the 'central components' of the movement in terms that sound familiar:

> The stress on community; local focus and decentralised organisation; the notion of participatory democracy and direct control of decisions; the emphasis on do-it-yourself direct-action politics; the extra-parliamentary character of the projects; the anti-paternalism and suspicion of 'do-gooding' (implying substantial self- and soul-searching); the belief in organising all the poor (inter-racially); and finally the concept of building counter-institutions. (Young, 1977, p. 56)

In response to their recognition of the difficulty of making major changes in the way in which American society was ordered, the young radicals scaled down their objectives. The focus shifted from the state to the 'grass roots', from the level of society to the level of individual lifestyle and the local community.

American community activism had a strongly individualistic outlook. As Jacobs and Landau (1967, p. 81) recognised, 'there is radical activity on many issues, but as yet no coherent intellectual force has replaced the moral obligation to put one's body and mind on the line in order to oppose large-scale and deep-rooted injustice and humanity'. The elevated subjectivity of the radical movement was expressed in its activists' courage and commitment – and also in their lack of ideological and organisational cohesion.

Given the middle-class origins of the radical activists and the gulf that separated them from a working class deeply divided along racial lines and long quiescent, they tended towards a condescending attitude towards the American masses. The recurrent themes in the writings of the New Left were of the need for education to overcome ignorance, of the moral corruption wrought by mass consumption and of the cultural impoverishment resulting from the influence of the mass media. The implicit (and sometimes explicit) assumptions were of a society made up of people who were at best apathetic and at worst bigoted, people who had been bought off by the consumer durables of the 'overdeveloped society' and duped by television. Concepts such as 'consciousness-raising' and 'empowerment', which emerged out this movement, presupposed a mass of people who lacked consciousness and power.

Another result of the lack of social weight of the radical movement was that, despite its anti-statist rhetoric, it tended to rely on the authority of the state to implement its policy agenda. Thus the central focus of Civil Rights agitation was on legislative reform and the feminist focus on the Equal Rights Amendment reflects a parallel juridical preoccupation. The subsequent emphasis on 'affirmative action', 'positive discrimination' and 'equal opportunities' policies reflects the continuing affinity of radical campaigners for the state enforcement of anti-discriminatory policies.

The radical social work diaspora

Although the ideals of the US radicals found a ready resonance in Britain, the context was significantly different.The most striking contrast was the existence in Britain of a labour movement, indeed one which was itself undergoing a remarkable rejuvenation in the rising tide of industrial militancy which reached a peak in the great strikes of the early 1970s. Despite the narrow focus of working-class activity, the high level of solidarity of the trade union movement made it a powerful force in British political life. Much of the activity of the early feminist and anti-racist campaigns in Britain was conducted under the umbrella of the labour movement.

The New Left in the USA emerged in a country in which the 'old left' had been crushed in the McCarthy era and in which the unions were generally conservative and corrupt bureaucracies. In Britain, however, the left had retained considerable vitality and it grew rapidly in the radical upsurge. Whereas in the USA radical community activists influenced the outlook of the left, in Britain the influence operated in the opposite direction.

Case Con was launched by a rank-and-file group in the local government workers' union. The leading activists were members of 'International Socialism' (IS), one of several radical left organisations which had expanded rapidly in the late 1960s. Mike Simpkin, a *Case Con* veteran, later explained the appeal of IS:

> It attracted support from many of the 1968 generation who had joined the public sector and wished to pursue activist politics outside the Labour Party. The essence of IS was an emphasis on rank and file activism which appealed to those social workers who were concerned with encouraging democracy and participation in their union, their department and their work with clients. (Simpkin, 1989, p. 165)

We see here some of the familiar themes of American community activism given a characteristically British labour movement inflection.

Given the strength of collectivism, the more individualistic features of American community activism appeared in Britain in a much weaker form – at least in the early years. Radical social workers placed the highest priority on the collective mobilisation of groups such as benefit claimants, council tenants, squatters and others, and explicitly disparaged the 'pseudoscience' of traditional 'casework':

> We are supposed to 'help' our 'clients' by making them 'accept responsibility' – in other words, *come to terms* as individuals with basically unacceptable situations. We must counterpose to this the possibility of *changing* their situation by *collective* action. We can only do this by acting collectively ourselves. (Bailey and Brake, 1975, p. 145)

A commitment to the 'self-activity' of the working class, almost an article of faith in the IS tradition, far outweighed any notion of radical activists 'empowering' working-class clients.

At a time when trade unionists were openly defying state legislation and even bringing down a government, the notion of youthful radicals conferring power on the working class did not have much appeal. For much of the ensuing decade, when American radicals were falling back on state power to push through their agenda, activists in Britain could still look to the labour movement as the agency of progressive reform.

By the late 1970s, however, the moment of radical social work had passed. The onset of recession in 1973 inaugurated a new era of mass unemployment and austerity. The election of a Labour government in 1974, which embraced fiscal orthodoxy and moved rapidly from restraining wages to curtailing welfare spending, proved disorienting for the left. Disillusionment with Labour paved the way for return in 1979 of a Conservative government, committed under the leadership of Margaret Thatcher to an abrasive free-market agenda. If, after 1974, radicals in social work and elsewhere were on the defensive, after 1979 they were in retreat. In the course of the 1980s, radical social work underwent a transformation, characterised by an increase in the influence of American radical ideas whose impact had previously been lessened by the peculiar strength of the labour movement in Britain.

The defeat of the labour movement resulted in a shift of radical social work away from the working class. Writing in 1981, Bolger criticised the Labour Party's approach towards social work on the grounds that it expressed a 'social democratic fear of the working class':

> In fact this probably reflects a more fundamental fear that the working class is racist, sexist, individualist and does not actually want the state services that are being imposed on it. (Bolger *et al.*, 1981, p. 12)

Labour's defeat in 1979, following the defection of many traditional Labour voters to the Conservatives, led some radicals to blame the working class for Thatcher's success. The tendency to disparage working-class people as racist, sexist and, worst of all, lacking in gratitude for state munificence, which Bolger recognised in the Labour Party, became increasingly influential in the world of social work.

Radical disillusionment with the working class led to a greater reliance on state agencies. Radical social workers tended to thin out at the grass roots as they rose up the social services hierarchy or went into teaching or the social work establishment. Like the American movement a decade earlier, British radicals now concentrated on working for improvements in the local community. The higher profile of, first, feminism and, later, anti-racism expanded the world of radical social work but also reflected a shift away from the labour movement towards an involvement with what became known as 'new social movements'. The collectivist outlook of the earlier radical movement was undermined by a new emphasis on difference and rights. Whilst many welcomed this shift, it also reflected the atomising trends of modern society and an increased reliance on juridical processes.

A more pedagogical approach now replaced the propagandist methods of *Case Con*. The emergence of 'race awareness training' illustrates the way in which this trend developed through the introduction of an approach developed in the USA in the 1970s into social work education – and into local government more widely in Britain in the 1980s. Based on Judy Katz' thesis that 'racism equals prejudice plus power', race awareness training insisted that the first step towards anti-racism is to recognise and eradicate our own racism (Katz, 1978; Dominelli, 1988). Because this technique sometimes unleashed angry confrontations, and because of its emphasis on inculcating 'correct' attitudes, it attracted media condemnation as a manifestation of 'political correctness'.

In its cruder forms, race awareness training has long been abandoned by most authorities and it is now regarded with some embarrassment by radicals who once championed it. Yet the basic approach survived: according to a book published by BASW in 1993, awareness training had 'a major part to play' in promoting anti-discriminatory practice and acted as 'a foundation for other forms and levels of training' (Thompson, 1993, p. 152). The most significant feature of the concept of race awareness training was how it revealed the shift in the attitude of radical social work. A movement which a decade earlier had regarded working-class people as the agency of the revolutionary transformation of society now assumed that the same people required professional training to eradicate their prejudices.

Radical social work in the 1980s was increasingly promoted from above. Whilst college lecturers conducted awareness training for social work students, radical policies on equal opportunities, harassment, anti-discriminatory practice and other issues were introduced by social work employers in local government and other agencies. Simpkin commented on the dramatic reversal experienced by a movement which had placed such emphasis on mobilising at the grass roots:

> Indeed much of the radical rhetoric which remains is at present experienced as being imposed from above, whether by progressive Labour councils or by senior managers. (Simpkin, 1989, p. 160)

The end?

The paradox of the 1990s is the apparent ubiquity of the rhetoric of radicalism at a time when the radical spirit seems to have long evaporated. To explain this paradox, we have to examine the convergence of different political trends in the peculiar ideological climate of the times.

The wider political context was set by the onset of the slump in the West shortly after the collapse of the Soviet Union and the Eastern bloc, and the ending of the Cold War. The resulting combination of social stasis and political exhaustion, with the attenuation of class allegiances and conflicts and the dissolution of traditional collectivities (affecting the right as well as the left), had a highly disorienting effect at all levels of society.

One thing that unites people today is the conviction that society is falling apart. At every level, there is a perception of social disintegration, of a growth in crime and a decline in civility, of a collapse of discipline in schools and an apparently unstoppable trend towards the breakdown of the family. The widespread sense of living in a society out of control leads inexorably to the quest for new ways of regulating society and of containing disintegrative trends. It has rapidly become apparent that traditional methods no longer work and no amount of sermonising about Victorian values or Blair-style homilies about family values is going to restore their influence.

One of the most significant trends of the past few years has been the deployment of formerly radical themes in a new framework of regulation.The use of the term 'empowerment' and the promotion of 'anti-discriminatory' practice in social work illustrate this trend.

Writing in 1991, Ward and Mullender commented that 'empowerment' had become such a 'bandwagon' term over the previous decade that it risked becoming meaningless. Emerging, as we have seen, in the US radical movement of the 1960s, the concept of empowerment enjoyed a new lease of life in the 1970s as an expression of right-wing commitment to liberate the individual through unleashing market forces. These trends now merged in a common hostility to the state as a barrier to individuality, creativity and enterprise.

What, then, does empowerment now mean? It implies an individualistic conception of power, which, by reducing social relationships to the interpersonal level, obscures the real power relations in society. Thus the playground bully appears as a major public menace, while the state, the real seat of power in society, appears powerless. Confusing the problem, empowerment offers illusory solutions. Measures of support or counselling make coping and surviving the ultimate objective. This is the crux of empowerment: once the perspective of social change is eliminated, just getting by becomes the zenith of aspirations (for an illustration of a parallel process in the sphere of health, see Wainwright, 1996).

Empowerment also means inviting people to participate in decisions over which they have no control. Thus, for example, parents are said to be empowered by being invited to attend child protection case conferences; they thus become complicit in measures of state intervention in their family life decided on by professionals and the police. Applicants for community care are empowered by the fact that their designated social worker is also the manager of a devolved budget which is limited by criteria quite independent of the applicant's particular needs.

Too often, empowerment means reconciling people to being powerless. For radical social work, this is the ultimate irony: in essence, it means returning to the traditional model of social work. According to Chris Jones, for all its 'rhetoric about user involvement and participation', social work 'has never been so antagonistic towards or dismissive of its clients' (Jones, 1996). In this climate, the élitist and paternalistic elements inherent in the concept of empowerment in its American origins came to the fore.

When, in November 1988, CCETSW adopted its anti-racist statement, it may not have examined the form of words chosen very carefully. This position had, however, in substance, already been adopted by the BASW, the profession's leading body, and the statement reflected the prevailing consensus (Bamford, 1990, p. 60).

In one of the few critical commentaries on CCETSW's anti-discriminatory policy to be written before the 1992–93 furore, David Webb noted 'an ironic resonance with the strident tendency in the Conservative party' in the council's 'claim to occupy the moral high ground'. He characterised the new morality as a form of puritanism, with 'an unswerving faith in the worth of certain actions':

> Judgement, censure, righteousness and watchfulness – all of which must perforce attend anti-sexism and anti-racism if they are to succeed – are also the defining attributes of the ideal-typical puritan. To the puritan falls the heavy obligation of practising extreme strictness in matters of morals and a developed sensitivity to breeches in the correct code of behaviour or thought. (Webb, 1990-91a, pp. 151–2)

The radical commitment to liberation appeared to have been transformed into a mechanism for regulation.

Given the subsequent furore over Paper 30 and its anti-racist appendix, a casual observer might be forgiven for losing sight of the main objective of the document: to promote a model of social work training with 'much greater employer involvement in training and assessment' (Cannan, 1994/95, p. 11). It marked the latest stage in

CCETSW's drive to subordinate social work education to the concerns of management, to marginalise academic social science and to elevate vocational training ('competencies model') over the pursuit of intellectual excellence. Cannan comments on how 'equal opportunities language and principles are used in a new way' to promote 'populist and anti-academic prejudices' and to 'encourage individualistic rather than egalitarian solutions'.

Conclusion

In a more recent article, Webb draws attention to the way in which 'exhortations to repudiate discrimination sit alongside what is in effect an endorsement of neo-liberalism' (Webb, 1996, p. 186). He endorses Brewster's view that CCETSW has become 'an almost perfectly designed vehicle' for the conservative modernisation of social work (Brewster, 1992). It is difficult to avoid the conclusion that, in addition to providing a mechanism for regulation, CCETSW's anti-discriminatory policy also offers a radical image for a highly conformist agency.

As for radical social work, Simpkin's judgement has proved prescient: ' while radical practice has in some ways become more integrated, radicalism itself has become diluted and fragmented' (Simpkin, 1989, pp. 171–2).

Further reading

Bailey, R. and Brake, M. (eds) (1975) *Radical Social Work* (London, Edward Arnold).

> The foundation text of the radical social work movement, edited by two key activists.

Cannan, C. (1994/95) 'Enterprise culture, professional socialisation and social work education in Britain', *Critical Social Policy*, **42**, Winter, pp. 5–19.

> A comprehensive critique of current trends in social work education by a veteran of the radical social work movement.

Dominelli, L. (1997) *Anti-racist Social Work: A Challenge for White Practitioners and Educators*, 2nd edn (London, Macmillan).

> The case for anti-racist social work in the 1980s by one of its leading advocates.

Jones, C. (1996a) 'Anti-intellectualism and the peculiarities of social work education', in Parton, N. (ed.) *Social Theory, Social Change and Social Work* (London, Routledge).

A spirited attack on the philistinism of CCETSW by one of the most consistent defenders of the radical tradition against the imperatives of managerialism.

Langan, M. and Lee, P. (1989) *Radical Social Work Today* (London, Routledge).

A review of radical social work from the perspective of the late 1980s, by two survivors of the early movement.

18

Feminist social work

JOAN ORME

Introduction and context

It might be assumed that, because social work is a female profession with its work being predominantly by women with women, it is at the very least woman-centred, if not totally accepting of feminist approaches. To assess how far social work has incorporated feminist analyses, it is necessary to explore feminist theories and to identify how these have contributed to developments in social work practice.

Research indicates that while the majority of staff employed in social services are female, a minority of senior management posts are held by women. Also, women were more likely to be unqualified or manual workers (Nottage, 1991). Most social work is undertaken with women, either as clients in their own right or as part of an infra-structure on which agencies depend to support services. Older women, women with disabilities or mental health problems and women in the criminal justice system receive services directly. More often, women are users of social services in their role as mothers or carers of older people, those who are sick, disabled people or those with mental health problems. In the criminal justice system, women are sometimes the focus of intervention simply because they are partners of delinquent males.

Despite the predominance of women as both providers and users of social services, a gendered perspective of both the profession of social work and service provision is relatively recent. Early studies by men included an historical and contextual approach to women's employment in statutory social work (Walton, 1975; Howe, 1986) but did not address the organisation and impact of service delivery. While acknowledged by the editor to be idiosyncratic, *Sex, Gender and Care Work* (Horobin, 1987) attempted to address the differential responses to women and men, and the constructions of masculinity and femininity implicit in legislation and policy which impacts on social work practice. However, none of these could be said to represent emergent feminist social work theory or practice.

The dual focus on women as direct users and as providers of care and support has led social work to be concerned with the 'condition' of being a woman, with an emphasis on explanations and expectations of female roles and behaviour. Traditionally, such explanations of service users have been gender neutral or have involved stereotypical views of women and men. Feminist analyses of social work have argued for greater attention to the conditions which women experience. For example, the economic position of women has meant that they are traditionally amongst the poorest in society. Although the participation of women in the labour force is increasing, their earnings are consistently lower than those of men (Central Statistical Office, 1995). Also, because of child care and other responsibilities, when women are not in paid work their entitlement to benefit or their dependence on male earners means that they constitute the poorest in society. Such socio-economic conditions often mean that women become dependent upon social services or are caught up in the web of service provision and regulatory practices. However, social workers rarely see the focus of their work with women as the alleviation of their poverty.

Attention to both the condition of being a woman and the conditions that women experience has been a feature of feminist analyses of social work since the 1970s. Initially associated with the radical critique (Statham, 1978; Wilson, 1980), a shared concern of both feminist thought and women in social work was the family and women's role. However, feminism was critical of women social workers, questioning whether they worked in a women-centred way. It was argued that opportunities for advice-giving led them, at best to reinforce roles as carers based on gendered stereotypes, and at worse to pathologise the women who were in touch with social work agencies, in relation to both their own problems and the problems of those for whom they had responsibility (Dale and Foster, 1986). While plotting the treatment of women on both sides of the social work encounter, and recognising the equal attention to the personal and the political, Brook and Davis (1985) eschew the notion of synthesising feminist theory for social work, suggesting that this would both institutionalise and marginalise feminist theory, thus negating its dynamism and creativity. This chapter argues that an articulation of feminist social work has occurred during the past decade, drawing on substantive feminist theory and providing a critique of mainstream social work. The contribution has to some extent been marginalised, but the influence is growing. In providing opportunities to understand and privilege the experiences of women, feminist theory has also contributed a reflexivity, a way of responding to the conditions of women drawing on a notion of a feminist social work praxis which demands attention from both women and men workers, and sees as its project understanding the situations of both women and men.

Attention to these issues does not mean that there is a consensus, nor are relevant writing and research confined to social work literature. Research in related disciplines (for example, criminological and psychiatric literature), as well as the traditional social work preserves of child care and other caring roles, has provided a focus on women's condition(s), and feminist social work, or women-centred practice, is now included in standard texts on social policy, welfare and health care. Work in the area of domestic violence (Hanmer and Maynard, 1987), child abuse (Hudson, 1992) and women offenders (Carlen and Worrall, 1987) has implications for social work practice. Dedicated texts have emerged (Dominelli and McLeod, 1989; Hanmer and Statham, 1988) identifying what is central and distinctive about feminist social work, providing both analysis and practice guidance. Significantly, feminist approaches are now addressing working with men (Cavanagh and Cree, 1996).

In the discourse of social work theory, feminist social work is described alternatively as a movement to raise consciousness and give women control of their lives (Howe, 1987) or as an analysis of oppression and modes of empowerment – for women (Payne, 1991). Such descriptions identify limitations of feminist social work theory for women who are providers and users of social work services. This chapter will, therefore, attempt to identify the contribution that feminist theories have made to social work practice, defining or clarifying distinctions between, for example women-centred and feminist practice. In doing this, it will address the critiques of feminist social work practice, arguing that it has both provided a commentary on mainstream social work and contributed to practice developments which have enhanced the profession of social work.

Feminist theories for social work

Feminist thought and its relevance for social work practice has been construed in a number of ways, but there are points of congruence between, for example, liberal, Marxist, radical and socialist (Wearing, 1986) and liberal reformist, separatist and socialist (Dale and Foster, 1986). In these analyses of the 1980s, there was agreement about the source of women's oppression, described alternatively as men or patriarchy. During the 1990s, postmodernism has precipitated a challenge to this analysis. The separate and cohesive category of women has been reframed by some feminist authors who argue that, to avoid essentialist notions of femininity and denying class, cultural and other differences, diversities within the category 'woman' have to be accepted. If there is no single category 'woman', there can be no single category 'man' (Butler, 1990). For social work, this has created both a crisis and a development. Some see postmodernism as part of a (white) male academic backlash against feminist thought and action (Hester *et al.*, 1996). Others see it as an opportunity for feminism to inform working with men, to challenge masculinist assumptions and to recognise the oppressions of patriarchy rather than expecting women to change their own conditions (Cavanagh and Cree, 1996).

This moves us ahead rapidly, but identifying the diversity of thought at this point helps to reflect on the correlation between feminist theory and social work practice. Any form of theorising is of limited value to social work if the understandings gained do not inform ways of intervening in the lives of service users to bring about some form of positive change. For feminism, the challenge is to identify how the analysis of both the nature and the source of women's oppression assist in addressing issues of empowering women through social work practice and interventions.

Liberal critiques

Liberal feminist approaches were concerned with equal rights for women and working towards equality opportunity to choose, seeing oppression as structural, linked to women's participation. This ignored the fact that, for some women, the actual choices or alternatives might be limited by, for example, a lack of child-care facilities. More fundamentally, the organisation of state welfare institutions such as benefit systems, housing policies and social services departments militates against any real opportunities for women to participate, if that is their choice. A more pertinent analysis reflects the failure to recognise the different experiences of women and the different oppressions precipitated by class, race and sexuality (hooks, 1984a).

Liberal strategies for intervention, while being criticised as individualist, short term and reformist, were attractive to social workers working constantly with the need to produce immediate solutions and imbued with a history of individual casework as a method of intervention. They focused on structural change but continued to regard women in their traditional roles and fulfilling caring functions.

Radical critiques

A more radical approach had two sources. Marxist feminism criticised orthodox Marxism as having ignored the particular position of women and argued that, whilst women and working-class men share a domination based on a class system, emphasis on monogamous marriage and the underpinning of the patriarchal family as the economic unit of society further affected women's situation. The welfare state sought to keep women in the role of housewife, mother and carer, and, as employees of that welfare state, social workers themselves were purveyors of the repression of the state (Wilson, 1980).

Marxist feminism drew attention to the oppressive function of individualised casework which pathologised women's problems, seeing the cause of their personal or socio-economic problems as being within the women themselves, their incapacity to manage resources or their propensity for depression being directly related to biological explanations, accepting an essentialist construction of definitions of gender. Women were assessed in isolation from interpersonal and interfamilial dynamics; their social situation and support networks were not considered. They were seen as the cause of the problem and the source of the solution – if they were considered at all.

Suggestions for practice include setting up collective self-help organisations which would evolve out of consciousness-raising, leading to collective political action outside state welfare provision. These suggestions confused women social workers who, at one level, agreed with the meta-analysis but wondered how to proceed in day-to-day practice when confronted with the immediate and urgent problems of women as wives, mothers and carers, defined within the welfare state and who, as Wilson rightly identified, have their powers and resources prescribed within the welfare state.

The limitations of Marxist concentration on class and the economic system as reflecting patriarchal underpinnings led some feminists to establish a radical perspective which identified the source of women's oppression as the social institution of gender. For social work, the recognition of sexual politics (Firestone, 1971; Millet, 1972) resonated because it emphasised the role of male power in interpersonal relationships within the family, which contribute to women's sense of personal and economic inferiority and helplessness. This analysis facilitated the identification of, and attempts to understand, domestic violence and sexual abuse. It also challenged heterosexist assumptions of state services which were predicated on women being in relationships with men. However, the solutions, which revolved around separating out from men, were of limited value to women in social work, both workers and users, who were in relationships with men and might have neither the inclination nor the means to ascribe to personal or political separatism.

Socialist critiques

It is because of its acceptance of both class oppression and male privilege as an explanation of women's oppression, seeing patriarchy and
capitalism as interrelated, that socialist feminism is identified as
giving a fuller analysis of the position of women in the context of
social work (Dale and Foster, 1986; Wearing, 1986). In keeping in
mind both class and gender, socialist feminism highlights the major
forces of society which contribute to the powerlessness of women.
Women social workers are subject to the same oppressive forces as
the women with whom they are working. This can be a source of
collective power but can also mean that the women workers are as
powerless as the women with whom they are working. In acknowledging that socialist feminism allows women to explore their
common and contradictory interests, Dale and Foster prepared the
ground for the analysis of women-centred practice in social work
(Hanmer and Statham, 1988).

Feminist social work practice

Early attempts to develop social work practice based on feminist
analysis recognised that women had been absent from social work
discourse (Hale, 1983). In identifying women's inequality in relation
to men, the initial focus for social work had to be at the micro level –
the enhancement of female clients' lives. Raising consciousness,
changing assumptions about, and perceptions of, women whilst
acknowledging structural oppression were themes reflected in
prescriptions for women-centred practice. These included codes of
practice which recognised the power of the social worker in individual interpersonal relationships (Hanmer and Statham, 1988) or
those which focused on constructing an anti-sexist environment and
mode of service delivery (NAPO, 1990). Maintaining a focus on the
individual, interventions often provided services for women in their
role as mothers and/or carers, for example mother and toddler
groups or prisoners' wives groups. A more sophisticated analysis of
feminist contributions to social work recognised that there had to be
moves beyond the individual as the focus for intervention and
change. Feminist social work requires the creation of social conditions
more reflective of feminist aims (Dominelli and McLeod, 1989). It is in
this approach that feminist social work has made its greatest contribution to social work practice by articulating debates about power
and its use and abuse in interpersonal relationships. Work in the area
of child abuse has highlighted that abuse can take many forms and
can be perpetrated by both women and men, but that interventions

must empower those who are oppressed, without any assumptions about the necessity or the therapeutic value of certain kinds of familial arrangement (Hudson, 1992). It is this concern for the way in which services are offered, as well as the actual services provided, which is the hallmark of feminism. For example, Carlen's work on a feminist jurisprudence starts from a recognition that women are adversely treated by the paternalism of the criminal justice system. In arguing for the appropriate treatment for women, she recognises that dehumanising and punitive custodial sentences are not appropriate for women or men (Carlen, 1989). For men to become less violent, there needs to be less violent treatment. Such approaches are not unproblematic. The urge to punish those men who have been violent to women and children, and the tensions brought about by finite resources which precipitate the need to choose between services for women and those for men, are not ducked by feminism. In putting them firmly on the agenda, feminist social work has been both influential, but also subject to criticism.

Issues

The most consistent criticism has been that adopting a separatist approach detracts from the need to permeate all practice. Feminist social work has been described as a form of crude reductionist sociology, with contradictory theories which create a hierarchy of oppression imposed by a form of ideological imperialism (Sibeon, 1991). In concentrating on the oppression of women, feminist social work is accused of avoiding or negating class, race and the imperative to work with men. It has also been suggested that insights into causes of oppression do not necessarily clarify how to intervene, that feminist theory has not informed social work practice (Payne, 1991). However, as we have seen, this is not the case. Whilst early women-centred practice focused on women's experiences, feminist approaches have provided substantive critiques of all social work activity.

The challenges, however, presented to workers by both women-centred practice and feminist social work practice should not be underestimated. Early critiques of social work by feminists were said to be simplistic in failing to recognise the care/control dichotomy present in much of social work practice (Wise, 1990). For example, women-centred practice presented an analysis that women are oppressed, and that, to avoid further oppression, social workers must accept women's accounts (Hanmer and Statham, 1988). In arguing that women do commit acts of violence and abuse, and girls do sometimes fantasise, Wise (1990) suggests that unquestioning acceptance is naïve and simplistic and can lead to essentialist interpretations of male/female behaviour which disadvantage women in all aspects of life. For example, arguing that women should always have custody of children could be seen to be reaffirming the myth of the naturalness of motherhood and explanations of depression which concentrate on the negative experiences of women, and fail to valorise women's strength. This does not mean that women should be blamed or punished, or that women-only facilities should not be provided. It is possible to listen to what women have done but to accept them, to recognise and work with inconsistencies, uncertainties and contradictions which are part of women's lived experience. This experience includes that, for good or for ill, women are in social situations where their needs have to be balanced against the needs of others, especially children, or that, because of socialisation or social situations, women experience conditions which severely limit their capacity to change.

The transformational nature of feminist social work, as opposed to women-centred practice, is to recognise the contradictions and, through a process of individualisation, accept that being a woman (be that a black woman or disabled woman) is part of the person-in-environment perspective core to all social work practice which resonates with the feminist claim that the personal is political (Collins, 1986). What is significant and has to be worked with is how individual women experience their situation. To tell a woman user she is oppressed is no more liberating than labelling her as depressed, unless there are ways of changing the situation. Having recognised the dilemmas and clarified the accounts, it is also necessary to be open about the social control contained in the social work role. This control often emanates from the legislative framework which reinforces gendered stereotypes or appears to circumscribe the work that has to be done. Such constraints are not unique to feminist social work, as Braye and Preston-Shoot discuss in Chapter 5 of this volume. Feminist social work, along with other paradigms for empowering practice, has sought to critique both the process of framing the legislation, and the interpretation of that legislation into service delivery (Dominelli and McLeod, 1989).

What is important, therefore, is the way in which situations are worked with, the praxis which incorporates feminist analysis. It is appropriate for feminists to intervene to protect vulnerable people, whoever they may be. The notion of praxis requires feminists to be part of the debate about acceptable standards of conduct, ensuring that these are not constructed on stereotypical gendered lines and arguing for the inclusion of users, especially women who constitute the majority of users, in the decisions (Wise, 1990). Hence feminist social work contributes to the transformation of social and structural relations.

The substantive issue for feminist social work is, therefore, to gain recognition as a force within social work, as a theory or set of theories contributing to an understanding of social work – as paradigmatic ways of understanding patriarchal culture (Collins, 1986) – or as a set of specific practices which differ in some way from other theories and modes of intervention without becoming marginalised (Dominelli and McLeod, 1989; Hudson, 1989).

Despite support for gender issues in the social work education curriculum (Phillipson, 1991), little progress is being made in social work training. Gender is often considered only in the context of anti-discriminatory practice, with no specific training on gender aware-ness, or any permeation of the curriculum with understandings of specific oppressions of women, nor as a specific social work practice (Kirwan, 1994). The twin themes of commonality and diversity explored in feminist social work literature (Hanmer and Statham, 1988) are not always helpful. Recognising commonalities can be expe-rienced as treating women as an homogenous group, reinforcing notions that women are the source of, and solution to, the problems they experience. Acknowledging diversities between women and users, and arguing that these should be transcended, denies the power relationship between these groups of women (White, 1995). Whilst recognising commonality as a way of expressing empathy (Hanmer and Statham, 1988), doing so raises crises over shared infor-mation. Lesbian women workers, in particular, may feel unable to disclose or share information about themselves for a variety of reasons. That feminist social work approaches have not permeated all practice is evidenced by (a lack of) appreciation of diversity. One study, of pro-feminist women workers, found that the traditional labelling of client groups persisted. Women as clients were identified predominantly in the child-care field, with no acknowlegement of the specific needs and oppressions of older women, women with disabil-ities or those with mental health problems (White, 1995).

Social work needs to respond to the richness of feminist theo-rising. Exploration of feminism as an ontology (Stanley, 1990) recog-nises that not all women share the state of being, nor does the state of being exist in relation to something essentially female, but to the social construction of 'women'. This construction, and the oppres-sions identified within the construction, recognises many forms of women's existence or condition which are incorporated in it, and indeed challenges the universalism of the social construction, thus allowing for the separate and different experiences of black women, lesbian women, disabled women and older women, for example, to be explored within and contribute to such a notion of ontology. More than most paradigms, the ideas explored in this chapter demonstrate that feminist social work has been reflexive in responding to the experiences and criticisms of those whose position it seeks to explore, explain and exhibit to ensure that women are both made visible within the organisation of service provision and empowered by individual interpersonal interventions. This emphasis on the transformational is now evident in debates within feminist social work about working with men.

The recognition of men's experience can lead to a deflection from focusing on the oppressions of women and undermine research which has stressed the material realities of women's lives and men's behaviour in these (Hester *et al.*, 1996). However, unless a dialogue occurs, unless work is done with men as users of services, as potential carers and as perpetrators of the abuse of women, there will be no challenge to constructions of masculine identity. Unless feminist theory and practice are used to undertake this challenge, there will be little change in the conditions and behaviour which women have tolerated.

Conclusion

Feminist thought in social work practice has moved from the woman-centred analysis that it is for women, by women and with women. That is not to say such a stance is not valid: women-only space is important, and women's thoughts and experiences should be actively heard. In working with women, feminist social work practitioners are only too aware that any one person's condition is influenced by the behaviour and expectations of others. For women users of social services, their lives are defined and constrained by malestream thinking and organisation and male behaviour. To focus solely on women, to attempt to empower them, leads to dilemmas, conflict and frustration, and holds them responsible for change in their own circumstances and those of others. It concentrates on their feminine condition but does not address the conditions which oppress them. Feminist praxis recognises the diverse experience of all users of social work services and seeks to challenge and transform policy, practice and the organisation of the service delivery which constrains people in gender-specific roles or oppresses them by the inappropriate exercise of power.

Further reading

Cavanagh, K. and Cree, V. E. (eds) (1996) *Working With Men: Feminism and Social Work, The State of Welfare* (London, Routledge).

A collection of practice accounts which explore the contribution that feminism has made to working with men.

Dominelli, L. and McLeod, E. (1989) *Feminist Social Work* (London, Macmillan).

An exploration of feminist approaches to both social work interventions and the organisations which deliver the services.

Hanmer, J. and Statham, D. (1988) *Women and Social Work: Towards a Woman-centred Practice* (London, Macmillan).

An introductory text which focuses on women-centred practice, offering opportunities for women workers to explore commonalities and diversities.

Langan, M. and Day, L. (eds) (1992) *Women, Oppression and Social Work: Issues in Anti-discriminatory Practice* (London, Routledge).

Focusing on women, a comprehensive edited collection of practice accounts of interventions in the lives of women by women workers, the complexities and the consequences.

19

Anti-oppressive practice

BEVERLEY BURKE and PHILOMENA HARRISON

Introduction

The complex nature of oppression is witnessed in the lives of people who are marginalised in this society. As social work practitioners, we have a moral, ethical and legal responsibility to challenge inequality and disadvantage. Historically, the profession, in attempting to understand, explain and offer solutions to the difficulties experienced by groups and individuals, has drawn from, amongst others, the disciplines of sociology, psychology, history, philosophy and politics. This multidisciplined theoretical framework, informed by anti-oppressive principles, provides social workers with a tool to understand and respond to the complexity of the experience of oppression.

This chapter explores how a theorised social work practice informed by anti-oppressive principles can be sensitively and effectively used to address the inequalities of oppression that determine the life chances of service users.

The writings of black feminists (hooks, 1981, 1984b, 1989, 1991; Lorde, 1984; Neale-Hurston, 1986; Morrison, 1987; Jordan, 1989; Hill-Collins, 1990; Russell, 1990; James and Busia, 1993) provides a rich literature that is theoretically based and informed by the disciplines of psychology, sociology, politics, history and anthropology. It incorporates existentialist ideas, liberatory educational principles, community activism and personal experiences provided by both autobiographical and fictional accounts. It thus expands understandings of oppression and lays the foundations for the exploration of the experience of power, powerlessness and oppression.

Black feminist thought is a dynamic perspective, derived out of 'diverse lived experiences', that not only analyses human interactions based on principles of equality, but also considers the interconnections that exist between the major social divisions of class, race, gender, disability, sexuality and age as they impact on the individual, family and community.

Black feminist thought has helped us to understand ourselves as black women. It has enabled us to make sense of the patterns of domination and oppression which characterise our professional and personal lives. We hold the view that personal experiences are inextricably linked to and determined by social, cultural, political and economic relationships within specific geographical and historical situations. This process of location allows us to challenge those who see only our race, gender or class, failing to understand that it is the interconnections between the social divisions to which we belong that defines who we are (Lorde, 1984).

The finding of solutions to and explanations of oppressive situations and practices poses a real challenge for those committed to making a difference. A starting point would, therefore, have to be a clear understanding of what is meant by anti-oppressive practice.

What is anti-oppressive practice?

There are a number of definitions, ranging in complexity and length. Anti-oppressive practice has been debated by a number of writers, whose works are informed by differing perspectives (Thompson, 1993; Clifford, 1994a; Braye and Preston-Shoot, 1995; Dalrymple and Burke, 1995; Featherstone and Fawcett, 1995; Dominelli, 1996). However, for the transformative potency of anti-oppressive practice to be realised, the reader needs to be critically aware that the choice of words used to define reveals not only the value and ideological base of the definer, but also the nature of the practice that will emanate from that definition.

Anti-oppressive practice is a dynamic process based on the changing complex patterns of social relations. It is, therefore, important that a definition is informed by research within academic institutions, practitioner research and the views of service users. For the purposes of this chapter, we provide below a 'definition' (with all the attendant problems of defining) which incorporates points already discussed providing a framework to clarify and inform practice.

Clifford (1995, p. 65) uses the term *anti-oppressive*:

> to indicate an explicit evaluative position that constructs social divisions (especially 'race', class, gender, disability, sexual orientation and age) as matters of broad social structure, at the same time as being personal and organisational issues. It looks at the use and abuse of power not only in relation to individual or organisational behaviour, which may be overtly, covertly or indirectly racist, classist, sexist and so on, but also in relation to broader social structures for example, the health, educational, political and economic, media

and cultural systems and their routine provision of services and rewards for powerful groups at local as well as national and international levels. These factors impinge on people's life stories in unique ways that have to be understood in their socio-historical complexity.

Within this definition, there is a clear understanding of the use and abuse of power within relationships on personal, family, community, organisational and structural levels. These levels are not mutually exclusive – they are interconnected, shaping and determining social reality. Clifford, informed by the writings of black feminist and other 'non-dominant perspectives' (Clifford, 1995), has formulated the following anti-oppressive principles, which provide the foundation for a social work assessment that is theorised and empowering:

- *Social difference.* Social differences arise because of disparities of power between the dominant and dominated social groups. The major divisions are described in terms of race, gender, class, sexual preference, disability and age. Other differences, such as those of religion, region, mental health and single parenthood, exist and interact with the major divisions, making the understanding and the experience of oppression a complex matter.

- *Linking personal and political.* Personal biographies are placed within a wider social context and the individual's life situation is viewed in relation to social systems such as the family, peer groups, organisations and communities. For example, the problems associated with ageing are not solely due to the individual but should be understood in relation to the ageist ideologies policies and practices that exist within the social environment in which the individual is located.

- *Power.* Power is a social concept which can be used to explore the public and private spheres of life (Barker and Roberts, 1993). In practice, power can be seen to operate at the personal and structural levels. It is influenced by social, cultural, economic and psychological factors. All these factors need to be taken into account in any analysis of how individuals or groups gain differential access to resources and positions of power.

- *Historical and geographical location.* Individual life experiences and events are placed within a specific time and place, so that these experiences are given meaning within the context of prevailing ideas social facts and cultural differences.

- *Reflexivity/mutual involvement.* Reflexivity is the continual consideration of how values, social difference and power affect the interactions between individuals. These interactions are to be understood not only in psychological terms, but also as a matter of sociology, history, ethics and politics.

The above principles relate to each other, interconnecting and overlapping at all times. Working from a perspective that is informed by anti-oppressive principles provides an approach that begins to match the complex issues of power, oppression and powerlessness that determine the lives of the people who are recipients of social care services. An understanding of these principles brings with it a funda-mental transformation in the relationship that exists between the assessment of a situation and the nature of the action that is required to change the existing state of affairs.

The driving force of anti-oppressive practice is *the act of chal-lenging*. Opportunities for change are created by the process of the challenge. Challenges are not always successful and are often painful for the person or group being challenged or challenging. A challenge, at its best, involves changes at macro and micro levels. If anti-oppres-sive practice is to provide appropriate and sensitive services that are needs-led rather than resource-driven, it has to embody:

> a person centred philosophy; and egalitarian value system concerned with reducing the deleterious effects of structural inequalities upon people's lives; a methodology focusing on both process and outcome; and a way of structuring relationships between individuals that aims to empower users by reducing the negative effects of social hierar-chies on their interaction and the work they do together. (Dominelli, 1994, p. 3)

Work in welfare organisations is constrained by financial, social, legislative and organisational policies. Social workers operating within such an environment will inevitably face conflicting and competing demands on their personal and professional resources. The use of anti-oppressive principles offers the worker a way of responding to and managing these sometimes hostile and disempow-ering situations which affect both worker and user.

The dynamic link between theory and practice will be demon-strated through the use of a case scenario, written in autobiographical form. It is through the action of practice that theories, principles and methods come alive. By reading the following scenario, you the reader are directly involved in a young black woman's 'lived experi-ences'. Through the very act of reading, you become both *participant* and *observer*. You begin to start the process of critical thinking, reflec-tion and analysis of her life, bringing with you to the interpretation of her story your values, assumptions and practice wisdom. It is impor-tant to remember, when reading Amelia's story, that it contains the stories of others – her son, the professionals involved, her community networks and her family.

A decision was made by a social services department that changed the life of a family. A young, single, 19-year-old black woman was told that the care plan regarding her 20-month-old son was that of adoption. The decision was based on evidence from extended social work involvement, which was ultimately influenced by information obtained from reports written by a white male psychologist and a white female psychiatrist.

Amelia's story as told to a friend

Leaving home at sixteen, I spent most of my time trying to find a place to live and make ends meet. I relied on shoplifting and my friends to survive. At seventeen I met a man who was twenty seven. We lived together; when I became pregnant, things began to change. He became violent towards me.

I was placed in a hostel for mothers with children, I wasn't very happy at the hostel, I disliked the racist name calling – no one in charge did anything about it. Drugs were easily available. I tried heroin.

My baby was born three months prematurely. While he was in hospital he nearly died, I was really frightened. I visited him every day for the two months he was in hospital. I kept asking for social work help. I needed money to travel to and from the hospital and I needed someone to talk to. The nurses asked for help for me. I never got any.

I returned to the hostel, with my son. He became ill. I took drugs to help me to stay awake so that I could look after him. Everything seemed too much. When he was in hospital I told one of the nurses that I had 'tapped' him when he would not stop screaming. They told social services. So when I tried to leave the hospital with him I was stopped. My son was placed in respite care for a couple of weeks I was told that I could have him back when I felt better.

When I wanted him back they said that they had to do an assessment to see if I was able to care for him. I began to scream and shout. I begged them to give my baby back, but they placed him with white foster carers; I did not agree, but there were no black foster carers. I saw him every day.

It was decided that I needed to have a psychological and psychiatric assessment. I felt that I needed someone to talk to. I know I am not mad. The social workers spent time with me and wrote a report saying I should have my son back. My son was put on a Supervision Order for a year.

I moved into a new house. I told my social worker that I really did not feel ready to live on my own. The social worker arranged for a child-minder two days a week and a home help. I wanted a nursery place.

I was lonely in the new house. I went out a lot. I told someone I knew that I had tried six months earlier, whilst on drugs, to harm my son. She said we should tell the social services and they would help me sort it all out. I agreed, they took my son into care again.

A month went by. They were trying to find a place where I could live with my son and get the help I needed. They never really told me anything. I felt very frustrated. It was hard being without my son.

One day, after access, I did not return my son to the carer. I kept him overnight, they found me the next morning. They took him away. Now I can only see him for two hours a day at the foster carers, and at weekends.

I cannot think straight. I cannot be upset or depressed as this would go against me. All the time I was told that I was capable of looking after my son and that they were working on us being together. They knew I loved and wanted him very much. But now they have told me that they have plans for adoption. I am so angry and frightened, but I cannot be angry or this would upset the workers. My son has had so many changes.

I am not sure what to think or do. Should I start thinking about when I will not have him? I know that I need someone to talk to about all the things that have happened to me. But I cannot do this without my son. Why do they need to take him away when I know I can look after him with help. I do not know how I can fight any of this.

Theory into practice

Using anti-oppressive principles, which incorporates challenging as a central process, we will analyse Amelia's story, highlighting issues and dilemmas that workers face in attempting to empower a service user.

The anti-oppressive principle of *reflexivity* demands that workers continually consider the ways in which their own social identity and values affect the information they gather. This includes their understanding of the social world as experienced by themselves and those with whom they work.

Involvement in Amelia's life is not a neutral event. It is determined by the interaction between the personal biographies of the worker and Amelia, and will be expressed in the power relationships that arise from their membership of differing social divisions.

For example, a white male social worker brings to the situation a dynamic that will reproduce the patterns of oppression to which black women are subjected in the wider society. In this scenario, Amelia feels she is silenced. Her plea for 'someone to talk to', to be listened to and taken seriously, is neither understood nor acted upon. This is highlighted in the powerlessness expressed in the telling of her story.

The challenge to you, the worker, is to reflect on your social divisions membership, your personal and professional biography and the impact that this will have on your involvement with Amelia. Are you the right worker for her? If the answer is no, the challenge is not only to find a more appropriate worker but to look to ways in which you may minimise the potential for oppressive practice at the point of referral. In and through this process of thinking and reflecting, which should take place in supervision, team discussions and interactions with service users, you will begin to work in an anti-oppressive way.

Society is divided along the major divisions of race, class, gender, sexual preference, disability and age. There are also other divisions which occur as a result of inequality and discrimination, such as poverty, geographical location, mental distress and employment status. The *social difference* principle is based on an understanding of how the divisions interconnect and shape the lives of people.

Amelia is young, black, unemployed, female, of a particular class background, living in poverty and a single parent. Yet in the scenario, she is seen merely as a young woman suffering domestic violence and in need of accommodation. Her needs as a black woman from a particular background with a specific history are not fully considered. Amelia's experience of racism in the hostel compounded her overall experience of oppression, forcing her into independence before she was ready.

The challenge for you, the worker, is to understand both the specific and general nature of social division membership and how it may contribute to the individual's experience of oppression. As a worker, you must make a systematic analysis of the social division membership of all the individuals involved Amelia's life and understand the relevance of this for your intervention.

It is important to locate both Amelia's and her son's life experiences and events within an *historical and geographical context*. Those experiences need to be chronologically charted and their relevance clearly understood and applied to Amelia's story. In doing that, you, the worker, will get an accurate picture of how events within the family, community and society have influenced Amelia's current situation. Amelia's story will have been influenced by previous specific historical and geographical factors.

As the worker, you need to be aware of how prevailing ideologies have influenced legislation, agency policy and practice relating to child care, homelessness and parenting by single mothers. The challenge is to use that analysis to inform your assessment and decision-making. You need to question the agency's policies on work with homeless young women. Amelia's needs as a homeless, black young woman were never assessed with reference to research evidence which documents the oppression and lack of services faced by this specific user group.

The principle of historical and geographic context directs the worker to consider not only the individual worker's relationship with the service user, but also the team and agency practice. The following are some of the questions that need to be considered: 'How does a prevailing ideology of a mixed economy of care affect practice within the team?'; 'How does the team prioritise work with homeless young people?'; and 'How far has the historical development of service provision in the area determined current practices?' Such questions will help workers to understand what is constraining their practice. Anti-oppressive thinking moves the worker beyond the confines of agency policy and practice and directs the challenge more appropriately.

In understanding the *personal as political,* the everyday life experiences of individuals need to be located within social, cultural, political and economic structures which are historically and geographically specific. This process of location ensures that, in practice, the individual is not pathologised, and weight is given to the interconnections and interactions between that individual's story and the social systems they encounter.

Amelia, is defined in terms of the domestic violence she has experienced. The assessment is not placed in a wider context, failing to make sense of Amelia's whole life experience. You, the worker, need to take into account the structural factors that contribute to womens' experience of violence and how, for Amelia, the dimension of race and her membership of other social divisions added other layers to her experience of oppression.

The social workers' decision in the scenario to formulate a care plan which put forward adoption as a solution to Amelia's problems needs to be analysed. Their decision appears to be highly influenced by the expert evidence which focused on Amelia's psychiatric and psychological functioning. How did these assessments inform the workers' analysis of Amelia's ability to parent adequately? Here, we see a failure to locate assessment evidence within a framework that takes into account all aspects of Amelia's existence – her gender, her race, her poverty, her single parenthood – as well as making reference to assessment evidence from other professionals.

The challenge to the worker is to examine the range of evidence used in decision-making, asking questions about why any one piece of evidence is given more weight than another. Does that weighting pathologise the individual by not taking into account the assessments made by other professionals, such as the health visitor and the foster carers. For example, was the support offered by the extended family and informal community support networks considered? By ignoring the impact of oppressive social values and policies in the decision-making process, the worker can further devalue the service user's capacity to function.

In addressing *power and powerlessness*, it is essential to understand how the differential access to power shapes and determines relationships on an individual, group, community, organisational and societal level. We get a glimpse of Amelia's feelings of powerlessness when she says, 'I do not know how I can fight any of this.' Central to her powerlessness is the lack of access to many social resources. There is evidence in Amelia's story of her being denied access to the resources she feels will help her to parent effectively.

You, as the worker, need to take into account the professional and personal power (based on your particular social division membership) you hold. What power does the service user have from her previous life experiences?

How do you, as a worker, ensure that your assessment and intervention includes an analysis of power? The worker in this situation could have advocated on behalf of Amelia, working creatively to explore other options which would have supported her in her parenting. It appears that the workers ignored the personal strengths of Amelia, gained from her experiences of oppression, leading to practice which compounded her feelings of powerlessness. They failed to listen and work in partnership with Amelia.

The misuse of power by the worker culminates in a situation in which decisions can be made where the outcome labels Amelia as a non-deserving case. Amelia, however, is not alone in her powerlessness. There are clear differences of the power ascribed to the opinions of one professional group over another. It appears that extended social work practice had little impact on the overall decision regarding the future of the family. Explanations of Amelia's behaviour are reduced to the opinions of one professional group who are seen as 'expert', reducing complex explanations of her behaviour to psychology and psychiatry.

Social workers are well placed to make assessments that are theoretically informed, holistic, empowering and challenging. Anti-oppressive practice should not negate the risks posed to the child. Intervention based on anti-oppressive practice incorporates a risk and needs analysis of both mother and child.

To work effectively, it is important to have a perspective that:

- is flexible without losing focus;
- includes the views of oppressed individuals and groups;
- is theoretically informed;
- challenges and changes existing ideas and practice;
- can analyse the oppressive nature of organisational culture and its impact on practice;
- includes continuous reflection and evaluation of practice;
- has multidimensional change strategies which incorporate the concepts of networking, user involvement, partnership and participation;
- has a critical analysis of the issues of power, both personal and structural.

If the principles of anti-oppressive practice are to move the practitioners' thinking beyond agency policy and practice and make a difference, then they need to invest time and energy in the application of those principles, enabling them to systematically analyse situations and think through the action that needs to be taken. Anti-oppressive practice then moves beyond descriptions of the nature of oppression to dynamic and creative ways of working.

The principles of reflexivity, social difference, historical and geographical location, the personal as political, power and powerlessness, and the act of challenging provide a framework which can be used to inform work with people in need.

Further reading

Barn, R. (1993) *Black Children in the Public Care System* (London, Batsford).

   A research study which highlights the significance of race and racism on decisions made by social workers and on the care careers of black children.

Campion, M. J. (1995) *Who's Fit To Be a Parent?* (London, Routledge).

   This book, cutting across numerous professional boundaries and personal expertise on parenting, investigates what is deemed as fit parenting and how it is to be assessed.

Hugman, R. and Smith, D. (1995) *Ethical Issues in Social Work* (London, Routledge).

   A critical analysis of the ethical implications of recent legislation, trends in social work thought and policy such as user empowerment, feminism and anti-oppressive practice.

Humphries, B. (ed.) (1996) *Critical Perspectives on Empowerment* (Birmingham, Venture).

Interrogates the concept of empowerment and raises questions about the political context in which debates about empowerment take place.

Walker, A. (1983) *The Color Purple* (London, Women's Press).

A first-person account of domination and abuse, it is also a story of recovery and the love and support that women can offer to each other.

20

Postmodernism and discourse approaches to social work

NIGEL PARTON and WENDY MARSHALL

Introduction

The purpose of this chapter is to demonstrate that there have recently been a number of major debates in social theory associated with the notion of postmodernity that should be taken seriously by social workers. Our essential argument is that such debates provide important insights into helping us to understand and conceptualise contemporary social work in a way which can inform practice itself. While the chapter can provide no more than an introduction to the area, we hope to provide sufficient signposts for readers to find their way through an ever-expanding and increasingly complex literature in a way which they will want to take forward. In particular, we will suggest that such a way of thinking is very instructive for articulating and developing notions of reflective practice.

What is meant by postmodernity and postmodernism?

It is only in very recent years in the UK that postmodern perspectives have been drawn upon in thinking about and analysing social work (Rojek *et al.*, 1988; McBeath and Webb, 1991; Howe, 1994; Parton 1994a, 1994b; Pietroni, 1995; Aldridge, 1996; Dominelli, 1996). There is, similarly, an emerging literature in North America (Sands and Nuccio, 1992; Chambon and Irving, 1994; Pardeck *et al.*, 1994a; Pardeck *et al.*, 1994b; Pozatek, 1994; Meinert and Pardeck, 1996). In many respects, the starting point is a recognition that social work is currently experiencing a major period of change and uncertainty in its organisation and day-to-day practice such that it seems qualitatively different from what went before, thus requiring new skills and new forms of knowledge in order to practise. Social work's engagement with postmodern perspectives is a recognition that these changes and experiences are not particular to social work but reflect much wider transformations in Western societies and have been the subject of considerable and often heated debate within social theory. The significance of postmodern perspectives is that they draw attention to a number of areas of social transformation in terms of: the increasing pace of change; the emergence of new complexities and forms of fragmentation; the growing significance of difference, plurality and various political movements and strategies, and the pervasive awareness of relativities; the opening up of individual 'choice' and 'freedom'; and the increasing awareness of the socially constructed nature of existence. Perhaps more centrally, such perspectives have reactivated a question which has lain dormant in social theory for many years but which touches the heart of much social work – what kinds of human being have we become (Rose, 1996)?

At the outset, however, it is important to recognise that the terms 'postmodernity' and 'postmodernism' have been hotly contested so that it is almost impossible to impose, by definitional fiat, an agreed set of terms for the debates (Turner, 1990). While the primary concern is to consider how far and in what ways 'current times' are different from what went before, a number of commentators have argued that it is inappropriate to periodise history in this way (Heelas *et al.*, 1996), that the changes and breaks have been exaggerated (Clark, 1996) and that, rather than characterise the present in terms of the postmodern, it is better characterised as high or late modern (Giddens, 1990, 1991). It is for this reason that one of us has previously very consciously used parenthesis for the '(post)modern', pointing to a provisional and somewhat sceptical use of the term (Parton, 1994a, 1994b), and has more recently argued that postmodern interpretations are in danger of not taking the situation of actually living human actors sufficiently seriously (Parton, 1998). Even so, the debates provide an important vehicle for developing our insights into the nature of the contemporary complexities, uncertainties and experiences, and for opening up new and creative ways of thinking and acting.

Certainly, reference to the postmodern is much older than the recent fashion in social theory might suggest and in art history and aesthetic theory goes back many years (Featherstone, 1988). Similarly, a number of commentators have argued that it is important to differentiate between modernism and modernity, and postmodernism and postmodernity (Boyne and Rattansi, 1990). *Modernism* is seen to refer to the set of artistic, musical, literary and more generally aesthetic movements that emerged in Europe in the 1880s, flourished before and after World War I and became institutionalised in the academies and art galleries in post World War II Europe and America. Whilst it was preoccupied with highlighting the means of representation, the disruption of narrative, contradiction and the increasing fragmentation in subjectivity and identity, there was a tendency in most modernist projects to cling to the belief that, in principle, the deep structures of reality are knowable, and are intellectually and culturally penetrable, but require complex, inventive and self-reflexive strategies to excavate reality.

The notion of *modernity,* however, is more concerned with the rationalist thinking that emerged in the post-enlightenment period often associated with science and the form and nature of society that subsequently developed. According to Boyne and Rattansi (1990, p. 80), 'defining modernity in the terms of *uncovering,* of ripping away of disguise, of disclosing and realising the promise or threat of the future *by moving on and through where we are now* enables us to reconcile the various sides of modernity' (original emphasis). The two crucial elements of modernity are seen as the progressive union of scientific objectivity and politico-economic rationality. However, Boyne and Ratansi argue that it is important to treat modernism and modernity separately because, whilst they are inevitably linked, modernism has always constituted something of a critique of modernity. It refused to endorse any simplistic beliefs in the progressive capacity of science and technology to resolve all problems and did not hold with positivism and the idea of the integrated individual subject that provides the underpinning for the celebratory 'grand narratives' of both capitalist and socialist visions of modernity.

The term 'postmodernism' was first used in the 1930s but became increasingly used in the areas of literature, architecture, philosophy and the arts more generally from the 1960s onwards. The perspective came to particular prominence with the publication of Lyotard's *The Postmodern Condition* in 1984. While, as we have seen, many doubt whether the term has any conceptual coherence, it is perhaps united by a number of cultural projects with a self-proclaimed commitment to heterogeneity, fragmentation and difference and, perhaps most significantly, their reaction to modernist perspectives. It is also useful to distinguish between 'postmodernism', which characterises a series of broadly aesthetic projects, and 'postmodernity' which refers to an emerging social, political and cultural configuration of which postmodernism is an element.

Social work and the postmodern

Howe (1994) has usefully outlined the possible significance of such debates for social work. His central argument is that, if social work was a child of modernity, it now finds itself in a world uncertain of whether or not there are any deep and unwavering principles which define the essence of its character and hold it together as a coherent enterprise.

He suggests that not only can the emergence of social work from the mid-nineteenth century onwards be seen as a particular manifestation of the development of the modern, but also that the three traditional cornerstones of social work – *care, control* and *cure* – can be seen as particular manifestations of modernity's three great projects. He suggests that 'in its own way social work has pursued the beautiful (aesthetics), the good (ethics) and the true (science) as it attempts to bring about a pleasing quality of life and a just society by using the insights of the social sciences' (Howe, 1994, p. 518). Howe and Parton (1994a, 1994b) suggest that the high point of modern social work came in the 1970s when major attempts were made to rationalise and reorganise social work's practices, skills and approaches. This was exemplified by the creation of unified social services departments and the generic social worker at the organisational and practice level and the search for a common base for social work (Bartlett, 1970) via the development of the systems approach (Pincus and Minahan, 1973) and integrated methods (Specht and Vickery, 1977).

However, Howe suggests that contemporary social work is, in many respects, experiencing a number of features which have been characterised as symptomatic of the postmodern condition. Modernism's promise to deliver order, certainty and security has been unfulfilled, and it is increasingly felt that there are no transcendental universal criteria of truth (science), judgement (ethics) and taste (aesthetics). The overriding belief in reason and rationality is disappearing as there is a collapse of consensus related to the 'grand narratives' and their articulation of progress, emancipation and perfection, and what constitutes the centres of authority and truth. The rejection of the idea that any one theory or system of belief can ever reveal the truth, and the emphasis on the plurality of truth and 'the will to truth', captures some of the essential elements associated with postmodern approaches.

Truth takes the guise of 'truth' centred neither in God's word (as in the premodern) nor in human reason (as in the modern), but is decentred and localised so that many 'truths' are possible, dependent on different times and places. Notions of 'truth' are thus related to context and are culture specific so that there is a refusal to accept that some groups have a monopoly on what constitutes truth, beauty and the good. Relativities, uncertainties and contingencies are no longer seen as marginal and problems to be overcome as yet beyond the reach of reason, but as central and pervasive. In fact, the modern approach, rather than being humanitarian, progressive and emancipatory, is seen as invariably exploitative and repressive because of its failure to recognise difference and its reliance on totalising belief systems, be these patriarchal, capitalist or socialist.

The importance of discourse and language

These developments have contributed to new ways of understanding the self in context which question the central assumptions of human nature and models of the person encoded in professional knowledge and derived from the modernist projects of sociology and psychology (Barrett and Phillips, 1992). Language is seen as central: 'An understanding of the part that language plays in the formation of human selves, human thought and human subjectivity underpins the post modern perspective' (Howe, 1994, p. 521). Instead of being described as a tool that simply reflects objects, language is seen as mediating and constituting all that is 'known'. Reality is not just obtrusive, but is also embedded within interpretation and 'language games' (Lyotard, 1984), so that 'truth' is a product of language. We cannot transcend the influence of interpretation and assume that reality is simply waiting to be discovered, it is constituted and constructed within language.

If it is the way in which language is structured that provides us with the basis for our notion of self-hood, personal identity and the way in which we relate to social 'reality', a central part of such approaches is to look at the way language is structured, used and accomplished in any situation. It is in this sense that the notion of discourse becomes key. For whilst such approaches give particular weight to the linguistically constituted character of reality, it does not mean that discourses are 'mere words'. Discourses are structures of knowledge claims and practices through which we understand, explain and decide things. In constituting agents, they also define obligations and determine the distribution of responsibilities and authorities for different categories of person, such as parents, children, social workers, doctors, lawyers and so on.

A discourse is best understood as a system of possibilities for knowledge and for agency which makes some actions possible whilst precluding others (Woolgar, 1986). It is a system of possibility that allows us to produce statements which are either 'true' or 'false'.

Thus whereas modernity assumes that increasing knowledge of the real world produces power, postmodernity reverses the formula, recognising that the formation of particular discourses creates contingent centres of power which define areas of knowledge and truth claims, and frameworks of explanation and understanding. Those with power can influence language and discourse and can therefore influence the way in which life is experienced, seen and interpreted.

However, because there is a range of different contexts, cultures and discourses available at any one time and place, there is also a plethora of different meanings, knowledges and truths available and many experiences and interpretations of self and identity. Notions of plurality and difference are widespread.

Possible implications of postmodern perspectives for practice

It has, however, been suggested that the implications for politics, policy and practice of such perspectives are at best ambiguous and at worst undermine many of the central values and principles of social work itself. Similarly, they may neglect the salience of issues of inequality in a simple celebration of difference (Williams, 1996). Post-modern perspectives have been criticised for being overly relativistic, nihilistic, negativistic and anarchistic, at the same time tending to exaggerate the breaks with the past, failing to recognise the importance of agency and resistance, and to overturn the past in a way which does not take heed of the positive and progressive elements that have previously gone on under the umbrella of social work (Smith and White, 1997). Such criticisms indicate that social work must be wary of such perspectives for it is essentially a practice where decisions have to be made and practitioners have to act. For whilst practitioners need to develop a critical reflexive awareness, they must also feel sufficiently confident to act. The contemporary challenge for social work is to take action, which demands that we have made up our mind, while being open minded.

In this respect, Rosenau (1992) provides an important contribution in characterising postmodern perspectives along a continuum from the *sceptic* to the *affirmative postmodernist*. Whilst it is difficult to accommodate the sceptic perspective, with its nihilistic stance on truth and other absolutes, within social work, the emphasis of the affirmative postmodernist on 'truth re-definition' rather than 'truth denying' is potentially much more suggestive. Rosenau's interpretation of an affirmative postmodern vision demonstrates that, whilst it cannot offer truth, it is not without content. It is interpretative and its focus is receptivity, dialogue, listening to and talking with the other. It reveals paradox, myth and enigma, and it persuades by showing, reminding, hinting and evoking rather than by constructing theories and approximating truth. It is suggested that our focus should be narrative, fragmented fantasies and different stories. Social work takes on the guise of persuasive fiction or poetry.

What such an approach demonstrates is that postmodern perspectives are not necessarily bleak or anti-social work but provide novel and creative insights that clearly talk to a number of themes and approaches which have been associated with social work for much of its history. It almost suggests that social work could be (re)interpreted as being (post)modern all along. Many social workers will identify with approaches which blur the difference between fact and fiction, history and story, art and science (England, 1986), and which take the view that what an individual perceives or experiences as her or his reality is *the* reality but a reality capable of change in an endless variety of ways.

There are now a number of attempts to develop and apply the positive elements of such an approach explicitly to social work practice. In the process, a number of themes and issues are illustrated which are of wide application and which can be developed further in different contexts. *Uncertainty* is central, Pozatek (1994, p. 399) suggesting that 'the acknowledgement of uncertainty is an essential element of the postmodern practice of social work' and that such a position can push workers to make the effort to understand a client's experience. A position of uncertainty is seen to represent a more respectful approach to cultural difference as certainty and objectivity are an illusion. Social workers should not expect, therefore, to know in advance what the outcomes of interactions will be. They can, at best, only trigger an effect. A position of uncertainty means that social workers will approach each situation respectful of difference, complexity and ambiguity. Words are understood by clients according to how they have constructed the reality embodied in the interaction. It is thus essential for practitioners to be aware of this and construct, through *dialogue* with the client, a shared understanding and reality which they agree is a representation of their interaction. It is an approach which recognises that *language* is crucial for constituting the experiences and identity of both the self and the interaction, and which takes seriously the diverse elements of power involved. It is similarly serious about notions of *partnership* and *participation,* and potentially enables the views of clients to be prioritised. This is not to say, however, that such issues are self-evident and clear cut. A commitment to uncertainty, indeterminacy and unpredictability will reinforce social workers' continual attempts reflexively to consider what they are doing, why and with what possible outcomes.

Sands and Nuccio (1992) have similarly identified a number of themes central to postmodern perspectives which can be drawn on in practice. Thus, rather than think and act according to *logocentrism,* assuming that there is a singular fixed logical order which is 'real' or 'true', practitioners need to recognise that there are no essential meanings. *Definitions and interpretations are historically contingent and context bound and hence fluid.* Similarly, logocentric thought promotes thinking in terms of binary opposites – male/female, black/white, adult/child, true/false – which are seen as mutually exclusive, categorical and hierarchical rather than interdependent. Such categories are usually embedded in language in a way which privileges some experiences and marginalises others. It is thus important explicitly to recognise the importance, but fluid and changing nature, of *difference* so that the oppressed and devalued can have a voice.

One way to recover suppressed meaning is through the key postmodern operation of *deconstruction* whereby phenomena are continually interrogated, evaluated, overturned and disrupted. Deconstruction is a way of analysing texts, language and narratives that is sensitive to contextual dimensions and marginalised voices. The process of deconstruction recognises that, whilst *multiple discourses* might be available, only a few are heard and are dominant, these being intimately related to the dominant powers/knowledges. When one deconstructs, one does not accept the constructs as given but looks at them in relation to their social, historical and political contexts. Constructs are 'problematised' and 'decentred'. Through deconstruction, the presumed fixity of phenomena is destabilised, and the perspective of the marginalised can be given voice. It involves, amongst other things, helping people to externalise the problem, examining its influences on their life, reconstructing and liberating themselves from it. The notion of *possibility* (O'Hanlon and Beadle, 1994) recognises that things can be changed. A vision of possibility can be used to mobilise people's potential and competence, and can empower them to reclaim and redefine who they are and how they want to act.

However, we should not assume that postmodern perspectives are concerned with giving suppressed subjects a voice in any simple way. The notion of *subjectivity* is itself complex. Whilst, within a logocentric tradition, the individual is autonomous and has an essential subjectivity, identity, personality and (if healthy) integrated, this is not the case with postmodern perspectives. In the latter, subjectivity is precarious, contradictory and in process, constantly being reconstituted in discourses (Weedon, 1987). Accordingly, the subject is multifaceted and speaks in many voices, depending on the sociocultural, historical and interpersonal contexts in which it is situated.

It is perhaps the emphasis on language and its intimate relationship with knowledge and power which provides the most distinctive message for practice arising from (post)modern perspectives. A focus on social work as text, narrative and artistry, as opposed to social work as science, moves centre-stage. Whereas science looks for explanations and causes, the story or narrative approach is intent on finding a *meaningful* account. As Howe (1993) has demonstrated, via his in-depth analysis of studies of what clients say about what they value from counselling and therapy, it is the latter which is important.

Talking not only helps people to understand their experiences, but also allows them to control, reframe and move on. As Howe states, 'there are no objective fundamental truths in human relationships, only working truths. These decentred contingent truths help people make sense of and control the meaning of their own experience. This is how we learn to cope' (Howe, 1993, p. 193). Such approaches emphasise *process* and *authorship*. An open-minded engagement with people's stories and the possibility of helping them to re-author their lives using more helpful stories can be both an empowering and respectful way of understanding situations and bringing about change. The work of de Shazer (1991) and White and Epston (1990) demonstrates how stories can be used to prompt new and more positive versions of situations. A person's own language and metaphors can be incorporated into a less problem-saturated narrative which can, for example, tell of triumph, survival and heroism in the face of difficulties. A number of developments in feminist praxis clearly relate to such developments (for example, Hollway, 1989; Flax, 1990).

Similarly, the creative capacities of the social worker must be understood in a context, not as an artist who imposes order and creates beauty through domination but as a co-creator of harmony, particularly with those who are marginalised and excluded. Postmodernists emphasise the importance of seeing life not just as a fixed course towards a single end but as an artistic composition with room for improvisation. Experience is seen as multiple and ambiguous so that, in social work encounters, solutions are not as much arrived at but found in the making, the telling and the talking.

Conclusion

What we have attempted in this chapter is to outline some emerging debates in social theory and to demonstrate how these can be seen to relate to some important changes in the way we think about and practise social work. In particular, we have suggested that, rather than attempt to explain and intervene in situations via the development and application of rational and scientific methods, we need to engage with both our own and other's 'truths', 'stories' and 'constructions'. We would also suggest that such approaches are particularly pertinent to developing and refining our understanding of reflective practice. As Taylor has suggested, reflective practice and reflective learning may be conceptualised 'as a response to postmodernism, as a positive and creative approach to the prospect of living with contingency' (Taylor, I., 1996, p. 159). In a world of uncertainty and rapid change, reflective practice offers the possibility of developing strategies for learning how to learn and how to practise in a self-conscious way. The concern is less with developing our know-ledge than with developing and deploying our capacities for reflex-ivity and action.

Dedication

This chapter was drafted and planned with Wendy Marshall, who died on 26 March 1997. It is dedicated to Wendy's memory and her considerable contribution to social work education and practice. Much loved and missed.

NIGEL PARTON

Further reading

Howe, D. (1994) 'Modernity, postmodernity and social work', *British Journal of Social Work*, **24**(5), pp. 513–32.

Parton, N. (1994) 'The nature of social work under conditions of (post)modernity', *Social Work and Social Science Review*, **5**(2), pp. 93–112.

These two articles, published in 1994, offer a useful way of taking some of these ideas further.

Parton, N. (ed.) (1996) *Social Theory, Social Change and Social Work* (London, Routledge).

Contains further examination of these issues by Howe and Parton, and a number of other chapters explicitly address issues related to social work and postmodernity.

Gould, N. and Taylor, I. (eds) (1996) *Reflective Learning for Social Work: Research Theory and Practice* (Aldershot, Arena).

The links between social work, postmodernity and reflective learning figure centrally in this book.

White, M. and Epston, D. (1990) *Narrative Means to Therapeutic Ends* (New York, Norton).

A good source for anyone who is keen to explore the application of the use of 'narrative' to practice.

PART III

Social Work Practice

21

Social work processes

ROBERT ADAMS

Introduction

Efforts to arrive at a single, definitive statement about the ingredients of social work practice are likely to fail. The title of Martin Davies' book *The Essential Social Worker* might imply that there is an ineradicable core of social work roles and activities, but that book does not build on a general consensus about what constitute the essentials of social work. Part I of the present book illustrates the controversial and uncertain context in which social work is practised. Part II demonstrates the great diversity of approaches to practice, some of which contradict or conflict with each other. The postmodern scenarios depicted in Chapter 20 lie closer to Salman Rushdie's observation in *Midnight's Children* that 'reality is a question of perspective' (Rushdie, 1982, p. 165). Rushdie adds that the further you are from the present, the more concrete and plausible it seems, but the closer you get, the more incredible it becomes, a comment which applies with equal force to the past and the present of social work. From a distance, the outlines of the major areas of social work practice dealt with in this third Part of the book – social work with children and families, adults and offenders – seem firm and clear, but a closer study of the detail of each area shows how uncertain and problem-ridden it is.

The content of the first two parts of this book might seem more problematic because their diversity of perspectives makes definition difficult and consensus impossible. In contrast, the practice considered in Part III could be regarded as the tangible reality and therefore as unambiguous. Donald Schön, writing about reflective practice, casts doubt on the accuracy of such a generalisation:

In the varied topography of professional practice, there is a high, hard ground where practitioners can make effective use of research-based theory and technique, and there is a swampy lowland where situations are confusing 'messes' incapable of technical solution. The difficulty is that the problems of the high ground, however great their technical interest, are often relatively unimportant to clients or to the larger society, while in the swamp are the problems of greatest human concern. (Schön, 1983, p. 42)

Taking Schön's analogy a little further, this introductory chapter makes connections between the contexts, approaches and practical terrain of social work. In following these connections through, some parts of the three following chapters maintain the high ground of social work, whilst others negotiate its swamps. This is complicated further by the fact that social work contexts and approaches are subject to continuing and often rapid change. The first section of this chapter examines some key features of the changing relationship between social work practice and its contexts. The second section considers aspects of the changing relationship between social work approaches and practice. The final section brings together the implications of these for practice, focusing on the two somewhat conflicting themes of managerialism and user empowerment; it concludes by showing how practice-based research has attempted to address, and in some ways transcend, these difficulties.

Changing contexts and social work practice

There is a lack of consensus about the conditions in which social work is practised and understood. No single perspective exists, whether from the vantage point of the professional, worker, officer, staff member, client, service user or offender, from which to consider the core of the actual matters of practice. Since the late 1980s, this lack of consensus has been made more noticeable by many factors dealt with in Part I of this book, chief among which are the development of managerialism, the creation of a contract culture in the health and personal social services (the impact of which is apparent especially in Chapter 23, on work with adults), and the imposition on social work education and training of a competence-based approach. These factors have changed the nature of customary processes of practice, making them more procedurally governed and increasingly subject to service specifications in novel contractual relationships between commissioners, purchasers and providers. Staff training and appraisal focus increasingly on competent performance rather than on the theory-based and value-driven aspects of critically reflective and progressive practice.

Managerialisms

Managerialism is the term used to refer to the inroads made by management into professional autonomy and power. Clarke *et al.*

(1994a, pp. 6–7) argue that, whilst professional ideology pushes practice towards empowering service users, managerialist strategies locate professionals and service users, as consumers, in a commercial relationship controlled by managers. Doray describes how, under scientific management, workers became slaves to the machine and the production process (Doray, 1988, p. 2). But, of course, many modern managers are committed to bringing out the best in their workforce, using a whole battery of approaches to maximise output and productivity. Many managers in social services share common backgrounds, experiences and qualifications with members of their own workforce, which in theory equips them to anticipate and to control their subordinate professionals. Lines of demarcation between health and social services professsionals break down or are repositioned as professionals develop new ways of working together. Clarke *et al.* (1994a, p. 4) point out that managerialisms are plural, in the sense that they take many different forms. The nature of these continually changes in different settings. The new managerialisms express aspects of the government's 'promotion and support of the values of entrepreneurialism and methods of business management' (Kelly, 1991, p. 178). The new managerialist agenda – ensuring effective control of the professionals by the managers – is policed by an ever-increasing array of procedures and standards, based on the prominent ideology of quality assurance, with reference to both the processes and the products of the professionals' work. This contrasts with the traditional centralised organisation, in which social work was judged largely by the extent to which, for example, staff kept within budgets. Lewis and Glennerster (1996, p. 141) acknowledge, in their evaluation of the implementation of community care in the 1990s, that its broader aspects have been pushed along by managerial rather than professional considerations.

However, not all versions of managerialism undermine professional social work. In fact, a notable feature of managerialism in the personal social services is the close interweaving with professional work achieved by some government-sponsored managerialist initiatives (Adams, 1998, Ch. 3). The SSI, for example, mediates between state policies, the operations of local authorities and the professional practice of social work. The SSI has continued a working style evolved in the former Social Work Service of the Department of Health and Social Security in the 1970s. This, although responsible for implementing government policy, often responds sensitively to local practice issues. At the same time, commentators such as Shaw view the tight parameters of managerial control as dramatically curbing professional autonomy (Shaw, 1995, p. 132), for example in the support by the Chief Social Services Inspector of a shift to a working style where 'no individual fieldworker should be regarded as self-sufficient' (SSI, 1992, p. 13) (see in particular, Chapter 22 on social work with children and families).

A number of the trends occurring in the personal social services mirror wider similar changes going on in the public sector as a whole: first, rather paradoxically, towards larger and more complex organisations managed by local and central government, and a trend towards a greater diversity – and a greater number of smaller – service-providing organisations in the voluntary and private sectors; second, towards a separation of senior management in the organisation purchasing services from the professionals who provide those services; third, towards the reduction of the size of the permanent workforce in the large local authority social work and social services departments of the 1970s, more staff being bought in on short and temporary contracts around a decreasing core of full-time, permanent officials.

Far from statutorily based social work remaining the backbone of the social services, programme cuts have reduced the capacity of social services departments to provide services themselves. The implementation of community care in the 1990s (see Chapter 23) has sharpened debates about whether social work has a future as an autonomous profession. The importation into the personal social services of the language and culture of contracts – commissioning and costing, service specification – is a reminder of the business culture being nurtured in the social services. Practitioners cannot insulate themselves from these changes, but they may attempt to preserve their professional integrity by distancing themselves as far as possible from any negative impact they may have. Tensions exist within social work practice, from the vantage points of different stake-holders, whether managers, practitioners or service users. These are not necessarily discrete but may overlap and on occasions conflict with each other. There are also tensions in the ways in which social workers engage with practice, given the policy, organisational and managerial pressures which exist.

The contract culture

The introduction of internal markets in the health and social services sector since the 1990s represents the most radical change for half a century in the way in which services are organised and delivered (see Chapter 6 for more detailed discussion). The superimposition on the relationship between the social worker and the client of a contract between the local authority as purchaser and the providing agency or body has a significant effect on the interaction between them. The contract culture commonly displays deep-seated features of self-interest and individualism which are antithetical to mutual help, collaboration and cooperation.

It is possible to make a virtue out of necessity and claim that basing social work with people on a service specification with built-in targets, standards and performance criteria by which to judge them improves the quality of the work done. However, such work runs the risk of decisions about what to do and how to achieve it being shaped by financial rather than professional considerations (Adams, 1996b, Chapter 3). For example, the widespread trend towards recommending residential care for older people was reported by the Audit Commission in 1996 to be due to the perverse incentive that it was cheaper for a local authority to place people in residential care because they qualified for state benefits, such as those in independent sector homes who qualified for the residential allowance (Audit Commission, 1996b, para. 70, p. 6). This was due to the pressure of shortages of community care resources rather than based on needs-led assessments and care and planning.

Competence-based approaches

Competence-based approaches (see Chapter 6 for discussion of the organisational context) have been likened to the driving test, which judges performance without regard to the process by which that level of expertise is reached. One such approach is embodied in the revised CCETSW Paper 30, which reflects an emphasis on outcomes and performance. Competence-based approaches to social work have a somewhat ambiguous significance. They may be perceived as empowering practitioners and services users, or as being used to reinforce managerialist practices. Dominelli (1996) argues that the adoption of a competence-based approach in social work contradicts the development of anti-oppressive practice.

There has been a widespread move in the health and social care field in the UK since the early 1980s towards developing occupational standards based on competence approaches. A competence-based approach involves assumptions about the appropriateness of identifying an inseparable common base of values, knowledge and skills. The value base of practice derives from the examination of the ethical dimension of practice. The base of knowledge for practice includes the wide range of aspects referred to in occupational standards. The use of the knowledge base includes not only the ability to repeat relevant memorised facts, but also a critical understanding which workers can apply to practice. For example, in drawing upon knowledge of the law, it is anticipated that the competent social worker will appreciate its problematic nature. Skills include such areas as engaging with people, assessing needs, planning, carrying out the work and evaluating work done. However, the location of such a competence-based approach in the contract culture implies that processes are regarded merely as instrumental means by which to attain valued goals.

A competence approach uses task analysis to define what workers do. It is based on assessing what people do – and how they perform – rather than on their qualities or their professional judgement and grasp of relevant issues. It involves three essential features. First, it rests on an assessment of what people actually do rather than on their critical understanding. Second, it builds on an analysis of people's existing jobs, matching personal specifications to lists of key roles which amount to occupational standards (Mangham and Silver, 1986). Boyatzis (1982), an influential advocate of a competence-based approach in management development, deduces necessary or desired qualities in performance at work from observing and measuring what workers do and distinguishes 'threshold' competences inherent in all competent performance from that level of competence demonstrated by the outstanding person (Salaman *et al.*, 1994, pp. 33–4). Third, it assumes a correlation between a person's actions, value commitment and critical awareness, with the crucial emphasis of judgments about professional expertise resting on performance.

Competence-based approaches are prone to six main criticisms.

1. They tend to focus on areas of expertise that are most appropriate in stable, bureaucratic work settings, rather than being directed towards future job requirements.
2. They encourage fragmentation, that is, a somewhat artificial atomisation of components of activities which could otherwise be viewed holistically.
3. They are convergent, in that they may bring about a narrowing of ideas consistent with outcome-based activity rather than encouraging divergent thinking and an emphasis on the value of the process of the activity, accompanying creative practice.
4. They focus mainly or wholly on those easily measurable aspects of people's performance.
5. They concentrate on techniques and skills, and this relegates considerations of values, critical evaluation and the deployment of front-line knowledge, particularly at more advanced levels, into second place.
6. They emphasise students acquiring specified techniques rather than developing approaches based on critically reflective practice.

Hayman also argues that, apart from the risk that competences may reduce complex professional issues to banal simplifications (Hayman, 1993, p. 182), competences 'can become frozen in time' and produce technicians rather than professionals (Hayman, 1993, p. 181). They are fundamentally contradicted by the requirement that the critical professional should constantly re-evaluate accepted practice and thereby achieve 'a constant openness to redefining what competent, effective practice is'. Hayman concludes: 'It is hard to see how to devise competences that call themselves into question in this way' (Hayman, 1993, p. 181).

Where practice is complex, uncertain and inherently problematic, a purely empirically driven competence-based approach is less likely to produce an adequate analysis of key roles. There is not much encouragement for the kind of reflective practice to which Payne refers (Chapter 10). Where changes in the context of practice are very rapid, a purely descriptive approach, without consultation with relevant – probably diverse and possibly conflicting – interests in the field of practice, inevitably falls short of representing complex reality. In social work, a wide range of advice from different interests and groups would be necessary, including different stake-holder managers and professionals in the statutory, voluntary and private and informal sectors, as well as services users and carers. There is a risk that the empirical analysis of competence may neglect 'soft' personal qualities such as 'assertiveness, impact, creativity, sensitivity and intuition [which] are difficult to measure under any circumstances' (Jacobs, 1989, quoted in Salaman *et al.*, 1994, p. 35) in favour of hard areas of activity and skill, such as finance budgeting. Job analysis based on limited consultation may not exclude bad practice, based on a distorted or flawed value base.

Changing approaches and social work practice

Practice is an extremely complex activity, rooted in the contexts set out in Part I of this book and drawing on many of the approaches examined in Part II. The impact of the factors reviewed above varies greatly according to the approaches adopted in local settings.

Inseparable from their context, changing views about what constitutes the core of the practice of social work since the 1960s mirror wider debates about how professional social work's knowledge base has evolved and how theory, practice and research into social work should be conceived. As Part II of this book shows, these debates have intensified since the 1960s as the legal basis and knowledge and value bases for social work have extended and become more complex and controversial.

Practice does not derive from an unchanging, agreed base of theories and knowledge. New social work approaches have tended to overlay rather than extinguish existing ideas about practice. Practice is a feature of constantly changing circumstances in which professionals and clients interact, and realities are fragmented and diverse, with few, if any fixed, unchanging or agreed points of reference. Social work has traditionally leaned heavily on psychological and sociological theories and researches with a bearing on work with individuals and groups, including families (Woodroofe, 1962). Until the 1950s, in Britain at any rate, practice related in large measure to psycho-analytic and psycho-therapeutic theory and practice. Influences from social psychology were evident in the growing popularity of groupwork and group-based approaches to work with families, including family therapy and group counselling (Brown, 1988; Whitaker, 1989). From the 1960s, social work was increasingly influenced by work in and with community groups engaged in social and political action. Concepts such as empowerment, which from the late 1980s found their way into the UK social work literature, derived much of their impetus from the social action movements and pressure group politics of the 1960s. Consequently, in the 1990s, all of the approaches examined in the chapters in Part II co-exist in social work. The use of different social work approaches in different circumstances is not precluded by the fact that some are at variance or even in conflict with each other.

The considerable ambiguities inherent in notions of process in social work surface particularly at the interface with other professions, notably in health care. Social work has shifted since the 1980s towards multidisciplinary and multiprofessional working. Yura and Walsh (1967) used the term 'the nursing process' to encompass four component stages of nurses' work with patients – assessment, planning, implementation and evaluation – each of which had its own discrete processes. Conceptualisations of such processes vary greatly according to the model of nursing which is applied to practice (Aggleton and Chalmers, 1986). Traditionally, the nursing process informing what nurses and midwives did reflected a view of health care which was hospital-based and medically dominated. The growth of community care and the impact of hospital closure programmes in areas such as mental health and learning disability has contributed to a situation where more nurses now work outside than inside hospitals. Social perspectives on health care are diminishing the professional distance between health visitors, occupational therapists, community nurses and social workers. The complementary roles of care assistants and health-care assistants are often blurred. Lewis and Glennerster, 1996, p. 188) use as an example the blurring of roles of health and social care at the interface with service users. Some managers, for example, leave to the professional the negotiation of the demarcation of responsibilities concerning which worker makes the toast and who gives the insulin to the person on a home visit. We can add to this complicated set of issues which the professionals may have to resolve on the spot, at the interface with service users and carers – the debates about what is legitimate professional work. The blurring of the boundary around the traditional activities of doctoring and nursing reflects the increasing legitimacy within health care of professions allied to medicine, and complementary health care. There are moves to legitimise oriental practice such as acupuncture as complementary to Western medicine (MacPherson and Kaptchuk, 1996). This emphasises a process orientation. In fact, it is arguable that such complementary therapies are more appropriate than, for example, surgery, for working with people in an ongoing process rather than at a fixed point of intervention such as an operation. The increasing tendency for professionals in the health and social services to work together heightens rather than resolves differences of professional ideologies, cultures and practices. The many problems of developing collaboration between disciplines, professions and health and social services organisations require careful attention in practice and cannot be resolved by a quick-fix approach.

Implications for practice

The final part of this chapter selects three of the main implications of the above discussion of contextual factors and changing approaches for social work practice. The first two of these concern the tensions between the 'upward' or organisationally 'inward' accountability of the social worker through the line manager to the state and the employing organisation, and the 'downward' or 'outward' accountability to the client or services user. The third area – the interface between research and practice – shows that since *both* managers and service users have legitimate stakes in the practice of social work, there is merit in exploring ways of surmounting such tensions rather than fatalistically accepting them.

Engaging with managerialism

We saw earlier in this chapter how managerialisms tend to emphasise a sequence or cycle of activity, as conceptualised and laid down by line managers rather than professionals working within their own knowledge base. Thus, they tend to reflect legalistic and procedural imperatives. The language and culture of such perspectives on practice is administrative. They may also borrow from the industrial or commercial sectors. In the contract culture, products may be the focus, at the expense of production processes; financial and outcome-based performance indicators may predominate over qualitative evaluation. The significant impact of these factors on all the areas of social work covered in Chapters 22 to 24 is referred to now.

In child care and family-based social work (Chapter 22), whereas the notion of stages bypasses more sophisticated concepts associated, for example, with intrapsychic change – whether development or decay – it cannot be dismissed as less useful. The collaborative arrangements between agencies set out in the publication *Working Together under the Children Act, 1989* (1991b) date from the 1960s, although they have attracted higher-profile attention particularly since the inquiry (1974) into the death of Maria Colwell and, even more so, following the Cleveland inquiry (Report of the Inquiry into Child Abuse in Cleveland, 1988). The useful summary of outcomes of 20 research studies in 1995 provided the occasion for the process of child protection to be set out in four stages: pre-investigation, first enquiry, family visit, and conference and registration (DoH, 1995, p. 26). One of the most useful concepts associated with the child protection process is that of thresholds, often linked with particular actions performed by the practitioner, but in any case involving a specific decision being taken, as a consequence of which there is movement from one stage to the next (DoH, 1995, p. 33). The separation of the stage of pre-investigation from first enquiry draws attention to the processes by which children for whom services are immediately forthcoming are distinguished from those referred for further investigation. Inevitably, proceduralism in child care has the negative consequence of constraining, or even eroding, professional autonomy. The challenge for professionals is to use procedures as the basis for claiming the necessary resources to engage in progressive practice (Adams, 1998, Chapter 9).

There is ambiguity over the circumstances in which processes of care management examined in Chapter 23 are driven by either professional or managerial imperatives. These are reflected in, but do not altogether originate in, the rationale for the care planning process. Notably, there is a similarity between the managerial sequence of planning, implementation and review in care management since the NHS and Community Care Act, 1990, and various models of the therapeutic process.

Miller and Gwynne (1972) were subsequently attacked by advocates of non-oppressive work with people with impairments, for applying the metaphors of the industrial setting to the residential care of disabled people, likening it to processes of operating warehouse or greenhouse approaches to care.

Again, in criminal justice and youth justice, one consequence of the ironic convergence between radical and conservative views referred to in Chapter 24 is the development of systems-based approaches to the management of the processing of offenders. Such top-down approaches have been nourished by the same research which has stimulated an overhaul of traditional, functionalist criminologies. Critiques by sociologists of deviance of processes by which people become labelled as problems were applied first to social work with offenders and subsequently to work with other client groups, such as people with mental health problems. From the late 1960s, challenges to the welfare model in criminal justice and juvenile justice impacted upon criminology (Taylor *et al.*, 1974) and then upon social work in the UK (Thorpe *et al.*, 1980). Thorpe's work involving evaluating, amongst other things, key stages in the career processes of delinquents provided an influential critique of the failings of the Children and Young Persons Act, 1969 and stimulated efforts to develop correctional curricula of sufficient rigour and attractiveness to the courts to enable young offenders to be diverted from custody. Latterly, Thorpe developed a similarly evaluative approach to other client groups (see the section on research viewpoints below), notably children in the child protection system (Thorpe, 1994).

Since the 1970s, in the fields of criminal justice and youth justice, the term 'process' has acquired added significance from the extensive literature based on research concerning offenders' progress through, or diversion from, criminal careers. Since that period, work with offenders has been concerned with managing the tension between the agencies and professions – amongst which social work is prominent – and processes of signification (Matza, 1969) or labelling (Becker, 1963), with the goal of minimising the penetration of individuals into the criminal and youth justice systems. Ironically, policies of delinquency management based on protecting the public by controlling youth justice systems (Audit Commission, 1996a) tend to manage the boundaries of intervention rather than developing a correctional curriculum which empowers young people. They may become intrusive, like tagging, or may even be overtly controlling (Adams *et al.*, 1981, p. 22).

In probation work, the combined impact of the 1991 and 1993 Criminal Justice Acts and the 1994 Criminal Justice and Public Order Act (see Chapter 24), in England and Wales at any rate, has been to shift the balance of the work of probation officers towards buttressing correctional philosophies. The writing of pre-sentence reports (PSRs) tends to focus on questions such as the seriousness of the offence and the risk to the public, to the near-exclusion of personal history or cultural and social factors contributing to criminality. The increasing prominence in probation practice of a focus on 'what works' in terms of the relative effectiveness of different sentences and approaches to work with offenders follows research reviews which emphasise psychological rather than social and environmental factors contributing to criminality, such as unemployment, poor housing, poverty and environmental degradation (McGuire, 1995).

Engaging with perspectives on empowering service users and carers

Since the late 1980s, principles and practices of empowerment have become prominent matters for debate amongst politicians, managers and professionals in the health and social services. However, empowering social work relates to traditions of activism and advocacy which are well established and not generally circumscribed by professional discourse and practice. In the 1980s, the growth of user-led and self-advocacy movements in the UK, notably amongst disabled people and people who had experienced hospital-based treatment for mental health problems, drew on, and gave additional impetus to, concepts of personal and community action with long traditions in many other countries (Wolfensberger, 1997). Conventional wisdom has it that these ideas were imported from the USA into social work in the UK (see Solomon, 1985; Adams, 1996b, p. 15; Payne, 1997, p. 275). The most dramatic signs of this change were the take-up in the personal social services in the UK from the late 1980s of the concept of empowerment and its incorporation in official guidance from the Department of Health concerning the implementation of the NHS and Community Care Act, 1990. This comes close to Orem's (1985) self-care approach to nursing, which encourages an holistic view, focusing on empowering people, so that they can initiate and carry out their own strategies to maintain health and well-being.

Empowering practice has received most attention in the areas of child care and community care, whilst, in work with offenders, it is the least developed and, not surprisingly, least well articulated in the, almost by definition, professionally dominated social work literature. Even in community care, however, the adherence of official guidance to rhetorical statements about empowering service users is surprising, since people may in practice complain of feeling disempowered by, marginalised by, or excluded from the ways in which professional services are provided for them. A further complication is that much of the literature on user empowerment contributes to the field of interprofessional communication or education for students rather than empowering clients (Adams, 1996b, pp. 72–3).

Empowering practice is furthermore very often associated with 'bottom-up' processes of consciousness-raising or liberation as they affect individuals and groups, whereas a growing literature on anti-oppressive work (Ward and Mullender, 1991) proceeds at the same time from 'top-down', structural analyses of divisions and inequalities in societies. There is, therefore, some looseness of fit between these concepts and practices (Servian, 1996; Taylor *et al.*, 1992).

However, commentators in the field of citizen participation are increasingly taking on board the need to link areas of anti-discrimination and anti-oppression with discourse on empowerment.

Mullender and Ward locate their empowering practice in groupwork, outlining five stages of user-led group work, which they then augment into 12 stages as they apply anti-oppressive principles of practice (Mullender and Ward, 1991). The work of Beresford and Croft (1995) takes as axiomatic the link between issues concerning citizen participation in service planning, implementation and evalua-tion, and the case for extending human rights to all disempowered individuals and groups, including those excluded by virtue of such social problems as poverty or disability.

Engaging at the interface between practice and research

Tensions betwen managerial and user perspectives on social work processes are reflected in the diversity of approaches to research in practice. Research and practice go hand in hand, but, depending on its assumptions, research may either reinforce oppressive practice, or espouse the goal of empowerment (see Chapter 9). Research provides, amongst other things, an evaluation of services provided by the agency. Thorpe and Thorpe (1992, p. 24) offer a systems model for eval-uating what happens to clients after they become clients, with reference to three components of the systems model: 'input – information avail-able on records, for example, concerning how people became clients; process; and outcomes – information about the results of services in the short, medium and longer terms'. Thorpe and Thorpe define process in these terms as 'a simple description of the services provided by the agency and the reasons why those services (as opposed to any other service) are supplied' (Thorpe and Thorpe, 1992, p. 24). Whitaker and Archer (1989, pp. 12–15) identify some shared features of the processes of research and practice in social work, notably those involved in such activities as collecting data and drawing conclusions. However (see Chapter 9), they use the variety of practice-based research carried out by post-qualifying social workers on practice-based research programmes at York to distinguish in some significant ways the research process from the process of practice (Whitaker and Archer, 1989, p. 75). Their observations draw also on some unpublished work by Dixon of Barnardos (Dixon, 1984, p. 4) in which she draws parallels, paraphrased below, between processes of research and social work:

1. The social worker and the researcher are presented with a problem or question.
2. The social worker collects facts to illuminate the problem; the researcher carries out a literature search on the problem or question.
3. The social worker formulates a plan of action; the researcher designs a piece of research.

4. The social worker implements the plan, recording progress; the researcher implements the study by collecting and collating data.
5. The social worker reviews the work and may make fresh plans; the researcher analyses the data, draws conclusions and may make recommendations for further action.

Whitaker and Archer (1989, p. 13) identify important differences between research and practice: the pace of research is likely to be much slower than that of practice, with much more time, for example, spent reflecting on methodological issues and the interpretation of data; practitioners tend to receive feedback much more quickly than researchers, in terms of whether a particular action has been appropriate to a service.

The proximity of the research and practice processes is not just conceptual, but also interactive. Research and practice may co-exist in a symbiotic relationship. Learning and insights from practice – the phrase Whitaker and Archer use is 'practice wisdom', whilst Parton and Marshall (Chapter 20) refer to different forms of discourse – can form the basis for developing research, the equivalent term for this being 'academic wisdom'. The reverse is also true, of course. Research may produce new knowledge and stimulate fresh practice. Research may be regarded as integral to practice and useful to local policy developments (Whitaker and Archer, 1989, p. 13).

Many useful examples of empowering research approaches can be found in countries outside the UK. For example, empowerment evaluation, which originated in the USA, is an increasingly popular approach in many fields of the human services, including social work. It enables a creative convergence between empowering research and practice. Empowerment evaluation lies beyond collaborative evaluation and involves facilitating people engaging in what is essentially self-evaluation (Fetterman, 1996, p. 11). The worker plays a facilitating role as consultant, rather than acting as expert, during this process. This comprises what Fetterman, a leading exponent, identifies as four steps: taking stock – the existing strengths and weaknesses of the situation; setting goals – people themselves deciding where they want to go in future; developing strategies – people choosing and developing means of accomplishing their goals; and documenting progress – enabling people to use relevant, credible and rigorous means of evaluating their activities (Fetterman, 1996, pp. 18–20).

But we do not need to go so far afield. New paradigm research, as developed by Rowan and Reason, has a close affinity with the paradigm of empowerment which emerged in social work in the UK in the late 1980s (Adams, 1990, 1996a). New paradigm research is a cooperative approach to experiential enquiry, embodying a move to participatory and holistic knowing, critical subjectivity and knowledge in action. These are three key components in a fundamentally empowering approach – pre-dating the use of the term 'empowerment' in social work, but which nevertheless has recognisable conceptual antecedents 'rooted in a new world-view which is emerging through systems thinking, ecological concerns and awareness, feminism, education, as well as in the philosophy of human inquiry' (Reason, 1988, p. 3). Reason refers to Rowan's (1981) argument that orthodox scientific method alienates experimental subjects from the product of the research, from the work of the research, from other people and from themselves (Reason, 1988, p. 6). The process of cooperative research set out by Rowan in 1981 contrasts with traditional experimental method and with the implicitly professionally owned, practice-based model set out by Whitaker and Archer. Rowan defines the cooperative research process as follows:

Stage 1: A group of co-researchers and co-subjects meet to inquire into some aspect of their life and work.

Stage 2: The group take decisions about what research action to take into their lives and begin to record. This may involve 'self-observation, reciprocal observation of other members of the inquiry group, or other agreed methods of recording experience; it is primarily in the realm of practical knowledge' (Reason, 1988, p. 5).

Stage 3: The co-researchers engaged in this activity become fully immersed in their practice and may actually lose their distinct awareness of being engaged in an inquiry.

Stage 4: The co-researchers return to reflect and make sense of their experience. This may involve abandoning early assumptions and 'a whole range of both cognitive and intuitive forms of knowing; its expression may be primarily propositional, but may also involve stories, pictures, and other ways of giving voice to aspects of experience which cannot be captured in propositions. When this making sense has been completed, the co-researchers can consider how to engage on [sic] further cycles of inquiry' (Reason, 1988, p. 5).

The rigid segregation of stages in the above description does less than justice to Reason's point that movement between experience and reflection goes on; there are similarities between this flux and the existential process of reflective practice developed by Schön (1983) (see Chapter 10). Reflective practice emerges as less a technique and more a perspective, less a series of concrete actions and more a state of being. Thus, Schön uses the term 'reflection-in-practice' to convey the dynamism and holism of the concept. Interestingly, Krim, in Reason's 1988 edited collection of studies, explicitly refers to Schön's work (Krim, 1988, p. 145). Some useful similarities can be identified with personal consciousness-raising, group-based, community action or community development perspectives. Reason writes of the cooperative inquiry process, which involves:

> establishing relationships of authentic collaboration and dialogue; ideally we care for each other, and approach each other with mutual love and concern. While not ignoring the necessity for direction and the role of expertise, we eschew unnecessary hierarchy and compulsive control. The emphasis on wholeness also means that we are not interested in either fragmented knowing, or theoretical knowing that is separated from practice and from experience. We seek a knowing-in-action which encompasses as much of our experience as possible. This means that aspects of a phenomenon are understood deeply because we know them in the context of our participation in the whole system, not as the isolated dependent and independent variables of experimental science. Our holistic concerns lead us to a form of theory-building and understanding which is descriptive and systemic, what Geertz (1973) would call a 'thick description', or Kaplan (1964) a 'concatenated' theory. The essential quality of a pattern model is that it creates a dense... web of knowing. This kind of non-hierarchical thinking-in-action is quite foreign to formal Western thinking: we tend to see the world in terms of hierarchical cause-and-effect, rather than in networks of understanding. (Reason, 1988, p. 11)

Changes in the legal and policy basis for social work, and in approaches to practice and research, have sharpened rather than resolved fundamental clashes between traditional and critical perspectives on how social work practice should be described and evaluated. On one hand, as Heineman notes in a seminal article, there are traditionalists who may seek credibility by 'embracing an antiquated research model that philosophers of science and social scientists from other disciplines were abandoning', on the positivist assumption that 'core practice-related concepts can be defined by empirical or quantitative measures' (Heineman, 1981, p. 371). On the other hand, there is a growing cadre of commentators, practitioners and researchers, representing a diversity of perspectives but invariably united in their scepticism of the efforts of positivists to generate a 'scientifically determined knowledge base and research methods' (Reamer, 1993, p. 121) which are unique to social work. According to Reamer, much theorising and research based on positivist empiricial approaches is 'of relatively limited value and relevance to practitioners' (Reamer, 1993, p. 141).

Finding ways forward: sustaining progressive practice

So social work contexts, approaches and practices remain as controversial in the 1990s as they were two decades or more previously. However, as the questions and assumptions associated with them have been subjected to more open and critical scrutiny, so the areas of debate have become more apparent. Social workers are engaged in complex webs of social and institutional relationships, embracing multiple accountabilities: to the state, to their employers who provide social work services, to colleagues, to professional values and not least towards the client and the wider community. Within this history, different views of practice reflect broader debates about the nature of social work and its relationship with its contexts.

A delicate balance needs to be maintained between becoming enmeshed in the politics and practice of managerialism – challenging from the inside – and maintaining professional distance and developing areas of progressive, but fairly isolated, practice.

The co-existence of professional and managerial perspectives on the social work process is somewhat anomalous. However, there is no virtue in pretending that professional, managerial and research perspectives on process can be coalesced and their differences somehow dissolved. It is possible, however, that they may interact creatively. The most common approaches to practice have also become clear, and it may help to regard these as responses to the areas of uncertainty and debate that the first two parts of this book have highlighted, which have been revisited and to some extent reframed in this discussion of process in social work. We can use three terms to help to clarify the wide range of responses to these uncertainties and debates: *absolutism*, or retention of one perspective; *relativism* or a pluralistic tendency; and *transcendentalism*, or the attempt to find a meta-perspective which incorporates the desired features of others. Each of these simplifies and is thus inevitably untidy in some way, but the brief exposition of each of them perhaps helps to clarify the territory of this final part of the book.

Absolutism is a rather unsatisfactory term – in that it sounds extreme and authoritarian – but one which nevertheless conveys accurately the stance which ring-fences one perspective on theory, research and practice and, by definition, excludes all debate and serious consideration of other perspectives. Reamer, for example, implies that the social worker setting out to develop a behaviourally based theory of assessment and the social worker committed to developing a psychodynamically oriented treatment theory may be equally unable or unwilling to consider their work from a pluralistic viewpoint (Reamer, 1993, p. 152). The term 'relativism' may sound more dubious than words such as 'pluralism' or 'eclecticism' concerning the tendency towards practitioners being prepared to pick up a suitable approach in particular circumstances from a range of possibly divergent or even conflicting approaches. Reamer (1993, p. 149) acknowledges the comment by Wood (1990, p. 378) that competent social work depends on 'the ability of practitioners to be polyocular – to have a variety of lenses through which to view their cases... Indeed, in a given case – or even in one interview in a case – the competent practitioner may be utilizing several different descriptive and prescriptive theories in rapid succession or even simultaneously'. However, a supermarket or 'pick-and-mix' approach is not implied as the optimum. Reamer is careful to point out that:

> [A]narchy in research and extreme forms of relativism should be avoided; rather, social workers need to draw *systematically* on various research perspectives and techniques in order to produce the most lucid, illuminating, and compelling body of information required by varying practice circumstances. Thus, formal evaluation of a long-term residential program for emotionally disturbed adolescents may call for a combination of quantitative, empirically based, self-report data from checklists, questionnaire data, and academic performance data, *and* qualitative data based on extensive observation in several naturalistic settings. (Reamer, 1993, p. 149)

Unfortunately, though, the hierarchy of knowledges and power within qualitative and quantitative methodologies may operate to produce what Willis, in his ground-breaking but controversial ethnography of boys making the transition from school to work in the 1970s, called 'mere methodological variety' (1978). More significant, perhaps, this crititique of methodological soup-making may not tackle more insidious divisions and inequalities which have marginalised qualitative methodologies, for example, as a feature of a less desirable form of masculinity, of which Gherardi and Turner (1987) write in their ironically titled paper 'Real men don't collect soft data'.

There is no certain way of transcending the limitations of single-focus perspectives on social work practice and the dangers of extreme forms of pluralism or relativism. Many gaps and discontinuities exist between different ways of chunking up perspectives, theories and approaches to social work processes and practices, so it is unrealistic to expect that one approach can, as it were, provide a meta-framework for incorporating all the others.

Since the 1970s, accumulating experiences and research through theory and practice in the areas of empowerment and non-oppressive practice have emerged in key areas of social work. Three kinds of contribution are worth noting: creative (England, 1986), critical (Everitt *et al.*, 1992; Everitt and Hardiker, 1996) and participatory (Reason and

Rowan, 1981; Marsden and Oakley, 1990; Beresford and Croft, 1993; Marsden *et al.*, 1994). England (1986) addresses the one-dimensionality of instrumentality expressed in the more rigid, skill-based approaches to competence by amplifying the many ways in which expressive aspects of practice contribute to an holistic approach. The approach of Everitt and colleagues is informed by Marxian and Hegelian notions of a dialectical process which creates synthesis from opposed interests. The creative approach suggests that, beyond the dualism of positivism and anti-positivism, lies a transcendent position which harnesses instrumental/technical and expressive/artistic components of theory and practice. The new paradigm approach of Rowan and Reason assumes that the differentials of interest and power between different stake-holders in research and practice can be reduced or even abolished by a collaborative strategy. This involves maximising the participation of service users, for example by meeting with them at the outset of any research process to elicit their own goals for the study and, in effect, recruiting them as co-researchers throughout the subsequent process. Marsden and Oakley (1990) and Marsden *et al.* (1994) use experience in social development projects from many parts of the world to caution against segregating academics, managers and professionals – and the research project – from the social development activity itself. In the UK, Beresford and Croft (1993) have used collaborative research in their examination of the feasibility of, and barriers to, citizen participation in the planning, delivery and management of local services.

It is doubtful whether the gulf between positivist and non-positivist perspectives can be abolished by treating them as possible contributors to a multimethod approach. We are left with a mixture of ideas and practices entirely consistent with the postmodern conditions described by Parton (Chapter 20). However, the developments referred to in the previous paragraphs are having a significant impact in theory, research and practice, in particular through emancipatory and participatory research projects focusing on the involvement of people in social services. These initiatives present three forms of challenge: first, to managerialism, which undermines professional autonomy and reduces professional decision-making to the gatekeeping of rationed services; second, to contribute to knowledge and theorising as activities owned equally by service users, professionals and academics; third, to empower people through developing participatory action which integrates both research and practice, by not separating the ownership of research from service development.

Professionals can use their practice as the basis for self-evaluation and for reflections which in turn contribute to social work models and theories. Each of the three following chapters addresses this task by situating examples of practice in the context of current policy directions and research findings.

Conclusion

This chapter has set the scene for the detailed examination of practice in the three areas covered in the following chapters. It portrays the diversity of work with different individuals and groups of people and illustrates the inadequacy of any attempt to distil the essentials of social work into an artificially contrived, unified set of concepts. The integrity of the profession is likely to be better served by social work professionals and educators aspiring to a more sophisticated understanding of practice, located in its contexts and taking account of the complexity of professional values and approaches.

Further reading

Farnham, D. and Horton, S. (eds) (1993) *Managing the New Public Services* (London, Macmillan).

> Deals critically with the nature and impact of managerialism in the public services, in a way which enables their general analysis to be applied easily to the personal social services.

Le Croy, C. W. (ed.) (1992) *Case Studies in Social Work Practice* (Pacific Grove, CA, Brooks/Cole).

> A collection of very wide-ranging case studies in different settings, exemplifying a variety of therapeutic approaches to social work processes.

Marsden, D., Oakley, P. and Pratt, B. (eds) (1994) *Measuring the Process: Guidelines for Evaluating Social Development* (Oxford, INTRAC).

> A concise exposition of the process of empowering evaluation, viewed through a number of practical examples from different parts of the world.

Walsh, K., Deakin, N., Smith, P., Spurgeon, P. and Thomas, N. (1997) *Contracting for Change: Contracts in Health, Social Care, and Other Local Government Services* (Oxford, Oxford University Press).

> Chapter 1, especially pp. 17–21 on the personal social services, provides an excellent overview of assumptions embedded in the shift towards reinventing local government based on market principles.

Yelloly, M. (1995) 'Professional competence and higher education', in Yelloly, M. and Henkel, M. (eds) *Learning and Teaching in Social Work: Towards Reflective Practice* (London, Jessica Kinglsey), pp. 51–66.

> Explores the concept of competence as it applies in social work and relevant areas of higher education.

22

Social work with children and families

LORRAINE WATERHOUSE and JANICE McGHEE

Introduction

Social work with children and families raises public and professional concern. Inquiries into the fatal non-accidental injury and sexual abuse of children highlight the need for sound child-care decision-making and effective interagency and interdisciplinary collaboration, and for the child's best interests to have paramountcy at all times. From the mid-1970s in the UK, public accountability demanded and influenced the shape of social work services with children and their families, giving rise to an emphasis on investigation and surveillance mediated through detailed procedural guidance in local authorities and some voluntary agencies. Since 1990, major changes in child and family law have been enacted throughout the UK, leading to a greater emphasis on parental responsibility and ascertaining children's views.

A major review of child protection practices in the UK (DoH, 1995) introduces a radical reappraisal of child-care policy and practice. The importance of social work services supporting families to rear their children, of working in partnership with parents and other adult carers, and responding to child welfare as well as child protection needs, is receiving renewed attention. The challenge these goals bring is to change the public face of social work child-care services away from services of last resort to outreaching services which seek to work alongside families in improving the life chances of their children.

This chapter considers four aspects of social work with children and families which are important for understanding how social work might contribute to the health and development of children growing up in the UK today. These include information on the social circum-stances of children and families, on some of the different settings and legislation which underpin child-care services, on approaches to working positively with children and families, and on the issues which must be faced if child-care social work is to move forward. The importance of linking social science and social work research to social work intervention in child care is stressed. Child-care research provides social workers and their agencies with clear messages about where to focus their efforts. Social work has a vital contribution in practice to help children gain access to early years services, to support parents and adult carers in developing their parenting skills and to promote a range of flexible child-care services for children and families, balancing the need for support and protection.

Social context

The Joseph Rowntree Foundation Inquiry (Hills, 1995) into the distribution of income and wealth in the UK found that children comprise 30 per cent of the poorest tenth of the population. Single parents and their children, who make up 6 per cent of the population, are significantly overrepresented in the poorest fifth. Not surprisingly, 70 per cent of the gross incomes of families in the poorest two-tenths of households come from social security benefits. The proportion of children living in relative poverty in the UK has increased threefold since 1980, and almost a third of children come from homes below the EC poverty line, households with less than half the national average income (Wilkinson, 1994). Britain has no official poverty line. Between 1979 and 1989, the number of citizens living on the safety net was up by two-thirds and by a third for those living below the level which income support is intended to guarantee. Income inequality has been rising more rapidly in Britain than other westernised countries with the exception of New Zealand.

Absolute poverty further blights the life chances of children. Wilkinson (1994) points to the worrying effects which the widening differences in income distribution are having on the welfare and well-being of children and young people. Widening of income differences since 1985 appears to be matched by a marked slowing of the decline in national death rates for infants and children and an apparent decline in reading standards over the same period which are not adequately explained by differences in teaching methods. Between 1981 and 1991, mortality rates for adults in the prime parenting years widened (Wilkinson, 1994).

The rise in homelessness and the privations that this brings pose serious threats to the health and development of children and young people. It is estimated there are 33,000 children affected by homelessness in Scotland (Children in Scotland, 1995). The steady decline of public sector provision in favour of home ownership and the private rented sector is resulting in poorer standards of housing for families unable to compete in the new market economy. Ironically, the general rise in car ownership leaves the poorest families exposed to all the risks of pollution and road traffic accidents (still one of the highest causes of child mortality in the UK) without the benefits of good public transport, especially in rural areas.

The Rowntree Inquiry (Hills, 1995) and Wilkinson (1994) highlight the range of social problems associated with areas of low income and poverty. Problems in the poorest areas are found to have increased, with high rates of family break-up, high levels of crime, vandalism and youth unemployment, and growing numbers of children registered with local authorities as at risk of abuse. Hills (1995) identifies, since the 1970s, that council housing nationally has become concentrated on those with low incomes. This tenure policy locates council housing in particular estates and areas, creating a social polarisation on the ground. Lone parents surviving on the margins of society, high levels of crime and vandalism, sometimes involving very young children, poor education and some schools being rejected by the children as symbols of 'authority' are noted. Booth and Booth (1996) highlight that the most significant factors in a child's health and development is the uneven distribution of risk or exposure to adversity.

A study of children registered at risk in three local authorities in Scotland (Pitcairn and Waterhouse, 1996) found that the children were primarily children in need, only some of whom were in need of protection from physical or sexual abuse. The parents of the children were almost always unemployed and had been for at least a year. Few left school with any educational qualifications. A significant number of fathers had been in trouble with the law as children and continuing into adulthood. Poor physical health was reported in the parents and children, with about half the women describing themselves as depressed. Alcohol and drug problems were in evidence. Children growing up against these odds may come to share some of the social adversity which characterises the biographies of their parents.

The combined probable impact of poor physical and mental health in children and parents against a background of poverty and family disruption provides a disturbing threat to the safety, health and development of children known to social work services. Childcare social work intervention is largely targeted on estates and areas where the Joseph Rowntree Inquiry (Hills, 1995) identified a 'cycle of poor parenting' with an intergenerational lack of good experiences of parenting, often combined with youth. Few support networks or child-care facilities were found to compound isolation, which can lead to depression and health problems. These social problems present major challenges to social work with children and families, requiring a focus on community as well as individual interventions.

The debate about providing for children as developed legislatively ignores the reality of the growing disparity in the material and social circumstances of children in the UK and the consequent impact that this has on a child's health and development. The impact of poor parenting is also attracting wider recognition (Quinton and Rutter, 1988) as a significant factor in the safety, health and development of children. Holman (1988) observed that similar expectations of parenting are placed on parents irrespective of their social circumstances and resources; certainly, in legal terms, the standard is an objective one of 'best interests' of the child.

Changing family patterns

The traditional view of the nuclear family, with mother at home caring for children and father as breadwinner in full-time employment, no longer describes the reality of family life. The changing nature of adult relationships and women's growing participation in the labour market have resulted in diverse family patterns. Rising divorce rates have resulted in larger numbers of single parents and step-parenting. Childlessness, whether or not chosen, is an issue for many adults. The importance of adapting and developing services to meet the needs and reflect the experiences of families is vitally important. Existing policies and frameworks do not always recognise the diversity of families living in the UK today. Black and minority ethnic people are often disadvantaged on social and economic indicators, especially in relation to employment, housing and child care.

Understanding the changing patterns of partnership and the impact on parenting are central to the development of supportive social services for children and families. Utting (1995) observed that 40 per cent of marriages end in divorce, 20 per cent of families are headed by a lone parent and 8 per cent of dependent children live in step-families. However, step-families are not a new phenomenon, as Walker (1997) indicates: in the nineteenth century, two in every five children lost their father and almost the same proportion their mother by the age of 15 years. Step-families and lone-parent households were as common a feature of Victorian life as they are today, although death rather than divorce was the source of change. Divorce, as a different family transition, now has a significant effect on parenting, with consequences for children depending on their age, gender and post-divorce arrangements. Parenting in the context of adoption, foster care or where a child may have a disability has particular features and additional aspects to be considered in the provision of services to children and families. Recognition of the impact of all types of family transitions on children are important to child-care professionals.

The status of children

The United Nations (UN) Convention on the Rights of the Child was adopted in 1989 and ratified by the UK in 1991. The Convention contains 41 substantive articles which can be grouped around the four main themes of survival, development, protection and participation (Lindsay, 1992). Each state must, after ratification, report to the UN Committee on the Rights of the Child, the convention thus providing a universal standard against which to measure progress in each of the broad areas outlined. Within the UK, the Department of Health has been given lead responsibility for overseeing progress on the implementation of the convention. In 1994, they cited the Children Act, 1989 as one major achievement by government in promoting the rights of children, and since then the Children (Scotland) Act, 1995 and the Children (NI) Order, 1995 have continued to build on this tradition.

The underlying principles stress the paramountcy of the child's welfare, the child's right to express his or her views, the child's right to be free from discrimination, inhumane treatment and all forms of physical, sexual or mental violence, and the child's right to information, education and health care (Lindsay, 1992). Putting these principles into practice is not straightforward. The UN Committee on the Rights of the Child criticised the UK government (1995) for its failure to address the economic rights of children, reflected in growing levels of child poverty, homelessness amongst young people and the treatment of young offenders, especially by placement in secure training units (Franklin and Franklin, 1996).

Despite the ratification by the UK of the UN Convention on the Rights of the Child, Oppeneheim and Lister (1996) point to the long-standing marginalisation of children in political debates. When children do appear, they are mainly treated as objects of public attention rather than subjects who are able to contribute in a meaningful way to an understanding of circumstances which directly affect them. There is growing concern that children and young people are increasingly marginalised from mainstream society. Despite the growing emphasis on the participation of children in decision-making, increasing numbers of children and young people are excluded from employment, housing and other material aspects of life.

Setting

The legal basis and organisational settings for social work with children and families differ between the constituent parts of the UK. The Children Act, 1989 in England and Wales introduced major legislative reform; Scotland and Northern Ireland have recently adopted new children's legislation (Children (Scotland) Act, 1995; Children (Northern Ireland) Order, 1995). Whilst the policy focus of all three are similar, being informed by the promotion of child welfare and having a common emphasis on children 'in need' (Cohen and Hagen, 1997), the legislative content varies to take account of longstanding organisational and legal differences in the delivery of child-care services. There is also a long tradition of charitable and voluntary organisations providing services to children and families (the Royal Scottish Society for the Prevention of Cruelty to Children [RSSPCC], Barnardos, Save the Children Fund [SCF] and so on).

The Children's Hearings System is the nexus for child-care decision-making in Scotland. The system was established under the Social Work (Scotland) Act, 1968 as a direct result of the deliberations of the Kilbrandon Committee (Kilbrandon, 1964), which sought to find solutions to the rise in the rate of juvenile delinquency in post-war Scotland. Developments similar to Kilbrandon also arose in England and Wales with the production of the White Paper *Children in Trouble*, which 'embodied the new thinking including the conflation of the previous separate 'delinquent' and 'deprived' category' (Frost and Stein, 1989) and provided the basis for some of the main provisions of the Children and Young Persons Act, 1969. Northern Ireland was not affected by these major reforms, the Children and Young Persons Act (NI), 1968 still applying (Kelly and Pinkerton, 1996).

This legislative period in Scotland, England and Wales reflected a family-oriented approach where concern was focused on problems at the parenting level with an emphasis on prevention against a background of expansion of welfare and support services (Fox Harding, 1991a, 1991b; Packman and Jordan, 1991). However, key sections of the Children and Young Persons, 1969, Act were never implemented, reflecting the beginning, as Frost and Stein (1989) argue, of a shift in the balance towards justice away from welfare. The welfare principle has, however, remained the key focus of child-care decision-making in relation to children in Scotland regardless of the reason for their referral to the Children's Hearings System, whether 'delinquent' or 'deprived'. The central philosophy of the hearings system has a clear welfare orientation, 'needs' rather than 'deeds' being the basis for decision-making and intervention.

The children's hearing is not a court but a tribunal serviced by lay people drawn from the community of the child, with a knowledge of children and family life. It aims to work in partnership with parents to identify needs and solutions in the best interest of the child, assuming that most parents will want the best for their children. The local authority is responsible for providing social background reports to the hearing and the provision of social work services for the child and family if a supervision requirement is made. The intention of the legislation was to introduce a straightforward procedure, avoiding legal technicalities, with the lay panel taking appropriate action in the child's best interests' (Lord Cameron in McGregor *v.* D 1977 *Scots Law Times* 182 at 185). The courts are only involved where the facts of a case are in dispute, for appeals and for dealing with serious offences. The hearings system was intended as an early intervention system for those children who would benefit from compulsory measures of care and protection, and as a diversion system for those children for whom more harm than good would be done by being drawn into a juvenile justice system.

Since its inception, the Children's Hearings System has given rise to debate about the balance to be struck between natural justice and the welfare of children (Adler, 1985). This was brought into public focus by the Orkney (Scottish Office, 1992a), and Fife (Scottish Office, 1992b) inquiries, and the decision in O *v.* Rae 1992 SCLR 318, which drew further attention to a children's hearing using information which could have founded a condition of referral but had not been tested before a sheriff. Criticisms as in Orkney (Scottish Office, 1992a) questioned the ability of hearings to deal with complex cases of child abuse, especially where allegations of child sexual abuse are to the fore. All legal fora appear to have difficulty in dealing with this issue (see re H (Minors) (Sexual Abuse: Standard of Proof) [1996] 2 *WLR* 8), and there is as yet no empirical basis to evaluate the effectiveness of the hearings system in contrast to other child-care systems.

Child care in Northern Ireland is part of the UK state system but has unique arrangements for the delivery of personal social work services. The Health and Personal Social Services (Northern Ireland) Order, 1972 removed personal social services from local government control, making them part of the NHS (Kelly and Pinkerton, 1996). Since 1973, four integrated health and social service boards have been responsible for providing social work services within a regional strategic plan. The personal social services for each board have a particular responsibility with regard to children and young people, not unlike the Children's Hearings System in Scotland; lay representation is found on the area boards. This has potentially facilitated closer links between social services and health than elsewhere in the UK (Cohen and Hagen, 1997). Legislation in 1994 (Health and Personal Social Services (NI) Order) Belfast, 1994) allowed health and social service boards to delegate responsibility for statutory child-care duties to self-governing trusts (Cohen and Hagen, 1997).

Peyton (1997) argues that, despite organisational integration between health and social services, child-care services come second to the health agenda and acute sector spending. In order to improve the status of child care, an interdepartmental project has been established to ensure coordinated implementation of the 1995 Children (NI) Order. A five year package of financial investment geared mainly to the most vulnerable children in Northern Ireland (including children with disabilities) has been put in place. It remains to be seen whether this will change the emphasis within child care in Northern Ireland from surveillance to support. Tensions have arisen, since the implementation of the 1995 Order, between a business culture and children's needs (Peyton, 1997). Attempts have been made to address the complex contracting process, and additional mechanisms for monitoring, setting standards including joint assessments of local need and a joint child-care strategy are being explored (Peyton, 1997). The Audit Commission Report (1994) in England and Wales identified that most commissioning health authorities have yet to assess the full needs of children in their areas for community child health services.

Despite these differing legal and organisational contexts, all social work services for children and families throughout the UK depend on a mix between statutory local authority services, the voluntary and private sector. It is less than 30 years since Departments of Social Work were introduced in Scotland (under the Social Work [Scotland] Act, 1968) and their counterparts, Social Services Departments, in England and Wales (1971). Social services came of age during a political era of economic restraint without the benefit of professional traditions already well established, and social work services have remained selective to those families and children most in need, sitting uneasily against health and education with their universalist concerns.

Child-care policy and practice

Unlike the universalist services of health and education, social services for children and families is, by comparison, a residual service providing support when children and families are experiencing difficulties. Child-care social work has been highly concentrated on children in need, children in public care, children who offend and children in need of care and protection. Social work intervention may be on a compulsory or requested basis and may involve children being looked after away from home in foster or residential care either briefly or on a long-term and in some instances permanent basis. There is a tension in practice between the provision of support where requested by families and the possibility of compulsory intervention. This highlights the context within which modern social work child-care practice operates, influencing the types of service provided and the approaches to social work intervention. The role of social work intervention in family life is the subject of continuing debate within government, amongst professionals and publicly in the media, especially in the context of child abuse. It is important to remember that child protection is only one aspect of child care, albeit one which has been a major influence in shaping social work practice.

The management of child abuse in the UK has evolved since the mid-1970s to a national system of local area review committees to coordinate policy and interdisciplinary cooperation. All areas now have procedural guidelines for professions concerned with children's welfare, child protection registers to identify children at risk of harm and multidisciplinary case conferences led by social work/services departments as a forum to assess risk and formally identify children in need of registration. There is an increasing cooperation between the law enforcement, health and social work agencies, most recently exemplified by the moves towards the joint interviewing of children and their parents by police officers and social workers. Procedural guidelines and numerous governmental circulars on child abuse have been the consequence of enquiries into the deaths of children at the hands of their parents or guardians (Maria Colwell Inquiry; DHSS, 1974). The Cleveland (DHSS, 1988) and Orkney (Scottish Office, 1992) inquiries provided further impetus for the development of investigatory techniques in child sexual abuse to provide evidence admissible within an adversarial court system.

Government procedural guidance has increasingly shifted the emphasis in social work/services departments away from the universal principle of welfare established in the Kilbrandon and Seebohm committees to a focus in social work practice with the detection and identification of children at risk of physical and sexual abuse. Perhaps the most detrimental outcome of this shift to surveillance may be the stigma which families who are in receipt of social work child-care services are reported to experience (Farmer and Owen, 1995). The Department of Health review of child protection studies (1995) demonstrated that, for many families, their greatest fear was the possibility of the compulsory removal of their child into public care. The statistical analysis of pathways into public care for child protection referrals shows that removal of the child on initial investigation occurs for fewer than 1 per cent of all children referred. Furthermore, the numbers of children accommodated on a compulsory basis after a child protection conference are no greater than those on a voluntary basis (DoH, 1995, p. 28).

Good child-care practice dictates an acknowledgement with families of the anxieties which child protection investigations raise. This is important to ensure the open communication, as far as possible, between practitioners and families so central to assessment and working together. The majority of families, however, who are investigated for apparently transgressive behaviour are poor and are, in the main, filtered out of the system, receiving no services or family support (Gibbons *et al.*, 1995). Cleaver and Freeman (1995) found that these families were seldom advised of the outcome of investigation, reinforcing their wariness of professional intrusion. This would point to the importance of discussing outcomes with families providing an important opportunity to improve parent and professional relationships.

The Department of Health, in *Child Protection: Messages from Research* (1995), encourages social work policy-makers to recast the problem of child abuse in ways which emphasise child welfare needs as the primary factor in determining the child's best interests. This has led to an increasing policy emphasis on prevention and support to families and 'children in need'. However, in a context of diminishing resources where local authorities may have insufficient means to meet duties to children 'in need', the gateway to limited resources may become the legal or administrative procedures which define children as 'at risk'. A child's chances of gaining access to resources may, therefore, be likely to be significantly increased through the imposition of a legal order.

Professionals involved in child-care decision-making are aware of this dilemma in practice, and it seems naïve to assume that this will not influence their decisions. In an in-depth study of the way in which policies for children in need were defined and prioritised (Colton *et al.*, 1995, p. 204), it was found, in two Welsh authorities, 'that social service departments in Wales are clearly concentrating their effort on children at risk of abuse and neglect'. However, managers ideally wished to place a greater emphasis on family support work to enable a corresponding reduction in the need for statutory intervention. Similarly, in a SSI Report (1996) of local authority services to families, in seven out of eight authorities inspected it was 'very difficult' to gain access to services unless child protection concerns were expressed. Clearly, children 'at risk' and their parents may be reassured and benefit from access to support services, which is a positive contribution to the welfare of children. It remains important in practice, however, not to label children as 'at risk' unnecessarily when they are 'in need', recognising the problem that this may pose for practitioners on a day-to-day basis in a context of scarce resources.

The following example illustrates this dilemma of balancing risk and need in day-to-day practice. The authors visited a lone mother whose husband had left the family home after hitting the younger of two children, who was 18 months old at the time. After a child protection investigation, it was clear that the father would not be returning to the household, and the children were therefore not deemed to be at risk of abuse. However, at the home visit, the mother was clearly struggling to care adequately for her two children, the elder being seven years of age. There was a marked absence of play materials, hygiene standards were fairly low: for example the youngest child needed bathing and the nappy changing. This family were living in a materially deprived housing estate with few public amenities for either adults or children. It was clear that the mother was unable to provide sufficient stimulation for either child to enhance their development, as she herself recognised despite an apparent sense of depression. Family support was needed and wanted by this mother to enhance the life chances of her children and to support her parenting of them. She was disappointed social work services appeared to be no longer interested in her or her children once the immediate source of risk – 'her husband' – had left the household. Failing to address broader child-care needs leaves children vulnerable to further crises and poorer long-term outcomes for health and development.

Hallett (1993), comparing European and UK practices in relation to child protection, stresses the need to strike a balance between the paramountcy of the welfare of the child and the notion of justice within the wider community. This struggle is also played out in relation to children who offend. The law and social work practice have attempted to balance these competing claims against a growing background of public policy which seeks to isolate the young offender for the protection of the community.

Policy appears to be shifting from a concern with the social and personal needs of juvenile offenders to the frequency and nature of their offending. Anderson and Kinsey (1993), whilst finding no significant social class differences in offending amongst young people, confirm that infrequent, non-serious offending is the norm rather than the exception for young people. Cleland (1995) suggests that increased public pressure to make children accountable for wrongdoing plus a growing concentration on victim need have contributed to the public focus shifting from the welfare of the child to the offending behaviour and its consequences. These are not necessarily mutually exclusive, but a balance needs to be struck between addressing offending behaviour and responding to the needs of children in trouble.

There is growing concern, however, about young people who persistently offend, with a belief that these youngsters tend to be specialist criminals. Hagel and Newburn (1994), in their research, identified 531 10–16-year-olds in two areas in England who had allegedly committed at least three offences in 1992. The most common were road traffic offences, theft from shops and car theft. Violent and/or sexual crimes were unusual, and drug-related offences were apparently rare. Few of the children were employed, or in further education or training, and 50 per cent were already known to social services. Patterns of familial disruption characterised by alcohol and/or drug misuse as well as criminality within the family were reported. Adverse personal and social circumstances, rather than the nature of their offences, were the factors common to the children. Closeness of parental supervision and levels of parental expectation of behaviour regarding offending were more important predictors of offending behaviour (Farrington, 1993).

Support to families in their parenting responsibilities would appear to be a central concern for social work practice in relation to children who offend. Parenting education programmes are increasingly being utilised within practice for all ages of children. Furthermore, direct work with young offenders, especially to improve their social and personal skills, is relevant. The use of cognitive behavioural techniques has been widely used and has proved effective in reducing offending behaviour. The importance of education is vital, truancy often being related to offending and poor educational attainment (Farrington, 1993).

A young man aged 20 years was convicted of assault and robbery with two older co-accused when he was aged 17 years. He was placed on probation for three years, this being his first offence and clearly related to his drug-taking behaviour. He had left school with no qualifications and had, for the most part, been unemployed following some youth training. He spent most of his time with other young men in similar circumstances, often sleeping for much of the day and meeting at night. He became involved on the fringes of a local older group of men who had criminal histories and were involved in a local drugs trade. In the course of the probation order, he was encouraged to resume physical fitness training, which he had at one time had an interest in. This was also partly a way to address his drug-taking, providing some substitute activity, and to offer opportunities to make new friends outside the drug scene. The social worker supervising the probation order supported his application to the local further education college to begin further training, and he gained recognised educational certificates equipping him to become a trainer. He subsequently went on to gain employment in the local authority's recreation department working with young people. In the final review of his probation order, he felt his life had been turned around and he had been given 'something to live for, a future'. Most importantly, his own sense of self-esteem and self-efficacy had been improved through discovering he was good at something.

Partnership, prevention and support in practice

Direct involvement of a social worker with a child and their ᵢₐₘᵢₗᵧ remains the major context in which child-care social work is practised in the UK. This may be on an voluntary or compulsory basis. There has also been a move towards specialism, with the development of dedicated children and families teams within social work/services departments. A growing recognition is being given to the importance of social work services working alongside health, education, social security and housing (Audit Commission, 1994). This may lead to a clearer articulation of policies and planning requirements for children and their families. It is clear that policy and practice are moving towards a renewed interest in partnership, prevention and early intervention, family support, and an emphasis on interagency coordination (Hallet and Birchall, 1995).

Partnership

The model of partnership between parents and professionals, as set out in guidance, is a cornerstone of the Children Act, 1989 in England and Wales, the importance of which is emphasised by the Department of Health (1995) in relation to child protection practice. Guidance now issued in Scotland relating to the Children (Scotland) Act, 1995 emphasises that parents should normally be responsible for the upbringing of their children and promotes a partnership model. Similarly, the new Children (NI) Order, 1995 promotes partnership with parents if children are in care and specifically requires consultation with parents and children about any decisions made. The Department of Health, in *Working Together*, made it clear that agencies should work in partnership with families in all child-care cases.

Partnership in day-to-day practice means involving parents, and where appropriate children, in decisions about the welfare of the child, offering real choices to families, sharing information and keeping families informed about progress and procedures. Partnership involves the sharing of responsibility between professionals and families, and recognising the imbalance in power which the statutory role may bring. Clarity about social workers' powers and duties, especially in the context of child protection, is vital to open communication and equalising the power balance between the local authority and the parent. Cleaver and Freeman (1995) found, in their study of parental perspectives in cases of suspected child abuse, that parents, who later found that inquiries had been made prior to any exploration of concern directly with them, were subsequently alienated from the professionals who were trying to offer help or support.

Furthermore, organisational change is likely to be necessary to ensure child-friendly procedures as well as practice and a move towards a more cooperative model of working with families. An open complaints procedure is a further important step (BAAF, 1996).

Thoburn *et al.* (1995) found a clear link between better outcomes for children and greater involvement of parents. With greater parental involvement, parenting arrangements for the children seemed to be more settled, links with parents and important adults were maintained, and progress was made in the child's health and development. In contrast, where there was a failure to work in partnership with parents, outcomes were less favourable. In these cases, parents were less involved and identified less with child-care decisions. Yet it was rare that the difficulties facing parents and their children were so severe as to preclude any working together.

The attitude, skills and efforts of social workers were found to be critical in achieving participation in families where there were multiple problems. Creative thinking by practitioners to encourage participation in these worse-case scenarios was best supported when agency policies and procedures aimed for parental participation. Children, too, strongly welcomed involvement in decisions which affected their lives, as borne out by Thoburn *et al.* (1995) and Roberts and Taylor (1996).

A practical example concerns the admission of a young man into residential care as he had been consistently truanting and mixing with a group of older boys who were frequently involved in minor theft and drinking. The parents were initially relieved at his admission as they had found it difficult to control his behaviour, and this had resulted in physical aggression between father and son at times. However, after a short time, the parents began to feel distanced from their son and decisions being made about his education and future. Although they attended review meetings, they found it difficult to speak and felt they had very little influence over their son's life. The social worker and residential staff quickly became aware of this and utilised a number of strategies to ensure closer communication between all the parties and to rebuild the parent/child relationship. Residential staff agreed to contact the parents on a daily basis to keep them in touch with their son's activities; furthermore, the social worker supported the parents in keeping directly in touch with their son's school to monitor his progress and attendance.

The aim was to support parents in maintaining their parental responsibilities for their son even though he was not living with them. The young man became interested in golf, and his father was encouraged to take part with him, this joint activity becoming a positive focus in their relationship. At the same time, direct work was done with the parents in renegotiating their strategies for controlling and disciplining their children and developing more appropriate means of communicating with the children as they grew into adults. The father was helped by the social worker to explore his own childhood, which had been characterised by harsh parental discipline, causing him to fear and dislike his own father. He did not wish this to occur with his own son but had found it difficult to be open about his experiences and the effects on him.

Early years services

It has become increasingly clear that one of the most effective forms of primary prevention lies in early years services, particularly those encouraging parental involvement. Preschool education remains discretionary despite widespread recognition of its importance to future outcomes for children (Berrueta-Clement *et al.*, 1984) and a significant growth in demand arising from such factors as increasing women's employment and the wish to provide stimulating environments for children in the early years. Traditionally provided by the statutory and voluntary sectors, there has recently been a rapid growth in private nurseries and day-care centres, available at a cost to those families who can afford them. Britain still compares unfavourably with other European and Scandinavian countries, the majority of whom provide high levels of preschool services (Cohen and Fraser, 1991).

A variety of services, including childminders, play groups, family centres, day nurseries and nursery schools, are available, but choice is largely restricted to those who can afford to pay (Jones and Bilton, 1994). Children from families on low incomes in the UK are most likely to be placed in local authority social work provision, which may set them apart from other children but also brings vital resources and child-care services.

Black children, especially, are more likely to be referred to local authority child-care services for broader social and economic reasons. Barn (1990) found that black children were overrepresented in public care and little attention was paid to their specific needs. Black children were twice as likely as white children to be admitted into care within four weeks of referral, which indicates a shortfall in appropriate preventive work with black children and their families. Asian children are underrepresented in public care but also in relation to family-based services, especially for children with disability (Shah, 1992). It is clear that, in the planning and provision of social services to black children and their families, there has been a fundamental lack of systematic consideration of race and cultural pluralism in mainstream service provision and social work practice.

Headstart and Hi-Scope are particular forms of intervention and support to preschool children and their families which emphasise active learning by the child and the involvement of parents. Research provides evidence that these types of service are of particular benefit to the most disadvantaged children. Black children, when assessed some years after an early years intervention programme, appeared to secure the most benefit, especially in cognitive development (MacDonald and Roberts, 1995). Positive effects were also reported in mothers' attitudes towards their children's schoolwork and future aspirations (MacDonald and Roberts, 1995). In the short term, health promotion programmes concentrating on child development appear to contribute to reducing the likelihood of appearance on child protection registers (Barker *et al.*, 1994).

The longer-term outcomes for children participating in these types of service is less clear. The most systematic study (Berrueta-Clement *et al.*, 1984) of long-term benefits for children of high-quality preschool education concludes that cognitive and social development are enhanced. The Hi-Scope programme, which places particular emphasis on an active learning curriculum, appears to be associated with fewer arrests in adolescence and early adulthood and a lower percentage in receipt of social services at the age of 27 years (MacDonald and Roberts, 1995). The Headstart programme, however, found that progress was not always maintained, especially in families facing extreme social adversity. Advantages initially gained could be lost within a few years as the child progressed into the formal school system.

The Hi-Scope curriculum has been widely adopted throughout the UK. Barnardos, along with the Department of Health, have promoted its development. A Hi-Scope Institute was opened in London in 1990, with the aim of providing high-quality training and continuing support.

Social work is playing an increasing role in early years services. A key example, the MARS project, was jointly funded by Barnardos and by local authority social work and education departments in Scotland. Practitioners worked intensively with children and families deemed to be at high risk and in crisis, using traditional social casework methods. The intervention was found to prevent entry into public care and offset some of the harmful effects of poor parenting (Fuller, 1992). There is an increasing recognition of the importance of preschool education which involves parents and an ongoing development of family centres which seek to support parents and children. An example is the Stepping Stones project in Scotland, which aims to empower families with young children in the more severely disadvantaged communities to improve their lives.

Parenting

An important role for social workers is a focus on parenting education and providing complementary support services which aim to promote the health and development of children by assisting and encouraging positive parental child-rearing strategies. There are numerous organisations and services developing to support parents, such as Family Mediation, Parent Link/Parent Network and Parent to Parent Information and Adoption Services (PPIAS) for adoptive and long-term foster carers. Parenting education programmes are being developed, as are associated home visiting programmes (Home-Start UK), often involving volunteers to provide practical support, advice and role models. The importance of interdisciplinary and interagency collaboration in supporting parents is emphasised in recent government policy (Audit Commission, 1994).

In practice, social workers can assist parents in bringing up their children by drawing on their knowledge of child development and effective parenting strategies. There may be, however, conflicting views between parents and professionals on what constitutes 'good enough' parenting. The demands of parenting will also be influenced by general social expectations of parents and social workers in society.

There is evidence to suggest some intergenerational continuity in parenting, although the experience of poor parenting does not automatically result in parenting difficulties in the next generation (Quinton and Rutter, 1988). Findings suggest that people who have been brought up in institutional care, have experienced abuse or neglect in their own childhood or grew up in hostile discordant families are more likely to experience difficulties in parenting themselves (Quinton and Rutter, 1988). Critics of the notion of intergenerational continuity in parenting point to social class, rather than prior childhood experiences, as a key factor influencing parenting styles (Smith, 1991).

Parenting styles have been linked to children's behaviour and social development (Baumrind, 1971). The Department of Health review of research in relation to child protection (DoH, 1995) highlights families where there is low warmth and high criticism towards children as most damaging to their development. Physical chastisement has been shown in non-abusing families to be routinely used as a method of behavioural control (Newson and Newson, 1976), and this may have reinforced the notion of a continuum of physical disciplinary strategies where, in an abusive situation, normal limits may have been exceeded. In practice, social workers are seeking to encourage parents to relate to their children with warmth using effective disciplinary strategies to reduce discord. Parents can be helped by social workers to make links between their own past experiences of being parented and the present experiences of being a parent.

In Pitcairn and Waterhouse's (1993) study of parents whose children were registered as potentially at risk, difficulties in the control and management of the children clearly emerged. Surprisingly, the nature of these difficulties, as reported by the parents, reflected a failure to discipline the children consistently and routinely, even when the parents were clear that some intervention on their part was necessary. Lax disciplinary strategies appeared to predominate for parents, whilst the social workers' framework remained fixed on the idea that excessive discipline was central in parent/child relationships in the context of alleged abuse. Misunderstanding of this aspect of the problem may lead to inappropriate solutions which fail to influence the daily management of the child in a positive way, especially for parents overwhelmed by the demands of parenting young children. Information and strategies to manage difficult behaviour are increasingly available and provide a practical way forward.

Public care services

Providing a range of flexible public child-care services is essential to the implementation of an effective child-care strategy. Residential child care remains a major plank of child-care services for children and families despite the shift since the mid-1970s towards family-based care, especially for young children. This change was partly influenced by Rowe and Lambert's (1973) study showing the failure on the part of some social workers to plan vigorously for children in public care. Combined with an increasing awareness of the need for children to have a permanent home base, policy, not uninfluenced by financial imperatives, shifted to either rehabilitation with the natural family or placement in a permanent substitute family. These developments led to some patchy results. The pressure to reduce the use of residential resources led to some of the most disturbed and troubled young people being looked after in residential care when either family care or family placement broke down.

This swing against residential care coincided with a reduction in financial and training investment, lowering the morale of child-care staff. Despite these difficulties, research by Fisher *et al.* (1986) and a Department of Health Inspection (1994) found that young people and parents preferred residential care to foster care. Both the Utting Report on *Children in the Public Care* (1991) and Skinner (1992) strongly recommend the recognition of residential child care as a positive choice, especially for young people who are unable live at home and present challenging behaviour. However (Hill and

Aldgate, 1996b; Cliffe with Berridge, 1991) found that there was little choice of placement for children or parents, resource levels being limited in scale and range.

In practice, residential care remains an important resource for many young people. A key focus for social work practice is the maintenance of links between parents and children and between residential and field social workers (Millham *et al.*, 1986). Hill and Aldgate (1996b) also point to the importance of actively involving young people in significant decisions and ensuring that meetings which concern their future are not overly adult-dominated. There is a responsibility incumbent on social work to provide safe environments for children in public care and to ensure that there is an adequate complaints procedure. Some local authorities now employ Children's Rights Officers offering an independent service to children in public care. The need to promote educational opportunities for children in public care is a central practice concern.

More recent research outlines the poor educational outcome for many children in public care (Aldgate *et al.*, 1993). The loss of schooling in children who are already facing adversity appears to have further negative consequences for later life chances. Quinton and Rutter (1988), looking at outcomes for young people raised in institutions, have shown the importance of positive school experiences in mediating adverse adult outcomes where home circumstances are characterised by poor relationships. Schooling is of central importance to children who come from already difficult backgrounds. This is particularly relevant for girls, where research has shown that choice of partner is likely to reflect their own circumstances of disadvantage and further to limit their horizons (Quinton and Rutter, 1988). Girls who come from backgrounds of family discord and have experienced institutional care are more likely to select deviant partners, perhaps as a well-intentioned but misguided escape from discordant relationships at home. Positive educational experience can, in effect, widen the choice of partner, research having shown that a supportive marital relationship is a protective factor against stressful experiences (Brown and Harris, 1978) and may support reasonable child-rearing practice (Quinton and Rutter, 1988).

Young people in residential care generally report getting on well with staff whilst regretting the lack of continuity in relationships. They are looking for individualised care, privacy, attention and support with school work, control of bullying and wider peer contacts (Fletcher, 1993). Staff favouritism was disliked. There is increasing recognition of the importance of taking account of the views of children looked after by local authorities. In a Scottish local authority, a one day conference was organised by young people in care in conjunction with the Children's Rights Officer and other staff to explore issues of particular significance, the aim being to feed back to senior staff and elected officials.

Family placement is another public child-care service. It includes short-term or long-term foster care and adoption for those children in need of permanent alternative care. Sellick (1996) found that 65 per cent of all children in local authority public care for one year were fostered. Most of the children spent very short periods in care, that is, less than 14 days for 50 per cent of the children. Concern continues about the number of children who are placed in short-term foster care at times of emergency without clear future child-care plans (Stone, 1995). McAuley (1996), in her study of children placed in foster care, found that the majority of the children had experienced several previous care placements before long-term solutions were sought. Most of the children had experienced abuse and/or neglect. Despite these difficulties, regular access to birth parents and siblings was maintained. McAuley, like Millham *et al.* (1986) and Packman *et al.* (1986), stresses the importance of social workers helping children to maintain links with their families, friends and wider social networks. Children themselves are often the most vocal advocates for this continuing contact.

The family placement needs of black children have received greater attention in recent years, although much of the debate has centred around the debates between 'transracial' and 'same-race' placements, especially for children of mixed parentage (Caesar *et al.*, 1993). However, whilst it is generally accepted that children may be best placed with families or in residential settings reflecting the ethnic background of their own parents, the experience of young people who have been placed transracially varies, and it is not necessarily always a damaging experience (Tizard and Phoenix, 1989). A full assessment of each child's needs should be made in decisions about family placement.

Adoption is a child-care option for a small proportion of children who cannot live with their families. In a survey by Rowe *et al.* (1989) of placement patterns in six local authorities, only 0.8 per cent of children in care went on to be adopted. The pattern of adoption has changed radically in the past 30 years. Fewer babies are now available for adoption, reflecting changes in societal values relating to single parenthood. There are increasing numbers of older children for whom adoption is sought; many of these children have special health or educational needs or have been removed from their families after contested proceedings, usually against a background of abuse and neglect. Research focusing on disrupted family placements (Rowe and Thoburn, 1988; Borland *et al.*, 1991) has shown that higher disruption rates are associated with increasing age at placement. In the case of children adopted as infants, there are still ongoing issues of explaining adoption, of identity (Hoopes, 1990), which adoptive parents may also need support in approaching.

In the light of the changing patterns of adoption, there has been an increasing recognition of the need for continuing post-placement support for adoptive families beyond the initial adjustment period, especially in the context of the adoption of 'hard to place' children, (Macaskill, 1985; Yates, 1985; Rushton *et al.*, 1993). Macaskill (1985) demonstrated that it was frequently after the first two years of place-ment that more complex difficulties were recognised. She further found that, even in the most stable placements, adopted children still tended to show vulnerability in the face of unexpected change or crisis.

It seems clear that, for children who have had poor early experi-ences, a secure home environment is not always sufficient to compen-sate for early difficulties. If there are further complexities in the adoption process, for example continuing birth family contact as in the situation of 'open adoption', further social work support is likely to be necessary in the family's life.

A useful way of providing post-placement support to adoptive parents and foster carers was initiated by the British Agencies for Adoption and Fostering (BAAF) in Scotland. A series of training initiatives were organised for adoptive parents and foster carers, focusing on the types of difficulty that children and young people may bring to placement. The training courses were both knowledge- and skill-based in an attempt to increase understanding of the differing problems and to equip people with possible methods of approaching these issues. Participants from all courses saw the opportunity to meet other parents with similar concerns and to share experiences as helpful. The courses with more skills orientation were seen to offer parents practical ideas they could use in looking after their adoptive or foster child. This may be a helpful and cost-effective way to offer support to adoptive parents and foster carers.

Conclusion

There is an urgent need to protect children from the worst conse-quences of social and economic change over the past two decades, to recognise that many children are growing up in poverty, and that children who come from poor families may also face additional adversities which threaten children's social development. Social adversity, like poverty, is accumulative and is harder to fight as parental reserves diminish. Changing family patterns mean that many children will experience disruption in their upbringing, and many women will be lone parents, at least for a part of their child-bearing years.

Children in need and their families run the risk of falling between the priorities of mainstream schools and the highly selective provision of social work and social services departments (Wilkinson, 1994). The Audit Commission Report (1994) points to the importance of health, education and social work working together to define 'needs' and developing a joint strategy for children's services. Encouragement is given to the three agencies to take a more equal share in the responsibility to provide for 'children in need'. Social work/services departments' duties to provide 'children's services plans' detailing policy and service links between health, education and social work are seen as the way forward in the UK. They have already been implemented in England and Wales and appear in primary legislation in Scotland for the first time.

The Audit Commission (1994) calls for a rebalancing in practice towards a greater emphasis on family support services, drawing from a wider range of options in the community, including voluntary bodies, health and education professionals. Health is asked, especially through general practitioners, to take a full and active participation in responding to health matters for 'children in need'. Education is expected to accept joint ownership of the problem of disrupted education for children looked after by social work/services. Family centres are proposed as a suitable focus for developing joint ventures between health, social work and education. These could act as an integrated base for child health clinics, peer support groups, nursery classes and other preschool provision, and advice centres on housing and social security benefits. This recommendation is timely when many of the preventative and early intervention strategies, such as Homestart, play groups and youth work, are under threat. At present, there is no infrastructure to ensure interagency and interdisciplinary collaboration in setting the aims, philosophy and principles for children's services in the UK.

Three implications stand out as central to the development of effective social work practice with children and families. The first concerns partnership in developing services which are available to all families in society who may be experiencing difficulties. The emphasis on child protection investigations within social services may have detracted from the promotion of wider preventative services where the primary emphasis is on support rather than surveillance alone. Child protection will always be central to social work because of the legislative and policy framework and a recognition that some parents are unable to care for and protect their own children. Social work practice with children and families should be proactive, involving local communities in the development of practical services, especially those which may support lone parents. This would allow social workers to work alongside the communities they

are seeking to serve and may encourage families to turn to soci
work services for help, support and advice. Models of practice nee
to include a community orientation, which appears to have lost
ground to models of individual surveillance and supervision. Set
against the levels of poverty many families in the UK now face, the
need for community orientation has never been more pressing.

Second, social work practitioners have a key role in helping families to gain access to child-care and educational services. The importance of early years services for the health and development of
children cannot be overemphasised, nor can the significance of
education in preparing children for the future. As many of the families in receipt of social work services are adversely affected by
poverty, poor housing and unemployment, such services are critical
in improving the life chances of children in these circumstances. Such
services can act as a protective factor for vulnerable children and
point to social work not as a sole provider of services but as having a
role in supporting parents and children to get the most out of current
universal child-care provision. Whilst it is important that parents are
encouraged to see the value of education for their children, parental
attitude being an important factor in determining educational
outcomes, it is equally incumbent on schools and social work services
to reach out to parents and children in ways which let them participate and benefit from educational and social care systems.

Third, developing parenting programmes as well as providing
direct support remains an important goal for social worker practice.
Research consistently points to the importance of 'good enough'
parenting for the future development of children. Social work practitioners have a contribution to make alongside other disciplines in
helping parents to gain the skills and resources they need to carry out
their parental responsibilities. Research also suggests that the vast
majority of parents want the best for their children, but some may
not be able to provide it without public and professional support.
Against increasing financial constraints in public expenditure,
imaginative solutions and working together with families and
communities point the way forward. In future, the emphasis needs
increasingly to be on what social work services can offer children and
families alongside the other major services of health, housing, education and income support.

There is a renewed interest in prevention, family support and early
intervention. The Children Act, 1989, the Children (Scotland) Act, 1995
and the Children (NI) Order, 1995 all focus on the importance of partnership between the family and the state and of providing support to
'children in need'. Legislation alone is not the solution to the problems
that children face in our society, nor does it represent child-care policy,
but is an attempt to set out principles and practice to regulate public

and legal interventions in children's lives. Financial and economic policies for child-care provision are equally important, and services to support children and families require resources in cash and in kind which appear to be increasingly restricted.

Public confidence in social work services will only be achieved if our own institutions set an example of practices which promote the health and development of children and their families. This can only be ensured if social work can provide a safe environment for children, a matter which has been called into question by public scandals since the 1980s over the institutional abuse of children in public care. Social work has to be clear that policies and practices are truly child-centred and work towards the best interests of children and their families.

Further reading

DoH (1995) *Child Protection: Messages From Research* (London, HMSO).

> This book provides a review of over 20 child protection studies commissioned by the Department of Heath, drawing out direct lessons for practice in social work with children and families.

Fahlberg, V. (1991) *A Child's Journey Through Placement* (London, BAAF).

> A very readable book which draws well on theory and research to highlight issues for the child looked after away from home. The strength of Fahlberg lies in her practical focus and ability to link theory to practice.

Hill, M. and Aldgate, J. (eds) (1996) *Child Welfare Services: Developments in Law, Policy, Practice and Research* (London, Jessica Kingsley).

> An excellent collection of essays which provides an extended view of some of the issues outlined in this chapter.

Sinclair, R., Garnett, L. and Berridge, D. (1995) *Social Work Assessment with Adolescents* (London, National Children's Bureau).

> A useful addition to literature on assessment in social work giving good practical guidance.

Waterhouse, L. (ed.) (1996) *Child Abuse and Child Abusers: Protection and Prevention* (London, Jessica Kingsley).

> A key reading for any social work student or practitioner who needs to understand the social, legal and professional context of child abuse.

23

Social work with adults

NEIL THOMPSON

Introduction

Social work with adults is a vast topic covering a wide range of client groups, settings problems, challenges, approaches, resources and rewards. This chapter is therefore necessarily selective and introductory in nature. What it is intended to provide is an overview of the context in which such work takes place, differences between client groups and settings, and common themes in terms of the roles and tasks expected of social workers undertaking work with adults.

Of course, social work with adults takes place in the context of a complex legislative and policy framework, one that has undergone considerable change during the 1990s as a result of new legislation and changes of emphasis in political perspectives on the role of social welfare in modern society, as, for example, in an increasingly significant role for market forces. This policy framework will no doubt continue to evolve, so the discussions presented here should be seen in that context rather than as static entities that will not change over time.

Social work with children is often presented as if it were more skilled and more important than work with adults (Preston-Shoot and Agass, 1990). An important point to be emphasised in this chapter is the highly skilful nature of effective practice in social work with adults. To regard such work as routine, straightforward or unskilled is both inaccurate and unfair – inaccurate because it fails to take account of the challenges involved and the skills needed to rise to them; unfair because it undervalues the high-quality work of so many practitioners involved in adult services. The myth of social work with adults being the poor relation of child-care work is, therefore, something that will be challenged and 'debunked' in this chapter.

As we shall see, social work with adults is extremely diverse. However, this is not to say that there are no common themes. One such theme, and a very important one at that, is the importance of seeking to empower people, to support them constructively in their efforts to retain as much control as possible over their lives, to remain as independent and autonomous as possible, and to remove or avoid barriers to enjoying a quality of life free from distress, disadvantage and oppression. This theme should, therefore, be borne in mind in considering the discussions that follow.

The context for practice is the first set of issues to be addressed. This involves outlining the different sets of people or 'client groups' that are included under the umbrella term of social work with adults. Following on from this, I shall explore the significance of 'systematic practice' with adults and, in so doing, emphasise the importance of being clear about what we are doing and why. Next comes a discussion of the life course and an examination of the significance of life stages for adults as well as for children, and for families as well as individuals. This paves the way for an exploration of the roles and tasks required of social workers in their work with adults, a discussion of many of the duties involved in such work. Space does not permit a critical analysis of, or commentary upon, these roles and tasks, but this is not to say that they are unproblematic or not open to criticism. Indeed, it could be seen as a general rule of professional practice that no method, technique or approach to intervention should be accepted uncritically at face value. This is partly what is meant by critically reflective practice. Finally, the conclusion seeks to draw together the main threads of the chapter and present an overview of the principles of good practice.

Before launching into the main substance of the chapter, it is also worth noting that this chapter addresses adults as direct service users in their own right. It does not, therefore, refer to the work undertaken with adults in a child-care context (as parents, for example) nor as offenders within the criminal justice system.

The context for practice

Work with adults encompasses a number of client groups and a wide variety of settings. Figure 23.1 summarises the situation in terms of the *main* elements, but this is of course by no means comprehensive.

Such groups have a great deal in common but also significant differences. I shall comment here on some of the aspects that apply to specific groups and will return to the question of commonalities below under the heading of roles and tasks.

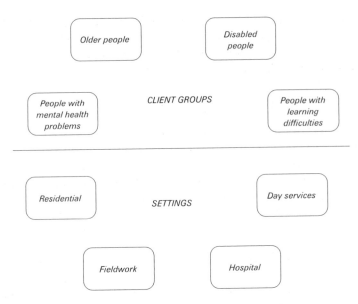

Figure 23.1 Client groups and settings

Older people

A fundamental basis for social work with older people must be the need to work consistently within a context of anti-ageist practice in order to ensure that the steps taken by the worker, or by others involved in the process of helping, act against the predominant tendencies to demean, marginalise and disempower older people without in any way reinforcing or condoning such tendencies. This involves recognising older people as a group who are subject to discrimination and oppression.

One particular example of ageist ideology is the tendency for older people to be excluded at times from the category of social work with adults. For example, services are often organised under the headings of services for children and families, services for adults, and services for 'the elderly' [sic], as if older people were not adults (Midwinter, 1990). It is, therefore, important to assert the right of older people to be included within the category of 'adults'.

Work with older people includes the assessment of need and provision (either directly or through purchasing from other sources) of appropriate services; advocacy and mediation; counselling and other problem-solving methods. However, it should be noted that ageist attitudes and structures can lead to the first item on this list becoming more or less the only item on the list for some practitioners or agencies, a point to which I shall return below.

People with physical disabilities

There are strong parallels here with the discussion above of social work with older people, in so far as disabled people also constitute a group who face discrimination and oppression (Oliver, 1990). A major factor in this regard is the importance of moving away from a medical model in which disability is confused with a form of illness, with the result that staff tend to focus too much on care and doing things *for* people, and not enough on rights and empowerment (a theme that will be explored more fully below). As Oliver (1996, pp. 76–7) comments:

> discrimination against disabled people is institutionalised through-out society and... welfare provision has compounded rather than alleviated that discrimination... The fact remains that providing welfare services on the basis of individual need has aided the process of excluding disabled people from society rather than facili-tated their inclusion.

Like older people, adults with disabilities can also face 'infantili-sation' (Hockey and James, 1993). That is, they too are often treated as if they were children, for example when they are not fully consulted about steps that are being taken on their behalf or services that are being provided. Recognising disabled people's status as full citizens is therefore an important part of social work with this group of adults.

Work with disabled people includes the assessment of need and the provision of appropriate services, as well as a range of other activities geared towards reducing risk, maximising independence and improving quality of life.

People with learning difficulties

The fact that we use terms such as 'learning difficulties' or 'learning disability' is in itself quite significant. It reflects the struggle that we have had in trying to move away from problematic terms such as 'mental handicap' or 'mental deficiency', terms that are profoundly stigmatising and unduly negative. Indeed, this is a criticism that can be levelled at traditional forms of practice with this client group – that it has tended to focus too much on the negatives and has thereby neglected the strengths and positive characteristics of people who have learning difficulties.

Support services for adults with learning difficulties include the promotion of employment, education and leisure opportunities, often as part of a programme of developing independence and life skills.

People with mental health problems

As with disabled people, a major feature of social work with people with mental health problems is the significance of the medical model, an approach which, although quite a dominant discourse in terms of influencing health and social welfare practice, can be seen to be quite destructive as a result of the disempowerment it engenders. The notion of 'mental illness' is one that brings with it considerable stigma as well as a number of other potentially problematic implications:

- Power is vested in members of the medical profession who do not necessarily have the appropriate training or experience for dealing with complex psychological processes and the sociopolitical context in which they occur.
- It implies that the remedies to the problems encountered lie primarily with the experts, and thus undermines self-determination and authenticity.
- By focusing on biologically based issues of 'illness', it fails to take adequate account of cultural and structural factors such as ethnicity, race, class and gender. It therefore runs the risk of exacerbating existing patterns of discrimination and oppression.

The work undertaken with people with mental health problems includes the assessment of need and the provision of appropriate services, statutory duties under the Mental Health Act, 1983 and related statutory provisions, and other activities geared towards reducing risk of harm, maximising independence and improving quality of life.

These categories are, of course, not mutually exclusive, as people can and do belong to more than one category at a time. For example, an older person may also be disabled, or a person with learning difficulties may also have mental health problems (depression, for example). This situation can at times lead to organisational difficulties, including conflict between specialist teams as to who is the most appropriate person to deal with a particular situation. At times, this may emerge as an example of territoriality, two or more individuals or teams competing with each other to play a lead role. At other times, the opposite may occur, a particular client finding that he or she is falling between two stools, with both service areas arguing that the other is the more appropriate. In view of the problems that such situations can cause, it is vitally important not to lose sight of the fact that each client is an individual in his or her own right and is not simply a representative of an abstract category. At all times, it is important to remember that the individual is precisely that – a *unique individual* with needs and rights – and should not, therefore, lose out as a result of the inability of teams to work effectively together where administrative or organisational categories overlap or conflict. A category should be an aid to understanding and helping people rather than a barrier to doing so.

This issue of 'territoriality' and boundary disputes is also an important consideration in relation to multidisciplinary collaboration. An important part of good practice in this respect is the ability to work cooperatively and constructively with colleagues from other disciplines without entering into unprofessional forms of behaviour that have more to do with professional rivalry than professional good practice. Difficult though it may be at times, it is vitally important that, where possible, professionals from different disciplines work together rather than against each other, so that the focus is clearly on the service user's needs and circumstances.

In addition to the above client groups, it is important to recognise a further category of people whose needs, rights and wishes also have to be taken into consideration, regardless of which of the particular groups is being dealt with. I am referring to carers – the friends, relatives, neighbours and others who provide day-to-day practical care. Carers have a right, under the Carers (Representation and Services) Act, 1995, to have an assessment of their ability to provide care. Consequently, it is very important that carers are part of the picture in working with any adult client group.

In work with all the client groups mentioned here, the common theme remains that of empowerment, working positively towards independence and autonomy while challenging factors, such as discrimination and oppression, that stand in the way of progress.

Systematic practice

One of the dangers that busy practitioners face is that of losing track of what they are trying to achieve or how they are going to achieve it – this is the problem of 'drift'. A proposed 'antidote' to drift is that of *systematic practice*. This can be seen to comprise two elements: working within the parameters of a clear and identifiable process, and retaining a clear focus on what is happening and why.

The phenomenon of drift is a well-known concept in child-care social work, as evidenced by the emphasis, especially in child protection, on clear planning, defined goals and comprehensive or holistic assessment (DoH, 1988). The extent to which such clarity and focus are carried through into the hurly-burly of the pressures of practice is something that probably varies considerably, but at least the emphasis is there in the policy and theory base, a base that provides a platform on which to build good practice. My argument in this chapter is that good practice in social work with adults should also be based on clear planning, defined goals and holistic assessment – in short, systematic practice.

In order to facilitate clarifying what is involved in systematic practice, I shall divide the discussion into two sections. The first addresses the importance of the social work process, with its focus on a clear, coherent and logical progression through a set of stages, each stage helping to provide guidelines for what the agenda for practice should be. The second relates to the vital role of clarity of focus, and it is in this section that I describe what I shall refer to as the three key questions of systematic practice.

The social work process

There are various conceptions of 'the social work process' (see Chapter 20), but the one I shall be presenting here consists of five stages within an 'iterative' framework (a term I shall explain below). These stages are as follows:

1. *Assessment.* This initial stage of the process involves gathering information about situation in order to establish, as far as possible the nature, extent and seriousness of the problems to be addressed, the needs of the people concerned, the risk factors involved, the strengths and resources available to the individual, family or group, and so on. However, the gathering of information is not enough on its own – such information has to be interpreted so that it can be of use in understanding the situation and planning a response to it. Assessment therefore consists of:

    *   gathering relevant information;
    *   constructing a 'picture' of the situation;
    *   considering possible courses of action;
    *   deciding upon the course(s) of action to be pursued.

    There is inevitably a subjective element to assessment, but this is not to say that the worker should not endeavour to be as objective as possible. Indeed, the principle of working in partnership should help to guard against personal bias as it necessarily involves taking account of the perspectives of all concerned and not simply the worker's.

2. *Intervention.* While assessment involves working together to recognise the problems be addressed and identifying possible solutions, the intervention stage involves implementing one or more courses of action geared towards resolving or ameliorating

the situation. A number of potential approaches to intervention are available to guide and inform practice, either as direct forms of intervention or as parts of a 'mix-and-match' approach based on experience and practice wisdom. It is important to recognise, as I shall emphasise below, that intervention should amount to much more than simply providing (or commissioning) services.

3. *Review.* Circumstances can and do change, and mistakes can be made at the assessment. It is therefore necessary to review our work from time to time in order to be able to respond appropriately to changing circumstances and to be able to rectify mistakes made in the assessment or fill in gaps in our understanding of the situation.

4. *Termination.* This stage of the process is one that is often neglected, both in practice and in the supporting literature base. This is a significant deficiency, as the termination stage can be a crucial one in ensuring that any good done is not undone by a mishandled ending of a piece of work (for example, by allowing it to 'fizzle out' without the loose ends being tied up carefully). The skills involved in effective and appropriate endings are ones that are well worth the investment of time and effort to develop them.

5. *Evaluation.* This is another stage in the process that tends to be neglected. It is not unusual to hear busy practitioners state that they do not have time to evaluate their work. While this seems understandable on the surface, a closer examination reveals a significant flaw in the logic. Evaluation involves examining our practice so that we can learn from our mistakes and build on our successes. It is therefore a very worthwhile investment of time that can save considerable time and energy in the medium and long terms. Neglecting to evaluate our work involves running the risk of repeating mistakes and failing to capitalise on the lessons to be learned from earlier successes. It is therefore a waste of time *not* to evaluate our practice.

The process is an *iterative* one. That is, it is not a mechanical, linear progression from one stage to the next. Systematic practice is not a rigid prescription for practice but rather a flexible framework to facilitate clarity and focus. An iterative process involves 'looping', returning to an earlier stage in the process as and when required, as Figure 23.2 illustrates.

It should also be recognised and emphasised that each of the five stages should operate on the basis of partnership. That is, each stage should be a shared endeavour rather than a one-sided process in which the powerful 'expert' diagnoses the problem and prescribes the solution, with little or no reference to the relatively powerless person

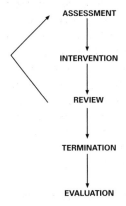

Figure 23.2   The social work process

or persons concerned – in short, a partnership model is to be preferred to a medical model. As Knibbs (1994, p. 19) puts it: 'professionals should be on tap not on top'. A clear benefit of working in partnership is that it promotes:

- working relationships based on openness and trust;
- opportunities for empowerment;
- shared responsibility for outcomes so that no individual is scapegoated for failures or receives undue credit for successes;
- the avoidance of dependency.

Partnership has achieved the status of something of a 'buzzword' in recent years, but this should not be allowed to detract from its role as an essential part of good practice if we are to avoid paternalistic and disempowering forms of practice.

Clarity of focus

A helpful way of developing and maintaining clarity of focus is to use a framework of three key questions. These questions make it easier to keep track of what we are doing and why. The three questions are:

1. What are you trying to achieve?
2. How are you going to achieve it?
3. How will you know when you have achieved it?

The first question refers to the process of clarifying the aims of the intervention – the needs, problems and rights to be addressed. It is not always possible to be precise about these, but the more clarity that can be gained the better, so that the focus of work does not become sidetracked. By establishing, through a process based on partnership, the overall aims and specific objectives of intervention, a firm basis for collaboration can be achieved. This can bring the benefits of reassurance for the client, confidence for the worker and clarity of purpose for both parties.

The second question refers to the courses of action decided upon with a view to achieving the objectives agreed in response to question 1. In other words, the answer to the first question determines the destination we wish to arrive at, while question 2 is intended to clarify the route to be taken to get there – the steps that need to be taken to achieve our ends. In this respect, the process has much in common with task-centred practice (Doel and Marsh, 1992; see also Chapter 16). However, where it differs is that the process I am describing here may involve identifying the specific tasks that need to be achieved, but it does not have to: the process of intervention may take a number of other forms (service provision, advocacy, counselling or other problem-solving activities).

The third question is perhaps the most difficult to respond to, and is, unfortunately, one that is often neglected in practice. Answering the question 'How will you know when you have achieved it?' involves considering in advance what success will look like and how we will recognise that we have arrived at our destination. This does not mean that we should attempt to use a (pseudo)scientific approach with precise, measurable indicators of success. Such an approach does not sit comfortably with the complexities and subtleties of social work practice, but this is not to say that it is not possible to measure or identify success – we just have to be more flexible and creative in our methodology. For example, as I. Shaw (1996, p. 21) points out, it is possible, and quite appropriate, to draw on 'humanist' forms of evaluation of practice which are:

> likely to adopt qualitative methods of inquiry and to stress the importance of discovering the meaning of events to the participants. Hence 'process' and the way in which meanings are constructed through negotiation are likely to figure largely.

The benefits of taking the trouble to seek to answer question 3 are:

- It helps to ensure that questions 1 and 2 have been answered appropriately. That is, if the answers to the earlier questions are too vague, unclear or ambiguous, it will be very difficult to answer question 3.

- It acts as a source of motivation for client and worker alike by providing a vision of how much better the situation could possibly be.
- It allows greater workload control as it avoids time and effort being wasted by pursuing inappropriate courses of action or continuing with intervention when it is no longer necessary or appropriate to do so. That is, it helps to prevent drift.

Systematic approaches to practice offer clarity and focus but without rigidity or tying people down to a particular method or technique of intervention. As such, then, the effort required to develop the necessary skills can be seen as a very worthwhile investment of personal resources. Systematic practice is not intended as a rigid, pseudoscientific approach to practice but rather as a structured framework which:

- provides focus and guidance but not at the expense of flexibility;
- enhances professional credibility by giving clients and carers a degree of confidence in the worker;
- acts as a firm basis for partnership;
- contributes positively to the avoidance of vagueness and drift;
- provides the basis for a coherent process of positive intervention;
- facilitates the review and evaluation of work undertaken.

The life course

It is well established that child development is an important part of the knowledge base that child-care workers need in order to practise in an informed way, with an understanding of the context of the child's thoughts, feelings and actions in relation to the stage of development within the life course that he or she has reached. However, what is not so well established is the significance of the life course for adults as well as children (see Chapter 7).

Perhaps the most salient example of the significance of the life course for work with adults is in relation to working with older people. Old age can be seen as the final stage in the life course (Sidell, 1993; Corr *et al.*, 1996). An important aspect of the life course is the predominance and influence of age-related expectations. This arises from the fact that age is not only a biological marker, but also a social division, an example of the many ways in which society is subdivided into more or less privileged groups (in much the same way as are class, race and gender). Age is used as a means of attaching significance to people and allocating power and life chances. Consequently, children and older people are assigned fewer rights and less power than young adults. As noted earlier, older people may even at times be excluded from the category of 'adults'.

Age-related expectations, when applied rigidly, become manifestations of ageism – the social division of age being used to marginalise and disempower older people. Our understanding of age-related expectations should, therefore, play a part in recognising and challenging ageist stereotypes. Consequently, we should not seek to explain people's behaviour by reference to their age – 'What do you expect at your age?' – as this runs the risk of relying on ageist assumptions or overgeneralisations.

Within the life course, there are a number of transitions to be encountered and dealt with, some of which are the recognised 'developmental crises' associated with ego psychology (Erikson, 1977), which contain within them an element of predictability: leaving the parental home and establishing an independent lifestyle, the menopause/mid-life crisis, retirement and so on. Other transitions involve the less predictable but nonetheless common experiences of grieving and significant losses (see the discussion below of loss and grief). An understanding of the significance and impact of such transitions should be a basic part of the social worker's repertoire of competence, for, without this, there is a danger that assessments may be significantly off-target and that interventions may be not only ineffective, but also positively harmful.

Similarly, while the importance of life stages needs to be considered in general, situations where they are different from the general picture also need to be taken into account. That is, such life stages are socially constructed and are therefore subject to considerable variation according to culture and other such social factors. It is important that they are not seen as biological stages that have to be experienced in a particular way. Such an approach would be ethnocentric and totally insensitive to issues of disability and sexual identity, for example. It is worth considering these questions under three headings: race, culture and language; disability; and sexual identity.

Race, culture and language

The life course is commonly depicted as if it were primarily or exclusively a question of biology. However, this is too narrow a perspective that fails to take account of the various processes – psychological, social, political and ontological – that are part and parcel of the life course. It is, therefore, necessary to take into consideration religious and cultural norms, values and folkways in understanding a person's 'trajectory' through the life course. The cultural and linguistic context of a person's lifeworld will, of course, have a major bearing on his or her perception of the world, the meanings attached to life events and experiences, the values that guide action and so on. A person's experience of the life course will therefore be largely shaped by his or her cultural and linguistic background (see Chapters 7 and 19). As Pugh (1996, p. 40) comments in relation to identity:

> Different languages reflect or construct different realities for people, and so logically it follows that language is a crucial mediator of reality... language mediates between the inner world of the person and the external world of other people. Language is the bridge that links us to the social world, but more than that, it constructs identity through its use; in one sense we find out and create who we are through the speaking of language.

However, while the importance of such ethnically and linguistically sensitive practice has to be recognised, it should not be allowed to overshadow the need to develop, in addition, forms of anti-racist practice. That is, while ethnically sensitive practice recognises the importance of cultural differences, anti-racist practice goes a step further in recognising the significance of assumed cultural (or 'racial') superiority. The significance of racism in the lives of black people will, of course, have an influence on their experiences of the life course and the various points of transition it involves (Robinson, 1995; see also Chapter 7).

Disability

One criticism of much of the literature on the life course is that it adopts an able-bodied perspective – that is, it fails to consider the life course experiences of people with a disability. The 'developmental milestones' of a person with one or more physical impairments may well be significantly different from those associated with non-disabled people. Conventional approaches can therefore contribute to the view that disabled people are not just different from non-disabled people but are actually inferior to them by virtue of the fact that they do not 'live up to' the developmental norms expected (Abberley, 1993). This is the equivalent of ethnocentric forms of racist thinking in which other cultures are seen as not only different, but also inferior (Ahmad, 1990).

Sexual identity

Davies (1996) points out that the stages of the life course are usually conceived in heterosexist terms – that is, they take heterosexual identity development as the desirable norm to be aimed for. Similarly, it can be argued that, for gay men and lesbians, there are two further stages in the life course. The first is that of 'coming out', bringing that identity into the public domain, and the second that of opting for a lifestyle (Plummer, 1981). Such transitions are not usually addressed in the mainstream literature on human development.

In some ways, perhaps, the most significant aspect of the life course is its ending. Issues of death, dying and bereavement can be seen as important factors in the ways in which they have a bearing on life. Death is, after all, a significant part of life. As Frank (1991) puts it:

> Death is no enemy of life; it restores our sense of the value of living. Illness restores the sense of proportion that is lost when we take life for granted. To learn about value and proportion we need to honor illness, and ultimately to honor death. (p. 120, cited in Corr *et al.*, 1996)

It is, therefore, fair to say that loss and grief play a key role in our life experiences and should therefore be taken into account in our practice as social workers. An awareness of, and sensitivity to, issues of grief and loss can, therefore, be seen as fundamental aspects of good practice.

Another aspect of the life course to be taken into account is that it is not simply individuals who go through life course transitions. The concept of 'life course', although not an entirely unproblematic one, can also be seen to apply at a familial or social network level. This is the case in two ways:

1. Life course development affects not only specific individuals, but also the whole family (or social group) in which each individual lives. For example, the situation of an older person reaching the stage where they may have to give up their home is one that will affect a number of people within the family or social network, rather than just the individual concerned.
2. Families also go through a form of life course, in the sense that there will be different stages in terms of the challenges they face, the resources they can draw upon and the losses and gains they face. For example, the situations faced by a family with young children are likely to be very different from those faced by a family where the children have grown up and moved out. Once again, it should be emphasised that the life course is not simply a

matter of biological development, despite the fact that many texts on developmental psychology give this impression.

Roles and tasks

Social workers engaged in work with adults are charged with a number of roles and tasks. We do not have space to explore these in the detail they merit, so it would be unrealistic to attempt to. I shall, therefore, restrict myself to outlining the key elements of such work, thereby laying the foundations for further learning and development.

The first element to consider is that of assessment. As outlined above, this involves gathering relevant information, forming an overview of the situation, identifying possible solutions or responses and determining the best way forward. There are various stages and levels of assessment, ranging from initial 'screening' to comprehensive analyses of very complex situations (Seed and Kaye, 1994). There are (at least) two potential problems associated with assessment practice, each representing the extremes of a continuum (Figure 23.3). The first is the tendency sometimes apparent for a very narrow perspective to be adopted, focusing primarily or exclusively on client need without taking sufficient account of a range of wider factors (see the discussion of care management below). The second, but less common, problem is that of gathering more information than is necessary for present purposes, thereby risking an infringement of civil liberties as well as a waste of time brought about by creating a situation of information overload. Good practice in assessment can therefore be seen to rely on achieving a constructive balance between the two destructive extremes illustrated in Figure 23.3.

Effective and appropriate assessment has a crucial role to play in 'setting the scene' for subsequent intervention. A mistake or oversight at the assessment stage can lead to significant difficulties later as services or other interventions may be misdirected or even wholly inappropriate. The price to be paid for mistakes or 'corner-cutting' at the assessment stage can, therefore, be very high indeed. This is particularly the case in relation to anti-discriminatory practice. For example, to make a racist assumption at the assessment stage may mean that subsequent actions have a profoundly racist impact.

| Insufficient information/ skimping | Constructive balance | Information overload/ intrusion |

Figure 23.3 The information balance

In addition to assessment, consideration needs to be given to planning. Complex situations require careful planning in order to prevent inappropriate responses or simplistic, ill-conceived answers that run the risk of making the situation worse. Planning begins from the moment of referral and continues through assessment and subsequent interventions. In this respect, planning is not a stage of the social work process *per se*, but instead a continuous aspect of practice. Indeed, it can be seen as an essential element of *reflective practice* in which routinised, uncritical practice is to be avoided.

If practice is to be systematic and effective, it needs to be goal-orientated; that is, there needs to be clarity about what is to be achieved. Consequently, practice needs to be *future-oriented* – constantly having an eye to the future and the steps that need to be taken to move towards the desired future outcomes. In this respect, planning has a key role to play.

Planning is also important in a broader sense. Above and beyond individual cases or pieces of work, there are broader patterns to be discerned and accounted for. That is, planning can and should relate to these broader patterns of need (particularly unmet need), service availability and shortfall, demographic or other changes (in relation to minority ethnic groups, for example), training requirements and so on. To a certain extent, this broader level of planning is the responsibility of managers and policy-makers, but this is not to say that practitioners should not operate on this territory at all. Practitioners have an important role to play in such planning in terms of:

- contributing to the policy monitoring and development role by providing information through the appropriate channels in order to ensure, as far as possible, that the process is informed by the perspective of staff involved directly in practice;
- recognising patterns in their own practice, for example in identifying opportunities for groupwork or other collaborative efforts with colleagues or partner agencies.

Planning, then, is more than the process that applies on an individual basis to managing particular cases or pieces of work.

Care management is a relatively new element to consider but nonetheless an important one. The development of care management in the UK owes much to the implementation of the NHS and Community Care Act, 1990, an Act which places a responsibility on local authorities to assess the needs of those members of the community who may require community care services. Care management, therefore, refers to the process of constructing a 'package' of care services designed to maintain the person in the community and thus avoid the need for residential care. As Orme and Glastonbury (1993, p. 187) put it, care management is:

> The label given in the UK to the task of organising and overseeing the provision of a care package for a client who has been assessed, and whose needs are considered of sufficient priority to warrant the allocation of services.

In principle, care management should provide an effective system for identifying and, as far as possible, meeting the needs of those members of the community who are in need of care services. However, one danger with this system is that it can easily become a form of service brokerage in which there is a narrow focus on needs and the services that may be able to meet them, without adequate consideration of:

- the factors that give rise to those needs (loss and grief, low self-esteem/ internalised oppression, relationship difficulties, discrimination, debt and so on);
- the strengths that people bring to their particular situations and their overall circumstances;
- the importance of rights, and the problems and injustices that can occur when rights are not upheld.

A key concept in relation to care management is that of the purchaser–provider split. This refers to the organisational practice of dividing the traditional social work role in two, care managers taking primary responsibility for purchasing or commissioning services, whilst a range of others in statutory, voluntary and private organisations have the task of providing such services. Care management is, in this context, therefore largely a process of commissioning services, hence the danger that other social work issues may be neglected or marginalised through an overemphasis on service brokerage at the expense of the broader processes of problem-solving, safeguarding rights, building on strengths, working towards social justice and so on. Care management should therefore be seen as a part of the overall social work role rather than as a substitute for it. Whilst seeking to meet someone's practical care needs within an organised and coordinated framework is clearly an important social work function, we should not make the mistake of limiting our vision of the social work task to this. This is for (at least) three reasons:

1. Failing to address broader issues may mean that, despite the provision of a substantial package of services, the client's quality of life may remain at a low level because more profound needs

have not been addressed, rights have been overlooked or strengths have not been recognised and consolidated.
2.   Failure to address broader issues or deeper needs (for example, in relation to self-esteem) or to safeguard rights can render intervention ineffective, thereby wasting precious resources that could have more appropriately been directed to other clients.
3.   A narrow focus on service brokerage can remove much of the job satisfaction of social work, thereby acting as a demotivating factor and a possible source of low morale.

Advocacy and mediation can also be seen as parts of the social worker's repertoire in working with adults. Social workers may, at times, be called upon to act as an advocate or mediate on behalf of a client or group of clients. This involves representing a person's or group's interests in circumstances where they are not able to do so themselves or where the support of a social worker may be of particular value. Phillipson (1993, pp. 182–3) describes advocacy in the following terms:

> The general understanding of advocacy is that it is concerned with the balance of power between the client as a member of a minority or other disenfranchised group and the larger society. From the advocate's point of view, the client's problems are not seen as psychological or personal deficits but rather as stemming or arising from discrimination as regards social and economic opportunities. Therefore, techniques of intervention, rather than focusing solely on the relief of individual clients, should challenge those inequalities within the system which contribute to or which cause difficulties for the... person.

Advocacy can, therefore, be an important form of empowerment in which relatively powerless individuals or groups are supported in their attempts to influence or challenge more powerful elements in society, such as official agencies. For a more detailed discussion of advocacy, see Bateman (1995).

Mediation is a process that has much in common with advocacy but is also crucially different. It parallels advocacy in so far as it tends to involve a process of negotiation, but differs in so far as mediation involves adopting a neutral role between two opposing parties (members of a family, for example) rather than taking up the case of one party against another. At times, particularly in very complex situations, the processes of advocacy and mediation can overlap, perhaps with very problematic results, as the worker loses clarity over his or her role. It is, therefore, important, if not essential, to maintain a clear focus in undertaking advocacy or mediation in order to ensure that the roles do not become blurred and therefore potentially counterproductive. For example, a mediator who 'takes sides' is likely to lose all credibility, as is an advocate who seeks to adopt a neutral position.

Responding to abuse is a further important part of social work with adults. Social workers have not only a 'duty of care', but also one of protection in certain circumstances, particularly protection from abuse. The most well-documented aspect of the abuse of adults is that of elder abuse, a phenomenon that was neglected for a long time but which is now beginning to attract a great deal more attention, both in the literature base (Pritchard, 1992; Bennett and Kingston, 1993; Eastman, 1994; Biggs *et al.*, 1995) and in emerging policy and practice. However, other groups of adults, of course, are also prone to abuse and exploitation, so it would be a mistake to focus exclusively on elder abuse. The potential for abuse is one that has to be borne in mind in working with any client group.

Responding to abuse can be difficult, complex and harrowing work, so it is not surprising that some people feel anxious or even reluctant when it comes to dealing with such issues. However, we should not see such work in an entirely negative light, as it is both very important work in terms of the harm that can be done if it is not undertaken properly, or not followed through at all, and can also be very rewarding in terms of job satisfaction. The time and effort required to develop the skills and knowledge required for responding to abuse are therefore a very worthwhile investment.

A further important element is that of counselling, although it is perhaps worth drawing a distinction between counselling and psychotherapy. The latter involves attempting to make major and sometimes radical changes to a person's psychological functioning and is generally well beyond the scope of a social worker in terms of both the expertise and time commitment required. The former, in contrast, involves helping clients to clarify their thoughts and feelings on their current circumstances, or a particular aspect of them, with a view to identifying and implementing possible ways forward. This is a skilled activity for which specialist training can be helpful. However, a qualified social worker should be equipped to undertake at least the basics of counselling.

It is worth stressing that counselling is not simply a matter of giving people the opportunity to talk about their situation or 'ventilate' their feelings, although these can be important elements of successful counselling. As Burks and Stefflre (1979) comment, counselling is:

> designed to help clients to understand and clarify their views of their lifespace, and to learn to reach their self-determined goals through meaningful, well-informed choices and through resolution of prob-

lems of an emotional or interpersonal nature. (p. 14, quoted in McLeod, 1993, pp. 1–2)

Counselling can at times be of tremendous benefit in helping to set people free from the barriers and restrictions that are preventing them from taking control of their lives and resolving the difficulties they face. In short, counselling can be empowering.

Social work is rightly included under the heading of the 'caring professions', but this is not to say that control is not also part of the social worker's duties. Indeed, it is often necessary to exercise control in order to care. Much of the control element of social work derives from the legal context and the statutory interventions that social workers are obliged to make under certain circumstances. Space does not permit a detailed account of these interventions, but we should at least note that social workers engaged in work with adults may be at times involved in statutory interventions that may entail a client being deprived of his or her liberty because of a danger to self or to others (for example, under the Mental Health Act, 1983).

Social action is perhaps an unfashionable approach in this day and age. However, 'unfashionable' should not be equated with 'non-existent'. Social action involves tackling problems at a broader level than the individual or family (Barber, 1991). This entails working in and with communities to identify problems affecting a range of people and exploring possible solutions that can be implemented by the community as a whole or by certain groups of people within the community. There are a range of schemes and projects that come under the heading of 'social action', for example community law centres, 'drop-in' resources or 'one-stop' shops where a range of community services are offered.

Social action can also involve taking up a political campaign, for example protesting against a particular plan or proposal or applying pressure to an organisation to influence policy or campaign for a particular service to be provided. The approach is, therefore, one that is often characterised by conflict. Nonetheless, such conflict can often be constructive and productive, especially if skilfully and creatively handled.

User involvement can also be seen as an aspect of social action. This involves taking whatever steps are possible to help clients to gain a voice in terms of assessment, service delivery, processes of intervention, review, termination and evaluation, as well as the broader processes of policy formulation, implementation, monitoring and evaluation (see Beresford and Croft, 1993; Beresford and Harding, 1993).

In addition to these elements, we also need to consider working in partnership as a form of practice in its own right. The point has already been made that good practice needs to be premised on partnership rather than the traditional model of the social worker as expert who 'diagnoses' the problem and 'prescribes' a 'cure'. A participative approach has far more to offer than a medicalised one in which barriers are erected between worker and client (Croft and Beresford, 1994). Wineman's (1984, p. 80) explanation of the need for 'two-way' approaches to practice is worth quoting in full:

> Professionals are taught to remain detached, not to become 'over-involved', not to get too 'emotional', certainly not to look to a client as a source of help. But one-way helping necessarily creates a power imbalance, and it communicates to the 'client' that s/he does not have the strengths and skills that it takes to be a source of support – or at the very least fails to actively recognize and affirm those strengths and skills. It thus cements the image of the 'client' as 'sick' and deficient. Two-way helping can create the shared power of mutual definition; can create a realistic perception of people as encompassing various combinations of strength and weakness, competence and troubles; can dignify and affirm people who have previously been defined in terms of their problems, deficiencies and 'pathologies' by also looking to them as sources of support and defining them as people with something to give as well as to receive.

However, it also needs to be recognised that working in partnership is a skilled activity. It involves communication, assertiveness and negotiation skills so that the possibilities for effective collaboration can be maximised.

Another broad approach is that of problem-solving. This is something of an umbrella term that describes a range of interventions geared towards resolving one or more difficulties. This may relate to practical problems, for example through adjustments made to the physical environment or the provision of aids that remove difficulties or enhance quality of life. However, problem-solving can be on a much broader basis, incorporating emotional, psychological, interpersonal and social problems. The breadth of this approach can act as a counterbalance to the narrow 'brokerage' approach associated with care management, as mentioned above.

Problem-solving involves working in partnership to:

- identify those aspects of a person's life or current circumstances (or those of a family, group or community) that are problematic;
- generate a range of possible solutions;
- evaluate the options;
- choose and implement the most appropriate solution.

The question of 'generating a range of possible solutions' is an important part of the process insofar as problem-solving is not simply a process of *finding* the right answer, as if there were one definitive answer to each problem encountered. It is more accurately represented as a process of *constructing* one or more solutions and considering the strengths and weaknesses, advantages and disadvantages of each option. This, then, makes it necessary to work in partnership so that the client(s) play an active part in dealing with their own problems. This enables them to share ownership of the proposed solution and to be empowered by the process, whereas an approach in which the social worker plays 'the expert' and prescribes a 'cure' is far more likely to encourage dependence (and recriminations if the proposed solution is not entirely successful).

Problem-solving is not an 'exclusive' approach. It is a framework that can be used in tandem with one or more other approaches (care management, counselling and so on).

Working together in a group context also offers considerable scope for addressing problems and unmet needs, safeguarding rights, enhancing quality of life and promoting empowerment (see Douglas, 1983; Preston-Shoot, 1987; Mullender and Ward, 1991; Brown, 1992). As Brown (1994, p. 34) comments, 'The essence of groupwork is the benefit that can be gained from being together with several other people who share something in common with you.'

Groups can exist in relation to a geographical community (for example, older people at a residential home), in relation to a particular set of issues (social skills development for people with learning difficulties, for example) or in other such areas in which a communal approach can have benefits for all concerned. Having the opportunity to express feelings in a safe, supportive and responsive environment, to discuss common problems and to identify ways in which they might be tackled can be a very constructive and empowering experience.

However, it should also be noted that groupwork can have destructive outcomes, leaving people feeling distressed and disempowered. It is a highly skilled form of practice, so it should not be entered into lightly, without being carefully planned and without the support of more experienced groupworkers.

I earlier identified empowerment as an overarching theme, but it too can be seen as an element of practice in its own right. As with 'partnership', empowerment has achieved the status of a 'buzzword', an overused word that is in danger of losing its meaning, potency and value (Gomm, 1993). Nonetheless, the concept of empowerment remains a central one. It can be defined as:

> the means by which individuals, groups and/or communities
> become able to take control of their circumstances and achieve their

own goals, thereby being able to work towards themselves and others to maximise the quality of their lives. (Adams, 1996a, p. 80)

The notion of social work practice 'giving' power to clients should not be interpreted simplistically as handing power to clients as if it were a commodity to be passed from one person to another. Power is not a 'zero-sum' concept – that is, social workers can empower others without necessarily being disempowered themselves (that is, losing control over their own circumstances), as if there were a finite sum of power that has to be shared or divided up. Indeed, as Adams (1996a) affirms, it is necessary for social workers to be empowered if they are to empower others.

Empowerment can be seen as both a specific strategy (or set of strategies) for increasing clients' control over their lives (through advocacy, for example) and an aspect of all practice – that is, all forms of good practice should be geared in some way towards helping people to increase their level of control. This is consistent with the discussion below of emancipatory practice and those above of partnership and participation.

Finally, emancipatory practice needs to be recognised as a central theme of social work with adults. In view of the fact that discrimination operates at personal, cultural and structural levels, good practice is not simply a matter of avoiding discriminatory actions, attitudes or language in our own work. It also involves the need to tackle discrimination in the work of others, in the cultural norms, values, stereotypes and assumptions that surround us and in the structural patterns and power relations that sustain them. Social work with adults therefore needs to be premised, first, on the recognition of the forms of discrimination to which adult client groups are subject, for example ageism and disablism, in addition to those that apply across the board, such as sexism, racism and heterosexism; and second, on a commitment to challenging these forms of discrimination in order to reduce, eliminate or counteract the oppression that such discrimination engenders.

Developing emancipatory practice involves challenging traditional assumptions about 'women's place', about racial superiority, about older people being 'past it', about disabled people being 'incapable' and so on. The process, therefore, involves 'unlearning' taken-for-granted assumptions and maintaining a focus on the need to counter discrimination wherever it is encountered.

Conclusion: developing good practice

As we have seen, social work with adults is diverse, complex and challenging. In this final section, I shall try to pull together the main themes and issues by teasing out what I see as the principles of good practice. These are not intended as simple formulae to be followed unthinkingly or uncritically. Social work is far too complex for such simple prescriptions to be of any value – indeed, such an uncritical approach can be dangerous. These guidelines, are instead intended as themes to be considered, debated and used as a stimulus to developing critically reflective practice. They should therefore be seen as the beginning or further step in a process of developing high-quality practice, rather than as a short cut.

1. *Systematic practice, based on clarity, focus and partnership, is the foundation of good practice.* Being clear, at all times, about what we are trying to achieve and how we are hoping to achieve it is a fundamental part of good practice in so far as it helps to prevent a drift, vagueness and wasted efforts.
2. *Assessment should not be narrow and service-orientated.* It is not simply a question of assessing need but rather of assessing circumstances, and such circumstances should include strengths as well as weaknesses, rights as well as needs.
3. *Interventions should not be routine or unimaginative.* Social work is a demanding job, so developing routines can be one way of coping with its pressures. However, where practice has become too heavily reliant on routines, opportunities for progress are likely to be missed through a failure to practise creatively.
4. *Social work with adults needs to be both ethnically sensitive and anti-racist.* Practice involves working with people from a range of ethnic backgrounds, some of which are regarded by many as inferior to dominant white cultures. Good practice, therefore, needs to recognise the specific customs, values and so on of the specific group being worked with at any one time (ethnically sensitive practice), whilst also taking account of, and responding to, the experiences of racism that so many members of minority ethnic communities are likely to have had (anti-racist practice).
5. *Good practice must be emancipatory practice.* Racism is not, of course, the only form of oppression that social workers are likely to encounter in their work with adults. Sexism, ageism, disablism, heterosexism and so on are also almost certain to feature in the day-to-day interactions of social work practice. It is important, therefore, that assumptions made and actions taken contribute to the undermining of such forms of oppression, rather than add to them or condone them.

Social work with adults is often regarded as less important, prestigious and rewarding than child-care work. It is to be hoped that the discussions in this chapter have helped to debunk the myth that adult services work is unskilled, unchallenging and unrewarding. Working with adults can be just as demanding as working with children and can also offer similar levels of stimulation, job satisfaction and opportunities for personal and professional development.

Further reading

Oliver, M. (1996) *Understanding Disability: From Theory to Practice* (London, Macmillan).

> Oliver's book explores some of the shortcomings of traditional approaches to social work with disabled people.

Payne, M. (1995) *Social Work and Community Care* (London, Macmillan).

> This book provides a clear and useful overview of community care issues in relation to adults.

Thompson, N. (1995) *Age and Dignity: Working with Older People* (Aldershot, Arena).

> A useful exploration of working with older people within a framework of anti-ageist practice is contained in this book.

Thompson, N. (1996) *People Skills: A Guide to Effective Practice in the Human Services* (London, Macmillan).

> This includes discussion of the importance of systematic practice.

24

Social work with offenders

DAVID SMITH

Introduction

Social work with offenders has a long history, as long as that of social work itself. Reformatory schools for juvenile offenders were established by legislation in the 1850s and 60s, the first of a long line of residential care institutions claiming to promote the well-being of young people in trouble and to prevent them from being contaminated by older, less tractable criminals (Carlebach, 1970). The year 1876 is often taken as the point at which the probation service was born, on the initiative of the Church of England Temperance Society (Bochel, 1976; Haxby, 1978). Probation entered the statute books in 1907, with the Probation of Offenders Act, and the special needs of juvenile offenders for 'rescue' as well as punishment were formally acknowledged by the creation of the juvenile court in the following year (Gelsthorpe and Morris, 1994). However, despite this venerable lineage, the status and purposes of social work with offenders have been and continue to be the subject of political and professional debate, often organised around such (supposedly) polar oppositions as welfare and justice, care and control, or help and surveillance. Although social work has long had a recognised place within the criminal justice system, this place has rarely been central or entirely secure: the image of the probation service 'moving centre-stage' which representatives of the Home Office frequently evoked in the early 1990s (Raynor *et al.*, 1994) was probably less characteristic of the general ministerial view of the service than was the well-attested puzzlement of one new Home Office minister of the late 1980s, who asked whether the probation service was, after all, quite a well-established organisation (rather than an unwanted child of the 1960s).

Social work with offenders is, then, a contested form of practice, and this chapter will necessarily deal with the arguments which it has aroused, in discussing their current versions and the ways in which they have influenced policy, legislation and practice in the recent past. Attention to the policy context is inevitable, because social work with offenders is, to a greater and more immediate extent than social work with many other client groups, both made possible and constrained by the law within which it operates and the associated guidelines, instructions and, in the 1990s, National Standards. The first section of the chapter, therefore, sets the scene by outlining in broad terms the important strands of recent criminal justice policy and their implications for social work practice. The chapter then discusses, in turn, some important contemporary themes in work with juvenile and with adult offenders, although, as will become clear, the line between the two is often blurred. The next section considers recent developments in the theory and practice of 'restorative justice' and the place of social work agencies in broader, community-based strategies on crime, in particular their potential contribution to 'community safety' (Home Office, 1991). Finally, the chapter argues for a more inclusive view of what counts as 'effective' practice than has featured in most recent debates. An attempt is made throughout to include Scotland within the scope of the discussion, since policy and practice in Scotland differ instructively from the pattern in England and Wales, and a better understanding of the differences is likely to be mutually helpful.

The policy background

Criminal justice policy is more liable to sudden, politically motivated changes of direction than is social policy in other fields, because of the high level of public concern and anxiety about crime and the fascination crime and its control exert upon the media (Downes and Morgan, 1994). It is, therefore, remarkable that, from 1980 (to go back almost to the start of the long period of Conservative government which ended in 1997) until early 1993, Home Office policy was as generally consistent as it was. It is possible to trace a fairly coherent line of development through successive policy statements, Criminal Justice Acts and the practice guidelines associated with them, which was broken only in 1993.

In that year, Kenneth Clarke, then Home Secretary, announced that the recently implemented Criminal Justice Act of 1991 required substantial modification. His successor, Michael Howard, quickly and enthusiastically confirmed that the policies of the previous years were to be abandoned. David Faulkner, who, as a senior civil servant at the Home Office, had been closely identified with the changes of the 1980s (Rutherford, 1996), wrote regretfully in the

Guardian that the change of line was 'probably the most sudden and the most radical which has ever taken place in this area of public policy' (Faulkner, 1993). As Hough (1996, p. 192)) notes, while 'in strictly legal terms' the changes to the 1991 Act looked minor, 'they were symbolically substantial, being widely interpreted as a rejection of the sentencing philosophy underlying the 1991 Act'. The wide interpretation was surely correct, and while the changes to the 1991 Act's sentencing principles were the most visible sign of the new temper of policy, and were to have a quick and serious effect, the change encompassed more than sentencing: new policies were to follow on (amongst other things) cautioning, probation training and the role of the police, accompanied by a radical reversal of the previous view that prison could be 'an expensive way of making bad people worse. The prospects of reforming offenders are usually much better if they stay in the community, provided the public is properly protected' (Home Office, 1990, p. 6).

The 1980s

What were the main elements of the policy pursued in England and Wales during the 1980s, which, according to McIvor (1996), were still being maintained, perhaps precariously, in Scotland in the mid-1990s? Three important and interrelated themes appeared right at the start, in the 1980 White Paper *Young Offenders* (Home Office, 1980). Despite its hard-line, anti-welfarist rhetoric and its reinstatement of punishment as the main aim of criminal justice (Blagg and Smith, 1989), there was embedded in the White Paper a strong statement in favour of cautioning rather than prosecuting juvenile offenders whenever possible, one side of the process which Bottoms (1977) called 'bifurcation' and which he correctly predicted would be an important principle of criminal justice policy in the coming years. Bifurcation entails distinguishing sharply between serious and less serious offences – usually interpreted as offences against the person and offences against property. In general, it prescribes that imprisonment should be reserved for those who have committed the most serious offences and that the others (the great majority of those who appear in court) should be dealt with by less punitive, less intrusive and less expensive measures, such as fines and the range of 'community penalties'.

The preference for cautioning minor juvenile offenders also reflected the influence of the labelling perspective, in an unusually clear example of sociological theory influencing policy (Smith D., 1995). The 1980 White Paper accepted that involvement in the criminal justice system was inherently likely to be damaging and should be avoided whenever possible. A second consistent theme of the policy of the 1980s was therefore a radical scepticism about the capacity of any measure available to the criminal justice system to make a positive difference to an offender, so that the justification for intervention of any kind, particularly of the most drastic form of intervention – imprisonment – came to be expressed primarily in terms not of the offender's needs or interests but of the requirements of the rest of us for protection from his or her misdeeds. A third theme, implicit in the 1980 White Paper but increasingly explicit, which exists in uneasy tension with the aim of public protection, is that of 'just deserts' or proportionality – the principle that the sentence should reflect the seriousness of the offence.

The commitment to diversion where possible was pursued through the 1980s by strong official encouragement to the police, notably in Home Office circulars of 1985 and 1990, to caution a higher proportion of juvenile offenders and to extend cautioning to a higher proportion of adults (Evans and Wilkinson, 1990). For younger offenders, the starting assumption was to be that a caution was the preferred response; prosecution should be recommended only if there was a good reason for not cautioning. The themes of bifurcation and just deserts both appeared in the legislation which followed the White Paper, the Criminal Justice Act of 1982. This was greeted gloomily by social workers and their allies in the liberal penal reform lobby because of its vigorous reassertion of punishment as a relevant aim of the juvenile justice system, its association with the 'short sharp shock' regime in detention centres and its apparent abandonment of a long process of increasing separation of juvenile and adult jurisdictions; early research (Burney, 1985) seemed to bear out their misgivings. However, the Act also contained the first serious attempt to use legislation to restrict the discretion of sentencers, particularly in relation to the use of custody. In doing so, it opened out an opportunity for social workers to increase their influence on criminal justice decision-making, by greatly widening the statutory place of pre-sentence reports (then called social inquiry reports). Briefly, the Act required sentencers, in all but exceptional circumstances, to consult a social inquiry report before sending anyone under the age of 21 to custody. It also stipulated that a custodial sentence could only be justified on the basis of the seriousness of the offence, the public's need for protection or the offender's inability or unwillingness to comply with a non-custodial measure. These 'criteria for custody', which were reinforced in the Criminal Justice Act, 1988, formed the basis of the more radical and thoroughgoing effort to restrict custodial sentencing which was a central part of the Criminal Justice Act, 1991.

The Criminal Justice Act, 1991

The 1991 Act followed the anti-custodial, bifurcatory logic of its predecessors, but its radical extension of it, and its particular version of just deserts, were to prove too much for some members of its judicial and political constituency. The Act extended the require- ment to consider a pre-sentence report for all offenders, and its criteria for custody laid greater stress on the seriousness of the offence (which could be combined with only one other offence to produce a total 'volume' of seriousness), restricted the public protec- tion criterion to violent and sexual offences (in what Cavadino and Dignan (1992, p. 108), referring to the preceding White Paper (Home Office, 1990) call a 'further twist in the bifurcatory spiral'), and replaced the criterion of unwillingness or inability to respond to a community penalty by the defendant's refusal of consent. The Act encouraged a view of sentences as falling into three broad bands, the lowest of which (in terms of restricting liberty, the Act's concep- tion of punishment) consisted of nominal and financial penalties (discharges, fines and so on). The next band, which the court should only consider if the offence (or a combination of two offences) was 'serious enough', contained the range of community penalties – supervision and probation orders with or without additional condi- tions, community service and the new 'combination order', which included elements of both community service and probation. The final band was that of custody, which courts should consider only if the offence was 'so serious' that, on just deserts grounds (or public protection grounds for violent and sexual offences), only a custodial sentence would be sufficient.

The Act introduced two other changes which have had a direct impact on social work agencies and which, unlike its attempt to restrict the use of custody, have survived subsequent legislation. First, it abolished parole in the form in which it had existed since the Criminal Justice Act of 1967. Parole meant that probation officers had to supervise in the community many more serious or persistent offenders than they had been used to dealing with, and it carried with it an expectation – the first of a series – that their supervision would be correspondingly more intensive and more concerned with public protection. Early research on the outcomes of parole suggested that it was successful, producing lower than predicted rates of reconviction (Nuttall *et al.*, 1977), although the supervision of parolees was not in practice strikingly different from that of probationers (Morris and Beverley, 1975). By the late 1980s, however, the system was widely thought to be in need of reform, to reduce the gap between the sentences imposed and the time actually served in prison, which had widened over the years as a result of various tinkerings with the original system. Following the recommendations of the Carlisle Committee (Home Office, 1988a), the 1991 Act substituted for parole a system of automatic conditional release (ACR) for all prisoners sentenced to over 12 months but less than four years. The scope of discretionary conditional release (DCR), the new version of parole, was restricted to longer-term prisoners, who would also become subject to ACR if not released under the discretionary scheme.

This change quickly had the effect of increasing the proportion of people on probation officers' caseloads who had not in any sense consented to be supervised by the service and with whom, therefore, it might be difficult to agree a basis for social work intervention. The first two years of ACR were evaluated for the Home Office (Maguire *et al.*, 1996; Maguire and Raynor, 1997), with mixed results: the system was thought to be fairer than parole by most parties, including offenders, and outcomes in terms of completed licences and reoffending rates appeared encouraging, but there was little consensus about the purposes of ACR, the expectations imposed by National Standards were thought to be impossible to meet and there was little connection between 'sentence planning' within prison and supervision after release. The researchers concluded that the system would work better if it allowed more scope for the professional judgement and discretion of probation officers rather than relying on a rigid set of rules on the conduct of supervision.

Second, the 1991 Act abolished the juvenile court and replaced it by the Youth Court. The most obvious change was in the scope of the new court's jurisdiction. Whilst the juvenile court dealt with offenders up to and including the age of 16, the Youth Court also dealt with 17-year-olds. Gelsthorpe and Morris (1994, p. 981) offer a rather cynical explanation of this reform: diversion from the juvenile court had gone so far and been so successful that 'expediency demanded some change "to keep courts busy"'. A less jaundiced view would see the change as one broadly in line with the Act's overall interest in reducing the use of custody, in this case by extending to 17-year-olds the benefits of the 'welfarist' tradition of the juvenile court. Although the criteria for determining the seriousness of offences were much the same as for adult offenders, there seems little doubt that this was at least one of the reasons for the Act's linking of 16- and 17-year-olds as 'near adults' (NACRO, 1991) and its requirement that sentencers should make a judgement on their maturity before deciding whether they should be sentenced as if they were adults or as if they were juveniles.

Developments in Scotland

In Scotland, the Children's Hearing System, established by the Social Work (Scotland) Act of 1968 to deal with offenders up to the age of 16 on the same welfarist principles as other children in difficulties, has been jealously maintained as a distinctive feature of the Scottish legal system (Kelly, 1996). It has been safeguarded by the lower salience of law and order as a political issue in Scotland (McIvor, 1996) and by the strong commitment to the system of those who work within it.

As a result, work with juvenile offenders in Scotland has been largely immune from the policy pressures described above, and even intensive programmes of work with persistent juvenile offenders can still operate on the basis of voluntary attendance. In contrast, services for 'adult' offenders (aged 16 and over) tended to be relatively neglected in the years following the 1968 Act. This had abolished the probation service as a separate agency, which meant that adult offenders were, in effect, in competition for the services of social work departments with other client groups more obviously deserving of help. In recognition of this imbalance, the Scottish Office took over full responsibility for funding community service in 1989 and for the whole range of services for adult offenders in 1991 (McIvor, 1996). This has enabled greater specialisation in work with adult offenders, and the revival of activity in this field has been supported by the introduction of National Standards (Social Work Services Group, 1991) which are noticeably more favourable to the values and methods of social work than were the Home Office's first version of National Standards for probation (Home Office, 1992), let alone the second version, which stresses strict adherence to rules for enforcement of orders and insists that work with offenders must not include anything which they might actually enjoy (Home Office, 1995). Nevertheless, and despite some important legal differences (including, during the 1990s, a greater scope for discretionary release from prison), social work with adult offenders in Scotland has come to resemble practice south of the border more closely than before, while work with juveniles, although at the level of immediate practice having many common features, is still carried out in a legal context which enables it to proclaim without embarrassment the virtues of help and support as valid aims of practice.

After the 1991 Act

The parts of the Criminal Justice Act, 1991 most relevant to social work were implemented in October 1992. Almost immediately, there came a chorus of complaint from powerful and authoritative figures, amongst them the Lord Chief Justice. It was claimed (unfairly) that the Act had been introduced without proper consultation and that its provisions to restrict the use of custody were illogical and unworkable (Feaver and Smith, 1994). A new Home Secretary, Kenneth Clarke, evidently felt little commitment to the Act and announced that crucial sections of it would be speedily amended. His successor, Michael Howard, quickly made it clear that he had no inhibitions about using public anxieties over crime for purposes of anticipated political advantage (hence, amongst other things, his announcement in October 1993 that 'Prison works'). It should be added that the Labour Party, in opposition, showed little inclination to oppose either the amendments to the 1991 Act which appeared in the Criminal Justice Act, 1993 or subsequent and increasingly extravagant declarations of the virtues of a punitive criminal justice policy.

As we saw above, Section 2 of the 1991 Act specified that, in assessing the seriousness of offences, sentencers could combine two, but no more, offences, and Section 29 sought to restrict the circumstances in which a defendant's previous record could be considered as aggravating the seriousness of the current offence. The sense of these two sections was, in effect, reversed by the 1993 Act, which allows courts to combine as many offences as they wish to arrive at a total measure of seriousness and to treat a previous criminal record as an aggravating factor. The 1991 Act's anti-custodial provisions were further eroded by a late amendment to the 1994 Criminal Justice and Public Order Act, which removed the general requirement to consider a pre-sentence report before imposing a custodial sentence. The Crime (Sentences) Act, 1997, with its provision for statutory minimum sentences for some repeat offenders, effectively completes the reversal of previous policy, although the new Labour government seems unlikely to implement it in full.

These measures, amongst other things, have reduced the influence which social workers and probation officers can have on sentencing. They have also led directly to a rapid increase in the prison population, a trend which will not be quickly reversed even if Labour proves less enthusiastic about prison in government than it did in opposition. The Home Office (1993) found that, in the first few months after the implementation of the 1991 Act, it was beginning to achieve the desired effect: less use was being made of custodial sentences, and the prison population was falling. The trend was reversed, however, even before the 1993 Act became law, as sentencers attended to the change of political line. The new trend continued, according to Greenhorn (1996, p. 10):

> At the magistrates' courts the proportionate use of immediate custody for indictable offences increased throughout 1995 to reach

9.4 per cent in the fourth quarter, the twelfth successive quarterly increase. This followed the sharp rises from around 5 per cent recorded in 1992... At the Crown Court, the proportionate use of immediate custody... rose... from 52 per cent in 1994 to 56 per cent in 1995. The figure for the fourth quarter was 58.3 per cent, the fifth successive quarterly increase.

The rhetoric of the 1991 Act may not have been much to social workers' taste, with its talk of just deserts and probation as a form of punishment in the community, but in view of what subsequently happened it became easier to identify its virtues. Whatever the limitations and oversimplifications of the just deserts model, the Act was 'drafted in such a way as to let social considerations back in through the space it leaves for the probation service to influence both individual decisions and system developments' (Raynor *et al.*, 1994, p. 13). This could not have been said of the legislation which followed. All the same, there are some grounds for cautious optimism, which paradoxically include the very failure of the 1991 Act.

Legislation, policy and practice

It is usual to think of legislation as marking the beginning of something new, but in some cases it may be better to think of it as representing the end of a process (Smith, 1984; Gelsthorpe and Morris, 1994), the high-water mark of a particular strand of thinking, after which a reaction is to be expected. The 1991 Act may thus be seen as the culmination of the influence of those who argued, in the Home Office and the Department of Health, for a reduction in the use of custody and the development of community-based measures, but by the time the Act was implemented, this influence was exhausted. Much the same can be said of the 1969 Children and Young Persons Act, which, with hindsight, looks very like the final expression of welfarist thinking about juvenile offenders and nothing like the start of a new era. It seems quite possible, with the change of government in May 1997, that the very different Crime (Sentences) Act may suffer part of the same fate, and that the punitive tide which dominated penal policy in the mid-1990s may now start to ebb.

One other point remains to be made about the policy context of social work with offenders, as it was until the early 1990s, which again can provide a source of hope. This is that among the major influences on policy was social work practice. This is worth stressing, because social workers, understandably enough, tend to think of national policy as something imposed on them from above, without their having much say in the matter. There are, however, several examples in the relevant period of policy following practice. One is the 1982 Act's extension of the range of conditions which could be attached to probation orders, so that offenders could be required to attend day centres (later probation centres) for a period of up to 60 days. There were complaints at the time that this represented an unwelcome shift towards control and surveillance and away from help and support, but the Act merely codified (and legalised) existing probation practice: it gave statutory warrant for something which probation officers had already shown themselves willing to do (Raynor, 1985). Another example is the explicit endorsement in the Green Paper *Punishment, Custody and the Community* (Home Office, 1988b) of developments in juvenile justice social work and its encouragement of the application of the same principles to adult offenders (Blagg and Smith, 1989). Even the principle of just deserts, which seemed to exclude social and individual factors in offending and to take account only of strictly legal definitions, had much in common with the 'back to justice' arguments of the late 1970s and early 1980s, many of whose keenest advocates were either social workers or academics closely associated with them (for example, Morris *et al.*, 1980). It seems reasonable to conclude that social workers have had a substantial influence on policy, even though the results have not always been quite what they would have wished, and if they had such an influence in the recent past, they may be able to have some again.

Working with juvenile offenders

In their summary of developments in juvenile justice in England and Wales since the 1969 Children and Young Persons Act, Cavadino and Dignan (1992) suggest that a period of 'system disaster' (1969–1982) was followed by a period of 'systems management', and that, during the latter period, it was plausible to claim that juvenile justice underwent a 'successful revolution'. The aims of this section are: first, briefly to summarise what the main elements of that revolution were and to assess how far the claim of success is justified; and second, to discuss what seem to be the most important issues facing social work with young offenders in the late 1990s and what lessons could be drawn from the experience of the 1980s.

Changing the juvenile justice system

The effects of the 'system disaster' of the 1970s are hardly disputable, if outcomes directly contrary to those intended by legislation and stated policy count as evidence of disaster. The 1969 Act had, albeit vaguely, envisaged the phasing out of custody for juveniles and the effective decriminalisation of offences committed by children under the age of 14. In spirit, although not in the detail of its letter, it was broadly in line with the Social Work (Scotland) Act of 1968, but its effects were to be very different.

During the 1970s, instead of becoming more welfare-orientated, the juvenile justice system became more dedicated to punishment; instead of an enhanced role for social work, the decade saw a reduction in social work's involvement with juvenile offenders and in its credibility and status. The use of community-based supervision declined while the use of custody massively increased (from 3,000 custodial sentences on 14–16-year-olds – or 6 per cent of sentences – in 1970 to over 7,000 – or 12 per cent of sentences – in 1978 (Cavadino and Dignan, 1992, p. 206). And while the proportion of care orders overall declined (a sign of reduced faith in social work, whatever the merits or otherwise of care orders), the number of children in secure accommodation increased from 150 in 1971 to well over 500 in 1981 (Muncie, 1984). What is strange, in retrospect, is that it took so long to recognise what was happening: nearly everyone, academics and politicians included, behaved until the end of the 1970s as if the juvenile justice system had fallen victim to 'an unconscionable softness' (Cavadino and Dignan, 1992, p. 205), when an unprecedented harshness would have been closer to the mark.

One of the first and most influential critiques of what had gone wrong was Thorpe *et al.*'s (1980) advocacy of targeted community-based resources which would provide intensive forms of supervision, with a focus on offending as the reason for social workers' involvement, for serious or persistent offenders, combined with what came to be known as 'systems management'. The latter entailed understanding the 'tariff' of sentencing in local juvenile justice systems and trying to manage it by consistent efforts to divert all but the most persistent offenders, through liaison with the police to increase cautioning, and recommending non-interventionist, or minimally interventionist, measures for juveniles at the early stages of a career in the courts. The argument was that well-intentioned recommendations for supervision and care for minor or transient offenders could quickly lead to the exhaustion of welfare measures in the minority of cases where offending turned out to be persistent, thus easing the passage into custody. Social workers were thus held partly responsible for the 'system disaster', compounding by their naïveté the damaging effects of the magistrates' dislike of the 1969 legislation and their distrust of social workers.

These arguments were reinforced by central government initiatives, including the support for cautioning and the restrictions on the use of custody noted above. The Department of Health also announced, in January 1983, that £15 million would be made available to voluntary organisations to develop 'intermediate treatment' facilities which would allow a higher proportion of persistent offenders to remain in the community. The intention was clear: to shift the balance of community resources from ill-defined 'preventative' work to more focused and specialised services for young people at risk of care or (more relevantly by this time) custody (Bottoms *et al.*, 1990). There is also no doubt that the arguments of Thorpe and his colleagues resonated with the concerns of many practitioners and local managers. For the latter, there was the promise of a reduction in the costs of residential care (largely discredited since the mid-1970s as a means of reducing delinquency (Cornish and Clarke, 1975); for the former, there was a new rationale for social work's presence in juvenile justice and a new hope that it could be made effective.

During the 1980s, social workers specialising in juvenile justice developed a distinct and theoretically coherent form of practice which combined a consistent commitment to diversion and minimum intervention with increasingly sophisticated face-to-face work with the most persistent juvenile offenders. They also developed an unmistakable sense of comradeship and shared purpose, exemplified in the formation of the Association for Juvenile Justice (now the National Association for Youth Justice). There were critics, of course, from within social work and elsewhere, of the 'minimalist radicalism' of the system's management approach and the alleged 'Pavlovian behaviourism' of offending-focused work (Pitts, 1988). Some practitioners certainly embraced a more rigorous version of the 'justice model' ('Do as little as possible because anything you do is likely to be harmful') than Thorpe *et al.* (1980) had ever imagined (for the limitations of this, see Raynor, 1993; Smith, D., 1995). Paradoxically, some of the most assured and confident social work practice of the time (and some of the most effective in pure 'systems management' terms) was based on the conviction that social work had been shown not to 'work'.

Youth justice in the 1990s

By the start of the 1990s, there were some signs that the enthusiasm and commitment which had fired the energies of social work in juvenile justice were beginning to wane. Local authorities were increasingly conscious of other priorities and the need to provide resources to more 'deserving' client groups under the NHS and Community Care Act, with its stress on purchasing services, ensuring value for money and staying within budgets. The attractions of allowing the prison service to bear the burden of dealing with recidivist young offenders started to become more apparent. The 1991 Criminal Justice Act's abolition of the juvenile court, while benignly intended, threatened to disrupt established relations with the juvenile court and required the renegotiation of responsibilities between social services departments and the probation service. From 1993 on, as described above, the coherence of policy began to break up, and juvenile justice social workers (or youth justice workers as they had by then become) found themselves in a less politically supportive environment than they had been used to. At least in some areas, the coherence of practice was also threatened, as tasks which had been marginal, such as acting as an 'appropriate adult' under the Police and Criminal Evidence Act, came to demand more of workers' time, and new areas of practice began to develop in response to anxieties about the adequacy of existing services, such as the growth of (highly labour-intensive) remand fostering and remand management schemes (NACRO, 1996).

To some extent, youth justice workers were the victims of their own achievements. The very success of diversion meant that some well-resourced youth justice centres looked rather short of customers by the early 1990s, which attracted the suspicious attention of hard-pressed staff in social services departments. Could they not, should they not, be working with more young offenders, if the local authority was to get value for money? I reviewed one such project, of which these questions were being asked, in 1995. The project had been established in 1984 and had become famous locally and in the professional community for having contributed to the achievement of one of a very few briefly celebrated 'custody-free zones' (Rutherford, 1986). From the review, it was clear (a) that some changes were needed if the local authority was to maintain its support for the project, and (b) that the principles developed during the 1980s were still viable and capable of producing the desired results. Members of the local youth justice system who knew of the project's work were unanimous in praising it. Project staff had the respect of the police, who were still prepared to listen to arguments for repeated cautions in spite of the restrictions introduced by a Home Office circular in 1994, which reversed the previous policy in favour of cautioning; they had the unstinting support of the leading members of the Youth Court bench, and, significantly, they were heartily resented by the local Crown Prosecution Service, one of whose staff remarked that he could not see why anyone bothered having magistrates in the Youth Court since they always did what the project asked anyway.

It is unlikely that the same degree of influence was ever possible everywhere, since the local magistrates in this case were plainly committed to doing good rather than harm, but it is worth summarising the main elements which contributed to this project's success. It was well-resourced and had skilled and experienced staff, whose senior members had been in post for some years; it had a high level of contact and credibility with other agencies, and related to them in a way which acknowledged the reality of conflicts of interest (Blagg *et al.*, 1988); its staff had long adopted an activist, interventionist style in court, which had come to be accepted as normal; its pre-sentence reports were clear and well focused, and promised nothing that could not be performed; and the project's direct work with young people was flexible, although always relevant, attentive to the young people's needs and delivered in an environment that conveyed a sense of care, comfort and safety.

Meanwhile in Scotland

The different political climate in Scotland has allowed social work with young offenders to continue to develop in a very different legal context. Almost incomprehensibly to the newly arrived visitor from south of the border, work with even the most persistent offenders can still be carried out on a voluntary basis, with the full support of the relevant agencies. This is the case, for example, with the Freagarrach Project (of which more below) in what was Central Region, which was funded by the Scottish Office for five years (until the year 2000) to work with the most persistent juvenile offenders in the region. The absence of statutory constraints and the willingness of others in the system, including the police and the Reporter to the Children's Hearings, to allow the project to experiment and to manage the young people's problems in flexible and creative ways make for a striking contrast with even the best practice now to be found in England and Wales. Another centrally funded project for persistent offenders, the Cue-Ten project in Fife, focuses its work not on offending behaviour but on improving young people's chances in the labour market through encouraging participation in training and education, illustrating the diversity of practice which is possible in a less punitive and more optimistic policy environment. More frequent visits to Scotland might hearten the many jaded veterans of the campaign for juvenile justice in England and Wales.

Working with adult offenders

There may seem to be something paradoxical about writing about social work with adult offenders at all, since the main agency involved (in England and Wales) – the probation service – has now officially shed its long-established links with social work, at least as far as qualifying training is concerned (Dews and Watts, 1994), and become something other than a social work agency. What that something will be is not yet clear, but there is no doubt that, unless the new government adopts a very different line, the probation service will be much more concerned with the supervision and enforcement of community penalties and much less concerned with helping, supporting and rehabilitating offenders than in the past. There is, however, another paradox here, because at the very time when it was losing the confidence of ministers, as penal policy shifted in the ways described above, the probation service was beginning to regain confidence in itself and its capacity to help offenders change. Social work, or something very like it, was beginning to look as if it 'worked', just as policy-makers had decided that social work was the last thing they wanted.

What if something works?

The origins of the gloomy faith that 'nothing works' have often been described (for example, Raynor *et al.*, 1994; McGuire, 1995), and there is no need to repeat the story here. Suffice it to say that pessimism as well as optimism can be naïve, and the widespread belief that nothing made any difference to offenders' likelihood of reoffending, which characterised the probation service and other agencies between, roughly, 1975 and 1990, was no more rational than the earlier belief that it was somehow obvious that well-intentioned and hard-working people would produce the desired results. Nevertheless, the jolt which the probation service felt from the negative findings of the IMPACT experiment (Folkard *et al.*, 1976), which seemed to show that 'intensive treatment' was less effective than everyday probation supervision, had some salutary effects and provoked some probably overdue new thinking about the aims and purposes of probation.

One of the first and most impressive products of this effort was the 'non-treatment paradigm' of Bottoms and McWilliams (1979). They argued that treatment on the medical model, which they saw as the dominant paradigm in probation practice, was neither ethically nor empirically defensible. In place of treatment, they argued for the provision of 'appropriate help'; in place of an allegedly expert diagnosis by the probation officer, they proposed a shared assessment of needs and problems; and in place of the 'client's dependent need' (of which the client might be perfectly unconscious), they suggested that the basis for social work intervention should be a collaboratively defined task. The other elements of their new paradigm were the statutory supervision of offenders, diversion from custody and crime reduction – through community development and the promotion of greater social cohesion rather than through individual change.

In reviewing the non-treatment paradigm 15 years later, Raynor and Vanstone (1994) concluded that its second and third elements – supervision of court orders and diversion from custody – were still entirely relevant as aims of the probation service. They argued, however, that research on effectiveness since 1979 meant that its separation of crime reduction from work with individuals could no longer be sustained and that its proposed scheme for individual work therefore required revision. Thus 'appropriate help', which for Bottoms and McWilliams meant that the client should determine what was to count as helpful, is glossed by Raynor and Vanstone (1994, p. 402) as 'help consistent with a commitment to the reduction of harm': there are limits to the extent to which client choice can be allowed to determine the nature of social work intervention. Similarly, 'shared assessment' might become 'explicit dialogue and negotiation offering opportunities for informed consent to involvement in a process of change', and the collaboratively defined task was qualified as one which is 'relevant to criminogenic needs and potentially effective in meeting them'.

Raynor and Vanstone's concern was to revise and update the non-treatment paradigm to take account of the research in the intervening period which had suggested that the 'nothing works' message was wrong (for an overview of this research, see McGuire, 1995). It was now possible to specify reasonably closely what kinds of work were most likely to be effective in reducing the risk of reoffending. Raynor and Vanstone argued that, if this is the case, to practise in ways which are less likely to be effective is not only wasteful, but also unethical, since the probation service has an obligation to potential victims as well as to offenders. The conclusions of the relevant research can be summarised as follows: other things being equal, work is more likely to be successful if it matches the intensity of intervention with the risk presented by the offender; is carried out in the community rather than in an institution; focuses on crime-related needs and problems; uses methods which are active and participatory; recognises the variousness of offenders' problems; aims to improve offenders' coping skills; has a cognitive-behavioural basis; maintains 'programme integrity' (that is, employs methods which are relevant to its stated aims); uses properly trained staff who are supported by their agency; and is systematically monitored and evaluated. Set out like this, the list may strike many readers as uncontentious, but the idea that 'something works', that we can more or less specify what this is, and that probation officers might try to adapt their practice accordingly, has not been universally welcomed in the service (for example,

Neary, 1992). There may have been some bleak comfort in the belief that nothing worked.

It is also important not to oversell the evidence of effectiveness. The most careful recent British evaluation of a programme consciously set up to meet the criteria for effectiveness outlined above – the STOP (Straight Thinking on Probation) programme in Mid-Glamorgan – showed promising rates of reconviction for those who had completed the programme one year on, but found that the two year reconviction rates were no better than predicted (Raynor and Vanstone, 1996; for the reconviction predictor, see Lloyd *et al.*, 1994). The authors suggest that the relatively disappointing two year results (which were still, it should be said, better than those for a comparison group who had received custodial sentences) may reflect the lack of reinforcement of what had been learned during the programme in one-to-one supervision and the absence of any 'after-care' which would have allowed offenders to return to the programme for further support.

The recent findings on effectiveness have undoubtedly influenced practice in groupwork (that is, in probation centres) much more than in individual work, about which little reliable is known (Underdown, 1996), and it would be difficult to argue that the 'what works' findings have yet had a decisive impact on probation practice, or on work with offenders more generally, although their broad outlines have been clear for some time (McIvor, 1990). Arguably, too, the narrow focus of much of this research has led to a neglect of what works in other aspects of work with offenders. For example, the collection edited by Drakeford and Vanstone (1996) includes discussions of the possibilities of working for change within the criminal justice system and the implications for practice of poverty, unemployment and housing and health problems, all wearyingly familiar to practitioners as common features of the lives of offenders (Stewart *et al.*, 1994). The following section suggests how social work with offenders might be conceived more broadly, to include social change as well as indi-vidual change among its aims, and the conclusion argues for a corres-pondingly larger view of what should count as effective practice.

Social work, restorative justice and community safety

In recent academic and professional discussions of the aims and purposes of work with offenders, it has become usual to find at least some reference to victims, actual or potential, and to the responsibili-ties of social work towards them and towards the communities in which they and the offender-clients of social work live. Successive reports of the British Crime Survey (most recently Mirrlees-Black *et al.*, 1996) have shown that, for most offences, the victimisation risks are highly concentrated in areas where the poorest and most vulnerable of the population are disproportionately likely to live, and ethnographic work has vividly conveyed the extent of the social and personal damage which high crime rates can cause (Robins, 1992; Campbell, 1993). It is inconceivable, in the light of this knowledge, that social workers should be indifferent to the implications of their work with offenders for the local public – the community of which offenders themselves must be counted as members (Currie, 1988) – and, indeed, the principle that part of the probation service's brief should be 'wider work in the community' featured in both the non-treatment paradigm (Bottoms and McWilliams, 1979) and in the first systematic attempt by the Home Office to define national objectives for the service (Home Office, 1984).

These considerations, and the idea that if something works it is arguably unethical to do something else, have informed some recent thinking about what the values of probation practice might be. Nellis (1995a) has suggested that the traditional 'personalist' values of social work, such as respect and care for persons, are, although not irrelevant, inadequate as a basis for social work with offenders and that they should be augmented by the more social values of anti-custodialism, restorative justice and community safety (see also James, 1995; Nellis, 1995b; Spencer, 1995). As Nellis points out, anti-custodialism was more explicitly espoused as a value by juvenile justice practitioners during the 1980s than by probation officers, but there is little doubt that most probation officers would, in practice, be prepared to own a version of it. Its implications for practice were outlined above, and nothing more will be said about them here. The two remaining values, which are linked by a concern for the status of victims and by some sense of the importance of 'community', are discussed below.

Restorative justice

In the 1980s, the probation service was involved in some of the pioneering attempts in Britain to make sense of the concept of restorative justice, in the form of victim–offender mediation (Smith *et al.*, 1988; Marshall and Merry, 1990) and, more tentatively, as a means of involving members of local communities who had been affected by an offence in its resolution (Celnick, 1985). The flurry of activity in the mid-1980s attracted the interest and, for a time, the support of the Home Office, but, despite some promising results, there were difficulties in reconciling the interests of victims and offenders when the mediated settlement of disputes was additional to, and not a substitute for, the standard process of prosecution and sentencing, and these, combined with concerns about resources, meant that the government's enthusiasm was short-lived. The enthusiasm of some practitioners proved more durable, and the practice of victim–offender mediation continued, for example, as an element of 'caution plus' schemes for juveniles, in which form it has recently won praise from the Audit Commission (1996a) as a positive and economical alternative to prosecution. By the early 1990s, a new theoretical basis for restorative justice had emerged in John Braithwaite's account of 'reintegrative shaming' (Braithwaite, 1989), which, when its implications for practice were considered, turned out to support a more communitarian, less private form of victim–offender mediation than had been tried in the 1980s. At first in New Zealand, under legislation which consciously drew on Maori practices in dispute settlement (e.g. McElrea, 1994) and then in Australia and elsewhere (Braithwaite and Mugford, 1994; Braithwaite, 1995), the Family Group Conference became the model for practitioners interested in a more positive and less stigmatising response to offending, particularly by juveniles.

A Family Group Conference is a vehicle for a ceremony of reintegration as opposed to one of degradation (Braithwaite and Mugford, 1994). The offender and his or her supporters meet the victim and his or her supporters, in the presence of a mediator who will try to guide the meeting towards a responsible reconciliation (McElrea, 1994). The offender is shamed not by any deliberate process of humiliation or public denunciation but by being confronted with the victim's suffering and the hurt the offence has caused to his or her own family and friends. Any attempt to add to the shame inherent in the situation would be redundant and probably harmful (Smith *et al.*, 1988). The offender's action is condemned – not the offender him- or herself ('He's a good lad really, although he made a bad mistake') – in a way which recalls the involvement of Quaker and other Christian groups in the origins of victim–offender mediation (Burnside and Baker, 1994). The aim is to reach an agreed means of putting right the wrong done by the offence, in which the offender and his or her supporters enter into various commitments intended to ensure that the offending is not repeated. In the process, both victim and offender lose the special outcast status bestowed by their relationship to the offence and are reintegrated as full participating members of the community.

No more than anything else is the Family Group Conference a panacea, and the account above ignores a number of practical and conceptual difficulties to which critics have pointed (for example, Morris *et al.*, 1993; Blagg, 1997). It would be a pity, too, if, in the present enthusiasm for Family Group Conferencing and the like, the lessons which ought to be drawn from the experience of the 1980s were to be neglected – for example, that confusion will arise if practitioners are not clear about their aims, and that successful mediation is a highly skilled activity. All the same, the strong revival of interest in restorative justice, on a more secure theoretical and empirical foundation, provides an opportunity for social work with offenders to discover a new sense of direction and purpose. The skills of good mediation are very much the skills associated with good social work, and, given a reflexive and self-critical spirit, social workers should be able to play a central part in a movement which holds out real hope for a more constructive response to offending.

Community safety

'Community safety', the term preferred to 'crime prevention' by the Morgan Committee (Home Office, 1991), has been criticised for being unhelpfully vague (Pease, 1994), but is now current not just in criminal justice agencies but increasingly in local authorities, and expresses a broad aspiration towards a social good from which few people would dissent. Despite official encouragement over recent years, social work agencies have not always found it easy to identify a distinctive niche in multi-agency initiatives on the prevention of crime (Sampson and Smith, 1992). It is, however, hardly conceivable that they should not try to be involved in such initiatives, if social work practitioners have some confidence, as they should, that they can contribute to community safety. Recently heightened awareness of the 'attrition rate', which suggests that only about 2 per cent of crimes with a personal victim produce an offender available to be sentenced (Barclay, 1993), has highlighted the relative unimportance of questions about sentencing compared with questions about crime prevention, and social work will deserve the marginalisation which will be its fate if it stands aloof from work on community safety.

Social work agencies can bring to community safety programmes knowledge, skills and values without which these programmes would be impoverished. For example, while multi-agency working is invariably more difficult in practice than it sounds on paper, social workers, by virtue of their structural position in the criminal justice system, have long experience of working cooperatively with other agencies and should have the skills to ensure that multi-agency initiatives avoid the pitfalls which lead to failure and frustration – such as a lack of a clear focus, inadequate resources, the absence of authoritative support, uneven levels of commitment, unrealistic expectations and so on (Geraghty, 1991; Raynor *et al.*, 1994, pp. 129–30). Social workers should also have faith in their own knowledge of offenders' lifestyles, the features of their daily experience which are criminogenic, and their patterns of offending – and be willing to share this knowledge and its implications for community safety programmes (Laycock and Pease, 1985). The values associated with social work, including a commitment to the social integration and inclusion of offenders, can also be an important influence on thinking and practice in community safety: purely 'situational' measures aimed at increasing physical security and/or surveillance are not only less effective than was once hoped (Smith, D., 1995), but are also potentially socially divisive and unjust, if safety and security come to depend on the ability to pay. The voice of social work needs also to be heard, amongst others, if community safety is not to slide towards punitiveness and repression (eviction orders, curfews and the like), without any compensating commitment to social measures such as support for parents under stress, the provision of services for young people at risk of delinquency and marginalisation, and efforts to reverse the upward trend of school exclusions (Graham and Bowling, 1995 – and see below).

Working in partnership

Community safety is one of a range of activities in which social work agencies must, of necessity, work in partnership with others. Reflecting the emphasis of policy, much recent work on partnerships has focused on the probation service's relationship with the voluntary or 'independent sector' (Smith *et al.*, 1993; James and Bottomley, 1994; Cross, 1997). There is a good argument, however, that partnership with other public sector agencies and services is more important if a strategic commitment to community safety is to be more than a rhetorical gesture. Partnership with health service agencies, for example, has usually been thought of as mainly relevant to the provision of specialist services for mentally disordered offenders and those with problems related to drug or alcohol abuse, but a broader conception of the relevance of the probation service to the health of local communities would involve, for example, the recognition that the service is in contact with many young men who make little use of health services but are at high risk of harm from drug misuse, HIV infection and suicide (Farrar, 1996). Farrar discusses the possible contributions of the service to shared care, notes its record of effective work in such fields as drink–drive education and the management of sex offenders, and suggests that the service's growing awareness of the needs of victims creates the possibility of earlier interventions which could reduce the long-term burden on the health service.

Another example of imaginative thinking (and action) on partnerships, in a different setting, is the strategy for young people at risk developed in Central Region in Scotland. Although the region disappeared in the local government reorganisation which took effect at the beginning of 1996, the police, who were the strategy's main sponsors, remained organisationally intact and have renegotiated it with the new unitary authorities. The strategy was designed to maximise diversion from the formal system of most juvenile offenders: police officers were encouraged to deal informally with minor offenders and to try to encourage them to participate in some positive recreational pursuit. The Education Department supported the strategy by (amongst other things) trying to reduce the level of exclusions from school by using special needs teachers to train their colleagues in mainstream education in the management of challenging behaviour, and by seconding two teachers to work in the Reporter's Department, where, it was hoped, they would be able to intervene quickly and effectively in school-related problems. The Social Work Department was to contribute by encouraging staff in residential care to deal with children's difficult behaviour themselves, as good parents would, calling the police only as a last resort. Social Work, with Education, also supported the Freagarrach Project discussed above. The Education Department guaranteed to provide six places in a special unit for young people attending the project, and the police gave practical support by allowing the project leader access to their information system (updated weekly), which she could use to identify the most serious or persistent offenders at any one time and thus offer the project's services to the intended target group.

The Scottish Office has also funded the Cue-Ten project in Fife, which aims to help persistent juvenile offenders away from careers as adult offenders by encouraging more positive attitudes to education, training and employment. Even more than the Freagarrach Project, this approach relies on the active cooperation not only of formal agencies such as the Social Work and Education Departments but on the goodwill and support of lay members of the community. The project depends on the willingness of trainers and employers to see offenders as members of the community, as citizens who have rights and claims like the rest of us. As Stern (1996) has observed, this is not how they were being encouraged to think by the official rhetoric of punishment, exclusion and warfare. Describing the proceedings of a European Union conference held in Barcelona in April 1996 on employment and ex-offenders, Stern wrote that the participants:

> were all in favour of reintegrating ex-offenders into the labour market, and they talked about social cohesion, the dangers of social exclusion and the need to persuade employers to give jobs to ex-delinquents.

At the time, Home Office ministers were using terms not of integration and inclusion but of contempt and hatred: drug dealers were
'the lowest of the low'; the police were 'challenging the car thieves,
burglars and thugs at every turn'. We are told that we must 'stamp
out crime in car parks', that the government wants 'to turn the tables
on the criminal' and that 'Rural criminals are the weeds in their
communities. Countrywatch is the weed killer'. Stern wrote:

> the man with the small garage who takes a couple of ex-offenders on
> a training scheme and then gives them jobs if they do well thinks
> (quite rightly) that he is performing his civic duty and contributing to
> a safer society. It is hard for him to see it in that light if he hears
> constantly that in official eyes those he is helping into legitimate
> employment are crooks, thugs, bullies and weeds needing an appli-
> cation of weedkiller.

Against this background, the owners of a music shop and a
garden centre in Fife who accepted young offenders from the Cue-Ten
project on work placements could hardly feel that their efforts were
being positively recognised. Part of social work's contribution to
community safety must be to support the reintegrative and rehabilita-
tive impulses which many lay people feel towards offenders, recognising that 'decency' (Rutherford, 1994) is not confined to criminal
justice professionals.

Conclusion: towards a wider conception of effectiveness

One implication of all this is that, in thinking about the effectiveness
of social work with offenders, we need to move beyond an interest in
a particular kind of groupwork. Even at the level of work with individual offenders, little is known about the effectiveness of different
styles of one-to-one work or about variations in effectiveness among
workers. Community service has received nothing like the evaluative
attention devoted to groupwork, nor has the practice of community
service in England and Wales been much influenced by work in Scotland which at least suggests what factors are associated with positive
outcomes (McIvor, 1992). The same state of underdevelopment characterises research on court reports (although see Gelsthorpe and
Raynor, 1992) and on social work intervention in the court setting.
And while it is widely recognised that most offenders known to
social work agencies suffer from a range of stresses and difficulties,
mostly associated with poverty and marginalisation, little is known
about what works best in interventions designed to help them

manage these problems (Stewart *et al.*, 1994). Much of the recent debate on effectiveness has been limited by its relative or complete neglect of the ways in which offenders' performance on specific programmes may depend upon aspects of their lives which such programmes are powerless to influence. As Thurston (1997) notes, the debate has also tended to neglect issues of gender and masculinity, whose relevance to criminality is empirically and theoretically well established (Newburn and Stanko, 1994). The contribution of social work to community safety will also need to be informed by questions and answers about what counts as effectiveness in, for example, inter-agency and partnership work, and in crime prevention initiatives generally, in respect of which there is still little agreement about what the relevant measures of performance should be (Tilley, 1995).

This is not meant as the familiar academic plea for more research, although it is certainly true that social work with offenders went under-researched for too long, largely because it was assumed that the (negative) answers were already known. Nor is it meant to imply that everything can be measured or subjected to a key performance indicator. It is, rather, to argue that the sheer scope of social work with offenders should be more fully recognised when questions are asked about its effectiveness, and that evaluative research should be more than a technical exercise in identifying the outcomes of specific programmes. We can now be reasonably confident that we know in broad terms what programmes of groupwork with offenders should aspire to if their staff are committed to effective practice; evaluative work should now move on and begin to explore some of the areas which are still largely unmapped. This will require an extension of the intellectual curiosity and theoretical awareness which has distinguished social work with offenders since the start of the 1980s. Having outgrown both naïve optimism and naïve pessimism, we can begin to try to answer such questions as: why are males much more likely to offend persistently and seriously than females, and what does this imply for social work practice? Why are some courts more ready to listen to social workers than others? Is this a quality of the courts or of the social workers? Are the theoretical claims for restorative justice and reintegrative shaming borne out in practice? What is it that social work has distinctively to contribute to making community safety programmes work? Is our intuition that some social workers are better than others correct? What makes them better, and what can we learn from them? Some of the answers may be uncomfortable for some social workers, but then social work with offenders has never been the right job for those in search of a comfortable life.

Bibliography

Abberley, P. (1993) 'Disabled people and "normality"', in Swain *et al.* (1993).

Adams, R. (1990) *Self- Help, Social Work and Empowerment* (London, Macmillan).

Adams, R. (1994) *Skilled Work with People* (London, Collins).

Adams, R. (1996a) *Social Work and Empowerment*, 2nd edn (London, Macmillan).

Adams, R. (1996b) *The Personal Social Services: Clients, Consumers or Citizens* (London, Longmans).

Adams, R. (ed.) (1997) *Crisis in the Human Services: National and International Issues*, Selected Conference Papers (Hull, University of Lincolnshire and Humberside).

Adams, R. (1998) *Quality Social Work* (London, Macmillan).

Adams, R. and O'Sullivan, T. (1994) *Social Work With and Within Groups* (Birmingham, BASW Trading).

Adams, R., Allard, S., Baldwin, J. and Thomas, J. (eds) (1981) *A Measure of Diversion? Case Studies in Intermediate Treatment* (Leicester, National Youth Bureau).

Adler, R. (1985) *Taking Juvenile Justice Seriously* (Edinburgh, Scottish Academic Press).

Aggleton, P. and Chalmers, H. (1986) *Nursing Models and the Nursing Process* (London, Macmillan).

Ahmad, B. (1990) *Black Perspectives in Social Work* (Birmingham, Venture).

Ahmed, S. (1986) 'Cultural racism in work with Asian women and girls', in Ahmed *et al.* (1986).

Ahmed, S., Cheetham, J. and Small, J. (eds) (1986) *Social Work with Black Children and their Families* (London, Batsford).

Ainsworth, M. D., Blehar, M. C., Walters, E. and Wall, S. (1978) *Patterns of Attachment: Psychological Study of the Strange Situation* (Hillsdale, NJ, Lawrence Erlbaum).

Aldgate, J., Heath, A., Colton, M. and Simm, M. (1993) 'Social work and the education of children in foster care', *Adoption and Fostering*, **17**(3), pp. 25–34.

Aldridge, M. (1996) 'Dragged to market: being a profession in the postmodern world', *British Journal of Social Work*, **26**(2), pp. 177–94.

Allan, M., Bhavnani, R. and French, K. (for the Department of Health Social Services Inspectorate) (1992) *Promoting Women: Management Development and Training for Women in Social Services Departments* (London, HMSO).

Allen, I. (ed.) (1988) *Hearing the Voice of the Consumer* (London, Policy Studies Institute).

Altrichter, H., Posch, P. and Somekh, B. (1993) *Teachers Investigate their Work: An Introduction to the Methods of Action Research* (London, Routledge).

AMA (1993) *Local Authorities and Community Development: A Strategic Opportunity for the 1990s* (London, Association of Metropolitan Authorities).

Amato-von Hemert, K. (1994) 'Should social work education address religious issues? Yes!', *Journal of Social Work Education*, **30**(1), pp. 7–11.

Anderson, L. and Kinsey, R. (1993) *Cautionary Tales, A Study of Young People and Crime in Edinburgh* (Edinburgh, Criminal Research Unit, Scottish Office).

Andrew, F. (1996) *Not Just Black and White: An Exploration of Opportunities and Barriers to the Development of Black Managers in Public Services* (London, Office for Public Management, 252B Gray's Inn Road, London WC1 8JT).

Anwar, M. (1976) *Between Two Cultures* (London, CRC).

Appleyard, B. (1993) 'Why paint so black a picture?', *Independent*, 4 August.

Askham, J., Henshaw, L. and Tarpey, M. (1993) 'Policies and perceptions of identity', in Evandrou, M. and Arber, S. (eds) *Ageing, Independence and the Life Course* (London, Jessica Kingsley).

Atkinson, D. R. and Hackett, G. (1995) *Counseling Diverse Populations* (Madison, Brown & Benchmark).

Audit Commission (1994) *Seen But Not Heard: Co-ordinating Community Child Health and Social Services for Children in Need* (London, HMSO).

Audit Commission (1996a) *Misspent Youth* (London, Audit Commission).

Audit Commission (1996b) *Balancing the Care Equation: Progress with Community Care* (London, HMSO).

BAAF (1996) *The Children (Scotland) Act 1995: A Training Programme* (London, British Agencies for Adoption and Fostering).

BAC (1985) *Counselling: Definitions and Terms in Use with Expansion and Rationale* (Rugby, British Association for Counselling).

Badham, B. (ed.) (1989) '"Doing something with our lives when we're inside": self-directed groupwork in a youth custody centre', *Groupwork*, **2**(1), pp. 27–35.

Bailey, R. (1988) 'Poverty and social work education', in Becker and MacPherson (1988).

Bailey, R. and Brake, M. (eds) (1975) *Radical Social Work and Practice* (London, Edward Arnold).

Bakhurst, D. and Sypnowich, C. (eds) (1995) *The Social Self* (London, Sage).

Ball, C., Preston-Shoot, M., Roberts, G. and Vernon, S. (1995) *Law for Social Workers in England and Wales* (London, Central Council for Education and Training in Social Work).

Bamford, T. (1990) *The Future of Social Work* (London, Macmillan).

Banks, S. (1995) *Ethics and Values in Social Work* (London, Macmillan).

Banks, S. (1996) 'Youth work, informal education and professionalisation: the issues in the 1990s', *Youth and Policy*, **54**, pp. 13–25.

Barber, J. G. (1991) *Beyond Casework* (London, Macmillan).

Barclay, G. C. (ed.) (1993) *Digest 2: Information on the Criminal Justice System in England and Wales* (London, Home Office).

Barclay Committee (1982) *Social Workers: Their Role and Tasks* (London, Bedford Square Press).

Barker, R. and Roberts, H. (1993) 'The uses of the concept of power', in Morgan, D. and Stanley, L. (eds) *Debates in Sociology* (Manchester, Manchester University Press).

Barker, W. E., Anderson, R. A. and Chalmers, C. (1994) *Health Trends over Time and Major Outcomes of the Child Development Programme* (Bristol, Early Childhood Development Unit and Belfast, Eastern Health and Social Services Board).

Barn, R. (1990) 'Black children in local authority care: admission patterns', *New Community*, **16**(2), pp. 229–46.

Barn, R. (1993) *Black Children in the Public Care System* (London, Batsford).

Barrett, M. and Phillips, A. (eds) (1992) 'Introduction', in *Destabilising Theory* (Cambridge, Polity Press).

Bartlett, H. (1970) *The Common Base of Social Work Practice* (Washington DC, National Association of Social Workers).

BASW (1979) *Clients are Fellow Citizens* (Birmingham, British Association of Social Workers).

BASW (1987) *A Code of Ethics for Social Work* (rev. ed.) (Birmingham, British Association of Social Workers).

Bateman, N. (1995) *Advocacy Skills: A Handbook for Human Service Professionals* (Aldershot, Arena).

Baty, P. (1997) 'Anita takes the plunge in Bath', *Times Higher Education Supplement*, 3 January, p. 5.

Baumrind, D. (1971) 'Current patterns of parental authority', *Developmental Psychology Monographs* 4, **1**(2).

Beck, A. T. (1976) *Cognitive Therapy and the Emotional Disorders* (New York, International Universities Press).

Beck, A. T. and Emery, G. (1985) *Anxiety Disorders and Phobias: A Cognitive Perspective* (New York, Basic Books).

Becker, H. (1963) *Outsiders: Studies in the Sociology of Deviance* (New York, Free Press).

Becker, S. (1988) 'Poverty awareness', in Becker and MacPherson (1988).

Becker, S. and MacPherson, S. (1986) *Poor Clients: The Extent and Nature of Financial Poverty Amongst Consumers of Social Work Services* (Nottingham, Nottingham University Benefits Research Unit).

Becker, S. and MacPherson, S. (1988) *Public Issues, Private Pain: Poverty Social Work and Social Policy* (London, Social Services Insight).

Beckford Report (1985) *A Child in Trust* (Wembley, London Borough of Brent).

Bennett, G. and Kingston, P. (1993) *Elder Abuse: Concepts, Theories and Interventions* (London, Chapman & Hall).

Bensted, J., Brown, A., Forbes, C. and Wall, R. (1994) 'Men working with men in groups: masculinity and crime', *Groupwork*, **7**(1), pp. 37–49.

Benzeval, M., Judge, K. and Whitehead, M. (eds) (1995) *Tackling Inequalities in Health: An Agenda for Action* (London, King's Fund).

Beresford, P. and Croft, S. (1993) *Citizen Involvement: A Practical Guide for Change* (London, Macmillan).

Beresford, P. and Croft, S. (1995) 'It's our problem too!: challenging the exclusion of poor people from poverty discourse', *Critical Social Policy*, **44/45**, pp. 75–95.

Beresford, P. and Harding, T. (1993) *A Challenge to Change* (London, National Institute for Social Work).

Beresford, P. and Trevillion, S. (1995) *Developing Skills for Community Care* (Aldershot, Arena).

Berrueta-Clement, J. R., Schweinart, L. J., Barnett, W. C., Epstein, A. S. and Weikart, D. P. (1984) *Changed Lives: The Effects of the Perry Preschool Program in Youths through Age 19* (Ypsilanti, High Scope Press).

Berthoud, R. and Ford, R. (1996) *Relative Needs* (London, Policy Studies Institute).

Biehal, N. (1993) 'Participation, rights and community care', *British Journal of Social Work*, **23**(5), pp. 443–58.

Biehal, N., Clayden, J., Stein, M. and Wade, J. (1992) *Prepared for Living? A Survey of Young People Leaving the Care of Three Local Authorities* (London, National Children's Bureau).

Biestek, F. P. (1961) *The Casework Relationship* (London, Allen & Unwin).

Biggs, S., Phillipson, C. and Kingston, P. (1995) *Elder Abuse in Perspective* (Buckingham, Open University Press).

Black Assessors (1994) DipSW 'Consultation a Sham', *Community Care*, October, pp. 13–18.

Blagg, H. (1997) 'A just measure of shame? Aboriginal youth and conferencing in Australia', *British Journal of Criminology*, **37**(4), pp. 481–501.

Blagg, H. and Smith, D. (1989) *Crime, Penal Policy and Social Work* (Harlow, Longman).

Blagg, H., Pearson, G., Sampson, A., Smith, D. and Stubbs, P. (1988) 'Inter-agency cooperation: rhetoric and reality', in Hope, T. and Shaw, M. (eds) *Communities and Crime Reduction* (London, HMSO).

Blakemore, K. and Boneham, M. (1994) *Age, Race and Ethnicity* (Buckingham, Open University Press).

Bland, R. (ed.) (1996) *Developing Services for Older People and Their Families* (London, Jessica Kingsley).

Bloch, A. (1997) 'Ethnic inequality and social security policy', in Walker and Walker (1997).

Blom Cooper, L. (1985) *A Child in Trust* (London, London Borough of Brent).

Bochel, D. (1976) *Probation and After-Care: Its Development in England and Wales* (Edinburgh, Scottish Academic Press).

Bolger, S., Corrigan, P., Docking, J. and Frost, N. (1981) *Towards Socialist Welfare Work* (London, Macmillan).

Booth, H. and Mallon, M. (1994) *Return Ticket* (Harpenden, Lennard Publishing).

Booth, T. and Booth, W. (1996) 'Parental competence and parents with learning difficulties', *Child and Family Social Work*, **1**(2), pp. 82–6.

Borland, M., O'Hara, G. and Triseliotis, J. (1991) *The Outcome of Permanent Family Placements in Two Scottish Local Authorities* (Scottish Office, Central Research Unit).

Bosanquet, B. (1901) 'Meaning of social work', *International Journal of Ethics*, **11**, p. 297.

Bosanquet, B. (ed.) (1905) *Aspects of the Social Problem* (London, Macmillan).

Bosanquet, H. (1906) *The Family* (London, Macmillan).

Bottoms, A. E. (1977) 'Reflections on the renaissance of dangerousness', *Howard Journal of Criminal Justice*, **16**, pp. 70–96.

Bottoms, A. E. and McWilliams, W. (1979) 'A non-treatment paradigm for probation practice', *British Journal of Social Work*, **9**(2), pp. 159–202.

Bottoms, A. E., Brown, P., McWilliams, B., McWilliams, W. and Nellis, M. (1990) *Intermediate Treatment and Juvenile Justice* (London, HMSO).

Boud, D. and Knights, S. (1996) 'Course design for reflective practice', in Gould, N. and Taylor, I. (eds) *Reflective Learning for Social Work* (Aldershot, Arena) pp. 23–34.

Bourn, D. F. (1993) 'Over-chastisement, child non-compliance and parenting skills: a behavioural intervention by a family centre worker', *British Journal of Social Work*, **23**, pp. 481–9.

Bowl, R. (1985) *Changing the Nature of Masculinity – A Task for Social Work* (Norwich, University of East Anglia, Social Work Monographs).

Bowlby, J. (1979) *The Making and Breaking of Affectional Bonds* (London, Tavistock).

Bowlby, J. (1988) *A Secure Base: Clinical Applications of Attachment Theory* (London, Routledge).

Boyatzis, R. E. (1982) *The Competent Manager: A Model for Effective Performance* (Chichester, Wiley).

Boyne, R and Rattansi, A. (1990) 'The theory and politics of postmodernism: by way of an introduction', in Boyne, R. and Rattansi, A. (eds) *Postmoderism and Society* (Basingstoke, Macmillan).

Bradshaw, J. (1993) *Household Budgets and Living Standards* (York, Joseph Rowntree Foundation).

Braithwaite, J. (1989) *Crime, Shame and Reintegration* (Cambridge, Cambridge University Press).

Braithwaite, J. (1995) 'Reintegrative shaming, republicanism and policy', in Barlow, H. D. (ed.) *Crime and Public Policy: Putting Theory to Work* (Boulder, CO, Westview Press).

Braithwaite, J. and Mugford, S. (1994) 'Conditions of successful reintegration ceremonies: dealing with juvenile offenders', *British Journal of Criminology*, **34**(2), pp. 139–71.

Braye, S. and Preston-Shoot, M. (1990) 'On teaching and applying the law in social work: it is not that simple', *British Journal of Social Work*, **20**(4), pp. 333–53.

Braye, S. and Preston-Shoot, M. (1991) 'On acquiring law competence for social work: teaching, practice and assessment', *Social Work Education*, **10**(1), pp. 12–29.

Braye, S. and Preston-Shoot, M. (1995) *Empowering Practice in Social Care* (Buckingham, Open University Press).

Braye, S. and Preston-Shoot, M. (1997) *Practising Social Work Law*, 2nd edn (London, Macmillan).

Brearley, J. (1991) 'A psychodynamic appraoch to social work, in Lishman, J. (ed.) *Handbook of Theory to Practice Teachers in Social Work* (London, Jessica Kingsley).

Brearley, J. (1995) *Counselling and Social Work* (Buckingham, Open University Press).

Breton M. (1994) 'On the meaning of empowerment and empowerment oriented social work practice', *Social Work with Groups*, **17**(3), pp. 23–38.

Brewer, C. and Lait, J. (1980) *Can Social Work Survive?* (London, Temple Smith).

Brewster, R (1992) 'The new class? Managerialism and social work education and training', *Issues in Social Work Education*, **11**(2), pp. 81–93.

Briggs, S. (1995) 'From subjectivity towards realism: child observation and social work', in Yelloly and Henkel (1995), pp. 103–19.

Broad, B. and Fletcher, C. (eds) (1993) *Practitioner Social Work Research in Action* (London, Whiting & Birch).

Broadbent, J., Dietrich, M. and Laughlin, R. (1993) *The Development of Principal-Agent Contracting and Acceptability Relationships in the Public Sector: Conceptual and Cultural Problems* (Sheffield, Sheffield University).

Brook, E. and Davis, A. (eds) (1985) *Women, the Family and Social Work* (London, Tavistock).

Brooks, G., Pugh, A. K. and Schagen, I. (1996) *Reading Performance at Nine* (Buckingham, NFER/Open University).

Brown, A. (1979) *Groupwork* (London, Heinemann).

Brown, A. (1986) *Groupwork*, 2nd edn (Aldershot, Gower).

Brown, A. (1992) *Groupwork*, 3rd edn (Aldershot, Ashgate).

Brown, A. (1994) 'Groupwork in Britain', in Hanvey, C. and Philpot, T. (eds) *Practising Social Work* (London, Routledge).

Brown, A. (1996) 'Groupwork into the future: some personal reflections', *Groupwork* **9**(1), pp. 80–96.

Brown, A. and Bourne, I. (1996) *The Social Work Supervisor: Supervision in Community, Day Care and Residential Settings* (Buckingham, Open University Press).

Brown, A. and Clough, R. (eds) (1989) *Groups and Groupings: Life and Work in Day and Residential Centres* (London, Tavistock/Routledge).

Brown, G. W. and Harris, T. (1978) *Social Origins of Depression: A Study of Psychiatric Disorder in Women* (London, Tavistock).

Brown, H. C. (1996) 'The knowledge base of social work', in Vass (1996), pp. 8–35.

Brown, R. (1988) *Group Processes: Dynamics Within and Between Groups* (Oxford, Blackwell).

Bryan, B., Dadzie, S. and Scafe, S. (1985) *The Heart of the Race: Black Women's Lives in Britain* (London, Virago).

Buckely, J. Preston-Shoot, M. and Smith, C. (1995) *Community Care Reforms: The Views of Users and Carers – Research Findings* (Manchester, University of Manchester School of Social Work).

Bullock, R., Little, M. and Millham, S. (1993) *Going Home: The Return of Children Separated from their Families* (Dartmouth, Dartington Social Research Unit).

Bulmer, M. (1982) *The Uses of Social Research: Social Investigation in Public Policy-Making* (London, Allen & Unwin).

Bunyan, A. (1987) '"Help, I can't cope with my child": a behavioural approach to the treatment of a conduct disordered child within the natural home setting', *British Journal of Social Work*, **17**, pp. 237–56.

Burgess, R. (ed.) (1993) *Educational Research and Evaluation for Policy and Practice* (London, Falmer Press).

Burke, B., Clifford, D. J., Cox, P. and Hardwick, L. (1995) 'The theory and practice of risk assessment', Paper given at ESRC Conference: Risk in Organisational Settings, London, May.

Burke, P. and Cigno, K. (1996) *Support for Families: Helping Children with Learning Disabilities* (Aldershot, Avebury).

Burkitt, I. (1991) *Social Selves: Theories of the Formation of the Personality* (London, Sage).

Burks, H. M. and Stefflre, B. (1979) *Theories of Counseling*, 3rd edn (New York, McGraw-Hill).

Burney, E. (1985) *Sentencing Young People* (Aldershot, Gower).

Burnside, J. and Baker, N. (eds) (1994) *Relational Justice: Repairing the Breach* (Winchester, Waterside Press).

Butler, J. (1990) *Gender Trouble: Feminism and the Subversion of Identity* (London, Routledge).

Butler, S. (1994) '"All I've got in my purse is mothballs!", The Social Action Women's Group', *Groupwork*, **7**(2), pp. 163–79.

Butler, S. and Wintram, C. (1991) *Feminist Groupwork* (London, Sage).

Cabinet Office, Office of Public Service and Science, Office of Science and Technology (1993) *Realising Our Potential: A Strategy for Science, Engineering and Technology*, Cm. 2250 (London, HMSO).

Caddick, B. (1991) 'Using groups in working with offenders: a survey of groupwork in the probation services of England and Wales', *Groupwork*, **4**(3), pp. 197–216.

Caesar, G., Parchment, M. and Berridge, D. (1993) *Black Perspectives on Services for Children and Young People in Need and their Families* (London, National Children's Bureau/Barnardos).

Campbell, B. (1988) *Unofficial Secrets* (London, Virago).

Campbell, B. (1993) *Goliath: Britain's Dangerous Places* (London, Methuen).

Campion, M.J. (1995) *Who's Fit To Be a Parent?* (London, Routledge).

Cannan, C. (1992) *Changing Families Changing Welfare* (Hemel Hempstead, Harvester Wheatsheaf).

Cannan, C (1994/95) 'Enterprise culture, professional socialisation and social work education in Britain', *Critical Social Policy*, **42**, pp. 5–19.

Cannan, C., Berry, L. and Lyons, K. (1992) *Social Work and Europe* (London, Macmillan).

Carlebach, J. (1970) *Caring for Children in Trouble* (London, Routledge & Kegan Paul).

Carlen, P. (1989) 'Feminist jurisprudence – or women-wise penology?', *Probation Journal*, **36**(3).

Carlen, P. and Worrall, A. (eds) (1987) *Gender, Crime and Justice* (Buckingham, Open University Press).

Carmichael, K. (1974) 'The relationship between social work departments and the DHSS: the use of the Social Work (Scotland) Act', in Adler, M. E. (ed.) *In Cash or In Kind* (Edinburgh, Social Administration Department, Edinburgh University).

Carnall, C. (1990) *Managing Change in Organizations* (Englewood Cliffs, NJ, Prentice Hall).

Carter, R. T. (1991) 'Racial identity attitudes and psychological functioning', *Journal of Multicultural Counseling and Development*, **19**, pp. 105–15.

Carter, P., Jeffs, T. and Smith, M. K. (1995) *Social Working* (Basingstoke, Macmillan).

Cavadino, M. and Dignan, J. (1992) *The Penal System: An Introduction* (London, Sage).

Cavanagh, K. and Cree, V. E. (eds) (1996) *Working with Men: Feminism and Social Work, The State of Welfare* (London, Routledge).

CCETSW (1990) '*Paper 30: Requirements and Regulations for the Diploma in Social Work* (London, CCETSW).

CCETSW (1990) '*Paper 31: The Requirements for the Post Qualifying Education and Training in the Personal Social Services* (London, CCETSW).

CCETSW (1991) *DipSW: Rules and Requirements for the Diploma in Social Work*, CCETSW Paper 30, 2nd edn (London, Central Council for Education and Training in Social Work).

CCETSW (1995) *Assuring Quality: in the Diploma in Social Work – 1: Rules and Requirements for the DipSW* (revised) (London, Central Council for Education and Training in Social Work).

CCETSW (1996) *Assuring Quality: in the Diploma in Social Work – 1: Rules and Requirements for the DipSW* (second revision) (London, Central Council for Education and Training in Social Work).

Celnick, A. (1985) 'From paradigm to practice in a special probation project', *British Journal of Social Work*, **15**(2), pp. 223–41.

Central Statistical Office (1995) *Social Focus on Women* (London, HMSO).

Chambon, A. and Irving, A. (eds) (1994) *Essays on Post Modernism and Social Work* (Toronto, Canadian Scholar's Press).

Chapillon, L. (1996) 'A behaviour management group for parents in a family centre', *Behavioural Social Work Review*, **17**, pp. 22–30.

Chaplin, J. (1988). *Feminist Counselling in Action* (London, Sage).

Charles, N. and Kerr, N. (1985) *Attitudes towards the Feeding and Nutrition of Young Children*, Research Report 4 (London, Health Education Council).

Cheetham, J., Ahmed, A. and Small, J. (1986) *Black Children and their Families* (London, Routledge).

Cheetham, J., Fuller, R., McIvor, G. and Petch, A. (1992) *Evaluating Social Work Effectiveness* (Buckingham, Open University Press).

Children in Scotland (1995) *Scotland's Families Today* (Edinburgh, HMSO).

Cigno, K. (1988) 'Consumer views of a family centre drop-in', *British Journal of Social Work*, **18**, pp. 361–75.

Cigno, K. (1993) 'Changing behaviour in a residential group setting for elderly people with learning difficulties', *British Journal of Social Work*, **23**, pp. 629–42.

Cigno, K. (1995) 'Helping to prevent abuse: a behavioural approach with families', in Wilson, K. and James, A. (eds) *The Child Protection Handbook* (London, Baillière Tindall).

Cigno, K. and Wilson, K. (1994) 'Effective strategies for working with children and families: issues in the provision of therapeutic help', *Practice*, **6**, pp. 285–98.

Clark, C. (1995) 'Competence and discipline in professional formation', *British Journal of Social Work*, **25**, pp. 563–80.

Clark, J. (1994) 'Should social work education address religious issues? No!', *Journal of Social Work Education*, **30**(1), pp. 12–17.

Clark, J. (1996) 'After social work', in Parton, N, (ed.) *Social Theory, Social Change and Social Work*, (London, Routledge), pp. 36–60.

Clarke, D. (1992) *Women at Work: The Essential Guide for the Working Woman* (Shaftesbury, Element).

Clarke, J. (ed.) (1993) *A Crisis in Care; Challenges to Social Work* (London, Sage).

Clarke, J., Cochrane, A. and McLaughlin, E. (1994a) 'Introduction: why management matters', in Clarke *et al.* (1994b).

Clarke, J., Cochrane, A. and McLaughlin, E. (eds) (1994b) *Managing Social Policy* (London, Sage).

Cleaver, H. and Freeman, P. (1995) *Parental Perspectives in Cases of Suspected Child Abuse* (London, HMSO).

Cleland, A. (1995) 'Legal solutions for children; comparing Scots law with other jurisdictions', *Scottish Affairs*, **10**, Winter, pp. 6–24.

Clegg, S. R. (1990) *Modern Organizations: Organization Studies in the Postmodern World* (London, Sage).

Clegg, S. R., Handy, C. and Nord, W. (eds) (1996) *Handbook of Organization Studies* (London, Sage).

Cliffe, D. with Berridge, D. (1991) *Closing Children's Homes: An End to Residential Child Care?* (London, National Children's Bureau).

Clifford, D. J. (1994a) Critical life histories: a key anti-oppressive research method, in Humphries, B. and Truman, C. (eds) *Rethinking Social Research* (Aldershot, Avebury).

Clifford, D. J (1994b) 'Towards anti-oppressive social work assessment method', *Practice* **6**(3).

Clifford, D. J. (1995) 'Methods in oral history and social work', *Journal of the Oral History Society*, **23**(2).

Cockburn, C. (1991) *In the Way of Women: Men's Resistance to Sex Equality in Organisations* (London, Macmillan).

Cohen, B. and Fraser, N. (1991) *Children in a Modern Welfare System: Towards a New National Policy* (London, Institute for Public Policy Research).

Cohen, B. and Hagen, U. (eds) (1997) *Children's Services: Shaping up for the Millenium: Supporting Children and Families in the UK and Scandinavia* (Edinburgh, Stationery Office).

Cohen, S. (1975) 'It's all right for you to talk: political and sociological manifestos for social work action', in Bailey and Brake (1975).

Cole-Hamilton, I. and Lang, T. (1986) *Tightening Belts* (London, London Food Commission).

Coleman, G. (1991) *Investigating Organisations: A Feminist Approach* (Bristol, University of Bristol, School for Advanced Urban Studies).

Collins, B. (1986) 'Defining feminist social work', *Social Work*, (May–June), pp. 214–19.

Collins, P. H. (1990) *Black Feminist Thought* (London, Routledge).

Collinson, D. L. and Hearn, J. (1996) *Men as Managers, Managers as Men* (London, Sage).

Colton, M., Drury, C. and Williams, M. (1995) 'Children in need: definition, identification and support', *British Journal of Social Work*, **25**(6), pp. 711–28.

Committee on the Rights of the Child (1995) *The Concluding Observations of the Committee on the Rights of the Child: United Kingdom of Great Britain and Northern Ireland* in Consideration of Reports Submitted by State Parties Under Article 44 of the Convention Eighth Session.

Community Care (1996) 'Cradle to Grave Campaign' (November/December).

Connell, R. W. (1995) *Masculinities* (London, Routledge).

Constable, R. and Metha, U. (1993) *Education for Social Work in Eastern Europe* (Vienna, International Association of Schools of Social Work).

Corby, B. (1996) Risk assessment in child protection work, in Kemshall, H. and Pritchard, J. (eds) *Good Practice in Risk Assessment and Risk Management* (London, Jessica Kingsley).

Cordon, J. (1980) 'Contracts in social work practice', *British Journal of Social Work*, **10**, pp. 143–62.

Cordon, J. and Preston-Shoot, M. (1987) 'Contract or con trick? A reply to Rojek and Collins', *British Journal of Social Work*, **17**, pp. 535–43.

Cordon, J. and Preston-Shoot, M. (1988) 'Contract or con trick? A postscript', *British Journal of Social Work*, **18**(6), pp. 623–34.

Cornish, D. B. and Clarke, R. V. G. (1975) *Residential Treatment and its Effects on Delinquency*, Home Office Research Study 32 (London, HMSO).

Corr, C. A., Nabe, C. M. and Corr, D. M. (1996) *Death and Dying, Life and Living* (New York, Brooks/Cole).

Corrigan, P. and Leonard, P. (1978) *Social Work under Capitalism* (London, Macmillan).

Coulshed, V. (1991) *Social Work Practice: An Introduction* (London, Macmillan).

Cowburn, M. and Modi, P. (1995) 'Justice in an unjust context: implications for working with adult male sex offenders', in Ward, D. and Lacey, M. (eds) *Probation: Working for Justice* (London, Whiting & Birch).

CRE Connections (1996) 'Twenty years of action for equality', *CRE Connections: Bulletin of Racial Equality*, 7 June.

Cree, V. E. (1996) 'Why do men care?' in Cavanagh, K. and Cree, V. E. (eds) *Working with Men* (London and New York, Routledge).

Croft, S. and Beresford, P. (1994) 'A participatory approach to social work', in Hanvey, C. and Philpot, T. (eds) *Practising Social Work* (London, Routledge).

Crompton, M. (1992) *Children and Counselling* (London, Edward Arnold).

Cross, B. (1997) 'Partnership in practice: the experience of two probation services', *Howard Journal of Criminal Justice*, **36**(1), pp. 62–79.

Cross, W. E. (1971) 'The negro to black conversion experience: towards the psychology of black liberation', *Black World*, **20**, pp. 13–27.

Cross, W. E. (1980) 'Models of psychological nigrescence: a literature review', in Jones, R. L. (ed.) *Black Psychology*, 2nd edn (New York, Harper & Row).

Cross, W. E. (1991) *Shades of Black: Diversity in African American Identity* (Philadelphia,, Temple University Press).

Cross, W. E. (1992) *Black Identity: Theory and Research* (Philadelphia, Temple University Press).

Crow, G. and Allen, G. (1994) *Community Life* (Hemel Hempstead, Harvester Wheatsheaf).

Cullen, C., Campbell, M., Connelly, D., Hutton, B., Beattie, K. and Robb, G. (1995) *Approaches to People with Challenging Behaviour* (learning pack) (St Andrews, University of St Andrews).

Culyer, A. A. (chair) (1994) *Supporting Research and Development in the NHS: A Report to the Minister for Health by a Research and Development Task Force* (London, HMSO).

Cumming, E. and Henry, W. E. (1961) *Growing Old: The Process of Disengagement* (New York, Basic Books).

Currie, E. (1988) 'Two visions of community crime prevention', in Hope, T. and Shaw, M. (eds) *Communities and Crime Reduction* (London, HMSO).

Dalal, F. (1988) 'The racism of Jung', *Race and Class*, **29**(3), pp. 1–22.

Dale, J. and Foster, P. (1986) *Feminists and State Welfare* (London, Routledge & Kegan Paul).

Dalrymple, J. and Burke, B. (1995) *Anti-oppressive Practice: Social Care and the Law* (Buckingham, Open University Press).

Dant, T. and Gulley, V. (1990) *Coordinating Care at Home* (London, Collins Educational).

d'Ardenne, P. and Mahtani, A. (1989) *Transcultural Counselling in Action* (London, Sage).

Davies, B. (1975) *The Use of Groups in Social Work Practice* (London, Routledge & Kegan Paul).

Davies, D. (1996) 'Homophobia and heterosexism', in Davies and Neal (1996).

Davies, D. and Neal, C. (eds) (1996) *Pink Therapy: A Guide for Counsellors Working with Lesbian, Gay and Bisexual Clients* (Buckingham, Open University Press).

Davies, M. (1984) *The Essential Social Worker*, 2nd edn (Aldershot, Gower).

Davies, M. (1994) *The Essential Social Worker*, 3rd edn (Aldershot, Arena).

Davis, A. and Wainwright, S. (1996) 'Poverty work and the mental health services', *Breakthrough*, **1**(1), pp . 47–56.

Deacon, B. (1992) *The New Eastern Europe* (London, Sage).

de Beauvoir, S. (1974) *The Second Sex*, trans. Pashley, H. M. (New York, Vintage Books).

de Shazer, S. (1988) *Clues: Investigating Solutions in Brief Therapy* (New York, Norton).

de Shazer, S. (1991) *Putting Difference to Work* (New York and London, W.W. Norton).

Dews, V. and Watts, J. (1994) *Review of Probation Officer Recruitment and Qualifying Training* (London, Home Office).

DHSS (1974) *Report of the Committee of Inquiry into the Care and Supervision Provided in Relation to Maria Colwell* (London, HMSO).

DHSS (1988) *Report of the Inquiry into Child Abuse in Cleveland* (Butler-Sloss Report) Cmnd 412 (London, HMSO).

Dixon, N. (1984) *Research and Planning in Barnardos* (unpublished paper) (Ilford, Essex, Barnardos).

Doel, M. (1994) 'Task-centred work', in Hanvey, C. and Philpot, T. (eds) *Practising Social Work* (London, Routledge).

Doel, M. and Lawson, B. (1986) 'Open records: the client's right to partnership', *British Journal of Social Work*, **16**(4), pp. 407–30.

Doel, M. and Marsh, P. (1992) *Task-centred Social Work* (Aldershot, Ashgate).

Doel, M. and Shardlow, S. M. (1998) *The New Social Work Practice* (Aldershot, Arena).

DoH (1988) *Protecting Children: A Guide for Social Workers Undertaking a Comprehensive Assessment* (London, HMSO).

DoH (1989) *Homes are for Living In* (London, HMSO).

DoH (1991a) *Care Management and Assessment: Practitioners Guide* (London, HMSO).

DoH (1991b) *Working Together under the Children Act, 1989* (London, HMSO).

DoH (1991c) *Patterns and Outcomes in Child Placement* (London: HMSO).

DoH (1992) *Committed to Quality: Quality Assurance in Social Services Departments*, (London, HMSO).

DoH (1993) *Guidance on Permissible Forms of Control in Children's Residential Care* (London, HMSO).

DoH (1994) *The Children Act 1989: Contact Orders Study* (London, HMSO).

DoH (1995) *Child Protection: Messages from Research* (London, HMSO).

DoH (1996) *Building Bridges: A Guide to Arrangements for Inter-Agency Working for the Care and Protection of Severely Mentally Ill People* (Yorkshire, Department of Health).

DoHSSI (1991a) *The Right to Complain: Practice Guidance on Complaints Procedures in Social Services Departments* (London, HMSO).

DoHSSI (1991b) *Women in Social Services: A Neglected Resource* (London, HMSO).

DoHSSI (1991c) *Practitioners and Managers' Guide to Care Management and Assessment* (London, HMSO).

DoH, Scottish Office, Welsh Office and Department of Health and Social Services, Northern Ireland (1996) *The Obligations of Care: A Consultation Paper on the Setting of Conduct and Practice Standards for Social Services Staff* (London, Department of Health).

Dominelli, L. (1988) *Anti-Racist Social Work* (London, Macmillan), 2nd edn published 1997.

Dominelli, L. (1990) *Women and Community Action* (Birmingham, Venture Press).

Dominelli, L. (1990–91) '"What's in a name?" A comment on "Puritans and paradigms"', *Social Work and Social Sciences Review*, **2**(3), pp. 231–5.

Dominelli, L. (1993) *Social Work: Mirror of Society or its Conscience?* (Sheffield, Department of Sociological Studies).

Dominelli, L. (1994) 'Anti-racist social work education', Paper given at the 27th Congress of the International Association of Schools of Social Work, Amsterdam, July.

Dominelli, L. (1996) 'Deprofessionalising social work: anti-oppressive practice, competencies and post-modernism', *British Journal of Social Work*, **26**, pp. 153–75.

Dominelli, L. (1997) *Sociology for Social Work* (London, Macmillan).

Dominelli, L. and Hoogvelt, A. (1996) 'Globalisation and the technocratisation of social work', *Critical Social Policy*, 47, **16**(2), pp. 45–62.

Dominelli, L. and McLeod, E. (1989) *Feminist Social Work* (London, Macmillan).

Doray, B. (1988) *From Taylorism to Fordism: A Rational Madness* (London, Free Association Books).

Douglas, T. (1978) *Basic Groupwork* (London, Tavistock).

Douglas, T. (1983) *Groups: Understanding People Gathered Together* (London, Tavistock).

Douglas, T. (1986) *Group Living: The Application of Group Dynamics in Residential Settings* (London, Tavistock).

Douglas, T. (1993) *A Theory of Groupwork Practice* (London, Macmillan).

Downes, D. and Morgan, R. (1994) '"Hostages to fortune"? The politics of law and order in post-war Britain', in Maguire, M., Morgan, R. and Reiner, R. (eds) *The Oxford Handbook of Criminology* (Oxford, Clarendon Press).

Downie, R. S. (1989) 'A political critique of Kantian ethics in social work: a reply to Webb and McBeath', *British Journal of Social Work*, **19**(6), pp. 507–10.

Downie, R. S. and Telfer, E. (1969) *Respect for Persons* (London, Allen & Unwin).

Drakeford, M. (1994) 'Groupwork for parents of young people in trouble', *Groupwork*, **7**(3), pp. 236–47.

Drakeford, M. (1996) 'Educating for culturally sensitive practice', in Jackson, S. and Preston-Shoot, M. (eds) *Educating Social Workers in a Changing Policy Context* (London, Whiting & Birch).

Drakeford, M. and Vanstone, M. (eds) (1996) *Beyond Offending Behaviour* (Aldershot, Arena).

Dryden, W. and Feltham, C. (1992) *Brief Counselling: A Practical Guide for Beginning Practitioners* (Buckingham, Open University Press).

Dryden, W., Charles-Edwards, D. and Woolfe, R. (eds) (1989) *Handbook of Counselling in Great Britain* (London, Routledge).

DSS (1996) *Households below Average Income: A Statistical Analysis 1979–1993/94* (London, HMSO).

Dunn, J. (1993) *Young Children's Close Relationships: Beyond Attachment* (Newbury Park, CA, Sage).

Durkin, K. (1995) *Developmental Social Psychology: From Infancy to Old Age* (Oxford, Blackwell).

Durrant, P. (1997) 'Mapping the future? A contribution from community social work in the community care field', in Cannan, C. and Warren, C. (eds) *Social Action with Children and Families* (London, Routledge).

Dwivedi, K. N. (1996) 'Introduction' in Dwivedi and Varma (1996).

Dwivedi, K. N. and Varma, V. P. (eds) (1996) *Meeting the Needs of Ethnic Minority Children: A Handbook for Professionals* (London, Jessica Kingsley).

Eastman, M. (ed.) (1994) *Old Age Abuse*, 2nd edn (London, Chapman & Hall).

Economic and Social Research Council (1996) 'Council to review priorities', *Social Sciences* **32**.

Egan, G. (1990) *The Skilled Helper*, 4th edn (Pacific Grove, CA: Brooks/Cole).

Eichenbaum, L. and Orbach, S. (1984) *What Do Women Want?* (London, Fontana).

Ellis, K. (1993) *Squaring the Circle: User and Carer Participation in Needs Assessment* (York, Joseph Rowntree Foundation).

England, H. (1986) *Social Work as Art: Making Sense of Good Practice* (London, Allen & Unwin).

Epstein, L. (1992) *Brief Treatment and a New Look at the Task-Centered Approach* (New York, Macmillan).

Eraut, M. (1994) *Developing Professional Knowledge and Competence* (London, Falmer Press).

Erikson, E. (1965) *Childhood and Society* (Harmondsworth, Penguin).

Erikson, E. (1977) *Childhood and Society* (London, Fontana).

Erikson, E. H., Erikson, J. M. and Kivnick, H. Q. (1986) *Vital Involvement in Old Age: The Experience of Old Age in our Time* (New York, Norton).

Erikson, H. (1964) 'Memorandum on identity and negro youth', *Journal of Social Issues*, **20**(4), pp. 29–42.

Erikson, H. (1968) *Identity: Youth and Crisis* (London, Faber).

Etzioni, A. (ed.) (1969) *The Semi-Professions and Their Organization* (New York, Free Press).

Evans, R. and Wilkinson, C. (1990) 'Variations in police cautioning policy and practice in England and Wales', *Howard Journal of Criminal Justice*, **29**, 155–76.

Everitt, A. (1995) 'Monitoring and evaluation: towards a culture of lying?', Paper given to NCVO Annual Research Conference, London, September.

Everitt, A. and Hardiker, P. (1996) *Evaluating for Good Practice* (London, Macmillan).

Everitt, A., Hardiker, P., Littlewood, J. and Mullender, A. (1992) *Applied Research for Better Practice* (Basingstoke, Macmillan).

Fahlberg, V. (1991) *A Child's Journey Through Placement* (London, BAAF).

Falloon, I. R. H. (1988) *Handbook of Behavioural Family Therapy* (London, Guilford Press).

Falloon, I. R. H., Laporta, M., Fadden, G. and Graham-Hole, V. (1993) *Managing Stress in Families: Cognitive and Behavioural Strategies for Enhancing Coping Skills* (London, Routledge).

Family Rights Group (1994) *Family Group Conferences* (London, Family Rights Group).

Farnham, D. and Horton, S. (eds) *Managing the New Public Services* (London, Macmillan.

Farrar, M. (1996) 'Probation in the community', Paper presented to the First Annual Colloquium of the Probation Studies Unit, Centre for Criminological Research, University of Oxford, 16–17 December.

Farrington, D. (1993) 'Juvenile Delinquency', in Coleman, J. (ed.) *The School Years* (London, Routledge).

Faulkner, D. (1993) 'All flaws and disorder', *Guardian*, 11 November.

Faulkner, D. (1995) 'The Criminal Justice Act, 1991: policy, legislation and practice', in Ward, D. and Lacey, M. (eds) *Probation: Working for Justice* (London, Whiting & Birch).

Featherstone, B. and Fawcett, B. (1995) 'Power, difference and social work: an exploration', *Social Work Education*, **15**(1).

Featherstone, M. (1988) 'In pursuit of the post modern: an introduction', *Theory, Culture and Society*, **5**(2–3), pp. 195–216.

Feaver, N. and Smith, D. (1994) 'Editorial introduction', Special issue on probation. *British Journal of Social Work*, **24**(4), pp. 379–86.

Feltham, C. (1995) *What is Counselling?* (London, Sage).

Feltham, C. and Dryden, W. (1993) *Dictionary of Counselling* (London, Whurr).

Fennell, G., Phillipson, C. and Evers, H. (1988) *The Sociology of Old Age* (Milton Keynes, Open University Press).

Fernando, S. (1991) *Mental Health, Race and Culture* (London, Macmillan).

Fetterman, D. M. (1996) 'Empowerment evaluation: an introduction to theory and practice', in Fetterman, D. M., Kaftarian, S. J. and Wandersman, A. (eds) *Empowerment, Evaluation: Knowledge and Tools for Self-Assessment and Accountability* (London, Sage), pp. 3–46.

Firestone, S. (1971) *The Dialectic of Sex* (London, Jonathan Cape).

Fischer, J. (1974) 'Is casework effective? A review', *Social Work*, **1**, pp. 107–10.

Fischer, J. (1978) *Effective Casework Practice: An Eclectic Approach* (New York, McGraw-Hill).

Fisher, M., Marsh, P., Phillips, D. and Sainsbury, E. (1986) *In and Out of Care: The Experience of Children, Parents and Social Workers* (London, Batsford).

Flax, J. (1990) *Thinking Fragments: Psychoanalysis, Feminism and Postmodernism in the Contemporary West* (Oxford, University of California Press).

Fleming, J. and Ward, D. (1996) 'The ethics of community health needs assessment: searching for a participant centred approach', in Parker, M. (ed.) *Ethics and Community* (Preston, Centre for Professional Ethics, University of Central Lancashire).

Fletcher, B. (1993) *Not Just a Name: The Views of Young People in Foster and Residential Care* (London, National Consumer Council/Who Cares? Trust).

Folkard, M. S., Smith, D. E. and Smith, D. D. (1976) *IMPACT Volume II: The Results of the Experiment*, Home Office Research Study 36 (London, HMSO).

Foster, B. and Preston-Shoot, M. (1995) *Guardians ad litem and Independent Expert Assessments* (Manchester, University of Manchester).

Foster, G. (1996) *Getting What You Want: A Short Guide to Career Development for Senior Women Managers* (London, National Institute for Social Work).

Fox Harding, L. M. (1991a) 'The Children Act in context: four perspectives in child care law and policy (1)', *Journal of Social Welfare and Family Law*, **3**, pp. 179–93.

Fox Harding, L. M. (1991b) 'The Children Act in context: four perspectives in child care law and policy (2)', *Journal of Social Welfare and Family Law*, **4**, pp. 299–316.

Frank, A. W. (1991) *At the Will of the Body: Reflections on Illness* (Boston, Houghton Mifflin).

Franklin, A. and Franklin, B. (1996) 'Growing pains: the developing children's rights movement in the UK', in Pilcher, J. and Wagg, S. (eds) *Thatcher's Children? Politics, Childhood and Society in the 1980s and 1990s* (London, Falmer Press).

Franklin, B. (1989) 'Wimps and bullies: press reporting of child abuse', in Carter, P. *et al.* (eds) *Social Work and Social Welfare Yearbook I* (Milton Keynes, Open University Press).

Freeman, I., Morrison, A., Lockhart, F. and Swanson, M. (1996) 'Consulting service users: the views of young people', in Hill, M. and Aldgate, J. (eds) *Child Welfare Services: Developments in Law, Policy, Practice and Research* (London, Jessica Kingsley).

Freeman, J. (ed.) (undated) *The Tyranny of Structurelessness* (Dark Star Press) (First US publication 1970).

Freeman, M. D. A. (1992) 'In the child's best interests? Reading the Children Act critically', *Current Legal Problems*, **45**(1), pp. 173–211.

Freire, P. (1972) *The Pedagogy of the Oppressed* (Harmondsworth, Penguin).

Freud, S. (1912–13) *Totem and Taboo* (Harmondsworth, Penguin Freud Library 13).

Freud, S. (1915) 'Thoughts for the times on war and death', *Imago*, **4**(1) pp. 1–21, trans. J. Strachey in *The Standard Edition of the Complete Psychological Works of Sigmund Freud*, vol. 14 (London, Hogarth Press).

Freud, S. (1930) 'Civilization and its discontents', in Strachey, J. (ed.) trans. Rivière, J. *The Standard Edition of the Complete Works of Sigmund Freud*, vol, 21 (London, Hogarth Press).

Frith, U. (1989) *Autism: Explaining the Enigma* (Oxford, Blackwell).

Frosh, S. (1987) *The Politics of Psychoanalysis* (London, Macmillan).

Frost, N. and Stein, M. (1989) *The Politics of Child Welfare: Inequality, Power and Change* (Hemel Hempstead, Harvester Wheatsheaf).

Frost, N. and Stein, M. (1990) 'The politics of the Children Act', *Childright*, July/August, p. 1.

Fuller, R. (1992) *In Search of Prevention* (Aldershot, Avebury).

Fuller, R. and Petch, A. (1995) *Practitioner-Research: The Reflective Social Worker* (Buckingham, Open University Press).

Gambe, D., Gomes, J., Kapur, V., Rangel, M. and Stubbs, P. (1992) *Improving Practice with Children and Families* (Leeds, Central Council for Education and Training in Social Work).

Gambrill, E. (1983) *Casework – a Competency-based Approach* (Englewood Cliffs, NJ, Prentice-Hall).

Gambrill, E. (1986) 'Social skills training with the elderly', in Hollin and Trower (1986).

Geertz, C. (1973) *The Interpretation of Cultures* (New York, Basic Books).

Gelsthorpe, L. and Morris, A. (1994) 'Juvenile justice 1945–1992', in Maguire, M., Morgan, R. and Reiner, R. (eds) *The Oxford Handbook of Criminology* (Oxford, Clarendon Press).

Gelsthorpe, L. and Raynor, P. (1992) 'The quality of reports prepared in the pilot studies', in Bredar, J. (ed.) *Justice Informed*, Vol. II (London, Vera Institute of Justice).

Gendreau, P. and Ross, R. (1987) 'Revisitation of rehabilitation: evidence from the 1980s', *Justice Quarterly*, **4**, pp. 349–406.

George, E., Iveson, C. and Ratner, H. (1990) *Problem to Solution: Brief Therapy with Individuals and Families* (London, Brief Therapy Press).

George, M. (1996) 'Figure it out', *Community Care*, 1–7 August, pp. ii–v.

Geraghty, J. (1991) *Probation Practice in Crime Prevention*, Crime Prevention Unit Paper 24 (London, Home Office).

Geva, J. and Weinman, M. L. (1995) 'Social work perspectives in organ procurement', *Health and Social Work*, **20**(4), pp. 241–320.

Gherardi, S. and Turner, B. (1987) *Real Men Don't Collect Soft Data* (Trento, Quaderno Dipartimento di Politica Sociale, Università di Trento).

Gibbons, J., Gallagher, B., Bell, C. and Gordon, D. (1995) 'Development after physical abuse in early childhood: a follow up study of child on protection registers', *Child Protection: Messages from Research* (HMSO), pp. 65–7.

Giddens, A. (1990) *The Consequences of Modernity* (Cambridge, Polity Press).

Giddens, A. (1991) *Modernity and Self Identity: Self and Society in the Late Modern Age* (Cambridge, Polity Press).

Gilder, G. (1984) *Wealth and Poverty* (New York, Basic Books).

Gilligan, C. (1982) *In a Different Voice* (Harvard University Press).

Ginsburg, N. (1997) 'Housing', in Walker and Walker (1997).

Glennerster, H. and Midgely, J. (eds) (1991) *The Radical Right and the Welfare State* (London, Harvester Wheatsheaf).

Gomm, R. (1993) 'Issues of power in health and welfare', in Walmsley, J., Reynolds, J., Shakespeare, P. and Woolfe, R. (eds) *Health, Welfare and Practice: Reflecting on Roles and Relationships* (London, Sage).

Gould, N. (1990) 'A political critique of Kantian ethics: a contribution to the debate between Webb and McBeath, and Downie', *British Journal of Social Work*, **20**(3), pp. 495–9.

Gould, N. (1996) 'Using imagery in reflective learning', in Gould, N. and Taylor, I. (eds) *Reflective Learning for Social Work* (Aldershot, Arena), pp. 63–77.

Gould, N. and Taylor, I. (eds) (1996) *Reflective Learning for Social Work: Research Theory and Practice* (Aldershot, Arena).

Gouldner, A. (1970) *The Coming Crisis of Western Sociology* (London, Heinemann).

Graham, H. (1992) 'Feminism and social work education' *Issues in Social Work Education*, **11**(2), pp. 48–62.

Graham, J. and Bowling, B. (1995) *Young People and Crime*, Home Office Research Study 145 (London, Home Office).

Greenhorn, M. (1996) *Cautions, Court Proceedings and Sentencing: England and Wales 1995*, Home Office Statistical Bulletin 16/96 (London, Home Office).

Greer, P. (1994) *Transforming Central Government: The New Steps Initiative* (Buckingham, Open University Press).

Griffiths, Sir Roy (1988) *Community Care: Agenda for Action* (London, HMSO).

Grimwood, C. and Popplestone, R. (1993) *Women, Management and Care* (London, Macmillan).

Grossman, K., Grossmann, K. E., Spangler, S., Suess, G. and Unzner, L. (1985) 'Maternal sensitivity and newborn attachment orientation responses as related to quality of attachment in northern Germany', in Bretherton, I. and Waters, E. (eds) *Growing Points of Attachment Theory: Monographs of the Society of Research in Child Development*, **50**(1–2) Serial No 209.

Guy, P. (1994) 'A general social work council – a critical look at the issues', *British Journal of Social Work*, **24**(3), pp. 261–71.

Hadley, R. and Clough, R. (1996) *Care in Chaos* (London, Cassell).

Hadley, R., Cooper, M., Dale, P. and Stacy, G. (1987) *A Community Social Worker's Handbook* (London, Tavistock).

Hagel, A. and Newburn, T. (1994) *The Persistent Offender* (London, Policy Studies Institute).

Hale, J. (1983) 'Feminism and social work practice', in Jordan, B. and Parton, N. (eds) *The Political Dimensions of Social Work*, (Oxford, Blackwell).

Hallett, C. (1993) 'Child protection in Europe: convergence or divergence?', *Adoption and Fostering*, **17**(4), pp. 27–32.

Hallett, C. and Birchall, E. (1992) *Coordination in Child Protection* (London, HMSO).

Handy, C. (1990) *The Age of Unreason* (London, Arrow).

Hanmer, J. and Maynard, M. (1987) *Women, Violence and Social Control* (London, Macmillan).

Hanmer, J. and Statham, D. (1988) *Women and Social Work: Towards a Woman-centred Practice* (London, Macmillan).

Harding, S. (ed.) (1987) *Feminism and Methodology* (Milton Keynes, Open University Press).

Harrison, A., Wilson, M., Pine, C., Chan, S. and Buriel, R. (1990) 'Family ecologies of ethnic minority children', *Child Development*, **61**, pp. 347–62.

Harrison, W. D. (1991) *Seeking Common Ground: A Theory of Social Work in Social Care* (Aldershot, Avebury).

Hart, E. and Bond, M. (1995) *Action Research for Health and Social Care: A Guide to Practice* (Buckingham, Open University Press).

Harwin, J. (1990) 'Parental responsibilities in the Children Act 1989', in Manning, N. and Ungerson, C. (eds) *Social Policy Review 1989–1990* (London, Longman).

Hawxhurst, D. and Morrow, S. (1984) *Living Our Visions: Building Feminist Community* (Tempe, Arizona, Fourth World).

Haxby, D. (1978) *Probation: A Changing Service* (London, Constable).

Hayman, V. (1993) 'Re-writing the job: a sceptical look at competences', *Probation Journal*, **40**(4), pp. 180–3.

Heap, K. (1977) *Group Theory for Social Workers* (Oxford, Pergamon).

Heap, K. (1985) *The Practice of Social Work with Groups* (London, Allen & Unwin).

Hearn, J. and Parkin, W. (1995) *Sex at Work: The Power and Paradox of Organisation Sexuality* (rev. edn) (London, Prentice Hall/Harvester Wheatsheaf).

Heelas, P., Lash, S. and Morris, P. (eds) (1996) *Detraditionalization Critical Reflections on Authority and Identity* (Oxford, Blackwell).

Heineman, M. (1981) 'The obsolete scientific imperative in social work research', *Social Service Review*, **55**(3), pp. 371–96.

Henriques, J., Holloway, W., Urwin, C., Venn, C. and Walkerdine, D. (1984) *Changing the Subject; the Subject, Psychology, Social Regulation and Subjectivity* (London, Methuen).

Herbert, M. (1987a) *Conduct Disorders of Childhood and Adolescence: A Social Learning Perspective*, 2nd edn (Chichester, Wiley).

Herbert, M. (1987b) *Behavioural Treatment of Children with Problems: A Practice Manual*, 2nd edn (London, Academic Press).

Hester, M., Kelly, L. and Radford, J. (eds) (1996) *Women, Violence and Male Power*, (Buckingham, Open University Press).

Hill, M. (1996) *Understanding Social Policy*. (Oxford, Blackwell).

Hill, M. and Aldgate, J. (eds) (1996a) *Child Welfare Services: Developments in Law, Policy, Practice and Research* (London, Jessica Kingsley).

Hill, M. and Aldgate, J. (1996b) 'The Children Act, 1989 and recent developments in research in England and Wales', in Hill and Aldgate (1996).

Hill-Collins, P. (1990) *Black Feminist Thought – Knowledge, Consciousness, and the Politics of Empowerment* (London, Unwin Hyman).

Hills, J. (1995) *Joseph Rowntree Foundation Inquiry into Income and Wealth*, Vol. 2 (York, Joseph Rowntree Foundation).

Hochschild, A. R. (1975) 'Disengagement theory: a critique and proposal', *American Sociological Review*, **40**, pp. 553–69.

Hockey, J. and James, A. (1993) *Growing Up and Growing Old: Ageing and Dependency in the Life Course* (London, Sage).

Hollin, C. R. and Trower, P. (eds) (1986) *Handbook of Social Skills Training*, Vol. 1 (Oxford, Pergamon).

Hollin, C. R., Epps, K. J. and Kendrick, A. J. (1995) *Managing Behavioural Treatment* (London, Routledge).

Hollis, F. (1972) *Casework: A Psychosocial Therapy*, 2nd edn (New York, Random House).

Hollis, M. and Howe, D. (1987) 'Moral risks in social work', *Journal of Applied Philosophy*, **4**, pp. 123–33.

Hollis, M. and Howe, D. (1990) 'Moral risks in the social work role: a response to Macdonald', *British Journal of Social Work*, **20**(6), pp. 547–52.

Hollway, W. (1989) *Subjectivity and Method in Psychology: Gender, Meaning and Science* (London, Sage).

Holman, B. (1988) *Putting Families First* (London, Macmillan).

Holman, R. (1983) *Resourceful Friends* (London, Children's Society).

Holman, R. (1993) *A New Deal for Social Welfare* (Oxford, Lyon Publishing).

Holman, R. (1996) *Children and Crime* (Oxford, Lyon Publishing).

Holmans, A. (1996) 'Meeting housing needs in the private rented sector', *Housing Review* 1996/7 (York, Joseph Rowntree Foundation).

Home Office (1980) *Young Offenders*, Cmnd 8045 (London, HMSO).

Home Office (1984) *Probation Service in England and Wales: Statement of National Objectives and Priorities* (London, Home Office).

Home Office (1988a) *The Parole System in England and Wales: Report of the Review Committee*, Cm 532 (London, HMSO).

Home Office (1988b) *Punishment, Custody and the Community*, Cm 424 (London, Home Office).

Home Office (1990) *Crime, Justice and Protecting the Public*, Cm 965 (London, HMSO).

Home Office (1991) *Safer Communities: The Local Delivery of Crime Prevention through the Partnership Approach*, the Morgan Report (London, Home Office).

Home Office (1992) *National Standards for the Supervision of Offenders in the Community* (London, Home Office).

Home Office (1993) *Monitoring of the Criminal Justice Act 1991: Data from a Special Data Collection Exercise*, Home Office Statistical Bulletin 25/93. (London, Home Office).

Home Office (1995) *National Standards for the Supervision of Offenders in the Community* (London, Home Office).

hooks, B. (1981) *Ain't I a Woman: Black Women and Feminism* (London, Pluto Press).

hooks, B. (1984a) 'Feminism: a movement to end sexist oppression', in Philips, A. (ed.) *Feminism and Equality* (Oxford, Blackwell).

hooks, B. (1984b) *Feminist Theory – from Margin to Center* (Boston, South End Press).

hooks, B. (1989) *Talking Back: Thinking Feminist, Thinking Black* (Boston, South End Press).

hooks, B. (1991) *Yearning: Race, Gender and Cultural Politics* (London, Turnaround).

Hoopes, J. L. (1990) 'Adoption and identity formation', in Brodzinsky, D. M. and Schechter, M. D. (eds) *The Psychology of Adoption* (Oxford, Oxford University Press).

Horobin, G. (ed.)(1987) *Sex, Gender and Care Work* (London, Jessica Kingsley).

Hough, M. (1996) 'People talking about punishment', *Howard Journal of Criminal Justice*, **35**(3), pp. 191–214.

Houston, G. (1984) *The Red Book of Groups* (London, Rochester Foundation).

Howard, M. (1997) 'Cutting social security', in Walker and Walker (1997).

Howe, D. (1986) 'The segregation of women and their work in the personal social services', *Critical Social Policy*, **15**, pp. 21–36.

Howe, D. (1987) *An Introduction to Social Work Theory*, Community Care Practice Handbooks (Aldershot, Arena).

Howe, D. (1989) *The Consumers' View of Family Therapy* (Aldershot, Gower).

Howe, D. (1993) *On Being a Client: Understanding the Process of Counselling and Psychotherapy* (London, Sage).

Howe, D. (1994) 'Modernity, postmodernity and social work', *British Journal of Social Work*, **24**(5), pp. 513–32.

Howe, D. (1995) *Attachment Theory for Social Work Practice* (London, Macmillan).

Hoyes, L., Jeffers, S., Lart, R., Means, R. and Taylor, M. (1993) *User Empowerment and the Reform of Community Care,* Studies in Decentralisation and Quasi-Markets 16 (Bristol School for Advanced Urban Studies, University of Bristol).

Hudson, A. (1989) 'Changing perspectives: feminism, gender and social work', in Langan and Lee (1989).

Hudson, A. (1992) 'The child sex abuse "industry" and gender relations in social work', in Langan and Day (1992).

Hudson, B. L. (1982) *Social Work with Psychiatric Patients* (London, Macmillan).

Hudson, B. L. and Macdonald, G. (1986) *Behavioural Social Work: An Introduction* (London, Macmillan).

Hughes, C. (1995) 'Really useful knowledge: adult education and the Ruskin Learning Project', in Mayo, M. and Thompson, J. (eds) *Adult Learning, Critical Intelligence and Social Change* (Leicester, NIACE).

Hugman, R. and Smith, D. (1995) *Ethical Issues in Social Work* (London, Routledge).

Hugman, R. and Smith, D. (eds) (1996) *Ethical Issues in Social Work* (London, Routledge.)

Humphries, B. (1993) 'Are you or have you ever been...?', *Social Work Education,* **12**(3), pp. 6–8.

Humphries, B. (ed.) (1996) *Critical Perspectives on Empowerment* (Birmingham, Venture Press).

Hutton, W. (1996) *The State We're In* (rev. edn) (London, Vintage).

Iannello, K. (1992) *Decisions without Hierarchy: Feminist Interventions in Organization Theory and Practice* (New York, Routledge).

IFSW (1988) *International Code of Ethics for the Professional Social Worker* (Vienna, International Federation of Social Workers).

Irvine, E. (1954) 'Research into problem families', *British Journal of Psychiatric Social Work,* **9**.

Itzin, C. and Newman, J. (eds) (1995) *Gender, Culture and Organisational Change: Putting Theory into Practice* (London, Routledge).

Iwaniec, D. (1995) *The Emotionally Abused and Neglected Child: Identification, Assessment and Intervention* (Chichester, Wiley).

Iwaniec, I., Herbert, M. and McNeish, A. S. (1985a) 'Assessment and treatment of failure-to-thrive children and their families: Part I. Psychosocial factors', *British Journal of Social Work,* **15**, pp. 243–59.

Iwaniec, I., Herbert, M. and McNeish, A. S. (1985b) 'Social work with failure-to thrive children and their families: Part II. Behavioural social work intervention', *British Journal of Social Work,* **15**, pp. 375–98.

Jackson, M., Kolody, B. and Wood, J. L. (1982) 'To be old and black: the case for double jeopardy on income and health', in Manuel, R. C. (ed.) *Minority Ageing* (Westport, CT, Greenwood Press).

Jackson, S. and Preston-Shoot, M. (eds) (1996) *Educating Social Workers in a Changing Policy Context* (London, Whiting & Birch).

Jacobs, M. (1988) *Psychodynamic Counselling in Action* (London, Sage).

Jacobs, P. and Landau, S. (1967) *The New Radicals* (London, Pelican).

Jacobs, R. (1989) 'Getting the measure of management competence', *Personnel Management,* **21**(6), pp. 32–7.

James, A. (1994) 'Reflections on the politics of quality', in Connor, A. and Black, S., *Performance Review and Quality in Social Care* (London, Jessica Kingsley).

James, A. L. (1995) 'Probation values for the 1990s – and beyond?', *Howard Journal of Criminal Justice,* **34**(4), pp. 326–43.

James, A. L. and Bottomley, A. K. (1994) 'Probation partnerships revisited', *Howard Journal of Criminal Justice,* **33**(2), pp. 158–68.

James, S. M. and Busia, A. P. A. (eds) (1993) *Theorizing Black Feminisms: The Visionary Pragmatism of Black Women* (Routledge, London).

Jannson, B. (1994) *Social Policy: From Theory to Policy Practice* (Pacific Grove, CA, Brooks/Cole).

Jehu, D. (1967) *Learning Theory and Social Work* (London, Routledge & Kegan Paul).

Jones, A. and Bilton, K. (1994) *The Future Shape of Children's Services* (London, National Children's Bureau).

Jones, C. (1978) *An analysis of the development of social work education and social work 1869–1977*. Unpublished PhD thesis, University of Durham.

Jones, C. (1983) *State Social Work and the Working Class* (London, Routledge & Kegan Paul).

Jones, C. (1993) 'Distortion and demonisation: the Right and anti-racist social work education', *Social Work Education*, **12**(12), pp. 9–16.

Jones, C. (1994) *Dangerous Times for British Social Work Education*. Paper presented at the 27th Congress of the International Association of Schools of Social Work, Amsterdam, 11–15 July.

Jones, C. (1996a) 'Anti-intellectualism and the peculiarities of British social work', in Parton (1996).

Jones, C. (1996b) 'Dangerous times for British social work education', in Ford, P. and Hayes, P. (eds) *Educating for Social Work: Arguments for Optimism* (Aldershot, Avebury).

Jones, C. (1996c) 'Regulating social work: a review of the review', in Jackson, S. and Preston-Shoot, M. (eds) *Social Work Education in a Changing Policy Context* (London, Whiting & Birch).

Jones, C. (1996d) 'Poverty, inequality and social division in contemporary Britain: implications for social welfare', *Representing Children*, **9**(4).

Jones, C. (1997) 'Social work and poverty', in Davies, M. (ed.) *Blackwell's Companion to Social Work* (Oxford, Blackwell).

Jones, F., Fletcher, B. and Ibbetson, K. (1991) 'Stressors and strains amongst social workers: demands, supports, constraints, and psychological health', *British Journal of Social Work*, **21**(5), pp. 443–69.

Jones, M. A. (1985) *A Second Chance for Families: Five Years Later: a Follow Up Study of a Program to Prevent Foster Care* (New York, Child Welfare League of America).

Jones, S. and Joss, R. (1995) 'Models of professionalism', in Yelloly and Henkel (1995).

Jordan, B. (1990) *Social Work in an Unjust Society* (Hemel Hempstead, Harvester Wheatsheaf).

Jordan, J. (1989) *Moving Towards Home: Political Essays* (London, Virago).

Joseph Rowntree Foundation (1996), 'Life on a low income', *Findings*, **97**, June.

Jung, C. (1950) 'On the psychology of the Negro', in McGuire, W. (ed.) *Collected Works of Carl Jung*, Vol. 18. (Princeton, NJ, Princeton University Press).

Kaganas, F., King, M. and Piper, C. (eds) (1995) *Legislating for Harmony: Partnership under the Children Act 1989* (London, Jessica Kingsley).

Kahan, B. (ed.) (1989) *Child Care Research, Policy and Practice* (London, Hodder & Stoughton).

Kant, I. (1785) 'Groundwork of the metaphysic of morals', in Paton, H. J. (ed.) (1948) *The Moral Law* (London, Routledge), pp. 53–123.

Kaplan, A. (1964) *The Conduct of Inquiry: Methodology for the Behavioural Sciences* (San Francisco, Chandler).

Katz, J. (1978) *White Awareness* (Oklahoma City, University of Oklahoma Press).

Kelly, A. (1991) 'The "new" managerialism in the Social Services', in Carter, P., Jeffs, T. and Smith, M. (eds) *Social Work and Social Welfare Yearbook 3 1991* (Milton Keynes, Open University Press), pp. 178–93.

Kelly, A. (1996) *Introduction to the Scottish Children's Panel* (Winchester, Waterside Press).

Kelly, D. and Warr, B. (1992) *Quality Counts: Achieving Quality in Social Care Services* (London, Whiting & Birch).

Kelly, G. and Pinkerton, J. (1996) 'The Children (Northern Ireland) Order, 1995', in Hill and Aldgate (1996).

Kelly, T. (1962) *A History of Adult Education in Great Britain from the Middle Ages to the Twentieth Century* (Liverpool, Liverpool University Press).

Kempson, E. (1996) *Life on a Low Income* (York, Joseph Rowntree Foundation).

Kempson, E. (1997) 'Privatisation of utilities', in Walker and Walker (1997).

Kemshall, H. and Pritchard, J. (1996) *Good Practice in Risk Assessment and Risk Management* (London, Jessica Kingsley).

Kilbrandon, L. (1964) *Children and Young Persons, Scotland*, Cmnd 2306 (Edinburgh, HMSO).

King, M. and Trowell, J. (1992) *Children's Welfare and the Law: The Limits of Legal Intervention* (London, Sage).

Kirby, P. (1994) *A Word from the Street: Young People Who Leave Care and Become Homeless* (London, Centrepoint and *Community Care*).

Kirwan, M. (1994) 'Gender and social work: will DipSW make a difference?' *British Journal of Social Work*, **24**, pp. 137–55.

Knibbs, S. (1994) 'User-run services', *Community Care*, 26 May.

Konopka, G. (1990) 'Thirty-five years of group work in psychiatric settings', *Social Work With Groups*, **13**(1), pp. 13–16.

Kotter, J. and Schlesinger, L. (1979) 'Choosing strategies for change', *Harvard Business Review*, March/April, pp. 106–14.

Krim, R. (1988) 'Managing to learn: action inquiry in city hall', in Reason (1988).

Krueger, R. (1994) *Focus Groups: A Practical Guide for Applied Research* (Newbury Park, CA, Sage).

Kurland, R. and Salmon, R. (1993) 'Groupwork versus casework in a group', *Groupwork*, **6**(1), pp. 5–16.

Lang, T. (1997) 'Dividing up the cake: food as social exclusion', in Walker and Walker (1997).

Langan, M. and Day, L. (eds) (1992) *Women, Oppression and Social Work: Issues in Anti-Discriminatory Practice* (London, Routledge).

Langan, M. and Lee, P. (1989) *Radical Social Work Today* (London, Routledge).

Law Commission (1995) *Mental Incapacity: Summary of Recommendations*, Consulting Paper 231 (London, HMSO).

Laycock, G. and Pease, K. (1985) 'Crime prevention within the probation service', *Probation Journal*, **32**, pp. 43–7.

Le Croy, C. W. (ed.) (1992) *Case Studies in Social Work Practice* (Pacific Grove, CA, Brooks/Cole).

Lee, J. (1994) *The Empowerment Approach to Social Work Practice* (New York, Columbia University Press).

Leonard, P. (1976) 'The function of social work in society', in Timms, N. and Watson, D. (eds) *Talking about Welfare* (London, Routledge & Kegan Paul).

Lewis, J. and Glennerster, H. (1996) *Implementing the New Community Care* (Buckingham, Open University Press).

Lindow, V. and Morris, J. (1995) *Service User Involvement* (York, Joseph Rowntree Foundation).

Lindsay, M. (1992) *An Introduction to Children's Rights*, Highlight No. 113 (London, National Children's Bureau).

Lishman, J. (1994) *Communication in Social Work* (Basingstoke, Macmillan).

Lloyd, C., Mair, G. and Hough, M. (1994) *Explaining Reconviction Rates: A Critical Analysis*, Home Office Research Study 136 (London, HMSO).

Local Government Management Board and Association of Directors of Social Services (1993) *Social Services Workforce Analysis 1992: Workforce Survey Main Report* (London, Local Government Management Board).

Loney, M. (1983) *Community Against Government: The British Community Development Projects, 1968–1978: A Study of Government Incompetence* (London, Heineman).

Looney, J. (1988) 'Ego development and black identity', *Journal of Black Psychology*, **15**(1), pp. 41–56.

Lorde, A. (1984) *Sister Outsider* (New York, The Crossing Press).

Lorenz, W. (1994) *Social Work in a Changing Europe* (London, Routledge).

Low Pay Unit (1996) 'Coming apart at the seams', *New Review*, **42**, pp. 8–10.

Lyotard, J. F. (1984) *The Postmodern Condition: A Report on Knowledge* (Manchester, Manchester University Press).

Mabey, C. and Mayon-White, B. (1993) *Managing Change* (London, Paul Chapman Publishing in association with the Open University).

Macaskill, C. (1985) 'Post-adoption support: is it essential?', *Adoption and Fostering*, **9**(1), pp. 45–9.

McAuley, C. (1996) 'Children's perspectives on long-term foster care', in Hill and Aldgate (1996).

McBeath, G. B. and Webb, S. A. (1991) 'Social work, modernity and postmodernity', *Sociological Review*, **39**/**40**, pp. 171–92.

McBrian, J. and Felce, D. (1992) *Working with People who have a Severe Learning Difficulty and Challenging Behaviour: A Practice Manual* (Clevedon: British Institute for Learning Disabilities).

Macdonald, G. (1990a) 'Allocating blame in social work', *British Journal of Social Work*, **20**(6), pp. 525–46.

Macdonald, G. (1990b) 'Moral risks? A reply to Hollis and Howe', *British Journal of Social Work*, **20**(6), pp. 553–6.

Macdonald, G. (1994) 'Developing empirically-based practice in probation', *British Journal of Social Work*, **24**, pp. 405–27.

MacDonald, G. and Roberts, H. (1995) *What Works in the Early Years?* (Ilford, Barnardos).

Macdonald, G., Sheldon, B. with Gillespie, J. (1992) 'Contemporary studies of the effectiveness of social work', *British Journal of Social Work*, **22**, pp. 615–43.

McElrea, F. (1994) 'Justice in the community: the New Zealand experience', in Burnside and Baker (1994).

McGuire, J. (ed.) (1995) *What Works: Reducing Reoffending: Guidelines from Research and Practice* (Chichester, Wiley).

Maguire, M. and Raynor, P. (1997) 'The revival of throughcare: rhetoric and reality in automatic conditional release', *British Journal of Criminology*, **37**(1), pp. 1–14.

Maguire, M., Perroud, B. and Raynor, P. (1996) *Automatic Conditional Release: The First Two Years*, Home Office Research Study 156 (London, Home Office).

McIvor, G. (1990) *Sanctions for Serious or Persistent Offenders: A Review of the Literature* (Stirling, University of Stirling, Social Work Research Centre).

McIvor, G. (1992) *Sentenced to Serve* (Aldershot, Avebury).

McIvor, G. (1996) 'Recent developments in Scotland', in McIvor, G. (ed.) *Working with Offenders*, Research Highlights in Social Work, 26. (London, Jessica Kingsley).

McLaughlin, E. and Muncie, J. (1994) 'Managing the criminal justice system', in Clarke *et al.* (1994).

McLeod, J. (1993) *An Introduction to Counselling* (Buckingham, Open University Press).

McMurran, M. and Hollin, C. R. (1993) *Young Offenders and Alcohol-related Crime*, (Chichester, Wiley).

MacPherson, H. and Kaptchuk, T. J. (eds) (1996) *Acupuncture in Practice: Case History Insights from the West* (Edinburgh, Churchill Livingstone).

Main, M. and Solomon, J. (1986) 'Discovery of an insecure disorganised/disoriented attachment pattern,' in Yogman, M. and Brazelton, T. (eds) *Affective Development in Infancy* (Norwood, NJ, Ablex).

Main, M., Kaplan, N. and Cassidy, J. (1985) 'Security in infancy, childhood and adulthood', in Bretherton, I. and Walters, E. (eds) *Growing Points of Attachment Theory and Research: Monographs of the Society for Research in Child Development* 50 (1–2, Serial No. 209).

Mama, A. (1995) *Beyond the Masks* (London, Routledge).

Management, Office of Public (1994) *From Margin to Mainstream: User and Carer Involvement in Community Care, Local Authorities Changing Themselves – Manager's Manual* (London, Office for Public Management).

Mandlestam, M. with Schwehr, B. (1995) *Community Care Practice and the Law* (London, Jessica Kingsley).

Mangham, I. L. and Silver, M. S. (1986) *Management Training: Context and Practice* (London, ESRC and DTI).

Marchant, H. and Wearing, B. (eds) (1986) *Gender Reclaimed: Women in Social Work* (Sydney, Hale & Iremonger).

Marris, P. (1974) *Loss and Change* (London, Routledge & Kegan Paul).

Marsden, D. and Oakley, P. (eds) (1990) *Evaluating Social Development Projects* (Oxford, Oxfam).

Marsden, D., Oakley, P. and Pratt, B. (eds) (1994) *Measuring the Process: Guidelines for Evaluating Social Development* (Oxford, INTRAC).

Marsh, P. (1991) 'Task-centred practice', in Lishman, J. (ed.) *Handbook of Theory for Practice Teachers in Social Work* (London, Jessica Kingsley).

Marsh, P. and Fisher, M. (1992) *Good Intentions: Developing Partnerships in Social Services* (York, Joseph Rowntree and *Community Care*).

Marshall, T. F. and Merry, S. (1990) *Crime and Accountability* (London, HMSO).

Martin, C. (1997) *The ISTD Handbook of Community Programmes for Young and Juvenile Offenders* (Winchester, Waterside Press).

Martin, L. (1994) 'Power, continuity and change: decoding black and white women managers' experience in local government', in Tanton, M. (ed.) *Women in Management: A Developing Presence* (London, Routledge).

Mattinson, J. (1975) *The Reflection Process in Casework Supervision* (London, Institute of Marital Studies).

Mattinson, J. and Sinclair, I. (1979) *Mate and Stalemate* (London, Institute of Marital Studies).Matza, D. (1969) *Becoming Deviant* (Englewood Cliffs, NJ, Prentice Hall).

Maxime, J. (1986) 'Some psychological models of black self-concept', in Ahmed *et al.* (1986).

Maxime, J. (1993) 'The therapeutic importance of racial identity in working with Black children who hate', in Varma, V. (ed.) *How and Why Children Hate* (London, Jessica Kingsley).

Mayer, J. E. and Timms, N. (1970) *The Client Speaks* (London, Routledge & Kegan Paul).

Maynard, M. (1994) 'Methods, practice and epistemology: the debate about feminism and research', in Maynard, M. and Purvis, J. (eds) *Researching Women's Lives from a Feminist Perspective* (London, Taylor & Francis).

Mayo, M. (1994a) *Communities and Caring* (London, Macmillan).

Mayo, M. (1994b) 'Community work', in Hanvey, C. and Philpot, T. (eds) *Practising Social Work* (London, Routledge).

Meinert, R. and Pardeck, J. (in press) *Social Inquiry*.

Midwinter, E. (1990) 'An ageing world: the equivocal response', *Ageing and Society*, **10**.

Miller, E. J. and Gwynne, G. V. (1972) *A Life Apart* (London, Tavistock).

Millett, K. (1972) *Sexual Politics* (London, Abacus).

Millham, S., Bullock, R., Hosie, K. and Haak, M. (1986) *Lost in Care* (Aldershot, Gower).

Mintzberg, H. (1989) 'The structuring of organizations', in Asch, D. and Bowman, C., *Readings in Strategic Management* (London, Macmillan).

Mirrlees-Black, C., Mayhew, P. and Percy, A. (1996) *The 1996 British Crime Survey: England and Wales*, Home Office Statistical Bulletin 19/96 (London, Home Office).

Mitchell, D. (1996) 'Fear rules', *Community Care*, 14–20 March, pp. 18–19.

Mitchell, J. (1974) *Feminism and Psychoanalysis* (London, Allen Lane).

Morgan, D. (1988) *Focus Groups as Qualitative Research* (London, Sage).

Morgan, G. (1986) *Images of Organization* (Thousand Oaks, CA, Sage).

Morris, A., Giller, H., Szwed, E. and Geach, H. (1980) *Justice for Children* (London, Macmillan).

Morris, A., Maxwell, G. W. and Robertson, J. P. (1993) 'Giving victims a voice: a New Zealand experiment', *Howard Journal of Criminal Justice*, **32**(4), pp. 304–19.

Morris, C. (1964) 'The future of the social services', *Almoner*, **17**(3).

Morris, J. (1991) *Pride Against Prejudice: Transforming Attitudes to Disability* (London, Women's Press).

Morris, P. and Beverley, F. with Vennard, J. (1975) *On Licence: a Study of Parole* (Chichester, Wiley).

Morrison, T. (1987) *Beloved* (London, Picador).

Moss Kanter, R. (1989) *When Giants Learn to Dance* (New York, Routledge).

Mulhall, S. and Swift, A. (1995) 'The social self in political theory: the communitarian critique of the liberal subject', in Bakhurst and Sypnowich (1995).

Mullender, A. (1996) *Rethinking Domestic Violence: The Social Work and Probation Response* (London, Routledge).

Mullender, A. and Ward, D. (1991) *Self-directed Groupwork: Users Take Action for Empowerment* (London, Whiting & Birch).

Muncie, J. (1984) *'The Trouble with Kids Today': Youth and Crime in Post-War Britain* (London, Hutchinson).

Murray, C. (1984) *Losing Ground: American Social Policy, 1950–80* (New York, Basic Books).

Murray, C. (1990) *The Emerging British Underclass* (London, Institute for Economic Affairs).

Murray, C. (1994) *Underclass: The Crisis Deepens* (London, Institute for Economic Affairs).

NACRO (1991) *Training Materials for the 1991 Criminal Justice Act* (London, National Association for the Care and Resettlement of Offenders).

NACRO (1996) *Remand Fostering*, NACRO Briefing, December (London, National Association for the Care and Resettlement of Offenders).

NAPO (1990) 'Working with women: an anti-sexist approach', in *Practice Guidelines*, edited by Probation Practice Committee (London, National Association of Probation Officers).

NASW (1990) *Code of Ethics* (Silver Spring, MD, National Association of Social Workers).

National Association of Race Equality Advisers (1993) *Black Community Care Charter* (Birmingham, NAREA, c/o Race Relations Unit, Central Executive Department, Congreve House, 3 Congreve Passage, Birmingham, B3 3DA).

National Urban League (1964) *Double Jeopardy, the Older Negro in America Today* (New York, National Urban League).

NCH Action for Children (1991) *Poverty and Nutrition* (London, NCH Action for Children).

Neale-Hurston, Z. (1986) *Their Eyes Were Watching God* (London, Virago).

Neary, M. (1992) 'Some academic freedom', *Probation Journal*, **39**, pp. 200–2.

Nellis, M. (1995a) 'Probation values for the 1990s', *Howard Journal of Criminal Justice*, **34**(1), pp. 19–44.

Nellis, M. (1995b) 'The "third way" for probation: a reply to Spencer and James', *Howard Journal of Criminal Justice*, **34**(4), pp. 350–3.

Newburn, T. and Stanko, E. A. (eds) (1994) *'Just Boys Doing Business?', Men, Masculinities and Crime* (London, Routledge).

Newman, T., Oakley, A. and Roberts, H. (1996) 'Weighing up the evidence', *Guardian*, 10 January, p. 9.

Newson, J. and Newson, E. (1976) *Seven Years Old in the Home Environment* (London, Allen & Unwin).

NISW (1992) *General Social Services Council Consultation Papers* (London, National Institute for Social Work).

NISW (1993) *Complaints: Getting Heard and Getting Things Changed*, Policy Briefings, No. 2 (London, National Institute for Social Work).

NISW (1995a) *Working in the Social Services*, Policy Briefings, No. 10 (London, National Institute for Social Work).

NISW (1995b) *Managing Innovation and Change*, Policy Briefings, No. 11 (London, National Institute for Social Work.

NISW (1996) *Social Exclusion, Civil Society and Social Work* Policy Briefings, No. 18 (London, National Institute for Social Work).

Noonan, E. (1983) *Counselling Young People* (London, Tavistock/Routledge).

Nottage, A. (1991) *Women in Social Services: A Neglected Resource* (London, HMSO).

Novak, T. (1997) 'Poverty and the underclass', in Lavalette, M. and Pratt, A. (eds) *Social Policy* (London, Sage).

Nuttall, C. P., Barnard, E. E., Fowles, A. J., Frost, A., Hammond, W. H., Mayhew, P., Pease, K., Tarling, R. and Weatheritt, M. (1977) *Parole in England and Wales*, Home Office Research Study 30, (London, HMSO).

Oakley, A. and Williams, A. S. (eds) (1994) *The Politics of the Welfare State* (London, University of Central London Press).

Office of Science and Technology (1994) *The Forward Look of Government-Funded Science, Engineering and Technology* (London, HMSO).

O'Hagan, K. (ed.) (1996) *Competence in Social Work: A Practical Guide for Professionals* (London, Jessica Kingsley).

O'Hanlon, B. and Beadle, S. (1994) *A Field Guide to Possibility Land* (Omaha, Possibility Press).

Oliver, J. P. J., Huley, P. J. and Butler, A. (1989) *Mental Health Casework: Illuminations and Reflections* (Manchester, Manchester University Press).

Oliver, M. (1990) *The Politics of Disablement: A Sociological Approach* (London, Macmillan).

Oliver, M. (1996) *Understanding Disability: From Theory to Practice* (London, Macmillan).

Onyett, S. (1992) *Case Management in Mental Health* (London, Chapman & Hall).

Oppenheim, C. (1997) 'The growth of poverty and inequality', in Walker and Walker (1997).

Oppenheim, C. and Harker, L. (1996) *Poverty: The Facts*, 3rd edn (London, Child Poverty Action Group).

Oppenheim, C. and Lister, R. (1996) 'The politics of child poverty 1979 to 1995', in Pilcher, J. and Wagg, S. (eds) *Thatcher's Children? Politics, Childhood and Society in the 1980's and 1990's* (London, Falmer Press).

Orem, D. (1985) *Nursing Concepts of Practice* (New York, McGraw-Hill).

Orme, J. and Glastonbury, B. (1993) *Care Management* (London, Macmillan).

Packman, J. and Jordan, B. (1991) 'The Children Act: looking forward, looking back', *British Journal of Social Work*, **21**, pp. 315–27.

Packman, J., Randall, J. and Jaques, N. (1986) *Who Needs Care? Social Work Decisions about Children* (Oxford, Blackwell).

Pahl, J. (1992) 'Force for change or optional extra? The impact of research on policy in social work and social welfare', in Carter, P., Jeffs, T. and Smith, M. K. (eds) *Changing Social Work and Welfare* (Buckingham, Open University Press).

Palmer, A., Burns, S. and Bulman, C. (1994) *Reflective Practice in Nursing: The Growth of the Professional Practitioner* (Oxford, Blackwell).

Pardeck, J. T., Murphy, J. W. and Choi, J. M. (1994a) 'Some implications of postmodernism for social work practice', *Social Work*, **39**(4), pp. 243–6.

Pardeck, J. T., Murphy, J. W. and Chung, W. S. (1994b) 'Social work and postmodernism', *Social Work and Social Sciences Review*, **5**(2), pp. 113–23.

Parham, T. A. (1989) 'Cycles of psychological nigrescence', *Counseling Psychologist*, **17**(2), pp. 187–226.

Parham, T. A. and Helms, J. (1985) 'Relation of racial identity to self-actualization and affective states of black students', *Journal of Counseling Psychology*, **28**(3), pp. 250–6.

Parker, R. (1990) *Safeguarding Standards* (London, National Institute for Social Work).

Parker, R. A., Ward, H., Jackson, S., Aldgate, J. and Wedge, P. (eds) (1991) *Looking After Children: Assessing Outcomes in Child Care* (London, HMSO).

Parmar, P. (1981) 'Young Asian women: a critique of the pathological approach', *Multi-Racial Education*, **9**(3), pp. 19–29.

Parton, N. (1991) *Governing the Family: Child Care, Child Protection and the State* (London, Macmillan).

Parton, N. (1994a) 'Problematics of government (post)modernity and social work', *British Journal of Social Work*, **24**(1), pp. 9–32.

Parton, N (1994b) 'The nature of social work under conditions of (post)modernity', *Social Work and Social Sciences Review*, **5**(2), pp. 93–112.

Parton, N (ed.) (1996) *Social Theory, Social Change and Social Work* (London, Routledge).

Parton, N. (1998) 'Advanced liberalism (post)modernity and social work, some emerging social configurations', *Social Inquiry*.

Patel, N. (1990) *A 'Race Against Time?' Social Services Provision to Black Elders* (London, Runnymede Trust).

Payne, M. (1991) *Modern Social Work Theory: A Critical Introduction* (London, Macmillan).

Payne, M. (1992) 'Psychodynamic theory within the politics of social work theory', *Journal of Social Work Practice*, **6**(2), pp. 141–9.

Payne, M. (1995) *Social Work and Community Care* (London, Macmillan).

Payne, M. (1996a) *What is Professional Social Work?* (Birmingham, Venture).

Payne, M. (1996b) 'The politics of social work theory and values', in IFSW, IASSW and HKSWA (eds) *Participating in Change – Social Work Profession in Social Development: Proceedings of the Joint World Congress of the International Federation of Social Workers and the International Association of Schools of Social Work* (Hong Kong, HKSWA, IASSW and IFSW), pp. 73–6.

Payne, M. (1997) *Modern Social Work Theory*, 2nd edn (London, Macmillan).

Pearson, G. (1975) *The Deviant Imagination: Psychiatry, Social Work and Social Change* (London, Macmillan).

Pearson, G. (1983) 'The Barclay Report and community social work: Samuel Smiles revisited?', *Critical Social Policy*, **2**, pp. 73–86.

Pearson, G., Treseder, J. and Yelloly, M. (1988) *Social Work and the Legacy of Freud* (London, Macmillan).

Pearson, R. E. (1990) *Counseling and Social Support: Perspectives and Practice* (London, Sage).

Pease, K. (1994) 'Crime prevention', in Maguire, M., Morgan, R. and Reiner, R. (eds) *The Oxford Handbook of Criminology* (Oxford, Clarendon Press).

Penna, S. and O'Brien, M. (1996) 'Postmodernism and social policy: a small step forwards?', *Journal of Social Policy*, **25**(1), pp. 39–61.

Perlman, H. H. (1957) *Social Casework: a Problem-solving Process* (Chicago, University of Chicago Press).

Pernell, R. B. (1986) 'Empowerment and social group work', in Parnes, M. (ed.) *Innovations in Social Group Work: Feedback from Practice to Theory* (New York, Haworth Press).

Perrott, S. (1994) 'Working with men who abuse women and children', in Lupton, C. and Gillespie, T. (eds) *Working with Violence* (London, Macmillan).

Peters, M. F. (1985) 'Racial socialization of young black children', in McAdoo, H. and McAdoo, J. (eds) *Black Children: Social, Educational and Parental Environments* (Newbury Park, CA, Sage).

Peters, M. F. (1988) 'Parenting in black families with young children: a historical perspective', in McAdoo, H. P. (ed.) *Black Families* (London, Sage).

Peters, T. and Waterman, R. (1982) *In Search of Excellence* (London, Harper & Row).

Peyton, L. (1997) 'Reorganisation; trends and issues in Northern Ireland', in Cohen, B. and Hagen, U. (eds) *Children's Services: Shaping up to the Millennium* (HMSO), pp. 61–4.

Phillips, M. (1993) 'An oppressive urge to end oppression', *Observer*, 1 August.

Phillips, M. (1994) 'Illiberal liberalism', in Dunant, S. (ed.) *The War of the Word: The Political Correctness Debate* (London: Virago).

Phillipson, C. (1993) 'Approaches to advocacy', in Johnson, J. and Slater, R. (eds) *Ageing and Later Life* (London, Sage).

Phillipson, J. (1988) 'The complexities of caring: developing a feminist approach to training staff in a residential setting', *Social Work Education*, **7**(3), pp. 3–6.

Phillipson, J. (1991) *Practising Equality: Women, Men and Social Work* (London, Central Council for Education and Social Work).

Phinney, J. S. and Rotheram, M. J. (eds) (1987) *Children's Ethnic Socialization: Pluralism and Development* (London, Sage).

Piachaud, D. (1997) 'The growth of means-testing' in Walker, A. and Walker, C. (eds) *Britain Divided: The Growth of Social Exclusion in the 1980s and 1990s* (London, Child Poverty Action Group).

Pietroni, M (1995) 'The nature and aims of professional education for social workers; a postmodern perspective', in Yelloly and Henkel (1995).

Pincus, A. and Minahan, A. (1973) *Social Work Practice: Model and Method* (Itasca, IL, Peacock).

Pinker, R. (1984) 'The threat to professional standards in social work education', *Issues in Social Work Education*, **4**(1), pp. 5–15.

Pinker, R. (1993) 'A lethal kind of looniness', *Times Higher Educational Supplement*, 10 September.

Pitcairn, T. and Waterhouse, L. (1993) 'Evaluating parenting in child physical abuse', in Waterhouse, L. (ed.) *Child Abuse and Child Abusers: Protection and Prevention* (London, Jessica Kingsley).

Pitcairn, T. and Waterhouse, L. (1996) 'Evaluating parenting in child physical abuse' in Waterhouse, L. (ed.) *Child Abuse and Child Abusers: Protection and Prevention*, pp. 73–90, Research Highlights in Social Work, 24.

Pitts, J. (1988) *The Politics of Juvenile Crime* (London, Sage).

Plomin, R. (1994) *Genetics and Experience: The Interplay Between Nature and Nurture* (Thousand Oaks, CA, Sage).

Plummer, K. (1981) 'Going gay: identities, life cycles and lifestyles in the male gay world', in Hart, J. and Richardson, D. (eds) *The Theory and Practice of Homosexuality* (London, Routledge).

Popple, K. (1995) *Analysing Community Work* (Buckingham, Open University Press).

Pottage, D. and Evans, M. (1994) *The Competent Workplace: The View from Within* (London, National Institute for Social Work).

Pozatek, E. (1994) 'The problem of certainty: clinical social work in the post modern era', *Social Work*, **39**(4), pp. 396–403.

Preston, P. (1996) 'When focus groups can be hocus-pocus', *Guardian*, 15 November.

Preston-Shoot, M. (1987) *Effective Groupwork* (London, Macmillan).

Preston-Shoot, M. (1996) 'Contesting the contradictions: needs, resources and community care decisions', *Journal of Social Welfare and Family Law*, **18**(3), pp. 307–25.

Preston-Shoot, M. and Agass, D. (1990) *Making Sense of Social Work: Psychodynamics, Systems and Practice* (London, Macmillan).

Preston-Shoot, M., Roberts, G. and Vernon, S. (1997) '"We work in isolation often and in ignorance occasionally": On the experiences of practice teachers teaching and assessing social work law', *Social Work Education*, **16**(4), pp. 4–34.

Preston-Shoot, M., Roberts, G. and Vernon, S. (1998) 'Working together in social work law', *Journal of Social Welfare and Family Law*, (2).

Priestley, P., McGuire, J., Flegg, D., Hemsley, V. and Welham, D. (1978) *Social Skills and Personal Problem Solving: A Handbook of Methods* (London, Tavistock).

Pringle, K. (1992/93) 'Child sexual abuse perpetrated by welfare personnel and the problem of men', *Critical Social Policy*, **12**(3), pp. 4–19.

Pritchard, J. (1992) *The Abuse of Elderly People: A Handbook for Professionals* (London, Jessica Kingsley).

Professional Social Work (1996) 'Parliamentary concern about social work stress', *Professional Social Work*, August, pp. 1–2.

Pugh, D. (1990) *Organization Theory* (Harmondsworth, Penguin).

Pugh, D. (1993) 'Understanding and managing organizational change', in Mabey, C. and Mayon-White, B., *Managing Change* (London, Paul Chapman).

Pugh, R. G. (1996) *Effective Language in Health and Social Work* (London, Chapman & Hall).

Quinton, D. and Rutter, M. (1988) *Parenting Breakdown: The Making and Breaking of Intergenerational Links* (Aldershot, Avebury).

Rafferty, A. M. and Traynor, M. (1997) 'Quality and quantity in research policy for nursing', *NTresearch*, **2**(1), pp. 16–27.

Raynor, P. (1985) *Social Work, Justice and Control* (Oxford, Blackwell).

Raynor, P. (1993) 'System purists, client refusal and gatekeeping: is help necessarily harmful?', *Social Action*, **1**, pp. 4–8.

Raynor, P. and Vanstone, M. (1996) 'Reasoning and rehabilitation in Britain: the results of the straight thinking on probation (STOP) programme', *International Journal of Offender Therapy and Comparative Criminology*, **40**(4), pp. 272–84.

Raynor, P. and Vanstone, M. (1994) 'Probation practice, effectiveness and the non-treatment paradigm', *British Journal of Social Work*, **24**(4), pp. 387–404.

Raynor, P., Smith, D. and Vanstone, M. (1994) *Effective Probation Practice* (London, Macmillan).

Reamer, F. G. (1993) *Philosophical Foundations of Social Work* (New York, Columbia University Press).

Reason, P. (ed.) (1988) *Human Inquiry in Action: Developments in New Paradigm Research* (London, Sage).

Reason, P. and Rowan, J. (eds) (1981) *Human Inquiry: A Sourcebook of New Paradigm Research* (Chichester, Wiley).

Rees, S. (1991) *Achieving Power* (Sydney, Allen & Unwin).

Reid, B. (1994) 'The mentor's experience – a personal perspective', in Palmer *et el.* (1994).

Reid, W. J. (1992) *Task Strategies: An Empirical Approach to Social Work* (New York, Columbia University Press).

Reid, W. J. and Epstein, L. (1972) *Task-centered Casework* (New York, Columbia University Press).

Reid, W. J. and Shyne, A. W. (1969) *Brief and Extended Casework* (New York, Columbia University Press).

Report of the Inquiry into Child Abuse in Cleveland, (1988) Cm 412 (London, HMSO).

Rhodes, M. L. (1986) *Ethical Dilemmas in Social Work Practice* (London, Routledge & Kegan Paul).

Ritchie, J., Dick, D. and Lingham, R. (1994) *Report of the Inquiry into the Care and Treatment of Christopher Clunis* (London, HMSO).

Roberts, J. and Taylor, C. (1996) 'Sexually abused children and young people speak out', in Waterhouse, L. (ed.) *Child Abuse and Child Abusers: Protection and Prevention* (London, Jessica Kingsley).

Roberts, R. (1990) *Lessons from the Past: Issues for Social Work Theory* (London, Tavistock/Routledge).

Robins, D. (1992) *Tarnished Vision: Crime and Conflicts in the Inner City* (Oxford, Oxford University Press).

Robins, S. (1990) *Organization Theory: Structure, Design and Applications*, 3rd edn (Englewood Cliffs, NJ, Prentice Hall).

Robinson, L. (1995) *Psychology for Social Workers: Black Perspectives* (London, Routledge).

Rochdale County Council (1986) *Report of Chief Executive to Social Services Committee, Study of Needs and Circumstances of Elderly Asians in Rochdale* (Rochdale, Rochdale Metropolitan Borough Council).

Rochford, G. (1991) 'Theory, concepts, feelings and practice: the contemplation of bereavement within a social work course', in Lishman, J. (ed.) *Handbook of Theory to Practice Teachers in Social Work* (London, Jessica Kingsley).

Roediger, D. R. (1991) *The Wages of Whiteness* (London, Verso).

Rogers, C. R. (1942) *Counseling and Psychotherapy* (Boston, Houghton Mifflin).

Rogers, C. (1980) *A Way of Being* (Boston, Houghton Mifflin).

Rojek, C. and Collins, S. (1987) 'Contract or con trick?', *British Journal of Social Work*, **17**, pp. 199–211.

Rojek, C. and Collins, S. (1988) 'Contract or con trick revisited: comments on the reply by Corden and Preston-Shoot', *British Journal of Social Work*, **18**(6), pp. 611–22.

Rojek, C., Peacock, G. and Collins, S. (1988) *Social Work and Received Ideas* (London, Routledge).

Rollinck, S. and Miller, W. R. (1995) 'What is motivational interviewing?', *Behavioural and Cognitive Psychotherapy*, **23**, pp. 325–34.

Rose, N. (1996) 'Authority and the genealogy of subjectivity', in Heelas *et al.* (1996).

Rosenau, P. M. (1992) *Post-modernism and the Social Sciences: Insights, Inroads and Intrusions* (Princeton, NJ, Princeton University Press).

Ross, R. R., Fabiano E. and Ross R. (1989) *Reasoning and Rehabilitation: A Handbook for Teaching Cognitive Skills* (Ottawa, Cognitive Centre).

Rowan, J. (1981) 'A dialectical paradigm for research', in Reason and Rowan (1981).

Rowe, J. and Lambert, L. (1973) *Children Who Wait* (London, Association of British Adoption Agencies).

Rowe, J. and Thoburn, J. (1988) 'A snapshot of permanent family placement', *Adoption and Fostering*, **12**(3), pp. 29–34.

Rowe, J., Hundleby, M. and Garnett, L. (1989) *Child Care Now* (London, British Agencies for Adoption and Fostering).

Rushdie, S. (1982) *Midnight's Children* (London, Pan).

Rushton, A., Quinton, D., Treseder, J. (1993) 'New parents for older children: support services during eight years of placement', *Adoption and Fostering*, **17**(4), pp. 39–45.

Russell, S. (1990) *Render Me My Song: African-American Women Writers from Slavery to the Present* (London, Pandora Press).

Rutherford, A. (1986) *Growing out of Crime* (Harmondsworth, Penguin).

Rutherford, A. (1994) *Criminal Justice and the Pursuit of Decency* (Winchester, Waterside Press).

Rutherford, A. (1996) *Transforming Criminal Policy* (Winchester, Waterside Press).

Rutherford, J. (1992) *Men's Silences: Predicaments in Masculinity* (London, Routledge).

Rutter, M. (1991) 'A fresh look at maternal deprivation,' in Bateson, P. (ed.) *The Development and Integration of Behaviour* (Cambridge, Cambridge University Press).

Rutter, M. and Rutter, M. (1993) *Developing Minds: Challenge and Continuity across the Life Span* (Harmondsworth, Penguin).

Rutter, M. and Smith, D. (eds) (1995) *Psychosocial Disorders in Young People: Time Trends and their Causes* (Chichester, Wiley).

Salaman, G., Adams, R. and O'Sullivan, T. (1994) *Managing Personal and Team Effectiveness Book 1: Managing Competently* (Milton Keynes, Health and Social Services Management Programme, Open University), pp. 29–38.

Salzberger-Wittenberg, I. (1970) *Psycho-analytic Insight and Relationships: A Kleinian Approach* (London, Routledge & Kegan Paul).

Sampson, A. and Smith, D. (1992) 'Probation and community crime prevention', *Howard Journal of Criminal Justice*, **31**(2), pp. 105–19.

Sands, R. G. and Nuccio, K. (1992) 'Postmodern feminist theory and social work', *Social Work*, **37**(6), pp. 489–94.

Sapsford, R. and Abbott, P. (1992) *Research Methods for Nurses and the Caring Professions* (Buckingham, Open University Press).

Schofield, G. (1996) 'Inner and outer worlds in child and family social work', Working paper (Norwich, Centre for Research on the Child and Family, University of East Anglia).

Schön, D. A. (1983) *The Reflective Practitioner: How Professionals Think in Action* (New York, Basic Books).

Schön, D. A. (1987) *Educating the Reflective Practitioner* (San Francisco, CA, Jossey-Bass).

Schorr, A. (1992) *The Personal Social Services: An Outsider's View* (York, Joseph Rowntree Foundation).

Scott, M. (1989) *A Cognitive-behavioural Approach to Clients' Problems* (London, Tavistock/Routledge).

Scott, M. J., Stradling, S. J. and Dryden, W. (1995) *Developing Cognitive-behavioural Counselling* (London, Sage).

Scottish Office (1992a) *The Report of the Inquiry into the Removal of Children from Orkney in February 1991*, the Clyde Report (Edinburgh, HMSO).

Scottish Office (1992b) *Inquiry into Child Care Policies in Fife*, the Kearney Report (Edinburgh, HMSO).

Scrutton, S. (1989) *Counselling Older People: A Creative Response to Ageing* (London, Edward Arnold).

Secker, J. (1993) *From Theory to Practice in Social Work: The Development of Social Work Students' Practice* (Aldershot, Avebury).

Seebohm Committee (1968) *Report of the Committee on Local Authority and Allied Social Services* (London, HMSO).

Seed, P. and Kaye, G. (1994) *Handbook for Assessing and Managing Care in the Community* (London, Jessica Kingsley).

Segall, M. H., Dasen, P. R., Berry, J. W. and Poortinga, Y. H. (1990) *Human Behaviour in Global Perspective* (New York, Pergamon).

Seligman, M. E. P. (1975) *Helplessness* (San Francisco, Freeman).

Sellick, C. (1996) 'Short-term foster care in research in England and Wales', in Hill and Aldgate (1996).

Senior, P. (1993) 'Groupwork in the probation service: care or control in the 1990s', in Brown, A. and Caddick, B. (eds) *Groupwork with Offenders* (London, Whiting & Birch).

Servian, R. (1996) *Theorising Empowerment: Individual Power and Community Care* (Bristol, Policy Press).

Shah, R. (1992) *The Silent Minority: Children with Disabilities in Asian Families* (London, National Children's Bureau).

Shakespeare, P., Atkinson, D. and French, S. (eds) (1993) *Reflecting on Research Practice: Issues in Health and Social Welfare* (Buckingham, Open University Press).

Shakespeare, T. (1996) 'Rules of engagement doing disability research', *Disability and Society*, **11**(1), pp. 115–19.

Shardlow, S. M. (1992) 'Abstracts (Philosophy)', *British Journal of Social Work*, **22**(5), pp. 588–92.

Shardlow, S. M. (in press) *Ethics and Values in Social Work* (London, Macmillan).

Shaw, I. (1995) 'The quality of mercy: the management of quality in the personal social services, in Kirkpatrick, I. and Martinez Lucio, M. (eds) *The Politics of Quality in the Public Sector* (London, Routledge).

Shaw, I. (1996) *Evaluating in Practice* (Aldershot, Arena).

Shaw, M. (1996) 'Out of the quagmire: community care-problems and possibilities for radical practice', in Cooke, I. and Shaw, M. (eds) *Radical Community Work* (Edinburgh, Moray House Publications), pp. 85–102.

Sheldon, B. (1982) *Behaviour Modification: Theory, Practice and Philosophy* (London, Tavistock).

Sheldon, B. (1994) 'Social work effectiveness research: implications for probation and juvenile justice', *Howard Journal of Crimninal Justice*, **33**(3), pp. 218–35.

Sheldon, B. (1995) *Cognitive-Behavioural Therapy: Research, Practice and Philosophy* (London, Routledge).

Sheppard, M. (1995) *Care Management and the New Social Work: A Critical Analysis* (London, Whiting & Birch).

Sibeon, R. (1991) 'Sociological reflections on welfare politics and social work', *Social Work and Social Sciences Review*, **3**(3), pp.184–203.

Sidell, M. (1993) 'Death, dying and bereavement', in Bond, J., Coleman, P. and Peace, S. (1993) *Ageing in Society: An Introduction to Social Gerontology*, 2nd edn (London, Sage).

Simons, K. (1992) *'Sticking Up For Yourself', Self-Advocacy and People with Learning Difficulties* (York, Joseph Rowntree Foundation).

Simpkin, M. (1989) 'Radical social work: lessons for the 1990s', in Carter, P., Jeffs, T. and Smith, M. (eds) *Social Work and Social Welfare Yearbook 1* (Milton Keynes, Open University Press).

Sinclair, R., Garnett, L. and Berridge, D. (1995) *Social Work Assessment with Adolescents* (London, National Children's Bureau).

Sinfield, A. (1969) *Which Way for Social Work?*, Fabian Tract 393 (London, Fabian Society).

Sinha, D. (1983) 'Cross-cultural psychology: a view from the Third World', in Deregowski, J. B., Dziurawier, S. and Annis, R. C. (eds) *Explorations in Cross-Cultural Psychology* (Lisse, Swets & Zeitlinger).

Skellington, R. with Morris, P. (1992) *'Race' in Britain Today* (London, Sage).

Skinner, A. (1992) *Another Kind of Home* (London, HMSO).

Smale, G. (1993) *Managing Change through Innovation: Workbook* (London, National Institute for Social Work, Practice and Development Exchange).

Smale, G. and Tusan, G. with Biehal, N. and Marsh, P. (1993) *Empowerment, Assessment, Care Management and the Skilled Worker* (London, HMSO).

Smith, C. and White, S. (1997) 'Parton, Howe and postmodernity: a critical comment on mistaken identity', *British Journal of Social Work*, **27**(2), pp. 275–96.

Smith, D. (1984) 'Law and order: arguments for what?', *Critical Social Policy*, **11**, pp. 33–45.

Smith, D. (1992) 'Puritans and paradigms: a comment', *Social Work and Social Sciences Review*, **3**(2), pp. 99–103.

Smith, D. (1995) *Criminology for Social Work* (London, Macmillan).

Smith, D., Blagg, H. and Derricourt, N. (1988) 'Mediation in South Yorkshire', *British Journal of Criminology*, **28**(3), pp. 378–95.

Smith, D., Paylor, I. and Mitchell, P. (1993) 'Partnerships between the probation service and the independent sector', *Howard Journal of Criminal Justice*, **32**(1), pp. 25–39.

Smith, G., Smith, T. and Wright, G. (1997) 'Poverty and schooling: choice, diversity or division?', in Walker and Walker (1997).

Smith, J. (chair) (1994) *A Wider Strategy for Research and Development relating to Personal Social Services*, Report to the Director of Research and Development, Department of Health, by an Independent Review Group (London, HMSO).

Smith, P. K. (1991) *The Psychology of Grandparenthood: An International Perspective* (London, Routledge).

Smith, T. (1995) 'Children and young people-disadvantage, community and the Children Act, 1989', in Henderson, P. (ed.) *Children and Communities* (London, Pluto), pp. 54–69.

Social Trends (1996) (London, HMSO).

Social Work Services Group (1991) *National Objectives and Standards for Social Work Services in the Criminal Justice System* (Edinburgh, Scottish Office).

Solomon, B. B. (1985) 'Community social work practice in oppressed minority communities', in Taylor, S. H. and Roberts, R. W. (eds) *Theory and Practice of Community Social Work* (New York, Columbia University Press), pp. 217–57.

Sone, K (1995) 'Get tough', *Community Care*, 6–12 March, pp. 16–18.

Specht, H. and Vickery, A. (eds) (1977) *Integrating Social Work Methods* (London, Allen & Unwin).

Spencer, J. (1995) 'A response to Mike Nellis: probation values for the 1990s', *Howard Journal of Criminal Justice*, **34**(4), pp. 344–49.

Spencer, M. B. (1988) 'Self-concept development', in Slaughter, D. T. (ed.) *Black Children in Poverty: Developmental Perspectives* (San Francisco, Jossey-Bass).

Spender, D. (1980) *Man Made Language* (London, Routledge & Kegan Paul).

SSI (1991a) *Care Management and Assessment* (London, HMSO).

SSI (1991b) *Care Management and Assessment: Managers Guide* (London, HMSO).

SSI (1992) *Concerns for Quality: The First Annual Report of the Chief Inspector Social Services Inspectorate 1991/2* (London, HMSO).

SSI (1994) *How Well are Children being Looked After? Agenda for Action Arising from the National Residential Child Care Inspection 1992–1994* (London, Department of Health).

SSI (1996) *Children in Need: Report of the SSI National Inspection of Family Support Services 1993/1995* (Leeds, Department of Health).

Stanley, L. (ed.) (1990) *Feminist Praxis: Research Theory and Epistemology in Feminist Sociology* (London, Routledge).

Statham, D. (1978) *Radicals in Social Work* (London, Routledge & Kegan Paul).

Stein, M. and Carey, K. (1986) *Leaving Care* (Oxford, Blackwell).

Stern, V. (1996) 'Let the ex-cons back in', *Guardian*, 2 May.

Stevenson, O. (1988) 'Law and social work education: a commentary on the "Law Report"', *Issues in Social Work Education*, **8**(1), pp. 37–45.

Stevenson, O. (1994) 'Social work in the 1990s: empowerment – fact or fiction?' in Page, R. and Baldock, J. (eds) *Social Policy Review 6* (Canterbury, Social Policy Association).

Stevenson, O. and Parsloe, P. (1993) *Community Care and Empowerment* (York, Joseph Rowntree Foundation and *Community Care*).

Stewart, J., Smith, D. and Stewart, G. (1994) *Understanding Offending Behaviour* (Harlow, Longman).

Stone, J. (1995) *Making Positive Moves: Developing Short-Term Fostering Services* (London, British Agencies for Adoption and Fostering).

Stubbs, P. (1988) *The reproduction of racism in state social work*. Unpublished PhD thesis, University of Bath.

Sue, D. W. and Sue, D. (1990) *Counselling the Culturally Different* (New York, Wiley).

Sutton, C. (1994) *Social Work, Community Work and Psychology* (Leicester, British Psychological Society).

Swain, J., Finkelstein, V., French, S. and Oliver, M. (eds) (1993) *Disabling Barriers – Enabling Environments* (London, Sage).

Tannen, D. (1996) *Talking from 9 to 5: How Men's and Women's Conversational Styles Affect Who Gets Heard, Who Gets Credit and What Gets Done at Work* (London, Virago).

Taylor, G. (1996) 'Ethical issues in practice: participatory social research and groups', *Groupwork*, **9**(2), pp. 110–27.

Taylor, I. (1996) 'Reflective learning, social work education and practice in the 21st century', in Gould, N. and Taylor, I. (eds) *Reflective Learning for Social Work* (Aldershot, Arena).

Taylor, I., Walton, P. and Young, J. (1974) *The New Criminology* (London, Routledge & Kegan Paul).

Taylor, M., Hoyes, L., Lart, R. and Means, R. (1992) *User Empowerment in Community Care: Unravelling the Issues*, Studies in Decentralisation and Quasi-Markets 11 (Bristol, School for Advanced Urban Studies University of Bristol).

Taylor-Gooby, P. (1994) 'Postmodernism and social policy: a great leap backwards?', *Journal of Social Policy*, **23**(3), pp. 385–405.

Thobani, M. (1995) 'Working for equality in the London Borough of Hounslow', in Itzin, C. and Newman, J. (eds) *Gender, Culture and Organizational Change: Putting Theory into Practice* (London, Routledge).

Thoburn, J., Lewis, A. and Shemmings, D. (1995) *Paternalism or Partnership? Family Involvement in the Child Protection Process* (London, HMSO).

Thomas, E. J. (ed.) (1974) *Behaviour Modification Procedure: A Sourcebook* (Chicago, Aldine).

Thompson, N. (1993) *Anti-Discriminatory Practice* (London, Macmillan).

Thompson, N. (1995) *Age and Dignity: Working with Older People* (Aldershot, Arena).

Thompson, N. (1996a) *People Skills: A Guide to Effective Practice in the Human Services* (London, Macmillan).

Thompson, N. (1996b) 'Opening the floodgates', *Professional Social Work*, November, p. 4.

Thompson, N., Stradling, S., Murphy, M. and O'Neill, P. (1996) 'Stress and organizational culture', *British Journal of Social Work*, **26**(5), pp. 647–65.

Thorpe, D. (1994) *Evaluating Child Protection* (Buckingham, Open University Press).

Thorpe, D. and Thorpe, S. (1992) *Monitoring and Evaluation in the Social Services* (Brighton, Pavilion).

Thorpe, D. H., Smith, D., Green, C. J. and Paley, J. H. (1980) *Out of Care: The Community Support of Juvenile Offenders* (London, Allen & Unwin).

Thurston, R. (1997) *Review, Vista: Perspectives on Probation*, **2**(3), pp. 200–2.

Tilley, N. (1995) *Thinking about Crime Prevention Performance Indicators*, Crime Prevention and Detection Series Paper 57. (London, Home Office).

Timms, N. (1983) *Social Work Values: An Enquiry* (London, Routledge & Kegan Paul).

Tizard, B. and Phoenix, A. (1989) 'Black identity and transracial adoption', *New Community*, **15**(3).

Tober, G. (1991) 'Motivational interviewing with young people', in Miller, W. and Rollnick, S. (eds) *Motivational Interviewing: Preparing People to Change* (New York, Guilford Press).

Tolson, E. R., Reid, W. J. and Garvin, C. D. (1994) *Generalist Practice: A Task Centred Approach* (New York, Columbia University Press).

Townsend, P., Phillimore, P. and Beattie, A. (1988) *Health Deprivation: Inequality and the North* (London, Croom Helm).

Tronick, E. Z., Morelli, G. A. and Ivey, P. K. (1992) 'The Efe forager infant and toddlers pattern of social relationships: multiple and simultaneous', *Developmental Psychology*, **28**, pp. 568–77.

Trowell, J. (1995) 'Working together in child protection, some issues for multi-disciplinary training from a psychodynamic perspective', in Yelloly and Henkel (1995).

Tuckman, B. (1965) 'Developmental sequences in small groups', *Psychological Bulletin*, **63**, pp. 384–99.

Turner, B. S. (1990) 'Periodisation and politics in the postmodern', in Turner, B. S. (ed.) *Theories of Modernity and Post Modernity* (London, Sage).

Turner, M. (1995) 'Supervising', in Carter, P. *et al.* (1995).

Twelvetrees, A. (1991) *Community Work* (London, Macmillan).

Twigg, J. (ed.) (1992) *Carers: Research and Practice* (London, HMSO).

Underdown, A. (1996) 'Practice and method', paper presented to the First Annual Colloquium of the Probation Studies Unit, Centre for Criminological Research, University of Oxford, 16–17 December.

Utting, W. (1989) 'Foreword', to Kahan (1989).

Utting, W. (1991) *Children in the Public Care* (London, HMSO).

Utting, W. (1993) 'Foreword', to Ellis (1993).

Utting, W. (1995) *Family and Parenthood: Supporting Families, Preventing Breakdown* (York, Joseph Rowntree Foundation).

Vanstone, M. (1995) 'Managerialism and the ethics of management', in Hugman and Smith (1995).

Vass, A. A. (1996) *Social Work Competences: Core Knowledge, Values and Skills* (London, Sage).

Veal, A. J. (1992) *Research Methods for Leisure and Tourism: A Practical Guide* (Harlow, Longman/ILAM).

Vernelle, B. (1994) *Understanding and Using Groups* (London, Whiting & Birch).

Verschelden, C. (1993) 'Social work values and pacifism', *Social Work*, **38**(6), pp. 765–70.

Wainwright, D. (1996) 'The political transformation of the health inequalities debate', *Critical Social Policy*, **49**(16), p. 4.

Walker, A. (1983) *The Color Purple* (London, Women's Press).

Walker, A. and Walker, C. (eds) (1997) *Britain Divided: The Growth of Social Exclusion in Britain 1979–1997* (London, Child Poverty Action Group).

Walker, A.and Walker, C. (eds) (1997) Britain Divided: The Growth of Social Exclusion in Britain 1979–1997. (London, Child Poverty Action Group).

Walker, J. (1995) 'Counselling in a social services area office: the practice behind the thoery', in Carter, P. *et al.* (1995).

Walker, J. (1997) 'Partnership and parenting', in Davies, M. (ed.) *The Blackwell Companion to Social Work* (Oxford, Blackwell).

Walsh, K., Deakin, N., Smith, P. *et al.* (1997) *Contracting for Change: Contracts in Health, Social Care, and Other Local Government Services* (Oxford, Oxford University Press).

Walton, R. (1975) *Women in Social Work* (London, Routledge & Kegan Paul).

Ward, A. (1993) 'The large group: the heart of the system in group care', *Groupwork*, **6**(1), pp. 64–77

Ward, D. (ed.) (1996) *Groups and Research,* Special edition of *Groupwork*, **9**(2).

Ward, D. and Hogg, B. (1993) 'An integrated approach to the teaching of social work law', in Preston-Shoot, M. (ed.) *Assessment of Competence in Social Work Law* (London, Whiting & Birch).

Ward, D. and Mullender, A. (1991) 'Empowerment and oppression: an indissoluble pairing for contemporary social work', *Critical Social Policy*, **32**, pp. 1–29.

Ward, H. (1995) *Looking After Children: Research into Practice* (London, HMSO).

Wardman, G. (1977) 'Social work: a communist view', *Marxism Today*, January, pp. 29–32.

Waterhouse, L. (ed.) (1996) *Child Abuse and Child Abusers: Protection and Prevention* (London, Jessica Kingsley).

Wearing, B. (1986) 'Feminist theory and social work', in Marchant and Wearing (1986).

Webb, D. (1990–91a) 'Puritans and paradigms: a speculation on the form of new moralities in social work', *Social Work and Social Sciences Review*, **2**(2), pp. 146–59.

Webb, D. (1990–91b) 'A stranger in the academy: a reply to Lena Dominelli', *Social Work and Social Sciences Review*, **2**(3), pp. 236–41.

Webb, D. (1996) 'Regulation for radicals: the state, CCETSW and the academy', in Parton (1996).

Webb, S. (1993) 'Women's incomes: past, present and prospects', *Fiscal Studies*, **14**(4), pp. 14–36.

Webb, S. A. and McBeath, G. A. (1989) 'A political critique of Kantian ethics in social work', *British Journal of Social Work*, **19**(6), pp. 491–506.

Webb, S. A. and McBeath, G. A. (1990) 'A political critique of Kantian ethics in social work: a reply to Professor R. S. Downie', *British Journal of Social Work* **20**(1), pp. 65–71.

Weber, M. (1947) *The Theory of Social and Economic Organization* (New York, Free Press). Reprinted in Pugh, D. (1990) *Organization Theory* (Harmondsworth, Penguin).

Webster-Stratton, C. and Herbert, M. (1994) *Troubled Families – Problem Children* (Chichester, Wiley).

Weedon, C. (1987) *Feminist Practice and Poststructuralist Theory* (Oxford, Basil Blackwell).

Westwood, S. and Bhachu, P. (1988) 'Images and realities', *New Society*, 6 May.

Whetham, W. C. D. (1909), *The Family and the Nation* (London, Longman & Green).

Whitaker, D. S. (1975) 'Some conditions for effective work with groups', *British Journal of Social Work*, **5**(4), pp. 423–39.

Whitaker, D. S. (1985) *Using Groups to Help People* (London, Tavistock/Routledge).

Whitaker, D. S. and Archer, J. L. (1989) *Research by Social Workers: Capitalizing on Experience*, CCETSW Study 9 (London, Central Council for Education and Training in Social Work).

White, M. and Epston, D. (1990) *Narrative Means to Therapeutic Ends* (New York, Norton).

White, V. (1995) 'Commonality and diversity in feminist social work', *British Journal of Social Work*, **25**, pp. 143–56.

Wilcox, S. (1996) *Housing Review 1996/97* (York, Joseph Rowntree Foundation).

Wilkes, R. (1981) *Social Work with Undervalued Groups* (London, Tavistock Publications).

Wilkinson, R. (1996) *Unhealthy Societies: The Afflictions of Inequality* (London, Routledge).

Wilkinson, R. G. (1994) *Unfair Shares: The Effects of Widening Income Differences on the Welfare of Young Children* (Ilford, Barnardo's).

Williams, F. (1989) *Social Policy* (Oxford, Polity Press).

Williams, F. (1996) 'Postmodernism, feminism and the question of difference', in Parton (1996).

Willis, P. (1978) *Learning to Labour: How Working Class Lads Get Working Class Jobs* (Farnborough, Saxon House).

Wilson, E. (1980) 'Feminism and social work', in Bailey, R. and Brake, M. (eds) *Radical Social Work and Practice*, 2nd edn (London, Edward Arnold).

Wilson, J. (1986) *Self-Help Groups: Getting Started – Keeping Going* (London, Longman).

Wilson, J. (1988) *Caring Together: Guidelines for Carers' Self-Help and Support Groups* (London, King's Fund).

Wilson, J. (1995) *How to Work with Self-help Groups* (London, Arena).

Wineman, S. (1984) *The Politics of Human Services* (Montreal, Black Rose).

Winnicott, C. (1964) *Child Care and Social Work* (Hitchin, Codicote Press).

Wise, A. (1985) *Becoming a Feminist Social Worker* (Manchester, University of Manchester).

Wise, S. (1990) 'Becoming a feminist social worker', in Stanley (1990).

Wolfensberger, W. (1997) 'Major obstacles to rationality and quality of human services in contemporary society', in Adams (1997), pp. 133–55.

Wood, K. M. (1990) 'Epistemological issues in the development of social work practice knowledge', in Videka-Sherman, L. and Reid, W. J. (eds) *Advances in Clinical Social Work Research* (Silver Spring, MD, National Association of Social Workers), pp. 373–90.

Woodroofe, K. (1962) *From Charity to Social Work in England and the United States* (London, Routledge & Kegan Paul).

Woolgar, S. (1986) 'On the alleged distinction between discourse and praxis', *Social Studies of Science*, **16**(4), p. 309.

Yalom, I. (1970) *The Theory and Practice of Group Psychotherapy* (New York, Basic Books).

Yates, P. (1985) *Post-placement support for adoptive families of hard-to-place children.* Unpublished MSc thesis, University of Edinburgh.

Yelloly, M. (1980) *Social Work Theory and Psychanalysis* (London, Van Nostrand Reinhold).

Yellolly, M. (1995) 'Professional competence and higher education, in Yellolly, M. and Henkel, M. (eds) *Learning and Teaching in Social Work: Towards Reflective Practice* (London, Jessica Kingsley).

Yelloly, M. and Henkel, M. (1995) *Learning and Teaching in Social Work: Towards Reflective Practice* (London, Jessica Kingsley).

Youll, P. (1996) 'Organisational or professional leadership? Managerialism and social work education', in Preston-Shoot, M. and Jackson, S. (eds) *Educating Social Workers in a Changing Policy Context* (London, Whiting & Birch).

Young, N. (1997) *An Infantile Disorder? The Crisis and Decline of the New Left* (London, Routledge & Kegan Paul).

Younghusband, E. (1970) 'Social work and social values', *Social Work Today*, **1**(4).

Yura, H. and Walsh, M. B. (1967) *The Nursing Process* (Norwalk, Appleton-Century-Crofts).

381

Subject Index